Prediction and Classification
Criminal Justice Decision Making

The University of Chicago Press

5801 S. Ellis Ave., Chicago, Illinois 60637

Crime and Justice

**Edited by
Michael Tonry
and
Norval Morris**

Prediction and Classification
Criminal Justice Decision Making

Edited by
Don M. Gottfredson and Michael Tonry

Crime and Justice
A Review of Research
Edited by Michael Tonry and Norval Morris
with the Support of The National Institute of Justice

VOLUME 9

The University of Chicago Press, Chicago and London

This volume was prepared under Grant Number 83-IJ-CX-K052 awarded to
the Castine Research Corporation by the National Institute of Justice, U.S.
Department of Justice, under the Omnibus Crime Control and Safe Streets
Act of 1968 as amended. Points of view or opinions expressed in this volume
are those of the editors or authors and do not necessarily represent the
official position or policies of the U.S. Department of Justice.

The University of Chicago Press, Chicago 60637
The University of Chicago Press, Ltd., London

ISSN: 0192-3234
ISBN: 0-226-80803-3

LCN: 80-642217

Library of Congress Cataloging-in-Publication Data

Prediction and classification.

(Crime and justice, ISSN 0192-3234 ; v. 9)
Bibliography: p.
Includes index.
    1. Criminal justice, Administration of—Decision
making.   2. Criminal behavior, Prediction of.
3. Classification of crimes.   4. Prisoners—
Classification.   I. Gottfredson, Don M.   II. Tonry,
Michael H.   III. Series: Crime and justice (Chicago,
Ill.) ; v. 9.
HV6001.C672   vol. 9   [HV7419]   364 s   [364'.068]   87-6016
ISBN 0-226-80803-3 (alk. paper)

The paper used in this publication meets the minimum requirements of American
National Standard for Information Sciences—Permanence of Paper for Printed
Library Materials, ANSI Z39.48-1984. ∞

Contents

Preface

Probably the most pervasive application of social science research in reform of the criminal justice system over the last twenty years has been the widespread incorporation into decision making of research-based prediction and classification methods.

Just a decade and a half ago, most decisions concerning defendants and offenders were ad hoc and intuitive. Whether the decision concerned bail, prosecution, plea bargaining, sentencing, parole release, prison security levels, assignment to treatment programs, or parole or probation revocation, decision makers made seat-of-the-pants decisions.

Today nearly every state has attempted to incorporate scientific knowledge about predictions—of future crimes, of violence, of suicide proneness, of victimization vulnerability, of amenability to treatment—into explicit decision standards.

Probation officers use "risk/needs-assessment" instruments. Prisons and jails use a variety of security and custody classification systems. Many states have adopted guidelines for bail, sentencing, and paroling that base decisions on classifications of defendants or offenders in terms of deserved punishment, predicted future crimes, or both.

An enormous literature has developed. Some is statistical and methodological and addresses the nature of prediction and classification methods. Some is descriptive and attempts to develop scientific bases for prediction and classification systems. Some is evaluative and investigates the operation and consequences of prediction and classification systems. Some is normative and policy focused.

Both the literature and practical application of science-based prediction and classification will continue to expand as institutions evolve to become more rational, more efficient, and more just. The social and political pressures conducing toward pursuit of these goals can only increase, and it is the goal of this volume to inform and guide those developments.

When classification or prediction methods are used in practice, problems of science and ethics become inextricably intertwined. The methods of science are limited but powerful in providing knowledge and information about what is and what might be. The dilemmas of ethics and philosophy provide compelling questions and strong arguments about what ought to be. The law inserts rules as to what is required at present. The resulting complex issues of science, ethics, and law present difficulties; but that does not require that we confuse them. The problems raised from scientific, ethical, and legal perspectives all must be identified and addressed.

These concerns stimulated the editorial board of *Crime and Justice* to commission the essays in this volume in order to examine major methods and applications of classification and prediction in the criminal justice system. The aim was to assess the state of the art, to review what is known, to identify promising next steps, and to consider some of the related legal and ethical issues. A first outline for the volume was examined in detail by the editorial board of the *Crime and Justice* series, then revised to incorporate the topics now included. When drafts were ready and had been reviewed independently by external referees, a two-day conference of writers and other scholars and practitioners was held at which the papers were presented, discussed, and criticized. The commentaries aided both the contributors and the editors in preparing the final versions of the essays included in this volume.

This collection of original essays, like its predecessors, was supported generously by the National Institute of Justice and its director, James K. Stewart. It is the second thematic volume in the *Crime and Justice* series. The first, *Communities and Crime*, edited by Albert J. Reiss, Jr., and Michael Tonry, was published in 1986.

The editors are grateful to the writers of the essays included in this volume, to the many anonymous reviewers, and to the staff of the National Institute of Justice. We believe, and hope others will agree, that the essays in this volume will stimulate the development and application of improved classification and prediction methods and, thereby, increase the fairness, efficiency, and effectiveness of the criminal justice system.

Don M. Gottfredson
Michael Tonry

Don M. Gottfredson

Prediction and Classification in Criminal Justice Decision Making

Prediction and classification occupy central positions in behavioral science, criminological research, and criminal justice decision making. They are fundamental to science and hence to the application of scientific methods to problems of crime and justice. They are critical to testing criminological theories and thus essential to verification of beliefs about crime and the criminal justice system. They are ubiquitous in criminal justice decision making and are central both to setting general policies and to making decisions about individuals. In these ways, classification and prediction are basic to efforts to prevent and control crime.

"Classification" refers either to the arrangement or division of entities into groups according to some system or principle or to the placement of entities into groups according to rules already determined. The concept is used in both these ways in this volume, but usually it means the allocation of persons to initially undefined classes in such a way that the persons in a class are in some way similar or close to each other (Cormack 1971). This definition is similar to the first meaning noted but is more specific: the aim is to develop groups whose members are similar to one another and who differ from members of other groups. This is very close to the statistical concept of minimizing within-group variability while maximizing between-group variability. The second meaning sometimes is used—as it often is in correctional practice—to refer to the process of choosing, for a new case, which of a number of already

Don M. Gottfredson is professor of criminal justice at Rutgers University.

assigned classes should be selected for an allocation. Sometimes the term "classification" is used in criminology or in criminal justice practice to refer instead to some method of categorizing persons according to theoretical types. This boils down to the first meaning: one may develop the groupings either empirically or theoretically, or both theoretical conceptions and observations may be used.

"Prediction" refers to an assessment of some expected future state. In criminology and criminal justice, prediction generally means an assessment of some expected future behavior by a person. Some criterion based on an assessment of future behavior (or sometimes of a future state of the criminal justice system) must be defined. Examples include criminal acts, arrests, or convictions (or rates of such incidents); probation or parole violations; appearance for trial when summoned; and escape from custody. Others include decisions by criminal justice functionaries including bail decisions by magistrates, sentencing by judges, or paroling by boards.

Whatever the criterion (the event or state to be predicted), this assessment must be made independently of any steps used in arriving at the prediction. Prediction requires two independent assessments separated over time. On the basis of the first assessment, a prediction method may be established. The second assessment establishes the classifications of the outcomes to be predicted. The predictions provide estimates of the expected values for the criterion categories. These estimates should be determined from earlier empirical investigations of the relations between the initial assessments and the criterion categories. The central idea of prediction is that previously observed relations between predictor and criterion classifications permit estimates of the most probable criterion outcomes for each category of persons or groups.

Prediction and classification are linked both conceptually and practically. Classifications in criminology and criminal justice may have many purposes, one being the prediction of offenders' behavior or officials' decisions. Prediction, however, is only one potential purpose of classification. In other classifications no predictive intent need be involved. The bail "guidelines" used in Philadelphia are an example of a classification with a predictive intent (see Goldkamp, in this volume). Minnesota's guidelines for sentencing convicted felons are an example of an analogous classification without primary predictive intent (Knapp 1984).

This essay introduces classification and prediction issues discussed in this volume, identifies critical problems in criminal justice applications of these methods, and points to some avenues toward their resolution. Why and how the concepts of classification and prediction are used should be explained.

When predictive classifications are under discussion, some first questions that naturally arise are, Can one predict? and then, How well can one predict? These necessarily precede the questions, How useful are classification and prediction methods? and, How ethically sound are proposed uses? The answers to such questions depend heavily on the purposes of the classification and prediction methods considered, and the questions therefore are not as simple as may first appear. Those purposes may be quite diverse, but major categories of use can be identified. For example, predictive classifications may have uses for research, program planning and evaluation, policy development, and individual case decision making. The answers to the preceding, seemingly simple questions may differ according to such purposes and in relation to specific dimensions of problem situations. Many of these questions arise when prediction methods are proposed for use in individual decision making or in setting policies that affect individuals or groups differentially.

This introductory essay discusses the questions posed in the preceding paragraph and considers what is known, what can be done to improve the "state of the art," and what is hoped may yet be achieved.

I. The Nature and Importance of Prediction and Classification

Classification has always played a central role in criminal justice research and policy development. Classification methods change continually in response to theoretical developments and to the changing needs of researchers and practitioners. Prediction is associated with classification in science generally and in criminology specifically. Carefully formulated and systematically tested classification methods are stimulating new research directions and policy developments. A general consideration of these various issues is presented in this section.

A. Why Classify?

Milestones in the history of research in criminology and criminal justice may be marked by advances in classification. Before Goring's 1913 publication *The English Convict* (Goring 1972), the state of affairs of criminology as described by Karl Pearson was that it was "on the one hand largely ruined by sentimentality and on the other by prejudice running riot" (Goring 1972, p. xvi). Goring's study focused on the alleged existence of a "physical criminal type," on the physiques of criminals, on age as an etiological factor in crime, and on other issues critical to an empirical examination of claims (he called them "superstitions") of the criminology of the day (Goring 1972, pp. 11–27). By careful measurement, classification, and hypothesis testing the study examined these claims, refuted many of them, and changed the course of criminology.

Lombroso's (1911) thesis of a criminal type, dating to 1870, had stimulated much of Goring's work. But another classification system based on skull configurations (later called phrenology) had been popular in society generally and in the criminal justice system. By 1855 the trustees of the Eastern Penitentiary at Philadelphia had linked the classifications of phrenology to categories of criminal behavior (Barnes and Teeters 1945, p. 160).

We can chuckle at these early efforts because the notion of external evidence of validity of classifications and predictions is now well understood and accepted. That does not deny their contribution; related lines of theoretical and empirical work in criminology have evolved from them. More recent investigators continued to relate physical types to propensities to delinquent or criminal behavior (e.g., Epps and Parnell 1952; Cortes and Gatti 1972).

As interest in classification developed in criminology, attention was given to the classification of offenders to examine whether different treatments are differentially effective for different categories of persons (e.g., Grant and Grant 1959; Adams 1961; Warren 1969). The notion underlying this work has been that some offenders may be favorably affected by a given treatment, others unfavorably, and others not at all. Much of this work, which is reviewed by Sechrest (in this volume), can be traced to the influences of psychiatry and particularly to psychoanalytic theory (e.g., Jenkins and Hewitt 1944; Erikson 1950; Redl 1956; Aichorn 1965). Some have origins in sociological theory (e.g., Schrag 1944; Sykes 1958). Other influential classification models have been related either to offense types or to conformity/nonconformity such as those of Reckless (1950), Ohlin (1951), Lejins (1954), and Gibbons and Garrity (1962). Meanwhile, classification methods were developed on the basis of assumptions about social perception or interpersonal interactions (e.g., Gough and Peterson 1952; Sullivan, Grant, and Grant 1956; Peterson, Quay, and Cameron 1959). Other classification methods have been related more to cognition (e.g., Venezia 1968). These classification methods have been developed from theoretical conceptualizations about the precursors to delinquency and crime or from theories about the relation of personality or social factors to differential effects of interventions.

Classification methods have also been developed that are largely atheoretical and empirically derived, mainly in relation to predictive objectives (Mannheim and Wilkins 1955; Gottfredson, Ballard, and Lane 1963; Fildes and Gottfredson 1971). Other empirical classification methods that may or may not be based on a predictive intent generally are called "numerical taxonomies."

Brennan (in this volume, a) describes the major methods of classification that have been developed. He emphasizes a necessary link between purposes and methods and that no single classification method may be considered best for all purposes. All the classification methods mentioned above are not equally valuable for all purposes. Some, even among those developed to aid in allocations to treatments, have more direct treatment implications than do others, some are demonstrably more reliable than are others, and some are more helpful than are others in generating testable hypotheses. The point to remember, in the words of William James (as apt now as in 1879), is that "every way of classifying a thing is but a way of handling it for some particular purpose" (Castell 1948, pp. 7–8).

The importance of classifications of individuals at each step of the criminal justice process should be emphasized. To the extent that criminal justice agencies seek to modify behavior to reduce the probability of crime, it is important at each point where placement decisions are made to know which methods are most likely to achieve that goal.

The centrality of classification is not limited to situations that involve crime control or other forward-looking goals. Were treatment, deterrence, and incapacitation to be rejected as bases for criminal justice decisions, even the requirements of an orientation limited to deserved punishment (e.g., von Hirsch 1976) would have to attend to the problems of classification of offenses, possibly prior records (von Hirsch 1981), and penalties. If the justification for a punishment system is that sanctions are imposed proportionately to the seriousness of the harm done by the crime and commensurate with the culpability of the offender, then reliable measures and classifications of seriousness of the offense, culpability, and the severity of sanctions are needed. Otherwise the notorious unreliability of individual judgments would foreseeably produce unwarranted disparity and inequity.

Much classification work in criminology and criminal justice has, however, had a predictive aim. Classifications for treatment, incapacitation, or supervision involve a predictive orientation. The determination of specific conditional factors that are relevant to expected values of the criterion classifications is thus a critical problem in the evaluation of effectiveness of treatment and control programs. The predictive nature of that orientation, with the determination best made by means of experimental designs or by inference from the results of quasi-experimental designs, is the topic of the essay by Richard Berk (in this volume).

B. Why Predict?

Prediction is a traditional aim of science. One tends to feel that one's understanding is increased when events can be predicted and controlled successfully. Prediction is thus often a requisite to control and is central to the application of scientific methods to understand and control crime. If one seeks to control crime behavior, one needs first to be able to predict it.

Much of our behavior is guided by the principle that relations observed in the past will hold in the future even though we believe there can be no guarantee of it. Change may be expected, but science requires that we assume that nature, subject to change, will change slowly. Thus we assume that some consistency will be found over time. Although we cannot write biographies in advance, it is clear that the observations of past relations can enable us to establish general expectations. We must live forward but seek to understand backward. Any prediction method can merely provide a way to summarize previous experience to guide future decisions.

Although it is common to hear that each person is unique (which is true), it is odd so often to hear that no formalized guides to making decisions can help because it is experience that counts. A systematic study, analysis, and condensation of that experience underlies classification and prediction methods, and that analysis and condensation is based on similarities and differences.

Critics of prediction methods sometimes argue that such procedures ignore individual differences among persons. It is the case, however, that individual differences, often assumed to be a source of error in other research problems, provide the basis for any prediction effort. If the persons studied are alike in respect to the predictor variables, no differential prediction can be made. If they are alike in respect to the criterion categories, there is no prediction problem. It is on analyses of differences that predictions must rely.

Classification methods in general and prediction methods in particular also can contribute to knowledge by providing tests of hypotheses (derived from hunches or more systematic theory) concerning the determinants of the behavior of offenders and of functionaries of the criminal justice system. The nature of classification and prediction problems and of the methods that have been developed to address them provide a framework within which hypothesized relations may be tested readily.

Classifications and predictions are involved in decisions made about offenders throughout the criminal justice system (Gottfredson and Gottfredson 1980). A victim's decision whether to report a crime to the authorities, a decision that usually determines whether the criminal justice system will be invoked, may hinge on the victim's prediction as to whether the police do anything. If the crime is reported, then the police must (besides determining whether there is reason to believe that a crime has occurred and locating a suspect) decide whether to make an arrest, issue a summons, or take the suspect into custody, each decision being influenced by the officer's predictions of the outcomes of his decision. If the suspect appears before a magistrate, the judge must decide whether to set bail and, if so, how much bail will be. Entering into this decision is the question whether the suspect can be expected to appear for trial (or whether there is a risk of new offenses being committed) if the suspect is released into the community. The magistrate may consider releasing the suspect "on recognizance." As part of that consideration the magistrate may consult a form that purports to separate the good risks for such release from those who are poorer risks. If the suspect is confined to jail to await trial, the correctional personnel must classify the person in ways related to prediction questions. Is the detainee an escape risk . . . suicidal . . . assaultive? What kind of person is this, presenting what kinds of risks? While the prosecutor is assessing the probability of winning the case if prosecuted and considering other classification and prediction questions such as whether this is a "career criminal" for whom special efforts should be made to ensure the protection of society, the probation officer may already be preparing a presentence investigation for the information of the judge. Besides similar prediction questions about the degree of risk of new offenses or of probation violation if placed under probation supervision, the probation officer may seek to determine the probability that the risk may be modified by placement in relevant treatment for alcohol or drug abuse, by educational or vocational training, or by assistance in employment.

The judge, at the time of sentencing, has myriad additional prediction questions. Will the sentence deter others from similar crimes? Will it deter this offender from future crimes? Is this the type of offender who needs to be locked up for a long time simply to incapacitate him? Again, what can be done to change the probabilities of additional crimes being committed by this person? Even within a context that might emphasize the administration of punishment because it is thought to be deserved, a multitude of prediction questions impinge on the decision.

If a sentence to prison is suspended and the offender placed on probation, the probation service has a new set of classification and prediction questions. How much risk does this new case present? What are his treatment needs? How closely must he be supervised? How shall he be classified? If a prison or jail sentence is not suspended, the correctional staff must make similar decisions.

When enough time has been served that the prisoner is eligible for parole consideration, questions of risk assessment arise again along with many of those considered before by the magistrate, prosecutor, probation officer, and judge. If paroled, there are new questions of classification for effective supervision and service. However the agencies that comprise the criminal justice system may differ, their members all have one thing in common; that is, they all make decisions about accused or convicted offenders, and those decisions require classifications and predictions.

Those who are required to make these decisions—such as prosecutors, judges, correctional personnel, and parole board members—typically do so with limited training about the difficult and complex predictive decisions confronting them. In the usual case the decisions must be made in the absence of information provided by classification and prediction tools such as those discussed in this volume. Rather, they usually are "clinical" predictions based on subjective judgments. These, in turn, are apt to rely on the decision maker's own experience, probably from biased samples and unsystematically observed, using combinations of evidence, conceptualizations, hunches, and untested hypotheses that are difficult to articulate. Viewed in this way it is not surprising that the available evidence strongly suggests that carefully and systematically derived statistical tools are more accurate than are trained decision makers (Meehl 1954; Monahan 1981; Morris and Miller 1985).

C. Can We Predict?

Two distinct but related lines of empirical research converge in the prediction studies discussed in this volume. First, a lengthy series of studies aims at the prediction of delinquency or crime or of probation or parole violation, that is, at defining the likelihood for various classifications of persons that they will engage in such behavior or be classified as violators. Second, there is a record of investigations of decisions of functionaries in the criminal justice system, such as judges or parole board members, that have had the objective of predicting their decisions.

The first line of research has been influenced markedly by studies that have sought to predict whether persons paroled from prisons or placed on probation will be classified later as successful or unsuccessful. Reviews of this research include Mannheim and Wilkins (1955), Gottfredson and Gottfredson (1980), Monahan (1981), and Farrington and Tarling (1985).

The studies aiming at predicting decisions are mostly more recent. Many of these have been motivated in part by interest in understanding the decision-making processes involved and in part by a desire to explain the decisions, including those that appeared to constitute an unwarranted disparity in outcomes. The question of empirical evidence of judicial disparities was raised as early as 1895 by Sir Francis Galton, who suggested that the comparison of different courts or judges might, for the same kind of offenders, reveal very different patterns of penalties imposed (Banks 1964). Many investigations seek to predict sentencing and paroling decisions. Many of the sentencing studies have been reviewed by Gottfredson and Gottfredson (1980) and Hagin and Bumiller (1983). Prediction of paroling decisions is discussed in Gottfredson, Wilkins, and Hoffman (1978). Some of these studies have been motivated by an interest in developing policy models or guidelines for these decisions. The review of sentencing and paroling decisions by Gottfredson and Gottfredson (1980) indicates the variables that typically have been found predictive; a summary of this work is given by Gottfredson (in this volume).

As interest in prediction studies developed in various disciplines and as the literature reporting specific studies grew, so did the literature addressing theoretical and technical issues. This includes a substantial body of writings on the logic of prediction in the study of personality (e.g., Meehl 1959), on related psychometric methods (e.g., Cattell 1937; Cronbach 1960), on statistical methods for combining predictors, and on the role of prediction methods in evaluating the effects of different treatments (Mannheim and Wilkins 1955; Wilkins 1961; Gottfredson 1963; Grygier 1964).

The general outline of steps usually followed in developing and testing prediction methods is not new, and they are widely understood and
used. Yet recommended procedures and attention to well-known pitfalls are not always reflected in reports of prediction studies, and this is
true even of some that have markedly influenced practice. The major
concerns are outlined by Gottfredson (in this volume).

D. Is Classification Useful?

As classification and prediction methods have developed, interest has
increased in the creation of tools for use in management, allocations to
treatments of different kinds, and policy development. This variety of
applications is addressed by Brennan (in this volume, b), Goldkamp (in
this volume), and Sechrest (in this volume). Correctional classification work has addressed diverse problems in jails, probation, prisons,
and parole supervision. This topic is discussed by Tim Brennan, who
focuses particularly on classifications for security and custody aims.
The general issue of classifications for treatment is taken up by Lee
Sechrest. It is clear from his review that there is yet much to learn
about the problem of differential classification and treatment, but it is
easy to agree also with his assertion of the importance of this problem
for applied corrections. Policy-model development to provide a structure and process within which individual decisions may be made more
rationally and fairly following a "guidelines" structure relies heavily on
issues of classification. John Goldkamp's essay reviews this development and the related research.

II. Applications of Classification and Prediction

Applications of classification and prediction methods often involve
research questions, planning problems, or decision situations. This
would not provide an adequate classification of such tools since the
ways in which they may be used are not mutually exclusive. Decision-
making applications in criminal justice can be said to be of two kinds,
namely, institutional policy decisions and individual decisions.

A. Classification in Research, Evaluation, and Planning

One research application involves the general question of "what
works" in the criminal justice system. The role that prediction methods
can play in gaining knowledge from program evaluations or other assessments of institutional decisions is often not thoroughly appreciated.

Rigorous experiments with random allocations to experimental and control groups are powerful but are of limited utility in the evaluation of criminal justice decisions. Their use often is beset with problems or is simply not feasible due, for example, to legal or ethical constraints or to strongly held beliefs in the efficacy of programs (e.g., Farrington 1983). When this is the case, statistical means of control must be substituted for the lacking experimental controls. Prediction methods can provide estimates of expected performance for any group of subjects, and the expected and actual outcomes for specific criterion classifications can be compared or other methods of statistical control used.

Planning problems often require estimates of outcomes of criminal justice decisions, including predictions of the persons who, in a given category, will have their probation or parole revoked, or who will not commit crimes at a high rate after release from confinement, or who may reasonably be expected to be paroled at first eligibility. Administrators may require estimates of the incarceration rates (dependent on discretionary sentencing by the courts) of various categories of offenders. And in the long run they often require conditional probability estimates dependent on effects (for different categories of persons) of differential handling for purposes of treatment or control.

Studies of the consequences of criminal justice system interventions rely heavily on predictions. From this perspective, however, Berk (in this volume) develops and explains the concept of "strong ignorability" and provides a framework for assessing the internal validity of such assessments.

B. Classification for Individual Decisions

Much attention has been focused on the problems of classification of offenders as to the risk of reoffending, probation or parole violation, or some similar criterion. The relevant studies and experiences are reviewed by Dan Glaser (in this volume), who points to obstacles and solutions to practical applications of the resulting predictive classifications.

Critical scientific and policy questions arise from recently popular but highly controversial crime-control strategies such as selective and collective incapacitation (Cohen 1983). These have stimulated much debate about both the scientific and the ethical issues involved (e.g., Cohen 1983; von Hirsch and Gottfredson 1984). Incapacitation concepts illustrate the relevance of classification and prediction topics to criminal justice policy choices. Under a collective incapacitation strategy, the same or a very similar sanction would be applied to all persons convicted of common offenses, but this would be informed by the expected future offense behavior for that group. A selective strategy involves sentences that are based on predictions of future rates of offending on the basis of individual scores on a prediction instrument. Either general strategy depends heavily on predictive power and the accuracy of the estimates made. The extent to which it is now possible to predict individual crime rates is the subject of the essay by David Farrington (in this volume).

What items of information may appropriately be used in prediction? If it is first assumed that the use of prediction in a decision situation is legally and ethically legitimate, this does not mean that the arguments are over. Questions arise in considering any intended application about the individual items of information used in arriving at the predictions.

Some obviously invidious items such as racial or ethnic classifications or gender may be thought to be easily dealt with; that is, simply leave them out. As usual, though, the case is more complicated (Fisher and Kadane 1983; Goldkamp, in this volume). Other items that may have predictive utility and thus are left in often are correlated with these invidious items. Thus an item that is seemingly acceptable such as "history of drug abuse" and that is seen as behavior for which the person may be held responsible may be perceived also as a "proxy" for the racial or ethnic classification since the predictor variables are correlated. The resulting ethical dilemmas provide a good example of the intertwining of scientific and ethical issues in this area and of the fact that both must be faced and addressed.

Does the choice of statistical methods for combining predictors or for classifying offenders affect the ethical concerns of bias and fairness at issue here? With a recent increase in the application of classification methods in criminal justice policy and decision making, assessments of the effects of the use of such methods on various groups is called for. Joan Petersilia and Susan Turner (in this volume) summarize and discuss their effort to examine the implications of use of descriptive guidelines on treatment of members of minority groups.

Most of the ethical concerns to be discussed in this volume are related to the use or the proposed use of classification and prediction methods in making decisions concerning individuals. The question whether to predict may be whether prediction methods should be used at all. Despite the centrality of the concept of prediction in criminal justice decision making, the question whether predictions should be used can be highly controversial. There is much less debate about uses of prediction methods in research or in planning. But when individual decisions (especially those that may involve liberty) or general policies that will set the context for such individual decisions are concerned, ethical controversies abound.

Errors in classification and prediction are inevitable because predictions cannot be perfect. There are only two ways to address this reality. First, reduce the errors. This can result only from increasing the correlation of a prediction method with the criterion classifications of interest, that is, from improving the validity of prediction (Einhorn and Schact 1975). Second, identify and face the ethical issues whenever applications to decision situations are proposed. Classification and prediction methods must rest on a basis in science, but they must be applied in a world of values. Thus they involve both research and ethics.

Controversies about the ethical and legal use of prediction in criminal justice decision situations are not limited to those surrounding sentencing. In the magistrate's decision concerning pretrial release, should the likelihood of new crimes being committed on release be considered in the decision? The ethical and, perhaps, the constitutional concerns must address the juxtaposition of the defendant's interest in liberty with the public's interest in safety. The defendant's right not to be a false positive must be balanced against the public's right not to be set on by a false negative (Monahan 1981).

Legal and ethical issues surrounding classification and prediction in criminal justice decisions are discussed by Michael Tonry (in this volume). He provides a general overview of the implications of these issues and suggests how some of them might be resolved.

III. What Do We Know? What Can We Do?
What Can We Hope?

In this final section I consider a number of important issues concerning what is known about prediction and classification research, how data quality and measurement can be improved, and how more use of theory can be made.

A. *Improving Prediction and Its Utility*

Predictive classifications with sufficient, although modest, validities that are useful for some purposes can be devised. A number of strategies are available for improving validities.

1. *Fitting Methods to Assumptions.* Currently used methods often do

not fit the necessary assumptions underlying the statistical methods used. Theoretically more powerful methods are available. Yet these theoretically better methods, when used, often do not improve validities (Gottfredson and Gottfredson 1987). This may result in part from the poor quality of available data in the criminal justice system and hence that used in the research. Data systems and thereby the reliability and validity of classifications used need to be improved.

2. *Measurement and Scaling.*   Serious measurement issues abound in the data used for classification and prediction work in criminal justice. Well-developed but little-used technologies are available for improving the scaling of variables of critical importance in many analyses and applications. Measurement of key concepts such as "seriousness of the offense" and "prior record" can be improved, and it can be hoped that this will improve validities.

3. *Outcome Criteria.*   Much work is needed on the definition and measurement of criteria in prediction studies. This is true whether the behavior of accused or convicted offenders or the decision-making behavior of criminal justice system authorities is to be predicted.

Criteria of delinquency, criminal behavior, probation or parole violation, and similar classifications have often been crude and easy to criticize. For example, a common criterion of delinquency has been confinement. If among the confined population some are wrongly convicted while the nonconfined group contains some who are engaged in delinquent behavior, the validity of the criterion classifications is reduced to that extent. Moreover, in predictions related to criminal justice decision making, criteria may depend not only on the behavior of the person about whom predictions are made but also on the behavior of others. The classification may also depend on the behavior of police, prosecutors, judges, or probation and parole officials. Commonly used criteria of parole violation, for example, may depend on both the parolee's behavior and the response of the parole officer or the paroling authority. The reliability and validity of criterion classifications often are related closely to the efficiency of law enforcement and the administration of criminal justice. They may be affected by policy changes in relevant social agencies and by changes in the categories of behavior that, in a changing social context, become defined as socially acceptable or unacceptable. Yet the criterion provides the standard for the identification of relevant predictor variables, constitutes the basis for determining the validity of the prediction method, and thereby determines whether the method will be useful for any practical applications.

The crudity of a simple dichotomous criterion of a concept such as success or failure on probation or parole or of recidivism is apparent; the behavior of interest almost always is a matter of degree, implying a need for measurement on a continuous scale. Moreover, the definition of "success" in many criminal justice problem situations may be not only debatable but also quite complex. If a person released from prison is convicted of a new, less serious crime, is that a total failure, or can it be argued that some measure of crime control has been achieved? If he stayed out of jail longer this time, is that a benefit? If he was returned to prison for a technical violation but not a crime and during his stay in the community paid taxes, supported his family, established a business, and was elected man of the year by the Chamber of Commerce, how should he be classified? If a burglar's rate of committing crimes in the community is reduced by half after incarceration, is that a desirable, if not wholly satisfactory, result?

What to predict depends on the problem and the specific purposes of the prediction study. In a sense, asking "what to predict" is like asking, What is the best dependent variable to study? The definition of the criterion classifications will depend on what one is trying to learn. But it is clear that one can do much to improve the current state of affairs and by this means also hope to improve validities.

4. *Dealing with Low Base Rates.*   Many prediction problems are complicated by the "low-base-rate problem" (described in the essay by Gottfredson [in this volume]), and this makes the task of improving validities especially difficult. This problem can be addressed in several ways. One can do the needed developmental work to provide continuous, rather than discrete, measures of the behaviors of interest. Or one can develop prediction methods as a sequential process in which homogeneous groups are first defined by classification methods and predictive measures are then devised for these groups separately.

5. *Developing and Applying Theory.*   Much work in classification and prediction is largely atheoretical. This likely decreases contributions to theoretical development and the utilities of the classification systems devised. The greater use of theory in developing classifications and of classification and prediction technology in testing theoretical propositions are important objectives for coming generations of research.

B. *Extending the Use of Statistical Designs*
Prediction methods provide a powerful tool for program evaluation research when experimental designs are not possible, yet they are

rarely used for this purpose. One can do so and can hope thereby to learn much more about the effects of criminal justice system interventions.

C. Comparing Classification Methods

Available technologies for classification studies provide a wide variety of competing methods, but there are few comparative studies of the replicability, validity, and utility of the differing methods for different purposes. Methods are available also for such comparisons, and they should be used. One can hope thereby to make the classification methods themselves more useful.

D. Developing New Variables

Most of the variables often used in classification studies or found consistently to be predictive (such as prior record variables or the offense of conviction) are "static" rather than "dynamic"; that is, they are not subject to change over time. More useful classification and prediction instruments and perhaps those more acceptable for use in individual decision making may include variables that are subject to change under the control of the subject and that are closer in time to the decision.

E. Measuring "Stakes" as Well as "Risk"

When there is a predictive component to the decision, the behavior of the decision maker is similar to that of an informed gambler with a decision made under uncertainty. Not only the odds of winning or losing a bet (risk) but also the amount of the wager (stakes) are considered by the prudent gambler. The expected value of a given bet may be taken as the product of the probability of winning and the amount at risk (the wager). Thus, in addition to measuring the risk of various outcomes of decisions about offenders in terms of discrete general criteria, one can develop measures of the societal stakes involved in the decision. One can hope that this may provide improved information for practical decision situations (Gottfredson and Gottfredson 1987).

F. Reducing Errors in Decisions

The only way to reduce errors in classification, including predictive classifications, is to improve the validities of the classification methods. The only way to reduce ethical mistakes in applying such methods is in the identification, analysis, and debate of the ethical issues that arise. It is hoped that this volume will contribute to the achievement of these goals.

REFERENCES

Adams, Stuart. 1961. "Interaction between Individual Interview Therapy and Treatment Amenability in Older Youth Authority Wards." In *Enquiries concerning Kinds of Treatment for Kinds of Delinquents.* Monograph no. 2. Sacramento, Calif.: Board of Corrections.

Aichorn, August. 1965. *Wayward Youth.* New York: Viking. (Originally published as *Verwahrloste Jugend*, 1925. Vienna: Psychoanalytischer Verlag.)

Banks, E. 1964. "Reconviction of Young Offenders." *Current Legal Problems* 17:74.

Barnes, Harry E., and Negley K. Teeters. 1945. *New Horizons in Criminology.* New York: Prentice-Hall.

Berk, Richard A. In this volume. "Causal Inference as a Prediction Problem."

Brennan, Tim. In this volume, *a.* "Classification: An Overview of Selected Methodological Issues."

———. In this volume, *b.* "Classification for Control in Jails and Prisons."

Castell, Albury, ed. 1948. *Essays in Pragmatism by William James.* New York: Hafner.

Cattell, Raymond B. 1937. "Measurement vs. Intuition in Applied Psychology." *Character and Personality* 6:114–31.

Cohen, Jacqueline. 1983. "Incapacitation as a Strategy for Crime Control: Possibilities and Pitfalls." In *Crime and Justice: An Annual Review of Research*, vol. 5, edited by Michael Tonry and Norval Morris. Chicago: University of Chicago Press.

Cormack, R. M. 1971. "A Review of Classification." *Journal of the Royal Statistical Society* 3:321–67.

Cortes, Joan B., and Florence M. Gatti. 1972. *Delinquency and Crime: A Biopsychological Approach.* New York: Seminar.

Cronbach, Lee J. 1960. *Essentials of Psychological Testing.* New York: Harper.

Einhorn, Hillel J., and Stephen Schact. 1975. "Decisions Based on Fallible Clinical Judgment." In *Human Judgment*, edited by Martin F. Kaplin and Steven Schwartz. New York: Academic Press.

Epps, P., and R. W. Parnell. 1952. "Physique and Temperament of Women Delinquents Compared with Women Undergraduates." *British Journal of Medical Psychology* 25:249–55.

Erikson, Erik H. 1950. *Childhood and Society.* New York: Norton.

Farrington, David. 1983. "Randomized Experiments on Crime and Justice." In *Crime and Justice: An Annual Review of Research*, vol. 4, edited by Michael Tonry and Norval Morris. Chicago: University of Chicago Press.

———. In this volume. "Predicting Individual Crime Rates."

Farrington, David, and Roger Tarling. 1985. *Prediction in Criminology.* Albany: State University of New York Press.

Fildes, Robert E., and Don M. Gottfredson. 1971. "Cluster Analysis in a Parolee Sample." *Journal of Research in Crime and Delinquency* 9:2–11.

Fisher, Franklin M., and Jay B. Kadane. 1983. "Empirically Based Sentencing Guidelines and Ethical Considerations." In *Research on Sentencing: The Search for Reform*, edited by Alfred Blumstein, Jacqueline Cohen, Susan E. Martin, and Michael H. Tonry. Washington, D.C.: National Academy Press.

Gibbons, Donald C., and Donald L. Garrity. 1962. "A Preliminary Typology of Juvenile Delinquents." *Journal of Criminal Law, Criminology, and Police Science* 53:27–35.

Glaser, Daniel. In this volume. "Classification for Risk."

Goldkamp, John S. In this volume. "Prediction in Criminal Justice Policy Development."

Goring, Charles. 1972. *The English Convict: A Statistical Study*. Montclair, N.J.: Patterson Smith. (Originally published 1913. London: Darling & Son.)

Gottfredson, Don M. 1963. "The Practical Application of Research." *Canadian Journal of Corrections* 5:212–28.

Gottfredson, Don M., Kelley B. Ballard, Jr., and Leonard Lane. 1963. *Association Analysis in a Prison Sample and Prediction of Parole Performance*. Vacaville, Calif.: Institute for the Study of Crime and Delinquency.

Gottfredson, Don M., Leslie T. Wilkins, and Peter B. Hoffman. 1978. *Guidelines for Parole and Sentencing: A Policy Control Model*. Lexington, Mass.: Lexington.

Gottfredson, Michael R., and Don M. Gottfredson. 1980. *Decisionmaking in Criminal Justice: Toward the Rational Exercise of Discretion*. Cambridge, Mass.: Ballinger.

Gottfredson, Stephen D. In this volume. "Prediction: An Overview of Selected Methodological Issues."

Gottfredson, Stephen D., and Don M. Gottfredson. 1987. *Behavioral Prediction in Criminal Justice*. New York: Springer-Verlag, in press.

Gough, Harrison G., and Donald R. Peterson. 1952. "The Identification and Measurement of Predispositional Factors in Delinquency." *Journal of Consulting Psychology* 16:207–12.

Grant, J. Douglas, and Marguerite Q. Grant. 1959. "A Group Dynamics Approach to the Treatment of Nonconformists in the Navy." *Annals of the American Academy of Political and Social Science* 322:135–46.

Grygier, Thaddeusz. 1964. "Treatment Variables in Non-linear Prediction." Paper presented to the joint annual meeting of the American Society of Criminology and the American Society for the Advancement of Science, Montreal, December.

Hagan, John, and Kristen Bumiller. 1983. "Making Sense of Sentencing: A Review and Critique of Sentencing Research." In *Research on Sentencing: The Search for Reform*, edited by Alfred Blumstein, Jacqueline Cohen, Susan E. Martin, and Michael H. Tonry. Washington, D.C.: National Academy Press.

Jenkins, R. L., and L. Hewitt. 1944. "Types of Personality Structure Encountered in Child Guidance Clinics." *American Journal of Orthopsychiatry* 14:84–94.

Knapp, Kay A. 1984. *The Impact of the Minnesota Sentencing Guidelines—Three Year Evaluation.* St. Paul: Minnesota Sentencing Guidelines Commission.

Lejins, Peter P. 1954. "Pragmatic Etiology of Delinquent Behavior." In *The Juvenile Delinquent,* edited by C. B. Vedden. New York: Doubleday.

Lombroso, Cesare. 1911. *Crime: Its Causes and Remedies.* Boston: Little, Brown. (Originally published 1876.)

Mannheim, Hermann, and Leslie T. Wilkins. 1955. *Prediction Methods in Relation to Borstal Training.* London: H.M. Stationery Office.

Meehl, Paul E. 1954. *Clinical vs. Statistical Prediction: A Theoretical Analysis and a Review of the Evidence.* Minneapolis: University of Minnesota Press.

———. 1959. "A Comparison of Conditions with Five Statistical Methods of Identifying MMPI Profiles." *Journal of Counseling Psychology* 6:102–9.

Monahan, John. 1981. *Predicting Violent Behavior: An Assessment of Clincial Techniques.* Beverly Hills, Calif.: Sage.

Morris, Norval, and Marc Miller. 1985. "Predictions of Dangerousness." In *Crime and Justice: An Annual Review of Research,* vol. 6, edited by Michael Tonry and Norval Morris. Chicago: University of Chicago Press.

Ohlin, Lloyd E. 1951. *Selection for Parole: A Manual of Parole Prediction.* New York: Russell Sage.

Petersilia, Joan, and Susan Turner. In this volume. "Guideline-based Justice: Prediction and Racial Minorities."

Peterson, Donald R., Herbert C. Quay, and G. R. Cameron. 1959. "Personality and Background Factors in Juvenile Delinquency as Inferred from Questionnaire Responses." *Journal of Consulting Psychology* 23:395–99.

Reckless, Walter C. 1950. *The Crime Problem.* New York: Appleton-Century-Crofts.

Redl, Fritz. 1956. *New Perspectives for Research in Juvenile Delinquency.* Publication no. 356. Washington, D.C.: U.S. Children's Bureau.

Schrag, Clarence A. 1944. *Social Types in a Prison Community.* M.A. thesis, University of Washington, Department of Sociology.

Sechrest, Lee. In this volume. "Classification for Treatment."

Sullivan, Clyde, J. Douglas Grant, and Marguerite Q. Grant. 1956. "The Development of Interpersonal Maturity: Applications to Delinquency." *Psychiatry* 20:373–85.

Sykes, Gresham M. 1958. *The Society of Captives.* Princeton, N.J.: Princeton University Press.

Tonry, Michael. In this volume. "Prediction and Classification: Legal and Ethical Issues."

Venezia, Peter S. 1968. "Delinquency as a Function of Intrafamily Relationships." *Journal of Research in Crime and Delinquency* 5:148–73.

von Hirsch, Andrew. 1976. *Doing Justice: The Choice of Punishments.* New York: Hill & Wang.

———. 1981. "Desert and Previous Convictions in Sentencing." *Minnesota Law Review* 65:591–634.

von Hirsch, Andrew, and Don M. Gottfredson. 1984. "Selective Incapacitation: Some Queries about Research Design and Equity." *New York University Review of Law and Social Change* 12:11–51.

Warren, Marguerite Q. 1969. "The Case for Differential Treatment of Delinquents." *Annals of the American Academy of Political and Social Science* 381:47–59.

Wilkins, Leslie T. 1961. "What Is Prediction and Is It Necessary in Evaluating Treatment?" In *Research and Potential Application of Research in Probation, Parole, and Delinquency Prevention.* New York: Columbia University, New York School of Social Work, Citizen's Committee for Children of New York.

Stephen D. Gottfredson

Prediction: An Overview of Selected Methodological Issues

ABSTRACT

A variety of statistical methods are available for making criminal justice predictions. None possesses a clear-cut advantage over the others, and this may be due to the poor quality of available data. Factors that affect the accuracy of predictions, regardless of the method used, include measurement reliability, base rates (the relative frequency of an event in the study population), selection ratios (the proportion of events identified by the prediction method as belonging to the outcome class), sample representativeness, and cross validation. The present ability to predict the decisions of criminal justice functionaries or offender behavior is modest. Predictions of decisions are more accurate than are predictions of behavior, and empirical studies indicate that statistical predictions outperform intuitive or clinical predictions. Predictive accuracy can be enhanced by improving data reliability, by improving measurement of prediction and outcome variables, by using both statistical and subjective bootstrapping models, by using theory-driven approaches, and, finally, by devoting greater attention to ethical implications of prediction methods and uses.

Any decision made under uncertainty with respect to future events, behaviors, activities, resources, trends, demands, or outcomes is a predictive one. Accordingly, a predictive component is pervasive in most decisions made in the criminal justice system, although this often is not

Stephen D. Gottfredson is associate professor of criminal justice, Temple University. Portions of this essay are adapted from Gottfredson and Gottfredson (1979, 1986).

recognized clearly; prediction is implicit in the decisions made but is rarely explicitly acknowledged.

This essay focuses on selected methods and problems of behavioral prediction in criminal justice settings. I am not concerned with predictions involving resource allocation, criminal population projections, estimation of rates of offending, or the length of criminal careers. Predictions based on aggregate data, forecasting problems, and time-series and simulation-modeling studies are ignored. Finally, psychological or psychiatric assessments of offenders are not discussed.

Critical reviews concerning several important issues recently have been published. Monahan (1978, 1981) and colleagues (Monahan and Klassen 1982) have given detailed attention to the prediction of violence, and longitudinal studies bearing on prediction issues have been reviewed by Farrington (1979, 1982). Recent reviews of work on the prediction of sentencing decisions are available in Hagan and Bumiller (1983) and Klepper, Nagin, and Tierney (1983). Gottfredson and Gottfredson (1986) review prediction studies concerning bail, pretrial detention, prosecution, and parole.

Section I of this essay discusses the nature of decisions generally and predictive decision making in particular. Section II discusses some of the recurring issues involved in assessing the value of predictions made. Section III describes what is known from prediction studies in a variety of decision areas. Section IV assesses how well one can predict. Section V describes some of the more common methods of behavioral prediction. The final section discusses ways in which the accuracy and utility of criminal justice prediction tools can be improved.

I. The Nature of Decisions

Decisions involve choice. Much of psychology, economics, and philosophy concerns the study of choices that people make. What determines the amount of money I will pay for a car? Why do I select a Labrador retriever over a Chihuahua as a family pet? Why do I generally obey the law? What is the role of altruism, of superstition, of morality, or of value in the choices made?

Detailed discussion of the nature of human choice behavior clearly is beyond the scope of this essay. Decision theory considers the rational person to be one who, when confronted with choice, makes the decision that is "best"; this decision is the "optimal" or the "rational" one (Lee 1971). This decision must be one of those available, will depend on the decision principles under study (different studies proceeding from different bases may identify different optimal choices), may differ among persons (e.g., due to differing values assigned to alternatives, differing subjective probability estimates, and so on), but must depend on the information available to the decision maker.

Behavioral decision theory (Hogarth 1980; Einhorn and Hogarth 1981; Pitz and Sachs 1984), "cognitive algebra" (Anderson 1974, 1979), utility theories (Lee 1971), and "game theories" and their assessments of strategies (Luce and Raiffa 1957) are examples of general considerations of ways in which the choice or decision behavior of the rational person may be modeled.

I note this literature to make two points. The first is that there is a distinction to be drawn between decision theories and studies that are "normative" and those that are "descriptive." Normative studies concern the decisions that people should make in a choice situation, while descriptive studies concern the decisions actually made. This distinction, although clear, may become blurred in practice; this is particularly so when the goal of the exercise is the improvement of rational decision making.

The second point is that human decision makers often do not appear to behave optimally. For this reason, among others, the provision of decision-making tools for criminal justice applications is necessary and desirable.

Any decision has three components, namely, a goal, alternative choices, and information. Decisions cannot rationally be made (or studied) if decision-making goals are neither stated nor clear. Unfortunately, goals for criminal justice decisions rarely are stated explicitly, and they often are complex. Rarely is a single goal for a decision given. Without alternatives, there can be no decision problem. Without information on which to base the decision, the "problem" reduces to reliance on chance.

Prediction is the use of information to estimate the probable future occurrence of some event or behavior. Prediction studies are of most value to decision makers in relating information to goals. Methods of using the information may be intuitive, clinical, or subjective, or they may be statistical or "actuarial." Any of a wide variety of statistical approaches may be used.

An obvious question to be asked when considering the value of predictive information is, How good is it? The answer is, It depends. Predictive accuracy is a function of several things, including the methods used to combine items of information and the reliability of the information used as well as of the outcome variable chosen, the base rate, the selection ratio used, and representativeness of samples employed. All these terms are defined in the following sections.

II. Methods of Combining Predictive Information

Many statistical methods have been used in criminological prediction studies, including the simple inspection of cross-classification tables (Warner 1923), multiple regression (Gottfredson, Wilkins, and Hoffman 1978), multiple discriminant function analysis (Brown 1978), multidimensional contingency table analysis (Solomon 1976; van Alstyne and Gottfredson 1978), Tobit analysis (Palmer and Carlson 1976), and a variety of clustering approaches (Fildes and Gottfredson 1968). Section V provides a brief nontechnical review of several of the more commonly used statistical methods. (For discussions of clinical methods of combining items of information, see Gough [1962] or Monahan [1981].)

For a variety of statistical and practical reasons, one or another of the approaches described in Section V may be preferred, and, in theory, the technique used can have dramatic consequences on the accuracy of resultant prediction devices. In criminal justice applications this potential unfortunately remains largely theoretical. Several attempts have been made to demonstrate the relative utility of different statistical approaches to criminal justice prediction problems (e.g., Babst, Gottfredson, and Ballard 1968; Farrington 1978), and potential advantages of different approaches have been enumerated several times (Wilkins and MacNaughton-Smith 1964; Gottfredson and Gottfredson 1980). Gottfredson and Gottfredson (1979) compared the relative utility of six of the more commonly used or promising methods and concluded that "no clear-cut empirical advantage in prediction is provided by one or another method" (p. 65). Several reasons for this have been suggested by Farrington (1978), Gottfredson and Gottfredson (1979), and Loeber and Dishion (1983). Principal among these is the fact that much criminal justice data is of such poor quality that the theoretical advantage provided by the more powerful methods simply cannot be realized.

Although there are no clear-cut empirical advantages of selecting one prediction method over another, there are several factors that do affect the utility of a prediction. These factors include measurement reliability, the base rate for the event, the selection ratio, sample representativeness, and cross validation. Each of these factors is considered below.

A. Reliability

Reliability refers essentially to the stability with which measurements may be made, and statistical validity—here imprecisely considered as "utility"—is constrained by the reliability with which both outcomes and predictor measurements are made. No prediction device can be better than the data from which it is constructed. Attention often is given to the reliabilities of the predictors, but the reliability of the outcome measure is neglected.

B. The Base Rate

The base rate for any given event is the relative frequency of occurrence of that event in the population of interest. Typically, base rates are expressed as proportions or percentages. In many criminal justice applications, where outcome measures often have been treated as a dichotomy (e.g., success or failure on parole), the base rate is the appropriate marginal distribution of the expectancy table.

The difficulty of predicting events of interest increases as the base rate differs from 0.5 (Meehl and Rosen 1955). Thus the more frequent or infrequent an event, the greater the likelihood of inaccurate prediction. (While this seems intuitively true for rare events, it must be remembered that the occurrence of very frequent events requires the simultaneous occurrence of very rare events unless the probability of an event is precisely zero or one.) As an example of the difficulty of such prediction, suppose that the base rate for failure on parole is .20. Given this information alone, it is known that a prediction that no one will fail will be correct 80 percent of the time. One will also be wrong 20 percent of the time, but one would have no way of estimating which 20 percent will fail.

Now assume that a predictive device has been developed that predicts parole outcomes with 78 percent accuracy. Even given this apparently powerful device, one would still be better off in expecting that no one will fail on parole, that is, in "predicting" performance on the basis of the base rate alone.

Developers of predictive tools often have failed to consider base rates and consequently have made classifications or predictions on the basis of criteria that produce larger errors than would the simple use of the base rate. In 1955 Meehl and Rosen summarized the consequences of failure to consider base rates and concluded that "almost all contemporary research reporting neglects the base rate factor and hence makes evaluation of . . . usefulness difficult or impossible" (p. 215). Although Reiss (1951b) clearly and dramatically illustrated this point over thirty years ago in a classic review of the Gluecks' *Unraveling Juvenile Delin-quency* (1950), failure to consider base rates remains an unfortunately common practice.

C. Selection Ratios

The selection ratio is the proportion of individuals or events studied and identified by the prediction method as belonging to the outcome classification of interest. In delinquency studies, for example, the selec-tion ratio is the proportion of persons studied and selected as expected delinquents by means of some prediction instrument (for a discussion, see Loeber and Dishion [1983]). Thus it may be seen that, while the base rate provides one marginal distribution for an expectancy table, the selection ratio provides the other; and, together, the marginal distri-butions determine the chance expectancies for the table. Selection ratios may be altered through manipulation of the cutting score with obvious but sometimes unrecognized consequences on prediction (Cronbach 1960). That is, as the point on the prediction scale above which a person is considered a likely "success" is changed (called the "cutting score"), the nature of the errors to be made is changed, and this may, particularly if the bivariate distribution is heteroscedastic, affect the accuracy of prediction as well (Fisher 1959).[1]

D. Representativeness of Samples

If accuracy of prediction is desired, then samples used in construct-ing selection devices must be representative of the population on which the device is intended to be used. This ensures that the appropriate base rate is considered and minimizes subsequent shrinkage of power from the construction to the operational samples.[2]

No two groups of people are identical. If, however, the groups have been selected by some appropriate mechanism (such as random sam-pling), they can be expected to have a great deal in common in terms both of their overall characteristics and of the interrelations of various

---

[1] One assumption requisite to the proper use of regression (and many other) methods is that of equality of variances about the regression line irrespective of where, on either the predictor or criterion scale, the measure is taken. Bi- or multivariate distributions (such as the normal) that meet this requirement are said to be "homoscedastic." When the requirement is not met, the distribution is heteroscedastic.

[2] The term "shrinkage" is used to describe the fact that prediction equations almost always are less powerful when applied to operational samples than they appear to be when constructed. The next section on cross validation describes a means of estimating shrinkage.

individual characteristics. All statistical predictions ultimately rely on this similarity of relations within different groups of people. If in one group of subjects the young do better in relation to some outcome, then it is assumed that, in a similar group of subjects, the young again will do better. Prediction methods are intended to estimate, on the basis of some group of people available for study, how members of other similar groups will behave. There is a danger, however, of overestimating the extent to which relations found in one sample can be used to explain relations in a similar sample.

Within the original sample alone, there is no adequate way to distinguish how much of the observed relation is due to characteristics and underlying associations that will be shared by new samples and how much is due to unique characteristics of the first sample. This is because the apparent power of a prediction device that is developed on a sample of observations derives from two sources, namely, from the detection and estimation of underlying relations likely to be observed in any similar sample of subjects and from the peculiar or individual properties of the specific sample on which the device has been created. Cross validation is important in estimating the relative importance of these two sources of predictive power. This is particularly advisable when the prediction study is intended for practical application in new samples.

E. Cross Validation

Cross validation is an empirical approach to the problem of attempting to obtain an unbiased estimate of the accuracy of predictions. Typically, this is accomplished by dividing the sample at hand in two, constructing the device on one, and using the other to estimate predictive accuracy. Horst (1966) refers to this general procedure as the "sample fractionation" approach and argues, quite correctly, that there are serious disadvantages to sample fractionation. First, the stability of estimates is dependent on the number of cases on which they are made. Thus dividing the sample reduces the reliability of the device constructed, which may reduce validity. Second, the approach gives only one estimate (from a potentially large universe of estimates). In effect, coefficients that result from cross validation are regarded as estimates of the average expected validity in independent samples. These validities are expected to be normally distributed.

There appears to be no "best" answer to the cross-validation problem. Sample fractionation procedures do constrain validity (unless the sample obtained is very large). A single estimate of shrinkage is not optimal, is unlikely to represent the actual mean validity, and is as likely to under- as it is to overestimate that value. As noted by Horst (1966), one can obtain two estimates by examining expected validities from each sample on the other (in the traditional fractionation approach) but is then left with deciding which of the devices actually to use. Similarly, one could further fractionate the sample and develop several empirical estimates. Again, however, we encounter problems of reliability as the sample size decreases. To meliorate this, one could then recombine the subsamples and create a device on the full sample, relying on the subsample estimators to provide an index of shrinkage (see Horst 1966, p. 380). The validity of the device developed in this fashion may be underestimated (perhaps seriously) because the samples from which validity is estimated are much smaller than the sample on which the final device is constructed. Jackknifing methods (in which a single case is omitted from the sample in all possible iterations and the resulting large sample of models combined) are meliorative but time-consuming and expensive (for a discussion, see Copas and Tarling [1984]).[3]

Some argue for a "longitudinal" validation approach (e.g., Horst 1963, 1966), in which the device is developed on the largest sample available and the device applied in operational use. Validity is assessed over time and research integrated into the administrative process. The appropriateness of this approach depends on the types of predictive decisions to be made and on the expected validities of the devices used. For certain relatively benign applications with relatively high expected validities, such a procedure might be acceptable. When the decisions involve liberty, however, and when expected validities are low (as commonly is the case in criminal justice applications), I would object. Wright, Clear, and Dickson (1984) recently illustrated that consequences (in terms of reduced validities) of the wholesale adoption in several jurisdictions of devices developed in one locale can be dramatic. In this example, a scale that was developed in the state of Wisconsin to be predictive of risk of recidivism for parolees and probationers was applied in the state of New York. Although the scale had some empirical validity in Wisconsin, it was found to have none in New York.

---

[3] Copas and Tarling (1984) also describe other methods beyond the scope of this essay (e.g., bootstrapping) and develop a method for the determination of a "preshrunk" model.

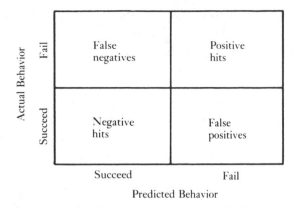

FIG. 1.—Prediction outcomes in a 2 × 2 contingency table

III. Measures of Predictive Accuracy

The issues considered so far can affect the accuracy of prediction, but I have not yet considered how best to assess that accuracy. This section focuses on such a consideration.

In most selection applications, prediction outcomes most fairly are represented by a 2 × 2 contingency table (fig. 1). The cutting score determines the selection ratio and the marginal distribution of the columns in figure 1. The base rate determines the row marginal distribution. Together these determine the distribution of cases within the table, subject to one degree of freedom.[4] They also determine the distribution of cases within the table to be expected by chance. Although statistics such as chi-square are useful in assessing independence in tables such as this, the value of chi-square is a function of the number of rows and columns in the table and the number of cases considered as well as of the relation beyond that expected by chance. Furthermore, chi-square is used to assess statistical significance; directly, it tells the investigator nothing about the magnitude of the effect discovered. It gives an assessment of "accuracy" to the extent that the investigator may feel confident in the reliability of the effect discov-

---

[4] Many statistical tests make an assumption that the marginal distributions observed are "fixed," that is, that they will not vary from sample to sample. In a fourfold table such as that under discussion, application of this assumption means that any given cell may take on any value allowed by the marginal distributions. Once a single cell is occupied by an allowable number, however, all remaining cells must be assigned a number determined by the difference between the "occupied" cell and the marginals. Accordingly, since only one cell is free to vary, we speak of "one degree of freedom." In general, a contingency table of r rows and c columns would have $(r-1) \times (c-1)$ degrees of freedom.

ered, but it does not tell one about the degree of relation implied by that effect. A variety of statistics are available to help in this assessment (e.g., Fisher's contingency coefficient and Cramer's V), but none completely overcomes the dimensionality problem, that is, the fact that expectancy tables may have different numbers of rows and columns.

One such contingency coefficient, phi, is formally identical to the familiar Pearson product-moment correlation coefficient. It is expressed as the square root of the quantity (chi square divided by N), where N is the number of cases in the sample. The use of phi is meliorative for problems such as those raised above when used for tables with one degree of freedom. Since the practical application of prediction tools for selection often reduces to such a table, phi would appear to be an attractive choice for an index of predictive efficiency. However, the marginal distributions of a table with only one degree of freedom place constraints on the phi coefficient by imposing an upper limit on the possible relation observed in the table (Guilford 1965). Finally, phi is subject to a limitation common to correlational measures; that is, it is sensitive to the base rate.

As noted by Richardson (1950) "the predictive value of a selection device has an immediate but highly incomplete and somewhat misleading answer in the standard error of prediction" (p. 192). Most selection applications of prediction devices use some cutting score that essentially reduces the predictor scale to a dichotomy. As commonly used, however, the standard error of prediction assesses the prediction device and the outcome measured continuously and may result in an underestimation of the power of the selection device since the device, as used, predicts only success or failure. The standard error of prediction, however, is a function also of degrees of success or failure; that is, it requires an assessment of the goodness of a success or the badness of a failure (Richardson 1950). Furthermore, the standard error of prediction also is sensitive to variations in the base rate and hence may be of little value in assessing the relative merits of devices used on different populations.

A number of indices attempt to provide an estimate of the "proportionate reduction in error" resulting from the use of a selection or prediction device. In general these indices attempt to offer an evaluation of predictive power above that afforded by the simple use of the chance rate. Ohlin and Duncan (1949) suggested an "index of predictive efficiency" (see also Horst 1941; Reiss 1951a; and Loeber and Dishion 1983), which is the percentage reduction in error gained by the use of a prediction device over that achieved by knowledge of the base rate alone. The index of predictive efficiency also has the limitation of sensitivity to the base rate. Thus it has little usefulness for the examination of accuracy across different situations.

Considering cases such as that diagrammed in figure 1 (in which one essentially wishes to predict membership in one or the other of two mutually exclusive categories), Berkson (1947) noted that there are "utilities" (defined as true positives and negatives) as well as "costs" (defined as false positives and negatives) associated with the decision made. Arguing that predictive devices should be evaluated with respect to a comparison of costs and utilities, he developed an index of effectiveness (which may be used at any utility) called "mean cost" and defined the "mean cost rating" (MCR) to allow the index to vary from zero to one. The MCR is less sensitive to the base rate than is phi or the point-biserial.[5] Berkson's index was introduced to criminologists by Duncan et al. (1952) and since has seen widespread use as a measure of the predictive efficiency of a selection device.[6]

For the 2 × 2 decision case (which represents the "fairest" test of a prediction device as used in selection decisions), Loeber and Dishion (1983) developed an index called "relative improvement over chance" (RIOC), which considers chance occurrence within the table as well as the maximum correct value that prediction could achieve given applicable selection ratio and base-rate conditions. Although not independent either of the base rate or of the selection ratio, the RIOC correlates much less highly with either than does the simple index of predictive efficiency (Loeber and Dishion 1983).

A. Which Index?

None of the indices described can answer completely the question of how accurate a prediction device is. Correlational indices suffer because they are affected by variations in the base rate. Thus they do not readily allow a comparison of devices or items across base-rate conditions. The MCR and RIOC indices do allow this, but it is not often that one wishes to evaluate a specific prediction device regardless of base-

---

[5] The point-biserial is another variation of the product-moment correlation coefficient. In this case one of the measures is measured continuously, and the other is a dichotomy. In applications such as those discussed, the "continuous" measure usually is the predictor scale and the dichotomy the criterion (such as success or failure on parole).

[6] It recently was shown that the MCR is related to Kendall's tau, providing a means of testing the statistical significance of the index (Lancucki and Tarling 1978); and Fergusson, Fifield, and Slater (1977) have shown the relation between the MCR and the familiar proportion of area under a "receiver operating characteristic" (ROC) curve, providing a grounding for the index in the framework of signal detection theory (Green and Swets 1966).

rate conditions, although this now is the most common application of such indices (Gottfredson and Gottfredson 1979).

Measures that are sensitive to base rates and those that are not can lead to dramatically different conclusions concerning the value of predictive devices (Fergusson, Fifield, and Slater 1977). The latter, such as the MCR, essentially give an indication of the general power of the device without respect to constraints of base rates and selection ratios. The former (e.g., correlation measures) describe the performance of the instrument in application with given populations and decision rules.

Which index to use depends on the question to be answered. If the relative power of different devices that are developed on different populations is an issue (for which the base rates may well be different), then indices that are less sensitive to base rates would seem preferable. However, if one wishes an estimate of the power of a particular device administered with particular decision rules on a particular population, then base rate–dependent indices will be more informative.

B. Other Problems concerning "Accuracy"

The practical application of prediction tools in criminal justice raises other problems related to the "accuracy" question. One almost always is attempting to construct, validate, and assess the accuracy of devices under circumstances that already have required some selection: thus true base rates often cannot be known nor "accuracy" assessed relative to them. One cannot, for example, know the true base rate for parole violation for all offenders considered for parole. Since not all are paroled, one can at best identify the base rate for known violations by paroled inmates.

Problems exist also in assessing the relative contributions of specific predictor variables to the overall accuracy of a prediction or selection device. Items that may be highly predictive under some base-rate conditions may be much less so under other base-rate conditions. Items that may prove predictive for some defined populations may be more or less predictive when examined in a different population (e.g., the item "race" may be predictive of criminal convictions in some large urban populations and not at all predictive in suburban or rural populations). Items that are predictive during some age ranges may not apply to other age ranges. "The greatest limitation of prediction methods is that the devices are developed and validated with respect to specific criteria, using available data, in a specific jurisdiction, during a specific time period. Thus, any generalizations to other outcomes of interest, or after modifications of the item definitions used, or to other jurisdictions or populations, or to other time periods, are to be questioned" (Gottfredson and Gottfredson 1979, p. 10).

C. Errors in Prediction

Two kinds of prediction errors are inevitable: some persons predicted to belong to outcome classification A will not (false positives), and some persons predicted to belong to outcome classification B will not (false negatives) (fig. 1). Each of the indices discussed above considers that the two types of errors are equivalent. In practice they may not be equivalent whether measured in monetary, social, or ethical terms. In most practical decision-making situations (and particularly those in criminal justice settings), the social, ethical, or programmatic consequences of one type of error may be dramatically different from those of the other. Although we typically evaluate devices without respect to this "weighting" of errors in a statistical fashion, political, ethical, and policy arguments tend not to ignore the differential consequences of the types of errors made (von Hirsch and Gottfredson 1984). Loeber and Dishion (1983) have demonstrated that the relative evaluation of predictions made can change dramatically depending on consequences assigned to one or the other type of error. Determining the expected utility of prediction devices on the basis of a differential weighting of errors is common in some contexts although not in justice system settings.

IV. How Well Can One Predict?

The present ability to predict the decisions of criminal justice system functionaries or the behavior of offenders is modest. Generally, descriptive decision studies are more powerful than are normative decision studies. One can better predict decisions made in practice than predict offender (or other) outcomes of interest. When normative prediction studies are considered, the proportion of outcome variance explained rarely exceeds .15–.20; it often is lower (for a review of this literature, see Gottfredson and Gottfredson [1986]).

Review of descriptive and normative decision studies across a variety of criminal justice system settings suggests that decision makers tend to rely on a few common items of information regardless of the decision being made (Gottfredson and Gottfredson 1986). Likewise, there is considerable commonality among items found useful in normative prediction studies—again, regardless of the decision-making arena for which the prediction is made. The descriptive and normative studies seem to recommend different items of information as predictive.

Table 1 provides a general summary of those variables found to

TABLE 1

Predictors of Criminal Justice Outcomes

Decision Stage: Outcome	Salient Predictors	
	Descriptive Studies	Normative Studies
Bail; pretrial release: Failure to appear for trial	Seriousness of charge Seriousness of prior charges Prior record "Community ties"	Offense type Prior record "Community ties" Drug use Prior F.T.A.s Pending charges
Cash bail	Seriousness of charge Weapons charge Juvenile record Age Personal victim of crime? "Community ties"* D.A. recommendation* Defense attorney recommendation*	N.A.
Recidivism on pretrial release	N.A.	Offense type Prior record Employment Age "Community ties" Weapons use Pending charges Prior F.T.A.s
Failure to appear or recidivism	N.A.	Type of release† Court disposition time† Offense type Age Pending charges Recent offense history Prior F.T.A.s
Prosecution: Charge	Witness and evidentiary factors Victim/offender relation Seriousness of charge	N.A.
Charge reduction	Seriousness of offense Type of offense Age Prior record	N.A.
Prosecute fully or dismiss	Charge reductions Offense type Number of charges Pretrial detention status	N.A.

TABLE 1 (*Continued*)

Decision Stage: Outcome	Salient Predictors	
	Descriptive Studies	Normative Studies
Prosecution:		
Conviction obtained	N.A.	Offense type
		Evidentiary and witness factors
		Pretrial status
		Age
Sentencing:		
Various‡	Seriousness of offense	N.A.
	Prior record	
	Pretrial status	
	Council and representation	
	Type of conviction	
	Various extralegal factors	
Parole:		
Time served	Seriousness of offense	N.A.
	Maximum term set	
	Subjective risk assessment	
	Institutional behavior	
	Prior record	
	Age	
	Sex	
	Socioeconomic status	
	Marital status	
	Juvenile record	
Parole/not parole	Seriousness of offense	Prior record
	Subjective risk assessment	Offense type
	Attributions regarding offender and offense	Age (particularly "age at onset")
	Institutional behavior	Employment
	Alcohol history	Marital status
	Age	Alcohol/drug use
		Education
		Institutional behavior
		Criminal associates

NOTE.—The first two or three entries in each column represent, in order, the most powerful predictors. Subsequent factors vary sufficiently from study to study to prohibit conclusions with respect to relative accuracy.

* Based on a simulation study.

† Not deemed useful for most practical applications of prediction tools.

‡ The most powerful predictors appear to be seriousness and prior record regardless of the particular criterion used (e.g., sentence type, sentence length, and measures of sentence "severity"). Accordingly, for purposes of this summary table criteria have not been differentiated.

predict the decisions of functionaries and those found to predict the behavior of offenders for a variety of criteria and decisions. Entries in table 1 are intended to represent "constructs"; these have been operationally defined in many different ways in the literature. This is true both for entries under the heading "Salient Predictors" and for those listed under "Outcome."

The first two or three entries in each cell represent, in order, the most powerful predictors of the relevant criterion. The power of variables represented by subsequent entries varies sufficiently from study to study to prohibit conclusions with respect to relative accuracy. Items of predictive information show remarkable consistency in different decision settings (with the possible exception of the prosecutorial stage, where evidentiary factors become important both to decisions made and to trial outcomes). This is true both for descriptive and for normative studies.

With some regularity, the descriptive and normative studies tend to recommend that attention be paid to different items of information. This particularly is true with respect to information concerning the offense: decision makers tend to focus on "seriousness" (which generally is not predictive of behavioral outcomes), while normative studies focus on "offense type," which is predictive of behavioral outcomes.

With respect to the criteria investigated, the data in table 1 suggest that criminal justice functionaries likely do not make optimal decisions. Normative studies also hardly may be said to be optimal in that by far the largest proportion of outcome variance remains unexplained. Still a number of factors appear to have some predictive utility in a variety of settings, and it appears that decision makers do not attend well to those factors. Rather they appear to focus on items of information that demonstrably are not statistically related to the behavioral outcomes of interest. Despite substantial base-rate problems, most investigators have achieved normative predictions that exceed the chance rate and that, if implemented, should improve criminal justice decision making.

In virtually every decision-making situation for which the issue has been studied, it has been found that statistically developed prediction devices outperform human judgments (reviews are available in Meehl [1954, 1965]; Goldberg [1970]; and Dawes [1979]). Meehl (1954) originally established the minimal "rules" for making comparisons of clinical and statistical predictions. One is that both the clinical predictions and those of the statistical model were to be made on the basis of the same information (for obviously the statistical model would be disadvantaged if information is not to be made available to it). In fact, this "rule" may not have been necessary since, even when it is disregarded, statistical models are almost always more valid. Even "bootstrapping" studies, in which a statistical model of clinical assessments is constructed, show that the models that are developed (even though these are of the decision makers' judgments) outperform the original judgments, often by substantial amounts.

The limited information available concerning criminal justice settings would not, I think, disappoint those on the "statistical" side of this continuing (but unproductive) argument. Notable are the studies by Glaser (1955, 1962), in which an actuarially derived device was shown superior to prognostic judgments made by sociologists and psychiatrists relative to a parole-violation criterion, and those of Gottfredson (1961) and Gottfredson and Beverly (1962), in which a statistical combination of items proved substantially more accurate than did judgments made by parole board members. Recently, Holland et al. (1983) found that a statistical composite consistently outperformed mental health professionals and correctional case workers in the prediction of recidivism.[7] Carroll et al. (1982) found that parole board members' judgments of risk were virtually uncorrelated with offender behavioral outcomes and that a simple statistical model, although not powerful, outperformed the decision makers.

The relative superiority of statistical to intuitive methods of predictions is due to many factors. Human decision makers often do not use information reliably (e.g., Ennis and Litwack 1974), they often do not attend to base rates (Meehl and Rosen 1955), they may inappropriately weight items of information that are predictive, they may assign weight to items that are not predictive, and they may be overly influenced by causal attributions (e.g., Carroll 1978) or by spurious correlations (Monahan 1981).

In fairness it should be pointed out that there may be advantages to intuitive judgments as well. For example, human decision makers can make use of information that cannot readily be made available to a statistical device. Demeanor during an interview may be one such example. Other factors in favor of intuitive judgments are reviewed in Dawes (1975).

Due in part to the demonstrable superiority of statistical prediction

---

[7] However, after a correction for range restriction was applied, the human judges did better than did the instrument in identifying indices of violent recidivism.

methods, a great deal of effort has been expended in attempts to provide criminal justice functionaries with tools to aid in decision making. When decision-making aids that incorporate an empirically based predictive component are implemented, there is little evidence that their use serves to reduce the prevalence of the outcome offender behaviors (Gottfredson and Gottfredson 1986). It must be noted, however, that little empirical evidence concerning this important question is available. It does appear that, when properly implemented, decision-making tools that have incorporated a predictive component indeed can provide advances relative to an equity criterion (Goldkamp and Gottfredson 1985; Gottfredson and Gottfredson 1986). With respect, then, to the goal of changing the behavior of functionaries, the devices appear more successful.

V. Methods of Prediction

Perhaps the most widely used actuarial predictive method has been the additive linear model. Models of this type assume that the relations between predictor variables and the criterion (and also among predictor variables themselves) can be represented adequately by a straight line and that the the effects of predictor variables are additive. This section describes the most commonly used additive prediction methods, clustering methods, and contingency table analyses.

A. Least-Squares (Multiple) Regression

The best known and most widely used additive linear model is least-squares regression (known in the bivariate case as correlation and in the multivariate case as multiple correlation or multiple regression). Recently, the term "ordinary least squares" regression has come into common usage to differentiate the standard method of regression from some of its variants (e.g., logistic regression). In general, the solution sought is the weighted linear combination of predictor variables that minimizes (the sum of squares of) errors about regression to some outcome variable. In its general form, the model is described as

$$Y = a + bXi + \ldots + e,$$

where (in this case) Y is the predicted outcome, a is some constant (actually, the intercept of the regression line), Xi is a predictor variable, and b is its weight. A random error term, e, completes the specification.

A potential advantage of the least-squares model is that it provides estimates of the effect of each predictor variable in terms of its relatively unique (i.e., nonoverlapping) contribution to explaining variability in the outcome. This typically results in a set of unequal weights, thus providing an indication (when standardized scores are considered) of the relative "importance" of each predictor in the context of the other variables used.

Regression analysis is a powerful and general class of methods, and the model defined above can be easily extended beyond the estimation of linear effects. While interaction effects (i.e., the extent to which the effect of one predictor variable is mediated or exaggerated by the state of one or several other predictors) can be estimated within a regression framework, the model can quickly become unwieldy (Cohen and Cohen 1975).

The power of least-squares regression in many applications is beyond question. It has been known for some time that least-squares models improve substantially over intuitive clinical approaches to prediction (Meehl 1954, 1965; Dawes 1979). Moreover, Dawes and Corrigan (1974) have shown that even linear regression models that use "random" regression weights do substantially better than do human predictions. Wainer (1976) demonstrated that a simple linear additive model (in which all regression weights are equal to .5) is essentially as good as, and in some important respects may be better than, an optimally weighted least-squares model.

B. The Burgess Method

The unweighted additive model in criminal justice has been patterned after the work of Burgess (1928). Each variable or item in the model can be scored as a "point," and the prediction is based on the aggregate number of points that apply in a particular case. The procedure involves the use of attribute data (or the dichotomization of predictor variables). Resulting attributes then are used in an unweighted, linear additive fashion to predict the outcome classifications. Thus the Burgess technique gives equal weight to all predictors even though there may be markedly unequal levels of association between the outcome and the various predictors used. It allows, therefore, no compensation for "overlapping" effects of the predictors, resulting in the further disadvantage that the technique does not give any indication as to which variables are redundant.

The general form of the model is specified as

$$Y = a + Xi + \ldots + e,$$

where Y is as before, a is an (arbitrary) constant, and Xi is some predictor attribute.[8] A similar model, generally attributed to the Gluecks (1950), weights predictor categories by the proportion of cases in the category that are considered as "successes" according to the outcome classification. Copas and Tarling (1984) have shown that both the Burgess and the Glueck "point-scoring" methods are in fact simple loglinear models in which all predictor variables are treated as independent.

A variety of criminal justice prediction studies have found that a simple, unweighted model had less shrinkage when applied to validation samples than did models derived from multiple regression (e.g., Gottfredson and Gottfredson 1979). Possible reasons for this are discussed in Farrington (1978), Gottfredson and Gottfredson (1979), and Loeber and Dishion (1983). Less shrinkage from the equal-weight model (compared with that from a weighted model) might be expected simply as a consequence of item unreliability if this is marked. The weighted models tend to rely heavily on a few items, so, if one is scored incorrectly, this makes a large difference in the prediction.

Other reasons for differential expected shrinkage are apparent. First, the weighted model may tend to overfit the original construction sample data to a greater extent than may the unweighted method. This is known as "capitalization on chance variation." Second, the weighted model capitalizes on the presence of any data points that deviate remarkably from bi- or multivariate normality; these are called "outliers." The equal-weights method may be meliorative since regression weights are not estimated from the construction sample data.

C. Clustering Models

Lack of power or shrinkage on validation in regression-based predictions may result in part from discrepancies between data characteristics and analytic assumptions. Usually, for instance, regression analyses do not include interaction terms in the prediction equations.[9] Indeed, in a study with a large number of variables, the examination of individual interactions is often impractical without clear theoretical guidelines

---

[8] Although the Burgess technique essentially is a "linear" model, it is difficult to say precisely what it is that is being treated as a straight line. This, however, also is true of many least-squares applications (see Cohen and Cohen 1975, p. 11).

[9] Interaction terms would be included in a regression equation in an effort to determine the extent to which the effects of predictor variables are mediated or exaggerated by particular states of other predictors.

(Mosteller and Tukey 1977). Also, inclusion of interaction terms in a regression framework usually results in substantial multicollinearity, making some model parameters unstable and uninterpretable.[10] Another possible limitation of regression analysis derives from the calculation of regression coefficients from the matrix of zero-order correlations among variables within the entire sample. The assumption is made (if implicitly) that the indicated relations hold in population subgroups, that is, that the population is homogeneous.[11]

Clustering methods have been used to compensate for the limitations of regression-based models "in circumstances where interactions and heterogeneities might be expected to reduce the power of multiple regression methods" (Wilkins and MacNaughton-Smith 1964, p. 613). Clustering methods allow for unspecified interactions and heterogeneities that may be present in a population and can be characterized as nonlinear.

A large number of clustering algorithms are available (see, e.g., Brennan 1980, chap. 7; Brennan, in this volume). Hierarchical clustering schemes generally are of two types: "divisive" methods proceed by successively partitioning or subdividing the sample into increasingly homogeneous groups, and "agglomerative" methods reverse this process. Other differences among methods lie in the specific rules for division or clustering, for termination of the process, or for item inclusion.

Numerical taxonomic approaches have a wide variety of uses in criminal justice research and application, and many of these involve classification for a predictive purpose. One advantage of using statistical clustering approaches may be that resulting devices are easier to implement in practice since the procedures may be more readily understood (and hence used) by decision makers. Indeed the method of combining information for any category of an expectancy table appears to be much more straightforward to nonstatisticians than is the use of, for example, regression scores (Babst, Gottfredson, and Ballard 1968). (For examples

[10] In an ideal world, predictor variables would be rather powerfully correlated with the criterion and not correlated with one another. This would be optimal for prediction since each predictor variable is rather uniquely correlated with the criterion and since the model is additive. Usually, however, this is not the case, and, in the extreme, predictor variables may be much more powerfully correlated with each other than with the criterion. This condition is known as "multicollinearity." Usually, the variables that are used to construct interaction terms already are included (independently) in the model. Accordingly, the interaction term(s) and the variables used to create them will correlate highly, thus resulting in multicollinearity.

[11] This demonstrably may be false when correlation matrices for subgroups are examined.

of the use of configural approaches to criminological prediction problems, see Wilkins and MacNaughton-Smith [1964] and Brennan [1980, chap. 7; Brennan, in this volume].)

Clustering approaches have been criticized for one lamentable failing: they often do not replicate from sample to sample. Critics argue that unstable clustering solutions or structures should not be the basis for practical decisions affecting people's lives. Recently, however, Gottfredson and Gottfredson (1982) have suggested that replication is far less important than is validation when clustering methods are used for a classification purpose with a predictive intent. If the principal purpose of the classification is predictive, then predictive utility and not replicability should be the primary concern. Gottfredson and Gottfredson demonstrated that the clustering methods that have been most often used in criminal justice do have predictive validity even though (as expected) attempted replications of obtained structures failed.

D. Multidimensional Contingency Table Analysis

These methods, developed by Goodman (1970, 1971) and others, require few assumptions about the nature of the variables under consideration (or about the nature of relations among them). The underlying rationale is relatively straightforward: rather than using a multiplicative model to account for potential interactions among predictor variables, the logit model uses logarithms of the odds ratios, resulting in an additive model.

The model inherently allows for nominal level measures, can estimate different "weights" for different predictors, can be conveniently used to estimate interaction terms, does not require the assumption of a particular multivariate distribution for significance testing (as does ordinary least squares regression, a closely related technique), and provides a means of estimating an "optimal" model. These advantages, plus the potential for identifying a parsimonious set of predictors, make the model worth a close examination.

The model predicts odds (e.g., ratio of successes to failures) as a multiplicative function of features of the predictor variables, each of which typically is measured at the nominal level.[12] The analytical form

---

[12] Nominal level measurement requires only the assumption of arithmetic equality. Accordingly, numbers assigned to values of the variable stand only as convenient labels: any other label would be just as acceptable (e.g., "apples" and "oranges"). At this level of measurement, distances between numbers are meaningless as is their order.

of the model is

$$S_{ijk} = a(bX_i)(bY_j)(bZ_k)(bXY_{ij})(bXZ_{ik})(bYZ_{jk})(bXYZ_{ijk}),$$

where X_i, Y_j, and Z_k denote the state (category) of the predictor variables X, Y, and Z, respectively, and S_{ijk} denotes the odds that obtain when variables S, Y, and Z are in states i, j, and k, respectively. The term a is a constant, which represents a basic odds rate (similar to a base-rate probability), from which the effects of the predictors are deviations. The second through the fourth terms (e.g., bX_i) represent the direct "main effects" of the predictors X, Y, and Z. The fifth through the seventh terms represent two-way interaction effects and the last term the three-way interaction effect of the predictors. It should be noted that this equation represents a "saturated" model; that is, it specifies all possible main effects and interaction effects of the independent variables. In the case of three independent variables (as illustrated here), the saturated model will have eight terms (including the constant) on the right-hand side of the equation.

Since technically we refer to a model of the log of the odds ratio, we can express the model in terms of logs:

$$O_{ijk} = T + TX_i + TY_j + TZ_k + TXY_{ij} + TXZ_{ik} \\ + TYZ_{jk} + TXYZ_{ijk},$$

where O_{ijk} is the log of S_{ijk}, and T's are logs of the corresponding a's and b's.

Examples of the use of logit analyses for predictive purposes in criminology may be found in Palmer and Carlson (1976), Gottfredson and Gottfredson (1979), and Goldkamp and Gottfredson (1985).

VI. Can Predictive Accuracy Be Improved?

If statistical prediction tools can improve criminal justice decision making, we clearly must work to improve the accuracy of those tools. This goal can be accomplished by improving the reliability of criminal justice data and the measurement of relevant variables, by statistical and subjective bootstrapping, by the use of theory-driven approaches, and, finally, by attention to ethical concerns.

A. Improved Reliabilities

The first effort should be to improve the predictor and outcome variables used. The reliability of many criminal justice data sources is notoriously poor. This often is recognized with respect to predictor variables but is forgotten with respect to the outcome variables used.

Hindelang, Hirschi, and Weis (1981) consider the accuracy of a variety of means of obtaining outcome data.

Case-specific information often is needed, and this typically is found only in case files available through parole and probation or correctional agencies. Although it has been observed that trained persons can code the information available in those files with respectable reliabilities, little is known about the reliability of that information in the first place. Commenting on Ohlin and Duncan's (1949) comparison of a number of prediction schemes, Vold (1949) lamented that "the most discouraging thing about the whole field of prediction in criminology is the continued unreliability and general worthlessness of much of the so-called 'information' in the original records. Opinions, hearsay, and haphazardly recorded judgments still constitute the bulk of any parole file. Statistics made of this can be no better than the original data" (p. 452).

Little appears to have changed in the past thirty-seven years: these data must be regarded with considerable skepticism. (Actually, one thing has changed; i.e., apparently unreliable information now is readily available in computerized form in many jurisdictions. This may be especially undesirable since investigators who are not familiar with the nature of this information may accept it uncritically.) Sparks (1983) has suggested that one seek to increase the reliability of information by collecting it prospectively rather than by relying on case records. This is attractive but will prove very expensive.

B. Improved Measurement

Improved measurement of both predictor and outcome variables is needed. Variously considered, prior record invariably proves of predictive value. Generally, however, this has been operationally defined in a crude fashion. Improved scaling of this construct potentially could improve the accuracy of predictions based on it. Offense seriousness scales have been developed but are not often used. We have experimented with seriousness scales considered as a criterion measure with demonstrable success (Gottfredson and Taylor 1986). Similarly, perhaps one should seek to predict criteria of interest other than recidivism considered as a dichotomy. For some purposes, the prediction of "time to failure" may prove advantageous (for illustration, see Schmidt and Witte [1979]; and Gottfredson and Taylor [1986]). Finally, multiple criteria of failure should be explored.

C. Use of the Most Appropriate Analytic Methods

Many prediction studies have not capitalized on the potential power of sophisticated analytic methods, and some studies may be subject to specification error resulting from inappropriate use of simple regression methods. When more appropriate methods are available, they should be used. However, little advantage is likely to result unless one first attends to measurement and reliability issues. If one is able to improve on the measurement and reliability of both predictor and criterion variables, the power of more sophisticated methods could well be realized.

D. Statistical Bootstrapping

Statistical bootstrapping models could increase the utility of prediction in criminal justice settings. The basic procedure would require the identification of relatively homogeneous subgroups of offenders, the construction of statistical prediction equations for each, and the combination of these into an "expectancy table" for the full sample.

E. Statistical/Subjective Bootstrapping

Just as decision makers may learn from statistically based information, the actuary may learn from the human decision maker. Models of subjective decisions can have more predictive accuracy than can the subjective decisions alone (e.g., Goldberg 1970), and recent evidence is suggestive that subjective judgments may be more accurate than are actuarial devices for some limited but important purposes (Holland et al. 1983). This has become known as the "clinical-versus-statistical" problem, and debate concerning the relative value of the two general approaches continues. I believe this debate to be counterproductive; prediction may be improved through a combined use of methods. An iterative bootstrapping process in which successive normative and descriptive devices are used to inform and modify each other may well prove productive.

F. Theory-driven Approaches to the Prediction Problem

Sparks (1983) noted that theoretical considerations could benefit those working on prediction but offered little guidance concerning directions such theories might take. Criminal justice prediction research has been rather atheoretical, although it seems to have been of some value in theory construction. Recently, Monahan (1981; Monahan and

Klassen 1982) has proposed ways in which situational approaches may aid in the prediction problem. This clearly represents a theory-driven approach to increasing predictive accuracy (and understanding the phenomena investigated). Gottfredson and Taylor (1986), following Olweus's (1977) person-environment integrity model, recently have demonstrated that recidivism predictions can be improved if person-environment interactions are included in the models developed. Furthermore, the magnitude and nature of the effects observed varied depending on the outcome variable used and on the nature of the offender and environmental variables considered.

G. Attention to Ethical Concerns

Finally, investigators must pay more sophisticated attention to ethical considerations involved in the construction of prediction devices intended for operational use (Fisher and Kadane 1983). Ethical concerns can be addressed within complex statistical models (although ethical choices always must be made), but this has not often been adequately done. Comparisons are needed of models that attempt to suppress unwarranted effects and of models constructed in a simpler fashion.

REFERENCES

Anderson, Norman. 1974. "Cognitive Algebra: Integration Theory Applied to Social Attribution." In *Advances in Experimental Social Psychology*, edited by Leonard Berkowitz. New York: Academic Press.
————. 1979. "Algebraic Rules in Psychological Measurement." *American Scientist* 67:555–63.
Babst, Dean V., Don M. Gottfredson, and Kelly B. Ballard. 1968. "Comparison of Multiple Regression and Configural Analysis Techniques for Developing Base Expectancy Tables." *Journal of Research in Crime and Delinquency* 5:72–80.
Berkson, Joseph. 1947. "Cost Utility as a Measure of Efficiency of a Test." *Journal of the American Statistical Association* 42:246–55.
Brennan, Tim. 1980. *Multivariate Taxonomic Classification for Criminal Justice Research*. Report prepared for the National Institute of Justice. Washington, D.C.: U.S. Government Printing Office.
————. In this volume. "Classification: An Overview of Selected Methodological Issues."

Brown, Lawrence D. 1978. "The Development of a Parolee Classification System Using Discriminant Analysis." *Journal of Research in Crime and Delinquency* 15:92–108.

Burgess, Ernest W. 1928. "Factors Determining Success or Failure on Parole." In *The Workings of the Indeterminate Sentence Law and the Parole System in Illinois*, edited by Andrew A. Bruce, Ernest W. Burgess, and Albert J. Harno. Springfield: Illinois State Board of Parole.

Carroll, John S. 1978. "Causal Theories of Crime and Their Effect upon Expert Parole Decisions." *Law and Human Behavior* 2:377–88.

Carroll, John S., Richard L. Wiener, Dan Coates, Jolene Galegher, and James J. Alibrio. 1982. "Evaluation, Diagnosis, and Prediction in Parole Decision-making." *Law and Society Review* 17:199–288.

Cohen, Jacob, and Patricia Cohen. 1975. *Applied Multiple Regression/Correlation Analysis for the Behavioral Sciences*. New York: Wiley.

Copas, John B., and Roger Tarling. 1984. "Some Methodological Issues in Making Predictions." Paper presented to the National Academy of Sciences Panel on Research on Criminal Careers, Woods Hole, Massachusetts, May.

Cronbach, Lee J. 1960. *Essentials of Psychological Testing*. New York: Harper & Row.

Dawes, Robyn M. 1975. "Case by Case versus Rule-generated Procedures for the Allocation of Scarce Resources." In *Human Judgment and Decision Processes in Applied Settings*, edited by Martin Kaplan and Steven Schwartz. New York: Academic Press.

———. 1979. "The Robust Beauty of Improper Linear Models in Decision-making." *American Psychologist* 34:571–82.

Dawes, Robyn M., and Bernard Corrigan. 1974. "Linear Models in Decision-making." *Psychological Bulletin* 81:95–106.

Duncan, Otis D., Lloyd E. Ohlin, Albert J. Reiss, Jr., and Howard R. Stanton. 1952. "Formal Devices for Making Selection Decisions." *American Journal of Sociology* 58:573–84.

Einhorn, Hillel, and Robert Hogarth. 1981. "Behavioral Decision Theory: Processes of Judgment and Choice." *Annual Review of Psychology* 32:53–88.

Ennis, Bruce J., and Thomas R. Litwack. 1974. "Psychiatry and the Presumption of Expertise: Flipping Coins in the Courtroom." *California Law Review* 62:693–752.

Farrington, David P. 1978. "The Family Background of Aggressive Youths." In *Aggression and Antisocial Behavior in Childhood and Adolescence*, edited by Lionel Hersov, Michael Berger, and David Shaffer. Oxford: Pergamon.

———. 1979. "Longitudinal Research on Crime and Delinquency." In *Crime and Justice: An Annual Review of Research*, vol. 1, edited by Norval Morris and Michael Tonry. Chicago: University of Chicago Press.

———. 1982. "Longitudinal Analyses of Criminal Violence." In *Criminal Violence*, edited by Marvin E. Wolfgang and Neil A. Weiner. Beverly Hills, Calif.: Sage.

Fergusson, D. M., J. K. Fifield, and S. W. Slater. 1977. "Signal Detectability Theory and the Evaluation of Prediction Tables." *Journal of Research in Crime and Delinquency* 14:237–46.

Fildes, Robert, and Don M. Gottfredson. 1968. "Cluster Analysis in a Parolee Sample." *Journal of Research in Crime and Delinquency* 5:2–11.

Fisher, Franklin, and Joseph B. Kadane. 1983. "Empirically Based Sentencing Guidelines and Ethical Considerations." In *Research on Sentencing: The Search for Reform*, edited by Alfred Blumstein, Jacqueline Cohen, Susan E. Martin, and Michael Tonry. Washington, D.C.: National Academy Press.

Fisher, Jerome. 1959. "The Twisted Pear and the Prediction of Behavior." *Journal of Consulting Psychology* 23:400–405.

Glaser, Daniel. 1955. "The Efficacy of Alternative Approaches to Parole Prediction." *American Sociological Review* 20:283–87.

———. 1962. "Prediction Tables as Accounting Devices for Judges and Parole Boards." *Crime and Delinquency* 8:239–58.

Glueck, Sheldon, and Eleanor Glueck. 1950. *Unraveling Juvenile Delinquency*. New York: Commonwealth.

Goldberg, Lewis R. 1970. "Man versus Model of Man: A Rationale, Plus Some Evidence for a Method of Improving on Clinical Inference." *Psychological Bulletin* 73:422–32.

Goldkamp, John, and Michael R. Gottfredson. 1985. *Policy Guidelines for Bail: An Experiment in Court Reform*. Philadelphia: Temple University Press.

Goodman, Leo A. 1970. "The Multivariate Analysis of Qualitative Data: Interactions among Multiple Classifications." *Journal of the American Statistical Association* 65:226–65.

———. 1971. "The Analysis of Multi-dimensional Contingency Tables: Stepwise Procedures and Direct Estimation Methods for Building Models for Multiple Classifications." *Technometrics* 13:33–61.

Gottfredson, Don M. 1961. *Comparing and Combining Subjective and Objective Parole Predictors*. Research Newsletter no. 3. Vacaville, Calif.: California Medical Facility.

Gottfredson, Don M., and Robert F. Beverly. 1962. "Development and Operational Use of Prediction Methods in Correctional Work." *Proceedings of the Social Statistics Section*. Washington, D.C.: American Statistical Association.

Gottfredson, Don M., Leslie T. Wilkins, and Peter B. Hoffman. 1978. *Guidelines for Parole and Sentencing: A Policy Control Method*. Lexington, Mass.: Heath.

Gottfredson, Stephen D., and Don M. Gottfredson. 1979. *Screening for Risk: A Comparison of Methods*. Washington, D.C.: National Institute of Corrections.

———. 1980. "Screening for Risk: A Comparison of Methods." *Criminal Justice and Behavior* 7:315–30.

———. 1982. "Numerical Taxonomies in Criminological Research: Replication of Structure vs. Validation for Predictive Intents." Paper presented to the joint meeting of the Classification Society and the Psychonomic Society, Montreal, June.

———. 1986. "The Accuracy of Prediction Models." In *Research in Criminal Careers and "Career Criminals,"* vol. 2, edited by Alfred Blumstein, Jacqueline Cohen, Jeffrey A. Roth, and Christy A. Visher. Washington, D.C.: National Academy Press.

Gottfredson, Stephen D., and Ralph B. Taylor. 1986. "Person-Environment

Interactions in the Prediction of Recidivism." In *Environmental Criminology*, edited by Robert Sampson and James Byrne. New York: Springer-Verlag.

Gough, Harrison G. 1962. "Clinical versus Statistical Prediction in Psychology." In *Psychology in the Making*, edited by Leo Postman. New York: Knopf.

Green, David M., and John A. Swets. 1966. *Signal Detection Theory and Psychophysics*. New York: Wiley.

Guilford, J. P. 1965. *Statistics for Psychology and Education*. New York: Prentice-Hall.

Hagan, John, and Kristin Bumiller. 1983. "Making Sense of Sentencing: A Review and Critique of Sentencing Research." In *Sentencing Research: The Search for Reform*, edited by Alfred Blumstein, Jacqueline Cohen, Susan E. Martin, and Michael Tonry. Washington, D.C.: National Academy Press.

Hindelang, Michael, Travis Hirschi, and Joseph Weis. 1981. *Measuring Delinquency*. Beverly Hills, Calif.: Sage.

Hogarth, Robin M. 1980. *Judgment and Choice: The Psychology of Decision*. London: Wiley.

Holland, Terrill R., Norman Holt, Mario Levi, and Gerald E. Beckett. 1983. "Comparison and Combination of Clinical and Statistical Predictions of Recidivism among Adult Offenders." *Journal of Applied Psychology* 68:203–11.

Horst, Paul. 1941. *The Prediction of Personal Adjustment*. Social Science Research Council Bulletin no. 48. New York: Social Science Research Council.

———. 1963. "The Statewide Testing Program." *Personnel and Guidance Journal* 41:394–403.

———. 1966. *Psychological Measurement and Prediction*. Belmont, Calif.: Wadsworth.

Klepper, Steven, Daniel Nagin, and Luke-Jon Tierney. 1983. "Discrimination in the Criminal Justice System: A Critical Appraisal of the Literature." In *Research on Sentencing: The Search for Reform*, vol. 2, edited by Alfred Blumstein, Jacqueline Cohen, Susan E. Martin, and Michael Tonry. Washington, D.C.: National Academy Press.

Lancucki, Leszek, and Roger Tarling. 1978. "The Relationship between Mean Cost Rating and Kendall's Rank Correlation Coefficient Tau." *Social Science Research* 7:81–87.

Lee, W. 1971. *Decision Theory and Human Behavior*. New York: Wiley.

Loeber, Rolf, and Thomas Dishion. 1983. "Early Predictors of Male Delinquency: A Review." *Psychological Bulletin* 94:68–99.

Luce, Robert D., and Howard Raiffa. 1957. *Games and Decisions*. New York: Wiley.

Meehl, Paul E. 1954. *Clinical versus Statistical Prediction*. Minneapolis: University of Minnesota Press.

———. 1965. "Seer over Sign: The First Good Example." *Journal of Experimental Research in Personality* 1:27–32.

Meehl, Paul E., and Albert Rosen. 1955. "Antecedent Probability and the Efficiency of Psychometric Signs, Patterns, or Cutting Scores." *Psychological Bulletin* 52:194–216.

Monahan, John. 1978. "The Prediction of Violent Criminal Behavior: A Methodological Critique and Prospectus." In *Deterrence and Incapacitation: Estimating the Effects of Criminal Sanctions on Crime Rates*, edited by Alfred Blumstein, Jacqueline Cohen, and Daniel Nagin. Washington, D.C.: National Academy Press.

———. 1981. *Predicting Violent Behavior: An Assessment of Clinical Techniques*. Beverly Hills, Calif.: Sage.

Monahan, John, and Deidre Klassen. 1982. "Situational Approaches to Understanding and Predicting Individual Violent Behavior." In *Criminal Violence*, edited by Marvin Wolfgang and Neil A. Weiner. Beverly Hills, Calif.: Sage.

Mosteller, Frederick, and John Tukey. 1977. *Data Analysis and Regression*. Reading, Mass.: Addison-Wesley.

Ohlin, Lloyd E., and Otis D. Duncan. 1949. "The Efficiency of Prediction in Criminology." *American Journal of Sociology* 54:441–51.

Olweus, Dan. 1977. "A Critical Analysis of the 'Modern' Interactionist Position." In *Personality at the Crossroads: Current Issues in Interactional Psychology*, edited by David Magnusson and Norman Endler. Hillsdale, N.J.: Erlbaum.

Palmer, Jan, and Paul Carlson. 1976. "Problems with the Use of Regression Analysis in Prediction Studies." *Journal of Research in Crime and Delinquency* 13:64–81.

Pitz, Gordon F., and Natalie J. Sachs. 1984. "Judgment and Decision: Theory and Application." *Annual Review of Psychology* 35:139–64.

Reiss, Albert J., Jr. 1951a. "The Accuracy, Efficiency, and Validity of a Prediction Instrument." *American Journal of Sociology* 61:552–61.

———. 1951b. "Delinquency as the Failure of Personal and Social Controls." *American Sociological Review* 16:196–207.

Richardson, Marion W. 1950. "Effectiveness of Selection Devices." In *Handbook of Applied Psychology*, vol. 1, edited by Douglas H. Fryer and Edwin R. Henry. New York: Rhinehard.

Schmidt, Peter, and Anne D. Witte. 1979. "Models of Criminal Recidivism and an Illustration of Their Use in Evaluating Correctional Programs." In *The Rehabilitation of Criminal Offenders: Problems and Prospects*, edited by Lee Sechrest, Susan White, and Elizabeth Brown. Washington, D.C.: National Academy Press.

Solomon, Herbert. 1976. "Parole Outcome: A Multidimensional Contingency Table Analysis." *Journal of Research in Crime and Delinquency* 13:107–26.

Sparks, Richard F. 1983. "The Construction of Sentencing Guidelines: A Methodological Critique." In *Research on Sentencing: The Search for Reform*, vol. 2, edited by Alfred Blumstein, Jacqueline Cohen, Susan E. Martin, and Michael Tonry. Washington, D.C.: National Academy Press.

van Alstyne, David J., and Michael R. Gottfredson. 1978. "A Multidimensional Contingency Table Analysis of Parole Outcome: New Methods and Old Problems in Criminological Prediction." *Journal of Research in Crime and Delinquency* 15:172–93.

Vold, George B. 1949. "Comment on 'The Efficiency of a Prediction in Criminology.'" *American Journal of Sociology* 54:451–52.

von Hirsch, Andrew, and Don M. Gottfredson. 1984. "Selective Incapacitation: Some Queries about Research Design and Equity." *New York University Review of Law and Social Change* 12:11–51.

Wainer, Howard 1976. "Estimating Coefficients in Linear Models: It Don't Make No Nevermind." *Psychological Bulletin* 83:213–17.

Warner, Sam B. 1923. "Factors Determining Parole from the Massachusetts Reformatory." *Journal of Criminal Law and Criminology* 14:172–207.

Wilkins, Leslie T., and P. MacNaughton-Smith. 1964. "New Prediction and Classification Methods in Criminology." *Journal of Research in Crime and Delinquency* 1:19–32.

Wright, Kevin, Todd Clear, and Paul Dickson. 1984. "Universal Applicability of Probation Risk-Assessment Instruments: A Critique." *Criminology* 22:113–34.

David P. Farrington

Predicting Individual
Crime Rates

ABSTRACT

There are great individual differences between offenders in their crime
rates. The chronic offenders who commit the most crimes tend to commit
them at the highest rates. High individual crime rates are predicted by an
early age of onset of offending, a serious first offense, and a high past
crime rate. Longitudinal surveys show that high individual rates are
predicted by early antisocial behavior, convicted parents and siblings, low
family income, and school failure. Cross-sectional surveys indicate that
they are also predicted by a poor employment record and drug use. The
prediction of individual crime rates should be investigated in prospective
longitudinal surveys, and predictor and criterion variables should be
selected on theoretical grounds rather than on availability in records. A
standard index of predictive efficiency is needed in studies of individual
crime rates, and this should be measured in validation samples.
Acceptance or rejection of a penal policy based on predictions of high-rate
offending depends on the choice of a utilitarian or just deserts approach to
criminal justice decision making and on a comparison of social costs and
social benefits. More research is warranted, rather than the adoption of a
new penal policy.

This essay reviews the prediction of individual crime rates—the
rates at which people commit offenses. Section I explains why this
research may have useful implications not only for explanations of
offending but also for penal policy, especially in regard to the selective
incapacitation of chronic offenders. Section II discusses the extent to

David P. Farrington is lecturer in criminology at Cambridge University. He is grateful
to Jacqueline Cohen, Peter B. Hoffman, Rolf Loeber, Michael H. Tonry, Andrew von
Hirsch, James Q. Wilson, and Marvin E. Wolfgang for helpful comments on an earlier
version of this essay.

53

which future crime rates can be predicted by criminal career features such as the age and type of the first offense and the past offending rate. Section III reviews early predictors of individual crime rates such as family environment and school failure and later ones such as drug use and unemployment. Methodological problems are discussed in Section IV. This essay is primarily concerned with research, but problems arising from the possible practical use of these predictions in the criminal justice system are examined in Section V. The final section summarizes major conclusions and outlines future research needs.

I. Why Predict Individual Crime Rates?

Prediction research in criminology is motivated by two major concerns: to provide predictive information that might be of use to criminal justice decision makers, especially in sentencing and parole, and to assist in the development and testing of theories of offending. Both of these concerns are addressed in this essay, although its primary aim is to review knowledge about prediction rather than possible practical applications of that knowledge.

A. Penal Aims and Chronic Offenders

Until recently, rehabilitation was generally considered the most important aim underlying sentencing and penal treatment. It was assumed that, if a prisoner had reformed, his likelihood of committing further crimes would be zero, and it would be safe to release him.[1] This idea led to research that aimed to predict whether offenders would commit further crimes during a specified follow-up period. Not all prediction research in criminology was inspired by rehabilitative concerns; for example, the use of base expectancy scores to group prisoners into risk categories assisted parole agencies in incapacitative decisions. However, the main objective of most research was to predict recidivism.

Interest in rehabilitation as a penal aim declined in the mid-1970s, as the influential reviews by Martinson (1974) in the United States and Brody (1976) in England suggested that existing techniques of penal treatment had no differential effects on recidivism. This conclusion was essentially confirmed by a National Academy of Sciences panel in an impressive, methodologically sophisticated review (Sechrest, White, and Brown 1979). As the emphasis on rehabilitation declined, interest

[1] Since most of the research reviewed in this essay has been concerned with male offenders, male pronouns and adjectives are used.

in retribution or just deserts, individual and general deterrence, and incapacitation increased.

Early research on incapacitation suggested that serious crime could be reduced significantly only at the cost of impractically large increases in prison populations (see Cohen 1983).[2] For example, on the basis of a random sample of convicted offenders in Denver, Colorado, Petersilia and Greenwood (1978) concluded that a mandatory minimum sentence of five years for any felony would have prevented 45 percent of the crimes but would have increased the prison population by 450 percent. Similarly, Cohen (1978) showed that California, New York, and Massachusetts would have to increase their prison populations by more than 150 percent in order to achieve a 10 percent reduction in Index crimes through incapacitation. However, a penal policy of incapacitation might be more effective if it could be targeted more narrowly on the offenders who commit crimes at relatively high rates. Using Greenberg's terms (1975), such a policy would have to be selective rather than collective, that is, targeted on types of offenders rather than on types of offenses.

In order to assess the incapacitative effects of penal treatment, it is essential to estimate how many offenses would be committed by a given offender during a certain period free in the community. This requires information about his rate of offending and about the residual length of his criminal career (the period of time during which he continues to commit offenses). Unfortunately, there has been little attempt to measure or predict career lengths. Incapacitation can prevent more offenses if the incarcerated person is a high-rate rather than a low-rate offender; and there is no incapacitative benefit gained from incarcerating people beyond the point at which they stop offending. In assessing incapacitative effects, it is also important to investigate other questions such as whether individual crime rates stay constant over time, whether the incarceration of one member of a group affects offending by the group as a whole, and whether incarceration causes an increase in crime rates or career lengths.[3]

---

[2] The primary focus of interest in this essay is on the more serious crimes: Index offenses in the United States and indictable crimes in England. Indictable crimes in England are slightly more inclusive than Index offenses in the United States since indictable crimes include the Index offenses of theft, burglary, robbery, aggravated assault, homicide, arson, and forcible rape and also fraud, receiving stolen property, vandalism, and several other sex offenses.

[3] Such an increase might occur, e.g., if prisons acted as "schools for crime" or if exprisoners were stigmatized and therefore could not get jobs.

Interest in incapacitation has focused attention on the minority of "chronic" offenders who commit large numbers of offenses. Their existence was first highlighted by Wolfgang, Figlio, and Sellin (1972) in their Philadelphia cohort study of 10,000 males born in 1945. Wolfgang and his colleagues found that 6 percent of their sample, who had each been arrested at least five times, were responsible for 52 percent of all the recorded juvenile offenses. These chronics constituted 18 percent of the offenders but accounted for substantial proportions of the serious offenses: 63 percent of all Index offenses, 71 percent of homicides, 73 percent of rapes, 82 percent of robberies, and 69 percent of aggravated assaults. Similar results were obtained in a second Philadelphia cohort of 13,800 males born in 1958 (Wolfgang and Tracy 1982).

Wolfgang, Figlio, and Sellin (1972) showed that their chronics committed large numbers of offenses but not that they committed offenses at high rates. However, Barnett and Lofaso (1985) demonstrated that an offender's future arrest rate in the Philadelphia cohort increased with the number of his prior arrests. Also, using data collected in a longitudinal survey of over 400 London males, Barnett, Blumstein, and Farrington (1987) showed that the average time interval between convictions decreased as the number of convictions increased. Therefore, in both the Philadelphia and London cohorts, the chronic offenders committed crimes at relatively high rates.

Self-report studies also reveal great variations in offending rates. In one Rand Corporation project based on prisoners in three states, Greenwood and Abrahamse (1982) reported that, while burglars committed burglaries at a median rate of 5.5 per year, the most active 10 percent of the burglars committed burglaries at a rate of over 230 per year. The comparable figures for robbery were five and eighty-seven. In another Rand project in which self-reports of offending were obtained from California prisoners, Peterson, Braiker, and Polich (1981) discovered that the median prisoner committed 2.8 serious crimes (homicides, rapes, robberies, burglaries, assaults, auto thefts, and forgeries) per year of street time, but that the most active 8 percent committed over sixty serious crimes per year. These 8 percent committed three times as many serious crimes per year in total as the least active half of these prisoners.

Information about crime rates and career lengths is potentially useful not only to investigate incapacitation but also to assess rehabilitative and individual deterrent effects of penal treatments. Whether recidivism occurred was always an unsatisfactory criterion. The absence of recorded offenses during a short follow-up period of one or two years does not necessarily indicate successful rehabilitation or deterrence because the person may have committed offenses that were not recorded or his offending may have occurred after the end of the follow-up period. Equally, the commission of one recorded offense during a follow-up period does not necessarily show the failure of rehabilitative or deterrent measures, because the measures may have caused an offender to commit fewer crimes. How far predictors of crime rates and career lengths are similar to or different from established predictors of recidivism is an important empirical question.

It would be more satisfactory to assess the effectiveness of rehabilitative or deterrent measures on the basis of changes in offending rates or residual lengths of criminal careers rather than recidivism. It may be that some penal measures affect crime rates while others affect career lengths. Of course, it would be necessary to disentangle the effects of the penal measures from those of other factors that might influence offending, such as aging or changing opportunities for crime. Also, it would be desirable to distinguish between rehabilitative and deterrent effects by interviewing the offenders to find out why their offending had changed. The prediction of individual crime rates and career lengths following different penal treatments might assist decision makers in choosing rehabilitative or deterrent measures as well as incapacitative ones.

B. The Criminal Career Approach

Traditionally, crime rates have been calculated on complete samples or populations. For example, in the Provo experiment, Empey and Erickson (1972) reported that the average number of recorded offenses per person (not per offender) in a four-year follow-up period was 1.32 for their experimental group and 1.42 for their control group. Blumstein and Cohen (1979) argued that samples or populations should be partitioned into offenders and nonoffenders and that crime rates should only be calculated for those who are active offenders (i.e., those who have begun a criminal career but not yet terminated). This would make it possible to establish whether changes in the total number of crimes committed by a population reflected changes in prevalence (the number of offenders in the population) or in the individual crime rate of offenders. Similarly, this approach could be extended to establish whether changes in the total number of crimes committed reflected a changing mix of offenders, for example, with low-rate offenders desisting more quickly than high-rate ones.

The traditional approach can be contrasted with the criminal career approach set out in greatest detail in the report of the National Academy of Sciences panel on criminal career research (Blumstein et al. 1986). A criminal career is a period during which a person's rate of offending is greater than zero and constant. The individual crime rate is only one feature of a criminal career, which also has an age of onset, a length, and an age of termination. The inverse of the rate of offending is the average time interval between offenses. In calculating either the rate or the time interval, it is desirable to eliminate periods when the person is not at risk of offending in the area under study: periods spent incarcerated in penal institutions, out of the area, in hospitals, and of course after death. At any given age, a variety of different types of crimes can be committed, and the rate of offending could be calculated separately for each type (as could other criminal career features).

The assumptions underlying the traditional approach have not usually been stated explicitly. However, with less serious Index or indictable offenses such as theft, it might be argued that every person (with the possible exception of young children) has a probability greater than zero of offending. Many criminologists have argued that offenders and nonoffenders are not sharply differentiated (see, e.g., Clarke and Cornish 1985). Therefore, theft rates should be based on a complete sample or population, and it may be more realistic to study increases and decreases in offending rates during theft careers rather than onset and termination. Hence criminal careers with clearly delineated starting and ending points do not exist, and the concept of career length is unnecessary, since the probability of offending only decreases to zero when a person dies.

The traditional approach is most applicable to research based on self-reports of less serious offenses. For example, in the London longitudinal survey, West and Farrington (1973) found that, at age fourteen or sixteen, 90 percent of their sample admitted traveling deliberately without a ticket or paying the wrong fare, and 82 percent admitted breaking windows of empty houses. When offending is almost universal, it is reasonable to divide a sample into more or less frequent offenders rather than into offenders and nonoffenders. The traditional approach is most applicable to fundamental research questions about why the average person commits common offenses.

The criminal career approach is most applicable to research based on official records or based on self-reports of more serious offenses. For example, in the London survey, West and Farrington (1977) found that, between ages fifteen and eighteen, only 7 percent of the youths were convicted of burglary, and only 11 percent admitted burglary. When offending is confined to a small deviant minority, it is best to divide a sample into offenders and nonoffenders. The criminal career approach is applicable not only to fundamental research questions about why offenders commit serious offenses but also to penal questions about how detected offenders should be treated.

The criminal career approach has the great advantage of quantification, and it could lead to a significant change in ways of thinking about offending. I generally follow it in this essay. However, because the two approaches apply to different types of crimes, I do not follow it to the exclusion of the traditional approach. In other words, I do not restrict my reviews of research only to projects that have measured the rate of offending by offenders.

In the criminal career approach, it is important to distinguish between a person's true and measured crime rate (Cohen 1983). The true rate is related probabilistically (i.e., according to random processes) to the actual number of offenses committed in a year because of unpredictable or chance factors such as the occurrence of criminal opportunities. For example, a person with a true rate of ten crimes per year may actually commit five crimes in some years and fifteen in others. The actual number of offenses is related probabilistically to the recorded number because of measurement biases. The most common methods of measurement are official records of arrests or convictions and self-reports of offending. The major problem is to draw conclusions from measured rates about true rates of offending.

One difficulty with this approach is to identify those who are currently active offenders. Some offenders—especially those with low crime rates—may commit no measured offenses during a given observation period. Therefore, the true individual crime rate cannot be calculated by simply dividing the total number of measured offenses by the number of measured offenders, although this is the usual method of calculation. This will lead to an overestimate of the true crime rate because every measured offender has at least one measured offense.[4]

---

[4] Cohen (1986, p. 338) has outlined a method of correcting estimates of individual crime rates to overcome this problem.

The problem of offenders with no measured offenses becomes less as the crime rate increases, as the measurement period increases, and with self-reports as opposed to official records (since self-reports capture a higher proportion of offenses committed).

As the measurement period increases, there is an increasing likelihood that an offender's crime rate will vary over time. If crime rates vary during the course of a criminal career, it would also be worthwhile to try to predict high-rate periods. In practice, such periods may be quite short-lived because of the likelihood of their being ended by a sentence of incarceration. If crime rates vary over time, it would also be useful to measure their acceleration and deceleration and to use these as predictive factors (Barnett and Lofaso 1985).

It might be thought that the aim should not be to predict frequency of offending but seriousness since one serious offense may be of more concern to the general public than several trivial ones. However, the most frequent offenders tend also to be the most serious. On the basis of the Rand self-report survey of prisoners in three states, Chaiken and Chaiken (1982) identified as the most serious offenders the "violent predators," those who committed robbery, assault, and drug dealing. They also found that these offenders tended to commit both more serious and less serious crimes at unusually high annual rates. Similarly, Peterson, Braiker, and Polich (1981) in their self-report survey of California prisoners showed that those who committed one type of crime at high rates tended also to commit other types at high rates.

It has been known for many years that frequency, seriousness, and variety of offending are highly correlated (e.g., Farrington 1973). In both the Philadelphia and London cohorts, those who committed more crimes tended also to commit more serious crimes (Barnett and Lofaso 1985; Barnett, Blumstein, and Farrington 1987). While it is rare for offenders in general to specialize (Wolfgang, Figlio, and Sellin 1972), it seems even more unusual for high-rate offenders to specialize. Hence, predictions of frequency tend also to be predictions of seriousness (and indeed also of variety of offending and of "career criminals").

This raises a question that is more compatible with the traditional approach, namely, whether there is one underlying theoretical construct of "criminal tendency" that determines all criminal career features. As criminal tendency increases, does the offending rate increase, the age of onset decrease, the age of termination increase, and the variety and seriousness of offending increase? This was an argument put forward by Hirschi and Gottfredson (1983). Or do these different career features have different underlying theoretical constructs? At the present state of knowledge, it is not possible to give a definite answer to this question.

If there were only one underlying theoretical construct that was constant over time, predictors of individual crime rates would be similar to predictors of onset, of career length, and of termination. It seems unlikely that predictors of onset would be the same as predictors of termination, if only because of the different ages at which these events occur. The child-rearing methods used by a person's parents will probably influence and predict onset but not termination, and getting married will probably influence and predict termination but not onset. These are essentially questions that can be resolved by empirical research.

While practical considerations and the criminal career approach require information about how well high-rate offenders can be predicted out of all offenders, theoretical considerations and the traditional approach suggest that it would also be useful to know which factors predict those persons in the general population who become high-rate offenders. Both issues are addressed in this essay.

II. Prediction Using Criminal Career Features

A number of projects have studied the extent to which the chronic offenders—persons who have committed a large number of offenses—can be predicted by criminal career features such as the age of onset of offending and the nature of the first offense. Not all of these have attempted to determine whether the chronic offenders commit crimes at high rates.

A. *Predicting Chronics and Persisters*

Important objections to the concept of identifiable chronic offenders were raised by Blumstein and Moitra (1980). They pointed out that every statistical distribution of rates of offending had a right-hand tail containing offenders with relatively high rates; it was only to be expected that those who became high-rate offenders accounted for a relatively high proportion of all the offenses. Even if all the arrested juveniles in the Philadelphia cohort had been identical in their prior criminal propensities, chance factors alone would have caused some to have had more arrests than others.

Blumstein and Moitra showed that a model assuming that all those with three or more arrests had identical recidivism probabilities yielded an arrest distribution quite similar to that of the Philadelphia cohort. Therefore, the chronics (arbitrarily defined as those with five or more arrests) could have been indistinguishable in advance from those who stopped at three or four juvenile arrests. The key theoretical and policy issue is not whether a small proportion of offenders account for a large proportion of offenses (to some extent, this is inevitable) but whether the high-rate offenders, however defined, can be predicted in advance.

The distinction between theoretical and empirical features of criminal careers has been illustrated by Blumstein, Farrington, and Moitra (1985). They were concerned to explain the measured probability of recidivism up to a certain cutoff age, a feature that probably reflects both the offending rate and the residual length of the criminal career. For example, in the Philadelphia cohort study of Wolfgang, Figlio, and Sellin (1972), the probability of recidivism up to the eighteenth birthday was .54 after the first arrest, .65 after the second, .72 after the third, and so on. Blumstein, Farrington, and Moitra (1985) proposed that offenders could be divided into two subpopulations, "persisters" with a high true probability of recidivism and "desisters" with a low probability. The assumptions that 44 percent of offenders were persisters and that the true recidivism probabilities were .80 for persisters and .35 for desisters produced an aggregate arrest distribution similar to that of the Philadelphia cohort. It followed that the measured recidivism probability increased after each successive arrest because desisters tended to drop out, so that the observed offenders consisted increasingly of persisters.

This model of offending has implications for prediction. The aim should be to identify persisters prospectively rather than chronics retrospectively. Because of essentially unpredictable probabilistic processes, some of the true persisters will not become chronics, and some of the true desisters will become chronics. These discrepancies should not be regarded as errors in prediction. In this context, an "error" only occurs when a predicted persister is not a true persister (or when a predicted desister is not a true desister).

In the London longitudinal survey, Farrington (1983b) reported that the 6 percent of the sample with six or more convictions (17 percent of the offenders) accounted for about half of all the convictions up to the twenty-fifth birthday. These persons could be regarded as the chronic offenders. The assumptions that 28 percent of the offenders were persisters and that the true recidivism probabilities were .87 for persisters and .57 for desisters produced an aggregate distribution of convictions close to that observed (Blumstein, Farrington, and Moitra 1985). It followed from this model that 24 percent of the London chronics were true desisters, while 17 percent of the nonchronic offenders with between one and five convictions were true persisters. Half of the true persisters achieved six or more convictions, in comparison with only 6 percent of the true desisters.

Blumstein and his colleagues also used a seven-point score designed to predict future offending. This was based on early antisocial behavior, convicted parents, social deprivation, low intelligence, and poor parental child-rearing behavior, all measured at ages eight to ten (before the first conviction). Coincidentally, 28 percent of the offenders had high scores of four or more, and therefore these were predicted to be persisters. It was then found that 35 percent of chronics were predicted desisters, while 20 percent of nonchronic offenders were predicted persisters. Just under half (41 percent) of the predicted persisters became chronics, in comparison with only 8 percent of the predicted desisters.

A major implication of this research is that it is important to partition observed "false positives" into those predicted in error and those caused by probabilistic processes. Assuming that the discrepancy between predicted persisters and chronics could be regarded as a false positive rate of 59 percent, most of this does not reflect error in prediction. According to the model, since each true persister has a .13 probability of ceasing to offend after each conviction, 50 percent of them do not survive to have a sixth conviction. An error occurs when a predicted persister is not a true persister, and the figures indicate that only 9 percent of the 59 percent rate is caused by prediction error. It can be calculated that the probability of a predicted persister being a true persister is .80. Similarly, only 2 percent of the 8 percent false negative rate reflects prediction error.

To explain the distribution of convictions but not their timing, Blumstein, Farrington, and Moitra (1985) concentrated on the recidivism probability and neglected the individual crime rate. More recently, Barnett, Blumstein, and Farrington (1987) have tested the adequacy of a model that assumes that there are two subpopulations of offenders, one with a high crime rate (an estimated 1.14 convictions per year free) and a low desistence probability (an estimated .10 chance of terminating after each conviction) and the other with a low crime rate (.41 per year) and a high desistance probability (.33). This model can explain the aggregate number of convictions, taking account of time at risk. It also provides information about expected lengths of criminal careers.[5]

B. Age of Onset

Hamparian et al. (1978) showed, in a retrospective longitudinal survey of violent juveniles in Columbus, Ohio, that the number of arrests after the age of onset increased linearly up to the eighteenth birthday. In other words, after this age, it seemed that these juveniles were offending at a constant rate.[6] In a similar survey of violent adults in the same city, Miller, Dinitz, and Conrad (1982) found that the age of onset was unrelated to the average interval between arrests. This also suggested that offending rates were constant after this age, although again an early age of onset predicted those who became chronic offenders. To the extent that an early age of onset is not predictive of a high crime rate, this casts doubt on the theory that all criminal career features reflect one underlying construct of "criminal tendency."

A retrospective longitudinal survey was carried out by the Home Office (1985) to investigate the conviction records of nationally representative samples of persons born in 1953, 1958, and 1963. As found in other studies, criminal convictions were heavily concentrated in a small minority. For example, 5.5 percent of the males born in 1953 (those with six or more convictions) accounted for 70 percent of all the convictions of this sample up to the twenty-eighth birthday. These chronic offenders tended to have been convicted first at an early age. Males in all three cohorts first convicted at age ten (the minimum age for conviction) averaged between five and six convictions by the eighteenth birthday. However, once a first conviction had occurred, the rate of offending was quite stable, at about 0.7 convictions per person per year.

In the London longitudinal survey, the total number of convictions of each youth decreased with increasing age of onset, from an average

[5] For example, with 1.14 convictions per year and a termination probability of .10 after each conviction, the probability of termination per year is 1.14 × .10, or .114. The expected length of the criminal career is the reciprocal of this probability, or 8.8 years in this instance (1/.114).

[6] There was no attempt in this survey (as usual) to assess when criminal careers began and ended. The average offending rate was calculated by reference to all juvenile offenders. It is conceivable that, if some criminal careers ended with increasing age, the number of currently active offenders became increasingly less than the number who had ever offended. Hence, those who continued to offend might have done so at an increasing rate. This explanation is implausible in the light of Barnett and Lofaso's (1985) research, quoted later, which suggests that criminal careers beginning in the juvenile years rarely end before age eighteen.

of 7.17 convictions for those first convicted at ages ten to twelve to 1.18 for those first convicted at ages twenty to twenty-four (Farrington 1983*b*). However, the earliest convicted youths had the highest rate of committing offenses at all ages. Furthermore, the average length of criminal career (measured simply as the time between the first and last convictions) was highest for the earliest convicted youths and then decreased with increasing age of onset (Farrington 1983*a*). In this study, then, an early age of onset predicted not only a high total number of offenses but also a high rate of offending and a long criminal career. Also, Blumstein, Farrington, and Moitra (1985) showed that a conviction at an early age was the best predictor of who would become chronics out of all the offenders. While 61 percent of the chronics were first convicted by age thirteen, only 41 percent of those first convicted by age thirteen became chronics. Therefore the false positive rate for this prediction was quite high.

Unfortunately, all the existing surveys are affected by the truncation of criminal careers at a certain age of measurement. A complete study of criminal careers would probably have to follow a sample until every member had died. The problem of truncation in the Philadelphia cohort study has been demonstrated by Barnett and Lofaso (1985). After the fifth arrest, 28 percent of the chronics had no further arrests up to the eighteenth birthday (and so apparently "desisted" from offending). The rate of "desistance" increased with the age at the fifth arrest, being 15 percent at age fifteen, 20 percent at age sixteen, and 41 percent at age seventeen. Barnett and Lofaso showed that, assuming that arrests occurred at a constant rate, virtually all the apparent "desistance" could be explained as time intervals between offenses that included the eighteenth birthday.[7] Hence they could not demonstrate that any of the delinquency careers in the Philadelphia cohort had truly ended by this age. It is important to establish in any project how far the ability of an early age of onset to predict a high total number of offenses is caused by truncation.

---

[7] They assumed that arrests occurred according to a Poisson probability process or, in other words, that all offenders accumulated arrests at random intervals at the same average rate when not incarcerated. For each offender, $P(x, t)$, the probability of exactly x arrests in an interval of t years, was given by

$$P(x, t) = \frac{(rt)^x e^{-rt}}{x!},$$

where r = individual crime rate (arrests per year).

C. The Nature of the First Offense

Several projects have investigated how far the nature of the first offense predicts subsequent offending, in most cases comparing status offenders with criminal offenders. An important policy issue is that, if status offenders tend also to commit criminal offenses, then decriminalizing status offenses will not necessarily reduce the prevalence of recorded juvenile offenders in the population.[8]

In a reanalysis of the Philadelphia cohort study, Clarke (1975) found that first offenders who committed theft or damage offenses were most likely to become juvenile chronics with five or more arrests (33 percent of blacks and 17 percent of whites). Violent first offenders were somewhat less likely, and status first offenders least likely (17 percent of blacks and 6 percent of whites). However, in a follow-up of over 2,000 juveniles appearing before the Virginia courts, Thomas (1976) reported that status first offenders were marginally the most likely to have three or more subsequent juvenile court appearances (9.1 percent of status first offenders, as opposed to 8.8 percent of felony first offenders, and 4.6 percent of misdemeanor first offenders). Different results were obtained by Kelley (1983) in a replication with over 2,000 juveniles appearing before the Detroit courts. Status first offenders were least likely to have three or more subsequent juvenile court appearances (5.3 percent), in comparison with felony (10.9 percent) and misdemeanor (12.4 percent) first offenders.

These apparently conflicting findings can be made more consistent by taking into account types of subsequent offenses. In the two juvenile court studies, there was some tendency for each type of first offender to repeat the same type of offense. For example, in the Thomas (1976) project, 43 percent of subsequent court appearances by felony first offenders were for felonies, and only 12 percent for status offenses; conversely, 41 percent of subsequent court appearances by status first offenders were for status offenses, and only 20 percent for felonies. The average number of subsequent felonies was twice as high for felony first offenders as for status or misdemeanor first offenders. Kelley (1983) also found that the average number of subsequent felonies was highest for felony first offenders, and Clarke's (1975) data show that the average number of subsequent Index offenses was highest for Index first offenders and lowest for status first offenders. It can be concluded that a

---

[8] Research concerned with the probability of recidivism rather than the frequency of reoffending (e.g., Meade 1973; Lab 1984) is not reviewed here.

relatively serious first juvenile offense predicts later persistent serious juvenile offending.[9]

Power et al. (1974), in London, followed up nearly 250 boys first convicted between ages eleven and fourteen. They reported that 41 percent of those first convicted for burglary had two or more subsequent juvenile convictions, in comparison with 28 percent of those first convicted for theft and 14 percent of those first convicted for other offenses. Similarly, Blumstein, Farrington, and Moitra (1985) found that boys in the London longitudinal survey who were first convicted for the more serious offenses of burglary or violence were slightly more likely to become chronics with six or more convictions than those first convicted for less serious offenses (primarily theft). However, the nature of the first offense was not an important predictor of chronics in this study.

D. The Past Rate of Offending

It might be expected that the best predictor of the future rate of offending would be the past rate of offending. Farrington (1983b) discovered a close relation in the London longitudinal survey between the number of juvenile convictions (ages ten to sixteen) and the number of adult convictions (ages seventeen to twenty-four). Over three-quarters of those with four or more juvenile convictions also had four or more adult convictions; conversely, 84 percent of those with no juvenile convictions also had no adult convictions. Nearly three-quarters (71 percent) of juvenile recidivists with two or more convictions became adult recidivists, but only 39 percent of adult recidivists had been juvenile recidivists.

Similar but less marked relations between juvenile and adult offending were reported by Shannon (1985) in his follow-up of three birth cohorts continuously resident in Racine, Wisconsin. As an example, for males born in 1949 and followed up to age twenty-five, one-third of those with three or more serious juvenile police contacts (for felonies or major misdemeanors) also had three or more serious adult police contacts, in comparison with only 3 percent of those with no, one, or two serious juvenile police contacts.

The most convincing demonstration of the predictive power of the past offending rate has been provided by Barnett and Lofaso (1985),

---

[9] Unfortunately, none of these studies extends the follow-up period into the adult years or takes account of the time at risk between the first offense and the eighteenth birthday.

using the Philadelphia cohort study data. Most of their analyses concentrated on predicting subsequent offending at the time of the fifth arrest, which was the cutoff point for the definition of chronic offending in the Philadelphia project. Holding age and the number of prior arrests constant, they showed that the future crime rate was best predicted by the past crime rate. Neither the number of prior arrests nor the acceleration of the past crime rate predicted the future rate independently of the past rate. Similarly, Barnett, Blumstein, and Farrington (1986) demonstrated that the past crime rate predicted the future crime rate in the London longitudinal survey.

E. Other Criminal Career Features

It is unfortunate that the predictive power of other features of criminal careers in regard to the individual crime rate has not been investigated. For example, in evaluating penal aims, it would be helpful to know the effect of different sentences on offending rates. Some projects have related dispositions to recidivism probabilities. For example, both in the Philadelphia cohort study (Wolfgang, Figlio, and Sellin 1972) and in the national English follow-up of birth cohorts (Home Office 1985), more severe dispositions were followed by higher recidivism probabilities than less severe ones. However, because of inadequate control of extraneous variables,[10] it cannot necessarily be concluded that there is any causal link between the disposition and recidivism, much less between the disposition and the offending rate. In contrast to the other studies, Miller, Dinitz, and Conrad (1982) reported that heavier sentences were followed by longer intervals between arrests, but this result could have followed artifactually from their failure to exclude time incarcerated from consideration.

There have also been a number of studies using measures of crime rates before and after the imposition of penal measures. Murray and Cox (1979), with a sample of Chicago youths, found that the number of arrests per year free declined from 6.3 just before their first commitment to an institution to 2.0 just after. The decline in the rate of offending was less for chronic delinquents treated in the community (from 5.7 to 2.7) or in group homes (from 5.5 to 2.2). Maltz et al. (1980) argued that this "suppression effect" of penal treatment could be caused by regression to the mean: the treatment was given just after an abnor-

---

[10] For example, those who received more severe dispositions may have been more frequent offenders beforehand or may have had a higher predisposition toward reoffending.

mally high rate of offending, and the normal variation in crime rates then caused an apparent decline afterward. Randomized experiments including before and after measures of crime rates have usually found little differential effect of correctional treatments (e.g., Empey and Lubeck 1971; Empey and Erickson 1972).

It is also unfortunate that there has been little research on the prediction of residual lengths of criminal careers. Blumstein, Cohen, and Hsieh (1982) estimated total and residual career lengths using cross-sectional data on the number of officially recorded offenders at each age, assuming that decreases in the number of offenders with age were caused by offenders terminating criminal careers. They found that careers of burglary and robbery were relatively short, averaging about four to five years, whereas careers of aggravated assault lasted about ten years on average. While the peak prevalence of Index crime tends to be in the teenage years (Farrington 1986a), in this study the average residual career length was greatest, and the dropout rate was lowest, for offenders aged between thirty and forty.

At the present time, the major conclusions that can be drawn about the prediction of individual crime rates using criminal career features are that the past offending rate, a serious first offense, and an early age of onset of offending all seem to be predictive. However, it is doubtful whether their predictive efficiency is sufficient to justify their use as predictors in criminal justice decision making. As already mentioned, in the London longitudinal survey only 41 percent of the earliest convicted youths became chronic offenders, although they constituted 61 percent of all chronics; and, while 71 percent of juvenile recidivists became adult recidivists, they constituted only 39 percent of adult recidivists. Decisions about the possible practical use of predictive information require consideration not only of predictive efficiency but also of the social costs and benefits of different outcomes.

III. Prediction Using Other Information

Section IIIA reviews what is known about the prediction of individual crime rates using early antisocial behavior, the family environment, school failure, and delinquent peers.[11] The most important results have been obtained in prospective longitudinal surveys, but few of these have been concerned to predict rates of offending. Section IIIB reviews the prediction of crime rates on the basis of later factors, such as drug

[11] For a more detailed review, see Farrington (1987a).

use and unemployment. Information about these has, in general, been obtained in retrospective surveys, casting doubt on the extent to which these factors are genuinely predictive. However, the retrospective surveys have followed the criminal career approach and provided direct information about individual crime rates of offenders.

Predictors of offending that cannot be modified in principle—notably age, gender, and ethnicity—are not reviewed in this essay. These variables cannot be manipulated, which makes it virtually impossible to demonstrate unambiguously any causal effects they might have on offending rates. Also, their potentially discriminatory nature and the fact that they are beyond the offender's control militate against their use in prediction exercises designed to assist criminal justice decisions. There are many existing reviews of the relation between these three demographic factors and offending (e.g., Blumstein et al. 1986; Farrington 1987b), showing, at least for age and ethnicity, that they are related to prevalence rather than to the individual crime rate.

A. Early Predictors

Many longitudinal surveys based on official records yield data about early differences between offenders and nonoffenders, but most such surveys based on self-reports have not studied early predictors. Consequently, more is known about the early predictors of offending as measured by arrests or convictions than as measured by self-reports. More is known about the onset of offending than about its persistence. The excellent review by Loeber and Dishion (1983) shows that the best predictors of onset are parental family management techniques, troublesome child behavior (such as stealing, lying, or truanting), criminality or antisocial behavior of other family members, poor educational achievement, separation from parents, and socioeconomic status, in that order (see also Loeber and Stouthamer-Loeber [1986] for a more recent and comprehensive review of this research). This essay, of course, is concerned with predicting crime rates rather than with predicting the onset of criminal careers.

In predicting crime rates, the most relevant longitudinal surveys are those comparing nonoffenders, nonchronic offenders, and chronic offenders, since chronic offenders tend to commit crimes at high rates. This classification makes it possible to study the predictors of both offending and chronic offending. Unfortunately, few studies of this kind have been conducted. Wolfgang, Figlio, and Sellin (1972) compared these three groups in their pioneering Philadelphia cohort study, but their conclusions were limited by the small amount of information available about each person. Blumstein, Farrington, and Moitra (1985) also compared these three groups, using the much wider range of variables measured in the London longitudinal survey, and so they could investigate the early predictors of chronic offending in more detail. They could carry out more extensive multivariate analyses to determine which factors predicted chronic offending independently of others. Apart from these two studies, most other results may reflect early characteristics of offenders in general rather than of high-rate offenders.

1. *Child Behavior Problems.* As Loeber and Dishion (1983) concluded, early troublesome, dishonest, aggressive, or antisocial behavior has always been found to be an important predictor of later offending. For example, in a follow-up of boys living in the center of Philadelphia, Spivack (1983) discovered that the majority of the most frequent offenders with four or more police contacts had been rated badly behaved by their teachers when they were in the first grade. Ensminger, Kellam, and Rubin (1983) showed that, for boys in an urban black ghetto of Chicago, teacher ratings of aggressiveness in the first grade at age six were significantly related to self-reports of offending by these youths at age fifteen. Also, in a high delinquency area of New York City, Craig and Glick (1968) reported that behavior problems in the first grade predicted later persistent serious offending.

In the London longitudinal survey, Farrington (1979a) found that troublesomeness, dishonesty, and daring between ages eight and ten, rated by teachers, peers, and parents, significantly predicted both official and self-reported offending during both the juvenile and young adult years. Farrington (1986b) investigated the precursors of official and self-reported offending at different ages. The best predictor of offending at any given age was the measure of offending at the immediately preceding age, showing the continuity in criminal behavior over time. Offending at ages twenty-one to twenty-four was best predicted by offending at ages seventeen to twenty, which in turn was best predicted by offending at ages fourteen to sixteen, which in turn was best predicted by offending ages ten to thirteen, which in turn was best predicted by troublesome behavior at ages eight to ten. In a very real sense, there appeared to be continuity between childhood troublesomeness and adult criminal behavior.

Blumstein, Farrington, and Moitra (1985) and Farrington (1987a) reported not only the extent to which different factors predicted offending but also the extent to which they identified the chronic offenders. Troublesomeness was an important predictor in both cases; 70 percent of the chronics had been rated troublesome at age eight to ten, in comparison with 33 percent of the nonchronic offenders. Furthermore, troublesomeness predicted the chronic offenders independently of all other precursors. Therefore it seems likely that childhood antisocial behavior before age ten predicts not only the onset of offending but also rates of offending, although these conclusions are limited by the failure in any of these surveys to measure lengths of criminal careers.

2. *Child-rearing Methods.*   Loeber and Dishion (1983) concluded that parental family management techniques predicted the onset of offending better than any other factor. West and Farrington (1973) found that harsh or erratic parental discipline; cruel, passive, or neglecting parental attitude; poor supervision; and parental conflict, all measured at age eight, all predicted later juvenile convictions. Furthermore, poor parental child-rearing behavior (a combination of discipline, attitude, and conflict) and poor parental supervision predicted both juvenile self-reported and official offending (Farrington 1979*a*). Harsh parental discipline and attitude at age eight also significantly predicted later violent as opposed to nonviolent offenders (Farrington 1978). However, poor parental child-rearing behavior was related to early but not later offending (Farrington 1986*b*). Bearing in mind that the chronic offenders typically began offending as juveniles and continued in their adult years, it was perhaps not surprising that early discipline and supervision did not significantly distinguish them from the nonchronic offenders (Blumstein, Farrington, and Moitra 1985).

3. *Antisocial Parents and Siblings.*   Robins (1979) found in her longitudinal studies that antisocial or alcoholic parents tended to have sons who later became criminals. For example, in her follow-up of over 200 black men in St. Louis, she showed that arrested parents (her subjects) tended to have arrested children and that the juvenile records of the parents and children contained similar numbers and types of offenses (Robins, West, and Herjanic 1975). Craig and Glick (1968) in New York City also showed that boys with criminal parents or siblings were especially likely to become persistent serious offenders later.

In the London longitudinal survey, West and Farrington (1973) found that, if a boy had a convicted mother, father, or brother by his tenth birthday, this significantly predicted his own later convictions. Furthermore, convicted parents and delinquent siblings were related to both self-reported and official offending (Farrington 1979*a*). Unlike most early predictors, convicted parents were less characteristic of those who offended at an early age (ten to thirteen) than of later convicted youths (Farrington 1986*b*). Also, convicted parents predicted which juvenile offenders would go on to become adult criminals and which recidivists at age nineteen would continue offending (West and Farrington 1977). While having convicted parents was one of the best independent predictors of offending, having convicted siblings proved to be one of the best independent predictors of chronic as opposed to nonchronic offending (Blumstein, Farrington, and Moitra 1985). Of course, boys with convicted parents tended also to be those with convicted siblings, so, if one of these factors emerged as an independent predictor of offending, the other would not.

4. *Broken Homes.* Power et al. (1974) investigated the extent to which broken homes predicted recidivism among London boys aged eleven to fourteen making their first court appearances. As in other studies (e.g., Wadsworth 1979; McCord 1982), boys from homes broken by death were no more likely to reoffend than boys from intact homes without stress. However, boys from homes broken as a result of disharmony had a high probability of reoffending, as had boys from intact homes characterized by serious and persistent stress.

West and Farrington (1973) also found that boys from homes broken by death were not particularly likely to be convicted, unlike boys from homes broken by parental separation or desertion. They concluded that homes broken at an early age were not especially criminogenic. Both permanent and temporary separations lasting more than one month predicted official delinquency, providing that they were not caused by death or hospitalization. Furthermore, such separations were related to self-reported as well as to official offending (Farrington 1979*a*). Separations proved to be an independent predictor of convicted as opposed to unconvicted persons, but not of chronic as opposed to nonchronic offenders (Blumstein, Farrington, and Moitra 1985).

5. *Social Deprivation.* More consistently than other types of studies, longitudinal surveys tend to show that children from socially deprived families are more likely to become offenders when they grow up than are children from nondeprived families. In the London survey, West and Farrington (1973) found that juvenile convictions were predicted by low family income, unsatisfactory housing, and an erratic paternal work record—but not by the occupational prestige of the family breadwinner. However, all of these measures predicted juvenile self-reported offending and adult convictions (Farrington 1979*a*). Also, low family

income at age eight was one of the factors that discriminated best between chronic and nonchronic offenders (Blumstein, Farrington, and Moitra 1985). Whereas only 28 percent of nonchronic offenders came from low-income families, this applied to 65 percent of the chronics.

6. *Low Intelligence and School Failure.* Loeber and Dishion (1983) concluded that poor educational achievement (including low intelligence and truancy) was an important early predictor of offending. The association between school failure and offending has been demonstrated consistently in longitudinal surveys. In the Philadelphia cohort study, Wolfgang, Figlio, and Sellin (1972) found that measures of intelligence and attainment in the first six grades (ages six to twelve) were significantly related to official juvenile offending. They concluded that these results largely reflected racial differences since the nonwhites were more likely to have low intelligence and attainment and to be arrested. However, in a reanalysis of their data, Jensen (1976) showed that achievement was more strongly related to offending than was race. Interestingly, Wolfgang and his colleagues demonstrated that their chronic offenders had much lower intelligence and achievement than their nonchronic offenders.

West and Farrington (1973), in the London longitudinal survey, found that low intelligence at age eight to ten (which was highly related to other measures of early school failure) was one of the best independent predictors of juvenile convictions. Furthermore, low intelligence was especially characteristic of the recidivists and those first convicted at the earliest ages (ten to thirteen). Low intelligence and attainment predicted both juvenile self-reported and official offending (Farrington 1979a). Also, truancy was one of the most important independent predictors of convictions as a young adult (Farrington 1986b), and low attainment at age eight to ten was one of the factors that discriminated not only between convicted and unconvicted persons but also between chronic and nonchronic offenders (Blumstein, Farrington, and Moitra 1985). Two-thirds of the chronics had low junior school attainment (based on arithmetic, English, and verbal reasoning tests).

7. *Peer Influence.* Elliott, Huizinga, and Ageton (1985) in their American national longitudinal survey concluded that bonding to delinquent peers was the most important proximate cause of delinquency. This conclusion was essentially based on analyses that showed that having delinquent friends was the most important independent correlate of self-reported offending. A major problem of interpretation arises because most delinquent acts are committed in groups and those who

commit such acts will almost inevitably tend to have delinquent friends. In other words, self-reports of a person's own offending and of his having delinquent peers may be measuring the same underlying theoretical construct of delinquent behavior. There is no demonstration in the literature that association with delinquent peers precedes or facilitates offending, although this may well be true.

In the London longitudinal survey, associating with delinquent friends was not measured until age fourteen, and so this was not investigated as a significant independent predictor of convictions as a young adult (Farrington 1986b). Also, the recidivists at age nineteen who ceased offending differed from those who persisted in their greater likelihood of stopping going around in a group of male friends. Furthermore, spontaneous comments by the youths indicated that withdrawal from the delinquent peer group was seen as an important factor in ceasing to offend (West and Farrington 1977). Therefore continuing to associate with delinquent friends may be an important factor in determining whether juvenile delinquents persist in offending as young adults and hence in predicting chronic offending.

8. *Summary*.   Early antisocial behavior, convicted parents and siblings, low family income, and school failure all predict chronic offenders, and by implication high rates of offending, among a population of offenders. Poor parental supervision, harsh or erratic parental discipline, parental conflict, and broken homes caused by parental conflict are all important predictors of the onset of offending. However, while they would discriminate between high-rate offenders and the remainder of a population that includes nonoffenders, they may not predict comparative rates of offending among a population of offenders. All these variables are important candidates for inclusion as causal factors in a theory of the development of high-rate offending.

Blumstein, Farrington, and Moitra (1985) investigated how far it might be possible to predict the chronic offenders by developing a combined score based on early antisocial behavior, convicted parents, social deprivation, low intelligence, and poor parental child-rearing behavior, all measured at ages eight to ten. The fifty-five youths with the highest scores (of 397 measured) included the majority of chronic offenders with six or more convictions (fifteen out of twenty-three), twenty-two of the 109 nonchronic offenders, and eighteen of the 265 unconvicted youths. This exercise gives some indication of how far it might be possible to predict high-rate offenders at age ten, in advance of any convictions. This prediction score was constructed and validated on randomly chosen halves of the same sample (Farrington 1985), and so needs to be validated prospectively on a different sample.

B. Later Predictors

The major retrospective surveys of individual crime rates have been carried out by Rand Corporation researchers with prisoner samples.[12] In the first of these, which was largely a pilot study (Petersilia, Greenwood, and Lavin 1978), forty-nine armed robbers serving at least their second prison sentences were asked about offending during their juvenile, young adult, and adult periods. Among the interesting findings was that, during their average twenty-year criminal careers, these offenders had committed serious crimes at a rate of about twenty per year when not incarcerated. The researchers divided the robbers into sixteen "intensive" and thirty-three "intermittent" offenders and found that the average intensive offender had committed about ten times as many crimes as the average intermittent offender. The intensives were more likely to have begun committing serious crimes before age thirteen, to be drug users, and to have a poor employment record.

In the second Rand survey (Peterson, Braiker, and Polich 1981), over 600 California prisoners were asked about crimes that they had committed while not incarcerated during the three-year period before their present sentence began. Multiple regression analyses (see, e.g., Blalock 1972) were carried out to investigate which factors predicted the total offending rate (across eleven categories of crime) independently of others. The best independent predictors were the extent of criminal identities (how far the person saw himself as a criminal), juvenile crime, criminal attitudes, race (white or Hispanic), drug use, and social instability (employment, residential, or marital).

Unfortunately, most of these "predictors" were not clearly predictive, in the sense of preceding offending. Criminal identities, criminal attitudes, and social instability could well be consequences or at least concomitants of frequent offending. Drug use was measured during the same period as the offending; one of the eleven categories of crime (the criterion variable) was drug selling. Only juvenile crime and race appear to be genuine predictors, and the racial result may reflect selection biases. As Peterson, Braiker, and Polich speculate (1981, p. 170), white and Hispanic prisoners may have had higher offending rates because

[12] For detailed reviews of these surveys, see Cohen (1986) and Visher (1986).

the California criminal justice system was more likely to imprison low-rate black offenders than low-rate white or Hispanic offenders.

The third Rand survey involved nearly 2,200 prison and jail inmates in California, Michigan, and Texas, selected to be representative of an incoming cohort of inmates. They were asked about crimes that they had committed while not incarcerated or hospitalized during the one to two years before their present sentence began. Greenwood and Abrahamse (1982) developed a seven-point prediction scale, based on items that were strongly associated with offending rates and considered suitable for use in sentencing. The items were a history of recent incarceration, a similar prior conviction, juvenile conviction or incarceration, heroin or barbiturate use recently or as a juvenile, and recent unemployment.

Each person was scored 0 or 1 according to the presence or absence of each item, leading to a prediction score between 0 and 7 for each offender. Greenwood and Abrahamse showed how these prediction scores were related to individual crime rates. For example, the median annual offense rate for burglary for California burglars was 1.4 for those scoring 0 or 1 on the scale, 6.0 for those scoring 2 or 3, and 92.9 for those scoring 4 or more. The scale was more successful in identifying low-rate offenders than high-rate ones. For example, their table 4.5 (1982, p. 53) shows that, of 209 offenders of all types predicted to be low rate (scoring 0 or 1), 76 percent actually were low rate. However, of 236 offenders predicted to be high rate (scoring 4 or more), only 44 percent actually were high rate.

The same data were analyzed differently by Chaiken and Chaiken (1982). They were concerned to predict the high-rate robbers, who tended also to be the violent predators—those who had committed robbery, assault, and drug dealing. The following variables appeared to predict the high-rate as opposed to low-rate robbers in a multiple regression analysis: juvenile violent crimes, juvenile drug addiction, a young age of onset of offending, juvenile incarceration, and the proportion of time unemployed. Among convicted robbers, the 20 percent with the lowest prediction scores had an average robbery rate of 0.9 per year, in comparison with an average rate of 37.5 per year for those in the highest 20 percent of prediction scores. Of twenty-five convicted robbers predicted to be high rate, eleven (44 percent) actually were high rate, in comparison with none of the twenty robbers predicted to be low rate.

The variables emerging in the Rand studies are quite similar to those included in the original Salient Factor Score developed in 1973 as a recidivism risk component of the parole guidelines developed by the U.S. Board of Parole (Gottfredson, Wilkins, and Hoffman 1978). Federal prisoners accumulated points on this scale if they had no prior convictions or incarcerations, had a first commitment at age eighteen or older, had a commitment offense not involving auto theft, never had parole revoked, had no history of drug dependence, completed twelfth-grade education, had been employed at least six months during the last two years, and planned to live with a spouse or children on release. High scores predicted parole success as opposed to failure.

Unlike the scales proposed by the Rand researchers, the original Salient Factor Score was validated prospectively on a new sample of prisoners (Hoffman and Beck 1976), with no significant decrease in predictive efficiency. In addition, its use to guide parole board decision making has led to a reduction in disparity (Gottfredson 1979). Perhaps it was not surprising that Janus (1985) argued that a policy of selective incapacitation was little more than a repackaging of the ideas underlying the Salient Factor Score and that such a policy had been operated by the federal prison system for more than ten years. Furthermore, "despite numerous challenges, the courts have yet to reject an SFS item on grounds of legal impropriety" (1985, p. 121). Nevertheless, later Salient Factor Scores developed in 1976 (Hoffman and Beck 1980) and 1981 (Hoffman 1983) concentrated more on criminal history variables and drug use and excluded such factors as education, employment, and marital status. This was true because the criminal history and drug use variables could be ascertained more validly, because the other factors did not add significantly to predictive efficiency, and because the later scores were more compatible with a just deserts approach.

Janus (1985) investigated the ability of the 1981 Salient Factor Score to predict individual crime rates in a validation sample of over 2,000 prisoners released from federal institutions. The probability of rearrest during a three-year follow-up period varied from 66 percent of the worst risks (scores 0–3) to 22 percent of the best (scores 8–10). Similarly, 23 percent of the worst risks had three or more rearrests, in comparison with only 4 percent of the best. The average arrest rate per inmate per year varied over the risk groups from 0.51 to 0.13. This average rate did not take account of the time spent in institutions, which would have been greater for the worst risks, and so the true difference between the groups in the aggregate arrest rate while free would have been greater. Janus calculated the arrest rate per inmate, not per active offender. Blumstein et al. (1986) allowed for both time incarcerated and career termination and concluded that the average arrest rate per year free for active offenders varied over the risk groups from 0.88 to 0.61.

Janus (1985) also estimated the current selective incapacitation effects of the use of the Salient Factor Score. This analysis was based on the 600 most serious offenders, in a rough attempt to equate them on just deserts sentencing. The worst risks in this group served 9.7 months longer than average and accumulated 0.035 arrests per month after release. Assuming a constant arrest rate, it could be argued that the use of the Salient Factor Score had saved 0.34 arrests for each of these inmates, in comparison with a collective incapacitation policy in which each inmate served the same length of sentence. Conversely, the best risks served 3.1 months less than average and accumulated 0.01 arrests per month, so the score had allowed 0.03 extra arrests for each of these inmates. Overall, it might be argued that the use of the score saved twenty arrests out of 371, or about 5 percent. Janus concluded that the federal prison system's policy of selective incapacitation represented an efficient use of available prison accommodation in comparison with collective incapacitation.

Parole prediction has a long history and has been responsible for most of the advances in the use of prediction methods in criminology (Farrington and Tarling 1985a). Parole studies show that, apart from features of the criminal career, unemployment, drug use, and marital status all predict recidivism. The Rand research represents a step forward in attempting to measure and predict individual crime rates, but its retrospective nature leads to formidable problems of interpretation. Nevertheless, emergence of similar variables in both types of studies suggests that unemployment and drug use, at least, would predict crime rates in a prospective validation. It is plausible that unemployment and drug use are causes of crime. This conclusion is strengthened by research showing that individual crime rates are higher during unemployment than employment periods (Farrington et al. 1986) and higher during drug addiction than abstinence periods (Ball, Shaffer, and Nurco 1983).

IV. Methodological Problems

Methodological problems of predicting individual crime rates include the research design, the sampling method, the selection and measurement of predictor and criterion variables, the combination of predictor variables into a prediction score, and the measurement of predictive efficiency.[13]

A. Research Design and Sampling

The best research design for investigating the prediction of offending rates is the prospective longitudinal survey. Most existing "prediction" studies do not involve true prediction since the predictors were not measured before the offending. This was true not only of the Rand studies by Greenwood and Abrahamse (1982) and Chaiken and Chaiken (1982) but also of the older comparison by Glueck and Glueck (1950) of 500 persistent serious offenders and 500 nonoffenders. The Gluecks developed a method of predicting offending based on five factors: the discipline of the boy by the father, the supervision of the boy by the mother, the affection of the father for the boy, the affection of the mother for the boy, and the cohesiveness of the family. Generally, families of offenders were characterized by unduly lax, harsh, or erratic discipline; poor supervision; low cohesiveness; and hostile or rejecting attitudes. The Gluecks advocated use of their prediction device to identify potential offenders at the time of school entrance (age six). However, commentators immediately perceived that it was "pure speculation" (Anderson 1951, p. 747) to assume that differences between offenders and nonoffenders observed at age fourteen to fifteen (on average) were present at age six.

A distinction can be drawn between historical information that is entirely retrospective (e.g., retrospective self-reports by offenders about their juvenile years) and historical information that was recorded prospectively but used retrospectively for research purposes (e.g., official records of juvenile offending). Problems of retrospective bias are obviously greater where the information is entirely retrospective. However, bias caused by knowledge of the criterion variable of offending can affect the extraction and coding of prospective data and its combination into a prediction instrument. Given that researchers wish to draw conclusions about the accuracy of prospective prediction, the best way to demonstrate this is in a prospective longitudinal survey (for reviews of such surveys in criminology, see Farrington [1979b, 1982] and Farrington, Ohlin, and Wilson [1986]).

---

[13] For detailed discussions of these problems, see Farrington and Tarling (1985a) and Gottfredson and Gottfredson (1986).

Sampling problems can arise when a prediction instrument is constructed on one sample and then applied to another. For example, in Greenwood and Abrahamse's research (1982), the predictions were based on a sample of inmates. However, they investigated the effect of using these predictions in sentencing. Clearly, predictions that apply to inmates do not necessarily apply to convicted offenders, who are likely to be a much less extreme group in many ways, especially in offending rates. Another sampling problem, particularly in self-report surveys, is attrition or nonresponse bias. For example, in the Peterson, Braiker, and Polich (1981) survey, only 57 percent of the inmates completed the questionnaire, and fewer were included in some analyses. This limits the ability to generalize to the population.

B. Predictor and Criterion Variables

In most prediction studies, the selection of predictor and criterion variables is determined primarily or exclusively by what is available in official records (see, e.g., Pritchard 1979). It would be better to choose such variables on theoretical grounds, according to what might be expected to predict what. For example, in predicting individual crime rates, it would be desirable to choose predictors on the basis of a theory of what causes high-rate offending and why people become high-rate offenders. Also, predictions would probably be improved if information from several different sources was combined since it might then be possible to overcome the errors and biases inherent in any one source. Predictor and criterion variables should be measured as validly and as reliably as possible. Interpretations are easier if each empirical variable measures one distinct theoretical construct.

To some extent, the choice of variables to measure depends on the purpose of the prediction exercise. If the purpose is theoretical or explanatory, then there need not necessarily be any restrictions on what variables are measured. However, if the purpose is to devise a prediction technique for use by decision makers in the criminal justice system, then it would be advisable to exclude certain categories of factors, such as gender and ethnicity. Interestingly, unacceptable predictors are often highly correlated with acceptable ones, and the inclusion of unacceptable predictors may not increase the efficiency of a prediction device based on acceptable ones (Gottfredson and Gottfredson 1985; Goldkamp, in this volume; Petersilia and Turner, in this volume).

Offending is usually measured either by official records or by self-reports. The most important predictive analyses in the Greenwood and

Abrahamse (1982) research were based on self-reports, but this may limit their practical usefulness. It may be impossible to obtain valid information from offenders who know that their answers will influence their processing in the criminal justice system. One solution to this problem might be to use official records instead of self-reports, but this may not be satisfactory. In the Rand research, Chaiken and Chaiken (1982) found that predictions based on official record data were less accurate than those based on self-reports.

Dunford and Elliott (1984) argued that official records and self-reports lead to different conclusions about offending rates. In their longitudinal survey of a nationally representative sample of 1,700 juveniles, they concluded from self-reports that most true high-rate offenders did not appear in official records. If this were correct, then the extent to which crime could be reduced by criminal justice system interventions directed at identified high-rate offenders early in their criminal careers would be small. Dunford and Elliott defined serious career offenders as those committing three or more Index offenses (according to self-reports) in at least two successive years out of the five covered by their longitudinal study. Only about a quarter of these offenders were arrested. Similarly, slightly less than a quarter of those admitting more than ten Index offenses during a three-year period were arrested. For the highest-rate offenders (those admitting twenty or more Index offenses), only one in forty offenses led to an arrest.

A number of objections can be raised to Dunford and Elliott's arguments. First, it is possible that the self-reported "Index offenses" would not be regarded as such by the police. Many of them consisted of strong-arming students, teachers, or others; gang fights; and minor assaults. Second, given that 27 percent of the target sample was not interviewed, the most persistent and serious offenders in the population may have been underrepresented in their sample. Their "serious career offenders" seem unlikely to be comparable to the Philadelphia chronics. Third, the police arrest data may be incomplete. The searches only included juveniles who consented to have their records searched (88 percent), and only covered jurisdictions within ten miles of a juvenile's home. Also, the arrest records extended over three years only, rather than covering the complete juvenile history.

In contrast, the London longitudinal survey of West and Farrington (1977) was based on an inner-city sample including 6 percent with six or more criminal convictions up to age twenty-five; 95 percent were interviewed at age eighteen (and higher proportions at younger ages), and the crime rate analyses were based on clearly serious criminal offenses such as burglary. West and Farrington found that the majority of those who admitted burglary during a three-year period (62 percent) had been convicted for it during that period. Only 13 percent of burglaries led to convictions, but most burglars were convicted sooner or later. About half (53 percent) of those who had committed one burglary had been convicted, in comparison with 58 percent of those who had committed between two and five burglaries, and 77 percent of those who had committed six or more. That these percentages did not increase more dramatically suggested that the high-rate offenders committed offenses in such a way that, on any given occasion, they were less likely to be convicted than the low-rate ones. Farrington (1983b) concluded that the official records and self-reports agreed quite well in identifying who were the burglars, although they differed greatly in their estimates of the number of burglaries committed.

In regard to a wider range of offenses, West and Farrington (1973) also found a considerable overlap between self-reported and official figures. Of the eighty youths (out of 409 interviewed) with the highest numbers of self-reported delinquent acts at ages fourteen and sixteen combined, twenty-two were convicted recidivists as juveniles, nineteen had one conviction, thirteen had some other police record (a conviction for a minor offense or a police caution), and only twenty-six had no official record. The majority of juvenile recidivists (twenty-two out of thirty-seven) were in this high self-report group. In contrast, of ninety-three boys with the lowest numbers of self-reported acts and no admissions of serious offenses, none were recidivists, only five had one juvenile conviction, only two had some other police record, and eighty-six had no official record. From these results, it seems likely that high-rate serious offenders identified by self-reports can overlap considerably with high-rate serious offenders identified by official records.

C. Methods of Combining Predictors

Methods of combining predictor variables into a prediction table have been reviewed by Farrington and Tarling (1985a). The simplest is the points score ascribed to Burgess (1928). This was used by Greenwood and Abrahamse (1982), but their method of selecting predictor variables seems rather arbitrary and subjective. The Burgess technique was criticized for its lack of statistical justification and for not taking account of intercorrelations between predictive factors. These criticisms led to the use of least-squares multiple regression techniques by such researchers as Mannheim and Wilkins (1955) in the 1950s. Peterson, Braiker, and Polich (1981) also used this method. However, there are some obvious problems in applying multiple regression techniques to criminological data, and these have been summarized by Palmer and Carlson (1976). In particular, difficulties are caused by variables that are not measured on interval scales and do not have normal distributions. Many criminological variables are dichotomous (e.g., recidivist/ nonrecidivist), categorical, or have highly skewed distributions (e.g., offending rates).

Disquiet with multiple regression led in the 1960s to the use of hierarchical clustering techniques such as predictive attribute analysis (Wilkins and MacNaughton-Smith 1964). These methods require less restrictive assumptions than multiple regression about the nature of the variables and hence are more suitable for use with criminological data. However, they are somewhat arbitrary and difficult to justify on statistical grounds. Dissatisfaction with these techniques led to the use of loglinear and logistic methods in the 1970s (e.g., Solomon 1976), which are statistically justifiable and applicable to the kinds of categorical data typically collected in criminological research. Unfortunately, neither they nor any other techniques appear to be more efficient than the Burgess method in validation samples (Farrington and Tarling 1985b). Furthermore, none of these techniques is designed for a criterion variable with a highly skewed distribution, such as the offending rate. One possible method of coping with the highly skewed offending rate is to use the logarithm of it as a criterion variable, as Chaiken and Chaiken (1982) did.

D. Measuring Predictive Efficiency

In most criminological applications, a dichotomous predictor is compared with a dichotomous criterion variable. If a prediction score is calculated, a cutoff point is chosen and all persons on one side of it are regarded as predicted offenders (or high-rate offenders), while those on the other side are regarded as predicted nonoffenders (or low-rate offenders). False positives are those predicted to be high-rate offenders who actually become low-rate offenders, while false negatives are those predicted to be low-rate offenders who actually become high-rate offenders. It is also interesting to look backward at the prediction problem and establish, for example, the percentage of high-rate offenders who were predicted to be low-rate offenders and the percentage of low-rate offenders who were predicted to be high-rate offenders. The incidence of correct predictions is also important, of course. As the cutoff point is increased to predict fewer and fewer high-rate offenders, the incidence of false positives can be decreased, but at the cost of decreasing the percentage of high-rate offenders who are correctly predicted.

There are various methods of measuring predictive efficiency. In the dichotomous prediction problem just discussed, the simplest measure is the percentage of predictions that coincide with outcomes. However, the disadvantage with this index is that it is greatly affected by the base rate of the outcome (e.g., the proportion of the population who are actually high-rate offenders). For example, if 5 percent of the population were actually high-rate offenders, a 95 percent accurate prediction could be achieved by predicting everyone to be a low-rate offender. However, this level of accuracy would be misleading, of course, since none of the high-rate offenders would have been correctly identified.

In order to overcome this base rate problem, Ohlin and Duncan (1949) proposed as an index of predictive efficiency the proportional reduction in error, calculated by comparing errors obtained with the prediction instrument and errors obtained with the base rate alone. In their research, 40.1 percent of parolees were violators and 32.5 percent of the predictions made by their Burgess-type instrument were incorrect, so the proportional reduction in error was 19 percent (40.1 minus 32.5, then divided by 40.1).

One problem with the Ohlin-Duncan measure is that the maximum reduction in error depends on the difference between the selection ratio (e.g., the percentage of the population who are predicted to be high-rate offenders) and the base rate. The proportional reduction in error can only reach 100 percent if the selection ratio and base rate are equal. In order to overcome this difficulty, Loeber and Dishion (1983) proposed a new measure of predictive efficiency—Relative Improvement over Chance (RIOC). This was defined as follows:

$$\text{RIOC} = \frac{(AC - RC)}{(MC - RC)} \times 100 \text{ percent,}$$

where AC is the actual number of correct predictions, RC is the randomly expected number of correct predictions, and MC is the maximum possible number of correct predictions. This takes account of both the selection ratio and the base rate. Copas and Tarling (1986) analyzed RIOC in some detail and advocated that confidence intervals should be calculated for measures of predictive efficiency.

In predicting individual crime rates in fundamental research, it may be unnecessary to dichotomize or categorize prediction scores. Predictive efficiency could be calculated by comparing predicted and actual rates directly, perhaps using the product-moment correlation or the paired t-test, if the nature of the variables permitted these statistics.[14] However, in prediction that is designed to assist criminal justice decisions (which are usually dichotomous or categorical in nature) it will probably be necessary to impose cutoff points on prediction scores. Also, results obtained with cutoff points may be more meaningful than summary statistics based on all offending rates. A standard method of measuring predictive efficiency in research designed to predict individual crime rates is needed.

One disadvantage with existing measures of predictive efficiency is that they give equal weight to the different kinds of errors and correct predictions. In setting cutoff points and in assessing the adequacy of any prediction technique, it may be desirable to take account of the different social costs of different errors. For example, if it is thought especially important not to predict someone as a high-rate offender who will not in fact become one, then the cutoff point should be set high and relatively few persons should be predicted. If, however, it is thought especially important to identify as many of the actual high-rate offenders as possible, then the cutoff point should be set lower. Blumstein, Farrington, and Moitra (1985) developed a "civil-libertarian ratio" that summarized the relative concern over false positives compared with false negatives and plotted a graph to show how the optimum cutoff point varied with this ratio.

The estimate of predictive efficiency in the sample used to construct the prediction instrument will always be too high, because of capitalizing on chance variations. In other words, in selecting predictors that are most closely related to the criterion in a construction sample, there will be a tendency to select variables that happen to be better predictors in the sample than in the population. In order to obtain an unbiased estimate of the efficiency of prediction in the population, it is desirable to apply the prediction instrument to a different (validation)

[14] The Pearson product-moment correlation summarizes the strength of the relation between two variables, ranging from -1 (a perfect negative relation) through zero (no relation) through $+1$ (a perfect positive relation). The paired Student's t-test can be used, where each person has a score on two variables, to investigate whether the difference between the variables is significantly different from zero. Both of these require interval-level variables such as height, where the difference between any two values has the same meaning throughout the scale. These concepts are discussed in statistics textbooks such as Blalock (1972).

sample of people. Greenwood and Abrahamse (1982) did not do this, and so the true predictive efficiency of their instrument is probably overestimated. The decrease in predictive efficiency between construction and validation samples is called "shrinkage" (see also Gottfredson, in this volume).

One way of estimating the shrinkage is to divide a total sample randomly into two halves and to use one half for construction and the other half for validation, as Chaiken and Chaiken (1982) and Farrington (1985) did.[15] Unfortunately, the shrinkage between two halves of a sample is not necessarily an accurate guide to the shrinkage between a construction sample and a totally different validation sample. Given that successful predictions require consistency over time, place, persons, and so on, it is important to establish how well predictions derived in one set of conditions will apply to another. Shrinkage is more of a problem with the more sensitive techniques than with the cruder Burgess points score (Farrington and Tarling 1985b).

In summary, it is desirable to investigate the prediction of individual crime rates in a prospective longitudinal survey. Predictor and criterion variables should ideally be selected in advance on theoretical grounds, rather than retrospectively according to availability in records. Predictive efficiency should be measured in a sample other than that used to construct the prediction instrument, and it would be desirable to give explicit consideration to the social costs and benefits of different outcomes. Several methods of combining predictor variables into a prediction score have been used, but none seems to be more efficient in validation samples than the simple Burgess points score. Finally, there is need for a standard method of measuring predictive efficiency in studies of individual crime rates.

V. Use of Prediction in Sentencing and Parole

The emphasis in this essay is on research on the prediction of individual crime rates and high-rate offenders. However, there have been many suggestions that such predictions should be used in the criminal justice system to guide sentencing and parole decisions, especially as part of a policy of selective incapacitation (e.g., Wilson 1983). The use of predictive information by criminal justice decision makers raises important ethical, legal, and practical issues. There is not space in this essay to

---

[15] Other methods of estimating shrinkage have been discussed by Copas and Tarling (1986).

discuss these in detail, but some will be mentioned in this section (see generally Tonry, in this volume).

A. *Arguments for the Use of Prediction*

Arguments in favor of the use of prediction rest mainly on a utilitarian approach to crime control. In dealing with offenders, it is argued that the criminal justice system should primarily aim to minimize crime. The major ways of achieving this are through rehabilitation, deterrence, and incapacitation. However, the choice of penal measures must be compatible with the more general aim of maximizing social benefits and minimizing social costs. For example, some efficient methods of minimizing crime, such as an expansion in the use of the death penalty, might be excluded because the social costs outweigh the social benefits. The weighing of costs against benefits is, of course, a subjective process.

One argument for the use of prediction is that a significant decrease in the total number of crimes committed in the community could be realized if high-rate offenders could be identified early in their offending careers and their crime rates decreased by preventive, incapacitative, deterrent, or rehabilitative methods.[16] The first opportunity for criminal justice system intervention occurs at the first conviction, so this could be a key point at which to identify potentially high-rate offenders.

In Great Britain and North America in recent years, there have been calls for special incapacitative sentences designed to protect the public. In the United States, Moore et al. (1984) argued that the criminal justice system should reserve its scarce prison space for the high-rate, serious, dangerous offenders. They proposed that there should be special investigative and prosecutorial efforts to solve crimes committed by these offenders, and especially long sentences. Similar ideas underlie career criminal prosecution programs (Greenwood 1980), although these often focus on the seriousness rather than the frequency of offending. In England, Floud and Young (1981) also proposed special protective sentences for dangerous offenders, in the context of more

---

[16] Cook (1986) has argued, however, that estimates of crime reduction from incapacitation must take into account various possible "replacement" phenomena; e.g., incarcerating high-rate offenders may reduce victimization risks that, in turn, may cause potential victims to reduce self-protection efforts. This may make criminal opportunities more attractive or lucrative and may attract new offenders who will partly or wholly replace those who are incapacitated.

general decreases in maximum sentences. Moore and his colleagues and Floud and Young recommended that the identification of dangerous offenders for special measures should be based not on predictions about future offending but on the present offense and the criminal record (including the juvenile record).

It is possible to argue in favor of prediction-based decision making in the criminal justice system using a medical analogy. Many illnesses can more easily and effectively be prevented than cured. One method of preventing the spread of diseases is through quarantine. This clearly involves some costs to the individual who is isolated. However, it is felt that the benefits to the community of preventing diseases outweigh the costs to the individual of being quarantined.

Even setting aside the issue of dangerousness, there are existing laws and penal measures that seem to be predictive and preventive. One example is the British breathalyzer law, which specifies that persons who drive a motor vehicle while their blood alcohol level exceeds eighty milligrams of alcohol per 1,000 milliliters of blood are liable to be disqualified from driving for at least a year. Such persons typically have not caused any harm to anyone. The legal penalty seems to reflect the belief that a high blood alcohol level predicts a high likelihood of causing a road accident, and the mandatory disqualification seems intended to prevent such an accident and the consequent harm.

It could be argued that the Anglo-American criminal justice system has always been engaged in the selective incapacitation of frequent or serious offenders. This has sometimes been explicit, as when parole boards have used prediction scores in deciding whether or when to release prisoners (Gottfredson et al. 1975; Nuttall et al. 1977). More often, however, it has been implicit. Explicit predictions seem preferable to implicit ones.

Since the best predictor of future criminal behavior is often past criminal behavior, it is important to establish empirically how far a prediction-based selective incapacitation policy might differ from existing sentencing practice. Greenwood and Abrahamse (1982) found that high-rate burglars and robbers in California were more likely to go to prison than low-rate ones but that the lengths of prison sentences were not related to individual crime rates. Hence, there was an existing association between the crime rate and the average time served, but it might be expected that this association would be much stronger if a policy of selective incapacitation were followed. Against this, Cohen (1983) concluded that Greenwood and Abrahamse's seven-point prediction scale was only slightly more effective than sentence lengths in distinguishing between high-rate and low-rate offenders.

B. Arguments against the Use of Prediction

Arguments against the use of prediction rest primarily on a retributive or just deserts approach to sentencing, which assumes that an offender should be punished because he deserves it (e.g., Walker 1980). This follows from the fact that penal punishment is an expression of society's censure. According to von Hirsch (1985, p. 50), "condemning people for the wrongful acts they commit is part of having a morality that holds people responsible for their behavior." In this approach, the penal punishment increases in proportion to the gravity of the offense and the blameworthiness of the offender. The imprisonment of an offender for a disproportionately long time because it is predicted that he will commit offenses at high rates in the community is repugnant essentially because the punishment is undeserved. The offender is being punished not for crimes he has committed but for crimes he might commit. A desert theorist could not support the use of predictive factors other than the current offense and the past criminal history because they have no bearing on the blameworthiness of the offender's choices.

Von Hirsch (1985) argued that a prediction-based policy of selective incapacitation would be quite different in practice from a just deserts approach. His approach gives primary weight to the gravity of the current offense and somewhat less weight to the criminal history, whereas a selective incapacitation approach would give primary weight to the criminal history and somewhat less weight to a number of "morally irrelevant" factors.

One problem with the just deserts approach is the subjective nature of the link between the gravity of the offense and the severity of the sentence. One of the few attempts to measure the coefficient of proportionality was completed by Fitzmaurice and Pease (1982). Von Hirsch (1985) pointed out that there was more agreement on the relative ordering of the seriousness of offenses (ordinal proportionality) than on how that order should correspond to sentence severity (cardinal proportionality). He advocated that the amount of available prison accommodation should determine cardinal proportionality, but there is a danger that this could lead to unequal treatment of offenders in states with differing amounts of prison space.

It is possible to compromise between the prediction-based and just deserts approaches, for example, if desert specifies a range of sentences and predictive considerations are used in choosing within that range (e.g., Monahan 1982). This option has been discussed in detail by Morris and Miller (1985), who argued that it was easier to specify which punishments were unjust rather than which were justly deserved and that there was often a range of not-unjust punishments in relation to the current offense and the offender's criminal record.

An important argument against the practical use of prediction centers on the availability and accuracy of the items likely to be included in a prediction score. Information may be routinely available to sentencers in the adult court about an offender's past criminal history, but there may be no details of his juvenile court history or of his unemployment record. These kinds of problems led to the successive modification of the Salient Factor Score. Reliable information probably could not be obtained from the offender, knowing that it could affect his sentence. In principle, it seems likely that such information could be collected from other sources routinely and reliably if necessary.

C. False Positives

Several of the arguments against prediction-based criminal justice decision making have centered on the high false positive rate—the proportion of predicted persons who do not become high-rate offenders. It is inevitably difficult to predict a rare phenomenon such as high-rate offending, and it seems both unjust and inefficient to apply penal measures to persons who neither deserve nor need them. It is important to consider not only the false positives but also the false negatives (the proportion of high-rate offenders who were not predicted), since both should be minimized to maximize the benefits of selective incapacitation.[17]

Greenwood and Abrahamse (1982) identified 25 percent of their burglars and robbers (195 out of 780) as high-rate offenders. Of the 236 with the highest prediction scores, 105 were high-rate. Thus the false positive rate was 56 percent and the false negative rate was 46 percent. Of course, there was no validation sample in this project, the predictors were not measured before the crime rate, and the predictors were obtained by self-report. Janus's (1985) study is not subject to these objections, but he did not measure crime rates directly. He found that

[17] The false negative rate is often defined as the proportion of those predicted to be low-rate offenders who become high-rate ones. For the purpose of this discussion, it refers to the proportion of high-rate offenders who were predicted to be low-rate ones.

24 percent of the prisoners had two or more rearrests in the three-year follow-up period. Of those with the lowest Salient Factor Scores, 38 percent had two or more rearrests. With this criterion of a high-rate offender, the false positive rate was 62 percent and the false negative rate was 64 percent.

Blumstein, Farrington, and Moitra (1985) included a much wider range of predictor variables and studied the accuracy of prediction of chronic offenders (with six or more convictions) at the time of the first conviction. Only 17 percent of the offenders were chronics on this definition, but this was true of 41 percent of those with the highest prediction scores. The false positive rate was 59 percent and the false negative rate was 35 percent in this project.

Assuming that about 15–25 percent of offenders will be designated as high rate, experience suggests that few well-designed prediction exercises will manage to keep both false positive and false negative rates below 50 percent. However, this need not necessarily prevent the use of prediction scores in criminal justice decision making. As Morris and Miller (1985) argued, what matters is not the absolute false positive rate but the predictive efficiency of the score. In deciding whether to use a predicting device, it would be desirable to give explicit consideration to the social costs and benefits of the correct and incorrect identifications, as did Blumstein and his colleagues (1985).

The measured false positive rate can sometimes be misleading. To take an example from predicting the onset of offending, West and Farrington (1973) attempted to predict juvenile convictions using five factors measured at age ten: convicted parents, low family income, large family size, poor parental child-rearing behavior, and low intelligence. Of sixty-three boys with adverse ratings on at least three of these factors, thirty-one were convicted as juveniles (including twenty of the thirty-seven juvenile recidivists). This prediction, therefore, appeared to have a false positive rate of roughly 50 percent.

When investigated more closely, the true false positive rate diminished. Eight of the thirty-two boys not convicted as juveniles were convicted at ages seventeen to nineteen. Another eight had police records as juveniles that did not extend as far as convictions for indictable crimes (i.e., convictions for minor offenses or official cautions). Another eight, while having no police record, admitted an above-average number of acts on a self-reported delinquency questionnaire, and so perhaps had been lucky in avoiding detection. The remaining eight were relatively good boys from relatively bad backgrounds. However, they all displayed some form of nervous disturbance, being variously described as anxious, nervous, highly strung, obsessional, timid, quiet, suspicious, inhibited, or apathetic. In other words, the genuinely non-delinquent "false positives" tended to be nervous and withdrawn, and it may be that delinquent and nervous-withdrawn behavior are two alternative reactions to a stressful early environment.

Obviously, the ethical issues raised by prediction are affected by the measures applied to predicted offenders. In the London survey, there might have been some justification for identifying these sixty-three boys as potential offenders and giving them special preventive or welfare services designed to help them—despite the apparent 50 percent false positive rate. It might be thought that this early identification could have undesirable labeling or stigmatizing effects, and there is indeed some evidence that official labeling tends to increase delinquency. For example, Gold and Williams (1969) and Farrington (1977) found that boys who were apprehended by the police or convicted in court tended to become more frequent offenders as a result. However, there seems to be no evidence that identifying people as probable high-rate offenders has similarly undesirable effects, although the degree of stigmatization may depend on the measures applied to the predicted offenders.

Acceptance or rejection of the use of prediction in criminal justice decision making depends largely on the choice between utilitarian and just deserts approaches to sentencing, which is essentially a moral or subjective choice. To some extent, a sentencing policy based on predictions of high-rate offending might merely be making explicit and systematizing what is now often implicit. In deciding whether to adopt such a policy, it is important to weigh the social costs against the social benefits. A number of penal aims—including just deserts, rehabilitation, deterrence, and incapacitation—could and should coexist in the criminal justice system. Some aims may be more applicable to some types of offenders and offenses than others. Selective incapacitation should not be put into practice unless and until well-designed research indicates that it would decrease crime more effectively than current penal policies.

VI. Conclusions

Research on the prediction of individual crime rates could be aimed either to advance fundamental knowledge about offending and its causes or to assist criminal justice system decision makers in dealing with offenders. Some research, of course, fulfills both aims, and both have influenced this essay. Ideally, methods of dealing with offenders should be based on fundamental knowledge about the causes of crime.

Previous prediction research has concentrated on the prediction of recidivism within a specified short follow-up period. However, studies of the prediction of individual crime rates would be more useful in evaluating the incapacitative, rehabilitative, or deterrent effects of penal measures, and in helping decision makers to choose appropriate sentences. Future research should aim to investigate predicted offending rates following specified penal measures, for different types of offenders. It would also be helpful to know how predicted offending rates were affected by the future circumstances of offenders (such as unemployment or marriage). This research could have both theoretical and practical implications.

Reviews of research in this essay show that the future crime rate is predicted by the past crime rate, by the nature of the first offense, and by an early age of onset of offending. While research on early precursors of offending has concentrated on the prediction of onset rather than of crime rates, it seems that early antisocial behavior, convicted parents or siblings, low family income, and school failure all predict later high-rate offenders. Indeed, a combined scale derived in the London longitudinal survey succeeded in identifying the majority of persistent or future chronic offenders. The studies of later predictors are limited by formidable methodological problems, but it seems likely that unemployment and drug use predict individual crime rates.

Discussions of methodological issues in this essay show that predictions constructed on one sample need to be validated prospectively on another. Predictive techniques designed for practical use need to be constructed on samples drawn from the population to which they are to be applied. In general, no method of selecting and combining predictors seems to be more effective in validation samples than the simple Burgess points score. There is need for a standard index of efficiency in predictions of offending rates. In assessing efficiency and in setting cutoff points for decisions, account needs to be taken of the social costs and benefits of different outcomes.

In basic research on prediction, the predictor and criterion variables should be selected on theoretical grounds (rather than according to availability in records) and measured reliably and validly. The extent to which each predictor is independently predictive of the criterion should be established, in the context of a prospective longitudinal study. In evaluating the feasibility of a policy of selective incapacitation, it is important to determine how far the high-rate offenders can be predicted in advance. This requires prospective longitudinal research based on samples of convicted offenders and measuring variables that are acceptable for use in criminal justice system decision making.

There are many advantages in following the criminal career approach, distinguishing between offenders and nonoffenders, and measuring crime rates only for offenders. More research is needed on the ability of different criminal career features such as the age of onset and the nature of the first offense, and other variables related to the criminal career, to predict individual crime rates and career lengths. In measuring offending rates, there should be a careful specification of time at risk of offending. It is important to carry out research that links the juvenile and adult offending careers, to avoid problems caused by truncation of the data at the eighteenth birthday. It is useful to distinguish between persisters and chronics and to predict persisters prospectively rather than chronics retrospectively. Persisters may fail to become chronics because of chance dropout processes rather than prediction errors.

Variations in offending rates during the course of a criminal career should be studied, using frequent data collection, including interviews. It may be possible to demonstrate that increases or decreases in offending reliably follow changes in other variables (such as unemployment or marriage), thereby suggesting causal relations. Additionally, it would be useful to study why predictions fail. For example, research on why some predicted high-rate offenders actually become low-rate offenders, to the extent that this does not reflect probabilistic processes, might indicate protective factors that can be used in crime reduction. Prediction assumes constancy over time, but instability over time can also be informative.

The use of prediction in criminal justice decision making might be justifiable within a utilitarian approach to penal treatment. Its acceptability may depend on the relative weighing of social benefits and costs. As far as possible, these concepts should be quantified and weighed explicitly.

It will be clear from this review that research on the prediction of individual crime rates, and of other features of criminal careers, is in its infancy. It is too early to use existing research results as a justification for large-scale penal policies. Nevertheless, more research on these topics is clearly warranted.

REFERENCES

Anderson, John E. 1951. Review of *Unraveling Juvenile Delinquency. Journal of Criminal Law, Criminology, and Police Science* 41:745–48.

Ball, John C., John W. Shaffer, and David N. Nurco. 1983. "The Day-to-Day Criminality of Heroin Addicts in Baltimore—a Study in the Continuity of Offense Rates." *Drug and Alcohol Dependence* 12:119–42.

Barnett, Arnold, Alfred Blumstein, and David P. Farrington. 1987. "Probabilistic Models of Youthful Criminal Careers." *Criminology* (in press).

Barnett, Arnold, and Anthony Lofaso. 1985. "Selective Incapacitation and the Philadelphia Cohort Data." *Journal of Quantitative Criminology* 1:3–36.

Blalock, Hubert M. 1972. *Social Statistics*. 2d ed. New York: McGraw-Hill.

Blumstein, Alfred, and Jacqueline Cohen. 1979. "Estimation of Individual Crime Rates from Arrest Records." *Journal of Criminal Law and Criminology* 70:561–85.

Blumstein, Alfred, Jacqueline Cohen, and Paul Hsieh. 1982. "The Duration of Adult Criminal Careers." Final report to the National Institute of Justice, Washington, D.C.

Blumstein, Alfred, Jacqueline Cohen, Jeffrey A. Roth, and Christy A. Visher, eds. 1986. *Criminal Careers and "Career Criminals."* Vol. 1. Washington, D.C.: National Academy Press.

Blumstein, Alfred, David P. Farrington, and Soumyo Moitra. 1985. "Delinquency Careers: Innocents, Desisters, and Persisters." In *Crime and Justice: An Annual Review of Research*, vol. 6, edited by Michael Tonry and Norval Morris. Chicago: University of Chicago Press.

Blumstein, Alfred, and Soumyo Moitra. 1980. "The Identification of Career Criminals from Chronic Offenders in a Cohort." *Law and Policy Quarterly* 2:321–34.

Brody, Stephen R. 1976. *The Effectiveness of Sentencing*. London: H.M. Stationery Office.

Burgess, Ernest W. 1928. "Factors Determining Success or Failure on Parole." In *The Workings of the Indeterminate-Sentence Law and the Parole System in Illinois*, edited by Andrew A. Bruce, Albert J. Harno, Ernest W. Burgess, and John Landesco. Springfield: Illinois State Board of Parole.

Chaiken, Jan M., and Marcia R. Chaiken. 1982. *Varieties of Criminal Behavior*. Santa Monica, Calif.: Rand.

Clarke, Ronald V., and Derek B. Cornish. 1985. "Modeling Offenders' Decisions: A Framework for Research and Policy." In *Crime and Justice: An Annual Review of Research*, vol. 6, edited by Michael Tonry and Norval Morris. Chicago: University of Chicago Press.

Clarke, Stevens H. 1975. "Some Implications for North Carolina of Recent Research in Juvenile Delinquency." *Journal of Research in Crime and Delinquency* 12:51–60.

Cohen, Jacqueline. 1978. "The Incapacitative Effect of Imprisonment: A Critical Review of the Literature." In *Deterrence and Incapacitation: Estimating the Effects of Criminal Sanctions on Crime Rates*, edited by Alfred Blumstein, Jacqueline Cohen, and Daniel Nagin. Washington, D.C.: National Academy of Sciences.

————. 1983. "Incapacitation as a Strategy for Crime Control: Possibilities and Pitfalls." In *Crime and Justice: An Annual Review of Research*, vol. 5, edited by Michael Tonry and Norval Morris. Chicago: University of Chicago Press.

————. 1986. "Research on Criminal Careers: Individual Frequency Rates and Offense Seriousness." App. B in vol. 1 of *Criminal Careers and "Career Criminals,"* edited by Alfred Blumstein, Jacqueline Cohen, Jeffrey A. Roth, and Christy A. Visher. Washington, D.C.: National Academy Press.

Cook, Philip J. 1986. "The Demand and Supply of Criminal Opportunities." In *Crime and Justice: An Annual Review of Research*, vol. 7, edited by Michael Tonry and Norval Morris. Chicago: University of Chicago Press.

Copas, John B., and Roger Tarling. 1986. "Some Methodological Issues in Making Predictions." In *Criminal Careers and "Career Criminals,"* vol. 2, edited by Alfred Blumstein, Jacqueline Cohen, Jeffrey A. Roth, and Christy A. Visher. Washington, D.C.: National Academy Press.

Craig, Maude M., and Selma J. Glick. 1968. "School Behavior Related to Later Delinquency and Non-delinquency." *Criminologica* 5:17–27.

Dunford, Franklin W., and Delbert S. Elliott. 1984. "Identifying Career Offenders using Self-reported Data." *Journal of Research in Crime and Delinquency* 21:57–86.

Elliott, Delbert S., David Huizinga, and Suzanne S. Ageton. 1985. *Explaining Delinquency and Drug Use*. Beverly Hills, Calif.: Sage.

Empey, LaMar T., and Maynard L. Erickson. 1972. *The Provo Experiment*. Lexington, Mass.: Heath.

Empey, LaMar T., and Steven G. Lubeck. 1971. *The Silverlake Experiment*. Chicago: Aldine.

Ensminger, Margaret E., Sheppard G. Kellam, and Barnett R. Rubin. 1983. "School and Family Origins of Delinquency." In *Prospective Studies of Crime and Delinquency*, edited by Katherine T. Van Dusen and Sarnoff A. Mednick. Boston: Kluwer-Nijhoff.

Farrington, David P. 1973. "Self-Reports of Deviant Behavior: Predictive and Stable?" *Journal of Criminal Law and Criminology* 64:99–110.

————. 1977. "The Effects of Public Labelling." *British Journal of Criminology* 17:112–25.

————. 1978. "The Family Backgrounds of Aggressive Youths." In *Aggression and Antisocial Behavior in Childhood and Adolescence*, edited by Lionel Hersov, Michael Berger, and David Shaffer. Oxford: Pergamon.

————. 1979a. "Environmental Stress, Delinquent Behavior, and Convictions." In *Stress and Anxiety*, vol. 6, edited by Irwin G. Sarason and Charles D. Spielberger. Washington, D.C.: Hemisphere.

————. 1979b. "Longitudinal Research on Crime and Delinquency." In *Crime and Justice: An Annual Review of Research*, vol. 1, edited by Norval Morris and Michael Tonry. Chicago: University of Chicago Press.

————. 1982. "Longitudinal Analyses of Criminal Violence." In *Criminal Violence*, edited by Marvin E. Wolfgang and Neil A. Weiner. Beverly Hills, Calif.: Sage.

————. 1983a. "Further Analyses of a Longitudinal Survey of Crime and Delinquency." Final report to the National Institute of Justice, Washington, D.C.

————. 1983*b*. "Offending from 10 to 25 Years of Age." In *Prospective Studies of Crime and Delinquency*, edited by Katherine T. Van Dusen and Sarnoff A. Mednick. Boston: Kluwer-Nijhoff.

————. 1985. "Predicting Self-reported and Official Delinquency." In *Prediction in Criminology*, edited by David P. Farrington and Roger Tarling. Albany: State University of New York Press.

————. 1986*a*. "Age and Crime." In *Crime and Justice: An Annual Review of Research*, vol. 7, edited by Michael Tonry and Norval Morris. Chicago: University of Chicago Press.

————. 1986*b*. "Stepping Stones to Adult Criminal Careers." In *Development of Antisocial and Prosocial Behavior*, edited by Dan Olweus, Jack Block, and Marian R. Yarrow. New York: Academic Press.

————. 1987*a*. "Early Precursors of Frequent Offending." In *From Children to Citizens*, edited by Glenn C. Loury and James Q. Wilson. New York: Springer-Verlag (in press).

————. 1987*b*. "Epidemiology." In *Handbook of Juvenile Delinquency*, edited by Herbert C. Quay. New York: Wiley (in press).

Farrington, David P., Bernard Gallagher, Lynda Morley, Raymond J. St. Ledger, and Donald J. West. 1986. "Unemployment, School Leaving, and Crime." *British Journal of Criminology* 26:335–56.

Farrington, David P., Lloyd E. Ohlin, and James Q. Wilson. 1986. *Understanding and Controlling Crime*. New York: Springer-Verlag.

Farrington, David P., and Roger Tarling. 1985*a*. "Criminological Prediction: An Introduction." In *Prediction in Criminology*, edited by David P. Farrington and Roger Tarling. Albany: State University of New York Press.

————. 1985*b*. "Criminological Prediction: The Way Forward." In *Prediction in Criminology*, edited by David P. Farrington and Roger Tarling. Albany: State University of New York Press.

Fitzmaurice, Catherine, and Ken Pease. 1982. "On Measuring Distaste in Years." In *Abnormal Offenders, Delinquency, and the Criminal Justice System*, edited by John Gunn and David P. Farrington. Chichester: Wiley.

Floud, Jean, and Warren Young. 1981. *Dangerousness and Criminal Justice*. London: Heinemann.

Glueck, Sheldon, and Eleanor T. Glueck. 1950. *Unraveling Juvenile Delinquency*. Cambridge, Mass.: Harvard University Press.

Gold, Martin, and Jay R. Williams. 1969. "National Study of the Aftermath of Apprehension." *Prospectus: A Journal of Law Reform* 3:3–12.

Goldkamp, John S. In this volume. "Prediction in Criminal Justice Policy Development."

Gottfredson, Don M., Peter B. Hoffman, Maurice H. Sigler, and Leslie T. Wilkins. 1975. "Making Paroling Policy Explicit." *Crime and Delinquency* 21:34–44.

Gottfredson, Don M., Leslie T. Wilkins, and Peter B. Hoffman. 1978. *Guidelines for Parole and Sentencing*. Lexington, Mass.: Heath.

Gottfredson, Michael R. 1979. "Parole Guidelines and the Reduction of Sentencing Disparity." *Journal of Research in Crime and Delinquency* 16:218–31.

Gottfredson, Stephen D. In this volume. "Prediction: An Overview of Selected Methodological Issues."

Gottfredson, Stephen D., and Don M. Gottfredson. 1985. "Screening for Risk among Parolees: Policy, Practice, and Method." In *Prediction in Criminology*, edited by David P. Farrington and Roger Tarling. Albany: State University of New York Press.

———. 1986. "Accuracy of Prediction Models." In *Criminal Careers and "Career Criminals,"* vol. 2, edited by Alfred Blumstein, Jacqueline Cohen, Jeffrey A. Roth, and Christy A. Visher. Washington, D.C.: National Academy Press.

Greenberg, David. 1975. "The Incapacitative Effect of Imprisonment: Some Estimates." *Law and Society Review* 9:541–80.

Greenwood, Peter W. 1980. "Criminal Career Prosecution: Potential Objectives." *Journal of Criminal Law and Criminology* 71:85–88.

Greenwood, Peter W., and Allan Abrahamse. 1982. *Selective Incapacitation*. Santa Monica, Calif.: Rand.

Hamparian, Donna M., Richard Schuster, Simon Dinitz, and John P. Conrad. 1978. *The Violent Few.* Lexington, Mass.: Heath.

Hirschi, Travis, and Michael Gottfredson. 1983. "Age and the Explanation of Crime." *American Journal of Sociology* 89:552–84.

Hoffman, Peter B. 1983. "Screening for Risk: A Revised Salient Factor Score (SFS 81)." *Journal of Criminal Justice* 11:539–47.

Hoffman, Peter B., and James L. Beck. 1976. "Salient Factor Score Validation—a 1972 Release Cohort." *Journal of Criminal Justice* 4:69–76.

———. 1980. "Revalidating the Salient Factor Score: A Research Note." *Journal of Criminal Justice* 8:185–88.

Home Office. 1985. *Criminal Careers of Those Born in 1953, 1958, and 1963.* Statistical Bulletin no. 7/85. London: H.M. Stationery Office.

Janus, Michael G. 1985. "Selective Incapacitation: Have We Tried It? Does It Work?" *Journal of Criminal Justice* 13:117–29.

Jensen, Gary F. 1976. "Race, Achievement, and Delinquency: A Further Look at Delinquency in a Birth Cohort." *American Journal of Sociology* 82:379–87.

Kelley, Thomas M. 1983. "Status Offenders Can Be Different: A Comparative Study of Delinquent Careers." *Crime and Delinquency* 29:365–80.

Lab, Steven P. 1984. "Patterns in Juvenile Misbehavior." *Crime and Delinquency* 30:293–308.

Loeber, Rolf, and Thomas Dishion. 1983. "Early Predictors of Male Delinquency: A Review." *Psychological Bulletin* 94:68–99.

Loeber, Rolf, and Magda Stouthamer-Loeber. 1986. "Family Factors as Correlates and Predictors of Juvenile Conduct Problems and Delinquency." In *Crime and Justice: An Annual Review of Research*, vol. 7, edited by Michael Tonry and Norval Morris. Chicago: University of Chicago Press.

McCord, Joan. 1982. "A Longitudinal View of the Relationship between Paternal Absence and Crime." In *Abnormal Offenders, Delinquency, and the Criminal Justice System*, edited by John Gunn and David P. Farrington. Chichester: Wiley.

Maltz, Michael D., Andrew C. Gordon, David McDowall, and Richard McCleary. 1980. "An Artifact in Pretest-Posttest Designs: How It Can Mistakenly Make Delinquency Programs Look Effective." *Evaluation Review* 4:225–40.

Mannheim, Hermann, and Leslie T. Wilkins. 1955. *Prediction Methods in Relation to Borstal Training.* London: H.M. Stationery Office.

Martinson, Robert M. 1974. "What Works? Questions and Answers about Prison Reform." *Public Interest* 35:22–54.

Meade, Anthony. 1973. "Seriousness of Delinquency, the Adjudicative Decision, and Recidivism—a Longitudinal Configuration Analysis." *Journal of Criminal Law and Criminology* 64:478–85.

Miller, Stuart J., Simon Dinitz, and John P. Conrad. 1982. *Careers of the Violent.* Lexington, Mass.: Heath.

Monahan, John. 1982. "The Case for Prediction in the Modified Desert Model of Criminal Sentencing." *International Journal of Law and Psychiatry* 5:103–13.

Moore, Mark H., Susan R. Estrich, Daniel McGillis, and William Spelman. 1984. *Dangerous Offenders.* Cambridge, Mass.: Harvard University Press.

Morris, Norval, and Marc Miller. 1985. "Predictions of Dangerousness." In *Crime and Justice: An Annual Review of Research,* vol. 6, edited by Michael Tonry and Norval Morris. Chicago: University of Chicago Press.

Murray, Charles A., and Louis A. Cox. 1979. *Beyond Probation.* Beverly Hills, Calif.: Sage.

Nuttall, Christopher P., Elizabeth E. Barnard, A. J. Fowles, A. Frost, Walter H. Hammond, Patricia Mayhew, Ken Pease, Roger Tarling, and Mollie J. Weatheritt. 1977. *Parole in England and Wales.* London: H.M. Stationery Office.

Ohlin, Lloyd E., and O. Dudley Duncan. 1949. "The Efficiency of Prediction in Criminology." *American Journal of Sociology* 54:441–51.

Palmer, Jan, and Paul Carlson. 1976. "Problems with the Use of Regression Analysis in Prediction Studies." *Journal of Research in Crime and Delinquency* 13:64–81.

Petersilia, Joan, and Peter W. Greenwood. 1978. "Mandatory Prison Sentences: Their Projected Effects on Crime and Prison Populations." *Journal of Criminal Law and Criminology* 69:604–15.

Petersilia, Joan, Peter W. Greenwood, and Martin Lavin. 1978. *Criminal Careers of Habitual Felons.* Washington, D.C.: National Institute of Justice.

Petersilia, Joan, and Susan Turner. In this volume. "Guideline-based Justice: Prediction and Racial Minorities."

Peterson, Mark A., Harriet B. Braiker, and Suzanne M. Polich. 1981. *Who Commits Crimes?* Cambridge, Mass.: Oelgeschlager, Gunn, & Hain.

Power, Michael J., Patricia M. Ash, Elizabeth Shoenberg, and E. Catherine Sirey. 1974. "Delinquency and the Family." *British Journal of Social Work* 4:13–38.

Pritchard, David A. 1979. "Stable Predictors of Recidivism: A Summary." *Criminology* 17:15–21.

Robins, Lee N. 1979. "Sturdy Childhood Predictors of Adult Outcomes: Replications from Longitudinal Studies." In *Stress and Mental Disorder,* edited by James E. Barrett, Robert M. Rose, and Gerald L. Klerman. New York: Raven.

Robins, Lee N., Patricia A. West, and Barbara L. Herjanic. 1975. "Arrests and Delinquency in Two Generations: A Study of Black Urban Families and Their Children." *Journal of Child Psychology and Psychiatry* 16:125–40.

Sechrest, Lee, Susan D. White, and Elizabeth D. Brown, eds. 1979. *The Rehabilitation of Criminal Offenders: Problems and Prospects*. Washington, D.C.: National Academy of Sciences.

Shannon, Lyle W. 1985. "Risk Assessment vs. Real Prediction: The Prediction Problem and Public Trust." *Journal of Quantitative Criminology* 1:159–89.

Solomon, Herbert. 1976. "Parole Outcome: A Multidimensional Contingency Table Analysis." *Journal of Research in Crime and Delinquency* 13:107–26.

Spivack, George. 1983. "High Risk Early Behaviors Indicating Vulnerability to Delinquency in the Community and School." Report to the National Institute of Juvenile Justice and Delinquency Prevention, Washington, D.C.

Thomas, Charles W. 1976. "Are Status Offenders Really So Different?" *Crime and Delinquency* 22:438–55.

Tonry, Michael H. In this volume. "Prediction and Classification: Legal and Ethical Issues."

Visher, Christy A. 1986. "The Rand Inmate Survey: A Reanalysis." In *Criminal Careers and "Career Criminals*," vol. 2, edited by Alfred Blumstein, Jacqueline Cohen, Jeffrey A. Roth, and Christy A. Visher. Washington, D.C.: National Academy Press.

von Hirsch, Andrew. 1985. *Past or Future Crimes*. New Brunswick, N.J.: Rutgers University Press.

Wadsworth, Michael. 1979. *Roots of Delinquency*. London: Martin Robertson.

Walker, Nigel. 1980. *Punishment, Danger, and Stigma*. Oxford: Blackwell.

West, Donald J., and David P. Farrington. 1973. *Who Becomes Delinquent?* London: Heinemann.

———. 1977. *The Delinquent Way of Life*. London: Heinemann.

Wilkins, Leslie, and Peter MacNaughton-Smith. 1964. "New Prediction and Classification Methods in Criminology." *Journal of Research in Crime and Delinquency* 1:19–32.

Wilson, James Q. 1983. *Thinking about Crime*. Rev. ed. New York: Basic.

Wolfgang, Marvin E., Robert M. Figlio, and Thorsten Sellin. 1972. *Delinquency in a Birth Cohort*. Chicago: University of Chicago Press.

Wolfgang, Marvin E., and Paul E. Tracy. 1982. "The 1945 and 1958 Birth Cohorts: A Comparison of the Prevalence, Incidence, and Severity of Delinquent Behavior." Paper presented at the National Institute of Justice conference on "Public Danger, Dangerous Offenders, and the Criminal Justice System," Harvard University, Cambridge, Mass.

John S. Goldkamp

Prediction in Criminal Justice Policy Development

ABSTRACT

Prediction methods have been employed to model criminal justice
decisions from arrest to parole and less frequently for policy review and
reformulation in areas marked by the exercise of broad discretion. The
development of decision guidelines is a principal example. A recent
bail-guidelines project in Philadelphia illustrates policy and
methodological issues that have been raised about the use of predictions in
decision making. Bail decisions under guidelines in Philadelphia, when
compared with a nonguidelines control group, revealed clear-cut
differences, particularly in disparity reduction. The seriousness with
which some of the methodological critiques have been viewed is not
commensurate with the likely impact of guidelines on actual cases.
Examination of the criticism that modeling practices may continue or
inadvertently generate biased decision making suggests that the impact of
poor modeling procedures may be much less than feared. There is
insufficient evidence to discredit the claims of the decision-guidelines
approach to policy reform.

Prediction methods have been used to model decisions including arrest,
charging, bail, sentencing, and parole release. Predictive approaches
have been used to examine the determinants of official decisions and
less frequently to reformulate policy and, by means of decision guidelines, to structure the wide discretion of criminal justice decision making.

The use of "voluntary" decision guidelines was pioneered in federal
parole practices in the early 1970s (Gottfredson, Wilkins, and Hoffman

John S. Goldkamp is associate professor of criminal justice, Temple University. The
author is grateful to Stephen Gottfredson and Michael Gottfredson for their helpful
comments.

1978). The federal parole guidelines were voluntary in two senses. First, they were developed by the U.S. Board of Parole voluntarily, that is, at its own initiative and not because legislation mandated that it do so. Second, they were intended for voluntary use by parole decision makers.

As initially conceived, decision guidelines were to be based partly on predictive modeling methods developed by the collaborative efforts of researchers and practitioners and voluntarily adopted by criminal justice decision makers (Gottfredson, Wilkins, and Hoffman 1978). The rationale was that significant criminal justice decisions were highly discretionary and suffered from confusing or contradictory goals, scarcity of relevant information, and scant feedback relating to the consequences of decisions made. This resulted in improvisational decision making, disparity among decisions and across decision makers, questions about fairness, and patterns of decisions whose effectiveness and efficiency were unknown.

The guidelines technology was intended to develop a policy framework to organize or structure the discretion so that it could be focused more rationally and deployed more effectively. In the early applications, the method of achieving this was important: the development of such decision guidelines presupposed a collaboration between social scientists and decision makers who sought to review and possibly revise their operating policy in a given area. Thus empirical modeling of decisions and their consequences has played an important role in rooting the discussion of practices on descriptions of "what is" as a springboard for discussion of "what ought to be."

As guidelines have become more common in sentencing and parole, some of the features of the original Gottfredson-Wilkins approach have been dropped or modified, such as the emphasis on collaborative development and on voluntary application by decision makers. Guidelines approaches to policy reform have taken on a different orientation as legislatures have sought to devise and impose sentencing reform and have specifically aimed at limiting judicial discretion.

This essay does not discuss all forms of guidelines but focuses on the initial Gottfredson-Wilkins approach because of questions that have been raised about it. Many of the questions raised concerning the development of "voluntary" guidelines are also relevant to nonvoluntary approaches.

Michael Gottfredson and Don Gottfredson (1984, p. 293) have suggested that the following components characterize the development of voluntary decision guidelines.

1. There is a general policy for decision making (articulated in explicit terms) within which individual decisions are made.

2. There are explicitly defined criteria for decision making with the specific weights to be given to these criteria also explicitly defined.

3. Within the general policy model, guidelines in the form of a grid are used in arriving at a particular decision. The most important policy concerns, decided by those responsible for the decision-making policy, are reflected in the dimensions of the grid.

4. The guidelines grid is intended to structure the use of discretion, not to eliminate it.

5. When departures are made, the decision maker must provide explicit reasons for the exceptional decision.

6. An established system of monitoring provides periodic feedback to the authorities responsible for the decision policy, giving the percentage of decisions falling outside each guideline category and the reasons given for these decisions.

7. The authorities may modify the guidelines at any time.

8. The general policy, including the guidelines incorporated within it, is not regarded as a "once-and-for-all" statement of a "right" policy; rather, the policy statement and the procedures are designed to facilitate an evolutionary system of policy development that changes in response to experience, learning, and social change.

9. The policy in general and the guidelines specifically are open and available for public review and debate.

Voluntary guidelines have been adopted throughout the United States for sentencing, parole, and bail and have been shown capable of realizing many of their proponents' objectives. Section I of this essay sets out a brief overview of the development of the guidelines concept and its applications from federal parole to bail. Section II examines criticisms that have been made of empirically derived voluntary guidelines. Section III describes the most recent major guidelines research concerning development and implementation of bail guidelines in Philadelphia with an eye particularly to demonstrating how that research addresses some of the major criticisms. Section IV reviews what is known about voluntary guidelines, their limitations, and their potential; comments on the persuasiveness of the outstanding criticisms of guidelines; and sets out proposals for next steps in research and practice.

I. An Overview of Voluntary Guidelines

The development of decision guidelines can be traced to the pioneering work of the Parole Decision-making Project led by Don Gottfredson and Leslie Wilkins in the early 1970s. The National Council on Crime and Delinquency and the (then) U.S. Board of Parole proposed to study parole decision making and to examine its implications for policy and practice. Using a variety of social science approaches, the researchers sought to examine the criteria relied on by parole board members in making their decisions and to facilitate an evaluation by the board of the appropriateness and efficacy of those criteria. As a result of this collaborative effort, guidelines were developed (based on policy debates) that adopted specific criteria to guide parole board members' decisions in the majority of cases.

The categories of offenders used in the guidelines were based on a ranking of offense severity and a "salient factor score" that classified defendants according to their probability of success on parole if released. These dimensions were constructed after careful study of the relative importance in past decision making of specific criteria, including ranking exercises by board members and hearing examiners to scale offense severities as well as actuarial analyses of failure on parole in large samples of parolees (Gottfredson, Wilkins, and Hoffman 1978).

The U.S. Parole Commission (the U.S. Board of Parole renamed) adopted guidelines in matrix format for voluntary use by parole decision makers. The hypothesis was that the decision makers would find the guidelines helpful in the vast majority of cases; discretion whether to grant parole would be structured according to specific criteria designed to reflect known policy goals. The guidelines also recognized that unusual cases would warrant exceptional decisions on the basis of criteria not built into the guidelines. Exceptional decisions would be accompanied by written reasons so that decision makers would be accountable for their decisions and so that the guidelines could later be analyzed for possible revision. The U.S. Parole Commission adopted parole decision guidelines fully in 1973. Experience with the federal parole guidelines has encouraged similar innovations in parole and sentencing in many states.

The second important stage of voluntary guidelines development was to determine whether the same collaborative strategy could be used to structure sentencing discretion. Feasibility studies were conducted by researchers working with Gottfredson and Wilkins to examine sentencing decisions in courts in Denver and Vermont. Empirical modeling of decisions was employed on samples of sentencing decisions, and these models were used to construct versions of guidelines that judges might choose to employ if guidelines were to be implemented (Wilkins et al. 1976). In a second phase, voluntary guidelines were developed or implemented by courts in Chicago, Phoenix, Newark, and Denver between 1976 and 1978 (see Kress 1980).

Since the initial parole and sentencing guidelines projects, parole guidelines have been adopted in a number of states (including Florida, Georgia, Maryland, Minnesota, New York, Oklahoma, Oregon, and Washington), and several states and many local jurisdictions have developed some form of voluntary sentencing guidelines. The Philadelphia Court of Common Pleas developed such guidelines as an offshoot of the Denver project. Michigan, Massachusetts, and New Jersey have engaged in the development of voluntary guidelines independent of the early research projects (Blumstein et al. 1983, pp. 126–83). Florida and Maryland undertook comparable guidelines-development processes (Carrow et al. 1985).

In the late 1970s, guideline development branched in two directions. Many jurisdictions continued to operate or to develop voluntary guidelines. Several states, however, elected to create presumptive sentencing-guidelines systems. They are "presumptive" in that the applicable guideline ranges are legally presumed to apply in every case; decision makers may impose some other sentence if they give their reasons for concluding that the presumption is overcome, and the sufficiency of those reasons is typically subject to review on appeal. In 1978 Minnesota created a sentencing commission and charged it to develop guidelines for felony sentencing. These guidelines were to be followed in any case unless "substantial and compelling" reasons justified a "departure," that is, imposition of some other sentence. Evaluation of the early years of Minnesota's experience with guidelines revealed high levels of compliance with the guidelines and reduction in sentencing disparities among felony cases (Knapp 1984a). Washington State and Pennsylvania developed and implemented presumptive sentencing-guidelines systems. Half a dozen other states have established sentencing commissions, and at the federal level the Comprehensive Crime Control Act of 1984 established the U.S. Sentencing Commission, which is charged to develop federal sentencing guidelines to take effect late in 1987. This essay is primarily about voluntary guidelines, and developments with presumptive guidelines are not discussed at length.

After completion of the early work with parole and sentencing, an effort was initiated to determine the feasibility of voluntary guidelines for bail decisions. This research, which is discussed in more detail below, culminated in the experimental implementation of guidelines for bail in the Philadelphia Municipal Court between 1981 and 1983 and in the formal adoption of guidelines as court policy in 1983 (Goldkamp and Gottfredson 1985). Before I discuss the Philadelphia project, however, the next section discusses a number of controversies associated with voluntary guidelines generally.

II. Critical Issues

Empirically based decision guidelines have been the subject of critical debate. Two broad sets of issues have been raised. The first involves the appropriateness of empirically based methods in guidelines development, and the second concerns the correctness of the statistical procedures employed in the construction of guidelines.

A. *The Role of Predictive Methods*

Three related questions lie at the heart of the debate concerning the use of predictive methods in developing decision guidelines: (1) Is it possible to infer "policy" meaningfully from predictive analyses? (2) What uses should and can be made of empirically based policy inferences in developing guidelines? (3) Have the statistical analyses used in guideline projects been appropriately selected and adequately performed?

1. *Inferring Policy from Statistical Description.*   The initial parole, sentencing, and bail-guidelines research projects collected and analyzed data describing samples of recent decisions. This was seen as facilitating discussion among the responsible decision makers of apparent operating policy and as setting the stage for constructing guidelines for future use (Wilkins et al. 1976; Gottfredson, Wilkins, and Hoffman 1978; Goldkamp, Gottfredson, and Mitchell-Herzfeld 1981; Wilkins 1981). This step employed multivariate statistical methods to model the decisions under study on the basis of knowledge of attributes of the cases (i.e., their demographic, legal, social, and criminal history characteristics) that would have been available to decision makers when making their decisions. The thesis was that, by finding commonalities in the ways that decision makers handle cases, researchers could identify underlying policies.

This key postulate has been challenged by a number of critics. The principal objection questions whether such statistical methods can capture inherent policy (Rich et al. 1982; Blumstein et al. 1983). The more general criticism questions whether meaningful inferences about policy may be drawn from aggregate statistics, which, critics contend, produce illusory and misleading results. What is obtained, it is said, is an "average" profile of decision making, which may be merely a statistical construct that reflects the actual policy of no individual judge (e.g., Rich et al. 1982, p. xx).

Proponents of the guidelines approach mean something different when they use the term "implicit policy." What they mean by use of that term is indeed a statistical aggregate. They reason that "empirical analyses of past decision practices are useful to policy development if they uncover sentencing (or paroling or bailing) behavior of the decision makers in the aggregate. . . . The bases of the estimates will capture as main determinants what we mean by policy—themes that seem to guide most decision makers in most cases" (Gottfredson and Gottfredson 1980, p. 300). Rough statistical indicators of policy correlates are all that is needed in the collaborative research process employed in guidelines development. The interpretation of the statistical results is not a task for researchers only. Models of decisions are examined and debated for sense by the decision makers who can confirm or refute the relevance of statistical correlates to decision policy.[1]

2. *Confusing Descriptive and Prescriptive Uses.* Some critics have objected to decision guidelines on the basis of a belief that empirical modeling of past practices leads inexorably to institutionalization of the status quo (e.g., Knapp 1984*b*). Similarly assuming that empirical description of justice decisions and construction of decision guidelines are the same thing, Fisher and Kadane write that "we are uncomfortable with the whole enterprise of empirically based sentencing guidelines . . . first, they are by their nature unthoughtfully conservative . . . [they] strike us as a species of computer-driven conservatism" (1983, p. 192; see also von Hirsch 1982, p. 173; Sparks 1983, pp. 232–33).

The developers of guidelines certainly conceived that guidelines could be designed solely to reflect and to better organize past decision practices,[2] but they also distinguished descriptive and prescriptive roles

---

[1] Discussions of the process by which descriptive findings were interpreted by decision makers for their meaning and relevance to understanding operating policy in the development of parole and bail guidelines are found in Gottfredson, Wilkins, and Hoffman (1978) and Goldkamp and Gottfredson (1985).

[2] See the discussion in Rich et al. (1982) of Wilkins et al. (1976). Concerning the bail guidelines in Philadelphia, see also Goldkamp and Gottfredson (1985).

for modeling by using empirical methods. In the descriptive phase, decisions are examined for patterns that suggest policies, the principal idea being that discussion of what "ought to be" may usefully be grounded on knowledge of what "is." In the prescriptive phase, descriptions of past practice can serve as the basis for identifying decision patterns that should be changed and for projecting the impact of alternative new policies. Proponents argue that the design of alternative models of decision guidelines that could be employed to shape future decisions is a distinct undertaking that involves the debate of the desirability of what "is" compared with competing visions of what "could be."

The distinction between the descriptive and the prescriptive empirical tasks is fundamental. Decision-making studies in other domains demonstrate that descriptions of what decision makers do often do not correspond with what they should do or even with what they believe they do (Gottfredson and Gottfredson 1986).

3. *The "Rationality-Cannot-Reform" Critique.* A third major critique is that decision guidelines are not an effective means for bringing about change. These doubts range from narrow criticisms of the guidelines method to more general, philosophical disagreements with the "rational-man" assumptions that underlie the voluntary guidelines approach.[3]

A "rational" conception of the human decision maker underlies the guidelines approach (Gottfredson, Wilkins, and Hoffman 1978). That conception assumes that decision makers voluntarily will seek optimal solutions to difficult choices, are interested in improving their understanding of the goals of their decisions, and see themselves as benefiting from information related to achievement of those goals and to the consequences of their decisions.

Some critics plainly question these assumptions (Rich et al. 1982, p. 206). In a summary of an evaluation of the Maryland and Florida sentencing guidelines, both of which were to have had an empirical base, Carrow concludes that the major weaknesses of the guidelines systems she examined were not traceable to their "judicial origins or empirical design, but their voluntary implementation" (1984, p. 171).

Proponents cite the experience of the U.S. Parole Commission and the bail-guidelines experiment in Philadelphia as evidence that mean-

---

[3] For example, Rich et al. (1982) seek to discredit the concept of decision guidelines as a vehicle for policy reform by highlighting weaknesses of a specific application.

ingful and measurable change can be effectuated by the voluntary guidelines method. Perhaps some forms of "voluntariness" carry with them powerful influences toward compliance. For example, a guidelines innovation adopted by a court of its own accord may be motivated by external pressures. Judges may fear that if they refuse to revise sentencing practices the legislature will mandate changes with which they disagree. Similarly, jail-crowding crises and litigation may motivate judges to worry about bail decision making.

In practice, use of "voluntary" guidelines may not be entirely voluntary. Decision makers may be influenced by collegial pressure or have little choice but to comply if the policy becomes a formal or informal court rule. Even without legislative backing, guidelines may be "enforced" informally by strong court leadership; conversely, they may fall quickly into disuse in the absence of commitment from the top. To date, nevertheless, there is evidence that voluntary guidelines can produce effective and meaningful change (see Sec. III and Goldkamp and Gottfredson 1985).

B. Statistical Methods

Critics argue that serious methodological weaknesses have characterized voluntary guidelines research. A lengthy list of methods problems has been detailed: the descriptive models at the heart of the guidelines have been seriously flawed, the models' predictive power has been unimpressively weak, and the models devised have institutionalized the discriminatory effects of status variables such as sex, race, or economic status or have failed to attend to the anticipated effects of classifications resulting from their adoption (Galegher and Carroll 1983, p. 368).

1. *Flawed Models.*   Quality modeling is crucial. If researchers do not model decisions well, the examination of policy and practice will be faulty, and the resulting guidelines may be based on erroneous premises. Vigorous critiques of the statistical sophistication of some of the earlier guidelines have been offered (Rich et al. 1982; Blumstein et al. 1983; Sparks 1983).

Poorly specified models may stem from a number of problems. Sampling may insufficiently or inequitably represent the decision makers whose decisions are the foundation of the modeling exercise; extrapolations of policy from such a sample may be too narrowly based. Sampling may also inadequately include entire categories of cases that, although essential in any sentencing scheme, may appear only rarely. Murder, rape, and robbery cases are less common than are less serious cases. To learn how these kinds of cases are "typically" handled, it may be necessary to design a sample to "overinclude" them.

In addition, samples serving as the basis for guidelines development may be too small for meaningful analysis if the researchers wish to weigh the relative strength of variables related to decisions, to assess possible interaction effects, or to validate results (Sparks 1983, pp. 211–12). Rich et al. (1982, p. 71), for example, suggest that, by relying on a sample of 200 cases, the researchers who were developing sentencing guidelines in Denver employed a sample much too small for in-depth multivariate modeling.

Another problem is that variables included in empirical models may not reflect operating concerns (because of poor data, poor conceptualization, or spurious correlations), and others that do influence policy may be omitted (because of measurement difficulties, poor theorizing, or missing information). The models that are produced may best be explained merely by the availability of some information in archival data and the unavailability of other information.

A related difficulty involves poor conceptualization and measurement of variables (Blumstein et al. 1983, pp. 83–84; Sparks 1983, pp. 209, 226). The measurement of sentencing decisions, for example, has been examined as a quasi-, interval-level variable (Wilkins et al. 1976) in which zero represented nonincarcerative sanctions, and values of one or higher stood for periods of time to be served in incarceration. Such a measure may impractically combine qualitatively different decisions (the in/out decision and the length of sentence decision) in one criterion, serving neither well. Subsequent guidelines efforts have generally modeled the two aspects of sentencing decisions separately (see, e.g., Blumstein et al. 1983).

Bail decision making poses a similar measurement problem because of its different decision options (release on personal recognizance, cash bail, conditional release, and outright detention). Some researchers have employed an all-purpose criterion with values ranging from $0.00 (for personal recognizance) to positive dollar values (sometimes reaching into the millions) (Landes 1974). More recently, the dependent variable has been conceptualized as a bifurcated or trifurcated decision (e.g., "release on recognizance," yes or no?; then, if no, cash amount) (Roth and Wice 1978; Goldkamp 1979). In bail guidelines, each aspect has been modeled separately because of the apparent different orientations of the decision components and the difference in the factors that appear to predict each (Goldkamp 1979; Goldkamp and Gottfredson 1985).

The measurement of independent variables, particularly offense severity, has also posed problems (Blumstein et al. 1983, pp. 108–10; Sparks 1983, pp. 226–27). Statutory offense definitions vary from jurisdiction to jurisdiction, so it is difficult to employ a measure that both reflects the treatment of severity locally and can serve as the basis for comparisons across jurisdictions. When offense severity is scaled without reference to statutory gradings, the resulting classification may be quite different still, as in the case of the original federal parole guidelines (Gottfredson, Wilkins, and Hoffman 1978) and of the bail guidelines developed in Philadelphia (Goldkamp, Gottfredson, and Mitchell-Herzfeld 1981). Similarly, measurements of criminal history suffer reliability and validity weaknesses (Is an individual's record accurate or even available? When available, does the conviction offense correspond well with the crime committed?).

Misapplication of statistical techniques has been described as a source of poor modeling in guidelines efforts (Blumstein et al. 1983, p. 80; Sparks 1983, pp. 218–19; Gottfredson and Gottfredson 1986, p. 127). Ordinary least squares regression, for example, has been applied to predictions of dichotomous criterion variables that have been treated as interval-level indicators without concern for the consequences. Often the distributions of these variables have been highly skewed (aggravating prediction errors) and nonlinear relations between the independent measures and the criterion variables not properly explored. Critics have urged that researchers pay more attention to the assumptions underlying specific statistical techniques in their application to guidelines modeling. However, because of the validity, reliability, and measurement difficulties characteristic of archival criminal justice data, comparisons of the relative power of simple versus "sophisticated" techniques have not shown a clear advantage to the preferred, more sophisticated techniques (Gottfredson and Gottfredson 1979).

In short, to the extent that the development of decision guidelines has relied on empirical modeling, the quality of statistical modeling tasks has become an important concern having implications for the final policy product. The various pitfalls have been well documented and debated in the critical literature. That specific errors have been made in the past does not mean they will be made again in the future.

2. *The Poor Predictive Power of Decision Models.* A second technical criticism questions the power of the predictive equations on the basis of which decision models are developed and suggests that basing future policy on models whose accuracy ranges from weak to modest is mis-

guided. Blumstein et al. (1983, p. 149), for example, note that "sentencing models seldom explain more than a third of the variance in sentences, often less, and consequently provide at best a blurred picture of
past patterns." The accuracy of predictive models may be linked to
many issues including sampling, reliability, measurement, and baseline
rates; often the behaviors of interest occur relatively rarely, thus increasing the difficulty of prediction.

Another explanation of the generally modest predictive power of
decision models is that the large amount of unexplained variance associated with the modeling of sentencing, parole, and bail decisions reflects
unpatterned or arbitrary decision practices, that is, "unwarranted variation."

Accuracy is also of concern when prescriptive guidelines classify
individuals according to risk as was done in the federal parole guidelines or the Philadelphia bail guidelines. To the degree that guidelines
decisions are based on empirical estimates of risk, legal, ethical, and
moral questions about the predictive validity of the models employed
assume critical dimensions (Cohen 1983; von Hirsch and Gottfredson
1984).[4]

The development of predictive devices to assist decision makers in
developing decision tools that are overtly predictive raises additional
questions. In the Philadelphia bail experiment, once judges decided
that prediction of flight and crime during pretrial release should be
guidelines functions, the limitations of prediction were discussed. The
judges decided that a validated predictive instrument would be valuable
because predictive judgments were unavoidable in deciding bail and

---

[4] In descriptive phases, the limitations of predictive analyses have important implications. If one concludes that the models predict poorly because data are highly incomplete,
then at least the courts or other officials may have been shown that they have a major
information problem. If, however, poor predictive models result from decisions that are
not characterized by measurable patterns, different implications arise. The first might be
that guidelines may provide structure for the exercise of discretion because inconsistency
or randomness reveal a great need for such a tool. The second implication arises from
difficulty in designing guidelines that are really only "descriptive." If the only detectable
patterns in sentencing decisions explain no more than one-third of the variance, for
example, then it is not possible to construct guidelines based only on knowledge of that
one-third variance and to have those guidelines produce decisions comparable to the
original decisions. Sentencing decisions resulting from such guidelines would differ
markedly from the decisions on which guidelines were modeled; if charge seriousness and
prior criminal history accounted for one-third of the variance in the decisions that were
being modeled descriptively, they would account for nearly 100 percent of the variance in
future guidelines-generated decisions. Use of such a "descriptive" formula in creating
new sentencing guidelines, thus, would amount to a normative decision to alter current
practices, to focus them more rigorously on what were found to be main themes in
current practices.

because the statistically derived instrument would be an improvement over ad hoc judicial decision making. Use of a prediction device did not change the need to worry about "bad" predictions at bail; this continued to be an important policy concern. There was hope, however, that the extent of such errors would be lessened.

3. *Classification and Suspect Models.* Reliance on predictive models of reoffending presents a number of classification issues. First, whatever the inadequacies of prediction devices, if they are used, offenders will be incarcerated as a result of predictive classifications. Second, failure to recognize and address (or "purge") the effects of ethically or legally inappropriate factors (such as race, sex, or economic status) in guidelines development may cause or aggravate distorted outcome patterns. Critics have noted that researchers who have tried to eliminate the influence of status-related variables from guidelines have failed to attend to methodological difficulties and may have institutionalized the negative effects of those variables into the guidelines. For example, guidelines may institutionalize the disadvantages experienced by minority groups under current decision practices (Petersilia and Turner, in this volume).

The significance of this issue depends on the frequency with which such status relations are encountered in descriptive modeling of decisions. It is a concern that ought to be carefully investigated, particularly when descriptive modeling will serve as the basis for guidelines construction. Particular attention is paid in Section IV to possible discriminatory effects of modeling in guidelines development because of the opportunity afforded by the Philadelphia data to move examination of the question from the abstract to the concrete.

III. Bail Guidelines in Philadelphia

The Bail Decision-making Project in Philadelphia is the most recent attempt to develop and implement judicial guidelines using the original Gottfredson-Wilkins voluntary approach. Although the Philadelphia project was begun shortly before the voluntary guidelines efforts came under severe criticism, it was designed as an experiment—the only experimental implementation of guidelines to date—that directly tested a number of the issues raised in the subsequent controversies.

The bail-guidelines experiment addressed four critical issues about voluntary guidelines, namely, the efficacy of voluntary reform measures, concern about poor or "flawed" modeling of decisions and outcomes, the predictive power of the models developed in guidelines construction, and concern that use of descriptive models in guidelines development has institutionalized discriminatory effects of status variables.

A. Decision Guidelines for Bail

In 1978 the National Institute of Corrections funded a feasibility study to determine whether voluntary guidelines might help address problems with bail and pretrial detention. After the feasibility research was completed in 1981, the National Institute of Corrections and the National Institute of Justice collaborated in funding an experimental implementation and evaluation of the Philadelphia bail guidelines.[5]

Philadelphia had much to offer as a site for the feasibility research. The municipal court judiciary were concerned about the fairness and effectiveness of bail. A pretrial services agency had struggled with pretrial release reforms for a decade. Most important, the local correctional institutions, known as the Philadelphia prisons, had been grappling with overcrowding and decrepit conditions since the 1960s. When the research began in 1978, overcrowding litigation was approximately eight years old, and pretrial detainees, comprising more than half of the city's 3,000 inmates, were a continuing source of difficulty.

The Philadelphia bail research was initiated when a small judicial steering and policy committee, consisting of six judges (of the twenty who were sitting at the time) and the director of the pretrial services agency, was appointed by the president judge of the court. The working agreement between the court and the research team included an understanding that the project could be discontinued by the court at any time and that there was no commitment by the court to adopt decision guidelines.

The researchers' role was to collect data related to bail decisions and their consequences, to analyze data in response to the specific interests and concerns of the steering committee, and to facilitate discussion of policy issues. For example, it was clear at the outset that the judges were concerned about unwarranted disparities in bail decisions. Second, they seemed eager to learn of the effectiveness of their decisions, complaining that they rarely had an opportunity to learn whether defendants were released or jailed and, if released, whether they ab-

---

[5] The National Institute of Justice has since funded the Bail Guidelines Project to develop and measure the utility of bail guidelines in three urban jurisdictions to follow up the Philadelphia experiment.

sconded or committed additional crimes—except as a result of negative media coverage of the rare defendant released on personal recognizance who was immediately rearrested for a brutal crime.

We designed a data-collection approach that permitted a focus on the decisions of individual judges (anonymously represented) and on specific categories of criminal cases. Because a random sample of recent bail decisions would not have included a balanced cross section of all the twenty judges who then had bail responsibilities nor a balanced selection of criminal cases (because misdemeanor charges were nearly three times more common than felonies in the population), a quota sample that was stratified by judge (twenty categories) and charge (six rankings) was employed. For each judge, the sample included forty cases for each of the six charge rankings, in other words, 240 cases for each judge. Data were collected for more than 200 items of information for each of 4,800 bail decisions occurring between 1977 and 1979.[6] The data collected included information relating to the current charges and to past criminal history, prior performance on pretrial release, social background, demographics, and subsequent performance on release.

B. The Descriptive Phase

Before modeling bail decisions, we confirmed with the judges the reasonableness of the bifurcated conceptualization of bail adopted in earlier research (Goldkamp 1979). Thus the first modeling task was to "explain" an initial decision to grant a defendant release on personal recognizance (ROR) (a yes-or-no choice), and the second, for defendants not receiving ROR, was to predict the judge's selection of an amount of cash bail.

Given the different levels of measurement associated with the two decisions to be modeled, different multivariate techniques were employed to predict them. For the modeling of the ROR decision, a number of logit models were fitted on the basis of an examination of underlying bivariate relations. The most parsimonious model predicted the granting of ROR based on knowledge of a defendant's current charge, prior arrests, prior felony convictions, prior failures to appear in court, pending charges, employment, and living arrangements. The current charge was by far the dominant independent variable in the

---

[6] For a full description of the research design and data collection, see Goldkamp, Gottfredson, and Mitchell-Herzfeld (1981).

prediction of ROR. The defendant's race was not found to be important, but gender was.[7]

Multiple regression was employed to predict cash-bail decisions. First, however, the criterion measure (i.e., amount of cash) was examined carefully. Cash bails were highly skewed (half of the cash bails were below $1,000, although the range extended from $50 to $625,000). Moreover, contrary to the assumptions of the regression technique, cash-bail patterns did not comport with an interval-level measure. Unlike a true interval measure, which is characterized by equidistant values ranging from $1.00 to $625,000, cash bail was set in nine or ten common amounts (e.g., $500, $1,000, $5,000, and $10,000) with other values rarely occurring. Bails of $279, for example, were never seen. To standardize the criterion measure and to allow the assumptions of multiple regression to apply, a logarithmic transformation of the criterion was employed. The final regression included ten predictor variables that explained 47 percent of the variance in the transformed bail measure.[8] These included victim injury, current charge, number of different charges, presence of charges involving crimes against the person, number of prior convictions for serious person crimes, number of pending charges, age of the defendant, and the identity of the judge determining bail.

Thus far, then, like other empirically based guidelines projects the Bail Decision-making Project had formulated "best" models that described the factors that apparently characterized decisions made by the judges. The important question was how these correlates were linked to bail policy for the judges of the Philadelphia Municipal Court. "Implicit policy" became "explicit" through discussion and debate of the meaning of the findings with the judges.

Discussion began with debate about the proper goals of bail.[9] Some

[7] For an in-depth discussion of the modeling of ROR and of cash bail, see especially the technical appendices of Goldkamp, Gottfredson, and Mitchell-Herzfeld (1981).

[8] For a discussion of the advantages and interpretation of a regression employing a dependent variable transformed into its logarithm, see Goldkamp, Gottfredson, and Mitchell-Herzfeld (1981, app. E).

[9] The debate concerning the proper goals for bail has been long and vigorous. Prior to 1970, when Congress enacted preventive detention legislation for the District of Columbia, the dominant view was that bail could be used only to assure the presence of a defendant in court, although public safety goals were hotly debated. The model bail reform legislation, that is, the Federal Bail Reform Act of 1966, specifically stated that assuring the defendant's presence at trial is the sole legitimate goal in noncapital cases. Since 1970, however, danger-related provisions have been added to the bail laws of thirty-four states and the District of Columbia. In 1984, as part of the Comprehensive Crime Control Act of 1984, Congress enacted preventive detention legislation for the federal jurisdiction (see Goldkamp 1979, 1985).

judges, for example, argued that failure to recognize bail's public safety function would be a sham. (The appropriateness of public safety as a goal of bail under Pennsylvania law was uncertain.) Others insisted that, until case law authorized judges setting bail to take "dangerousness" into account, the only acceptable bail goal was the appearance of defendants in court.

The multivariate findings were summarized and presented to the committee against this debate as a backdrop. The sense made of the findings by the steering and policy committee revealed what appeared to be two qualitatively different policy orientations of judges when considering ROR and when determining cash bail. The ROR decision represented a screening at which persons charged with offenses viewed as either very serious or not at all serious had probabilities of ROR that could not be modified by other factors. Persons in the first category were unlikely ever to receive ROR, and those in the second were very likely to receive it. For defendants with charges of moderate seriousness, secondary factors such as evidence of solid community ties played an important role. The ROR stage was seen by the judges as an opportunity to screen out the "good-risk" defendants so they could be immediately released and to pick from among the moderate risks those who could be trusted for outright pretrial release. This decision and its factors were more concerned with the defendant's potential for absconding than was the cash-bail-amount decision.

The cash-bail stage appeared reserved for defendants who posed a very high risk of flight or who appeared to present possible danger to victims, witnesses, or the community. The heavy emphasis on the seriousness of the current criminal charge (four of the ten predictors were related to current charge) in the cash-bail analysis seemed to make sense in light of this policy interpretation as did the relative importance of the defendant's prior record. In contrast with the ROR decision, at which community ties and the defendant's record of prior attendance at court seemed to play an important role, none of these appeared influential in the judge's choice of a cash-bail amount. However, whether a defendant was already on pretrial release at the time of the current charge was a marked concern.

One interesting finding was the relation between a defendant's age and the selection of cash bail (the younger the defendant, the lower the bail, other factors being equal). This was interpreted by the steering committee judges as reflecting the practice (engaged in by judges on some occasions) of not automatically giving young defendants ROR even if charged with nonserious offenses. Instead they would intentionally set bail at a very low amount so that the defendant would be compelled to call home for assistance, thus alerting the parents to a child in trouble—something that ROR release might not have accomplished.

Findings suggesting pronounced disparity in the assignment of cash bail had a major impact on the judges. Disparity was inferred from two findings. First, even after the analysis of 200 items of information, a great deal of variance remained unexplained. Although this might have resulted in part from failure to measure important variables, it was reasonable also to assume that bail decisions varied unsystematically. Second, after controlling for the effects of all other important correlates of cash bail, the identity of the judge deciding bail made a significant difference: an additional 10 percent of the variance was explained simply by adding the identities of the judges. Some of the judges' initial doubts about the equity of bail decisions in Philadelphia thus seemed to be supported by the modeling of cash-bail decisions. This finding was viewed as especially important because, since judges brought about the detention of defendants through the manipulation of cash-bail amounts, disparity in the use of cash bail by definition translated into disparity in the use of pretrial detention.

C. The Normative Phase

The consequences of the bail decisions were investigated, including the allocation of pretrial detention and the occurrence of absconding and rearrest of defendants during their pretrial release on bail or ROR. A follow-up study of the 4,800 defendants was conducted to learn the correlates of pretrial flight and crime.[10] We demonstrated widely different rates of failure during pretrial release among defendants released by the different judges and developed models predicting pretrial flight and crime. The judges were struck by the lack of correspondence between the factors found to influence judges' decisions and the predictors of defendants' performance during pretrial release: the correlation was not significant ($r = -.02$). Gottfredson and Gottfredson (1986, table 1) have demonstrated the consistency of this effect across a wide variety of justice decision settings.

At this point, with the support of the steering committee, guidelines

---

[10] For an in-depth discussion of the modeling of the performance of defendants during pretrial release, see the technical appendices of Goldkamp, Gottfredson, and Mitchell-Herzfeld (1981).

development shifted to an explicitly prescriptive phase in which both the goals of bail and the criteria that ought to guide the bail decision were examined. The research task became the development of alternative models of bail guidelines that represented different policy orientations.

The debate by the judges focused on three competing models. One, a "status quo" model, employed the ROR and cash-bail stages of the bail decision and scored and classified defendants on the basis of formulas derived from the final descriptive models of the ROR and cash-bail decisions. The presumptive bail decisions established for this version of bail guidelines were expressed in ranges of cash derived from study of how bail typically was set in the recent past for categories of defendants. (The "categories" were determined from a classification analysis, the goal of which was to locate a small number of classes of defendants treated differently in the awarding of ROR or cash bail.) The would-be presumptive decision ranges were fixed using the amounts between which the middle 50 percent of bails had been set in each category in the past.

A second, "actuarial" model was based on refinement of the predictions of absconding and pretrial crime developed during the descriptive guidelines phase. The refined actuarial model was validated on an independent sample of Philadelphia defendants.[11] This model would determine bail by classifying defendants according to their probability of engaging in misconduct during pretrial release. One of the difficulties associated with this model was that judges do not overtly decide to release or detain defendants but rather shape that outcome through the device of cash bail; the judges were reluctant to use such a framework to distinguish openly between release and detention. Thus the actuarial guidelines would have relied on an array of ROR, conditional release, and cash options aligned with increasing probabilities of misconduct during release. Nevertheless, the actuarial model was designed to address predictive aims of bail. If it had been adopted, it would have marked a dramatic departure from the then-current bail decisions by

[11] The final risk model included five categories of defendants ranked from low to high probability of failing to appear in court, being rearrested for additional crimes, or both. For a technical discussion of the development and validation of this model, see Goldkamp, Gottfredson, and Mitchell-Herzfeld (1981). For an application of this risk model to a jail population in the context of emergency release measures in Philadelphia, see Goldkamp (1983).

aligning future decisions more directly with the empirical correlates of risk.[12]

A third, "hybrid" model combined elements from the status quo and the actuarial models. The matrix was defined by two axes, one based on a measure of charge severity derived from the descriptive analysis of bail decisions and the other on a five-part risk classification of defendants taken from the actuarial model. The five-part risk dimension and the fifteen-part charge-severity dimension produced a grid of seventy-five cells with presumptive bail decisions established by examining what judges did with these categories in the past and the absconding, pretrial crime, and detention rates associated with them.

The policy implications of each model were debated by the steering committee. Although the status quo model might achieve greater consistency, the judges understood that this approach might institutionalize inequitable features of traditional practices and would rely on factors that were not highly correlated with risk of flight and pretrial crime. The actuarial model had the advantage of framing bail decisions in terms of the strongest predictors of pretrial misconduct. The judges were not ready, however, to "trust the computer" entirely, and they were sensitive to the controversy likely to surround bail practices that were based openly on predictions of future danger. The hybrid model seemed to offer statistical guidance from the actuarial research as well as some grounding in tradition, and it was this model that the judges elected for use in a subsequent guidelines experiment (see fig. 1).

D. Flawed Modeling and Poor Predictive Power

Empirical modeling played a central role in the development of alternative versions of bail guidelines in the Philadelphia research and in the format ultimately selected for implementation in the Philadelphia Municipal Court. Most of the issues outlined in the critical literature pertaining to the quality of modeling procedures were addressed. For

[12] The logit model predicting flight, crime, or both during pretrial release relied on knowledge of the age of a defendant (defendants over forty-four years of age were assigned a low probability of misconduct); whether defendants had a phone; prior record of absconding; the existence of pending charges (whether this charge occurred while the defendant was already on pretrial release); prior arrests; the kind (as opposed to the severity) of the current charge; and the interaction of age and prior absconding (a defendant over forty-four who had a record of prior absconding was an especially high risk) and distinguished between kind of current charge and prior record of arrests (a person charged with a serious crime against the person was a lower-probability risk, but such a person who also had a lengthy record of prior arrests was a high risk). See Goldkamp, Gottfredson, and Mitchell-Herzfeld (1981, chap. 6).

BAIL GUIDELINES: JUDICIAL DECISION

| Date | Log # | Name of defendant | Police photo # | Calculated by |

Guidelines Matrix

Probability of failure

Low ← ———————————————— → High

		Group I	Group II	Group III	Group IV	Group V
Low	1	ROR	ROR	ROR	ROR	ROR
	2	ROR	ROR	ROR	ROR	ROR
	3	ROR	ROR	ROR	ROR	ROR–$500
	4	ROR	ROR	ROR	ROR	ROR–$500
	5	ROR	ROR	ROR	ROR	ROR–$1,000
	6	ROR	ROR	ROR	ROR–$1,000	$300–$1,000
	7	ROR	ROR	ROR	ROR–$1,000	$300–$1,000
	8	ROR	ROR	ROR	ROR–$1,000	$500–$1,000
Charge Severity	9	ROR	ROR	ROR	$500–$1,500	$500–$1,500
	10	ROR	ROR	ROR–$1,500	$500–$1,500	$500–$2,000
	11	ROR–$1,500	ROR–$1,500	ROR–$1,500	$500–$2,000	$500–$2,000
	12	ROR–$1,500	ROR–$1,500	$500–$1,500	$800–$2,500	$800–$3,000
	13	$800–$3,000	$800–$3,000	$1,000–$3,000	$1,000–$5,000	$1,500–$5,000
	14	$1,000–$3,000	$1,000–$3,000	$1,000–$3,000	$1,000–$5,000	$1,500–$5,000
High	15	$2,000–$7,500	$2,000–$7,500	$2,000–$7,500	$2,500–$7,500	$3,000–$10,000

| Guidelines Decision _____ | / Judicial Decision: ☐ ROR | ☐ Financial (amount) $_____ |

☐ IF DECISION DEPARTS FROM GUIDELINES, REASON(S):

☐ High probability that prosecution will be withdrawn
☐ High probability of conviction   ☐ Low probability of conviction
☐ Defendant's demeanor in court room   ☐ Sponsor present at hearing
☐ Defendant's physical or mental health   ☐ Defendant's history of court appearance
☐ Defendant's relationship to complaining witness
☐ To cause guardian to be informed of defendant's arrest
☐ Defendant poses specific threat to witness or victim
☐ Presence of warrants, detainers, or wanted cards
☐ Other (explain): _____

Decision by _____

example, the sample was carefully crafted to reflect a balanced array of kinds of cases and to include equal numbers and kinds of cases for each of the presiding judges. Similarly, measurement of dependent and independent variables was attended to in the conceptualization of the bail decision, in the transformation of cash bail into a more useful (logarithmic) version, and in the careful analysis of charge severity.

Attention was paid to the assumptions underlying the application of analytic methods: logit analysis was applied to the analysis of the use of ROR and the prediction of pretrial misconduct, and regression procedures were used in the analysis of cash bail. Each of the solutions was validated on a separate sample before it was employed in developing descriptive-type guidelines alternatives.

Questions concerning the power of the predictive analyses were also important in the feasibility research. Although the analyses of decisions produced results generally stronger (e.g., in terms of R^2) than those reported in the sentencing literature (and the solutions validated well), unexplained variance was still a problem. For example, the best explanation of variance in cash bails accounted for less than 50 percent of the variance. If the judges had elected to implement "descriptive" guidelines for bail, this limitation could have become important. Bail decisions resulting from such guidelines would differ markedly from the decisions on which guidelines were modeled; if, for example, identified correlates of decisions accounted for one-half of the variance in the decisions that were modeled descriptively, they would account for nearly 100 percent of the variance in future guidelines-generated decisions. Use of such a "descriptive" formula would amount to a normative decision to alter current practices, that is, to focus them more rigorously on what were found to be main themes in current practices.

The predictive analyses of defendant flight and crime during pretrial release raised perhaps an even more important issue relating to the power of predictive models. Decision research in criminal justice and elsewhere has repeatedly demonstrated that statistical methods will better predict future events than will clinical or subjective methods (Morris and Miller 1985). Producing a trouble-free and powerful risk device is, however, not simple.

The study of defendant misconduct during pretrial release is hampered by several well-documented problems. First, samples are biased. Only defendants who achieve pretrial release can be studied; little is known about the risks posed by those who were detained. In Philadelphia, nearly 90 percent of all defendants entering the system in the sample were released before the completion of their cases; 10 percent were thus excluded.

Second, data may be poor. In Philadelphia, a great deal of data was available because of elaborate interviews before initial appearances conducted by pretrial services staff and because criminal histories are reasonably accurate. Yet the reliability of some of the items stemming from defendant self-reports, such as the defendant's drug history, was questionable.

Third, the outcomes of concern (i.e., flight from court or crime) are rare occurrences and thus, from a statistical point of view, are difficult to predict. In the Philadelphia sample, 12 percent of released defendants were recorded as willful failures to appear in court, and 16 percent were rearrested for new crimes within a 120-day follow-up period (less than half for serious crimes).

Fourth, because of the sample and data limitations final predictive solutions are not powerful. They result in more inaccurate than accurate predictions. However, and crucially, though the resulting predictions may be near failures when compared with perfect predictions, they are modestly successful when compared with the uneven record of judges who make predictions.

Many of these problems are, of course, well known. The solution involves two approaches: the careful validation of results of predictive analyses before implementation and the recognition of the limitations of predictive devices. Although predictive devices can help decision makers frame their decisions, they will produce errors that must be addressed, if possible through careful reviews and other due process measures. Only after discussing the strengths and weaknesses of actuarial information did the Philadelphia judges decide to incorporate a risk dimension in their bail guidelines.

E. Testing the Impact of Voluntary Reform

Perhaps the principal criticism of empirically derived guidelines has been the charge that voluntary guidelines cannot achieve positive or meaningful changes. In its second phase, the Bail Decision-making Project sought to test this criterion directly through a controlled experiment.

Development, selection, and refinement of a version of bail guidelines acceptable to the committee of judges was one matter; implementation of guidelines using an experimental research design was quite another. Guided by the president judge of the municipal court, the researchers developed a plan to implement the guidelines through a rigorous experimental format to learn whether hypothesized benefits would occur.

The obstacles to conducting experiments in courts are formidable. The biggest complication is to devise a method for randomizing the treatment among incoming criminal defendants so that the experiences of comparably situated defendants can be contrasted and inferences drawn about the new procedures. One approach would have been for each judge to set bail, alternating between the new bail guidelines and the normal methods. This had two drawbacks. The logistics of conducting and monitoring such a system would be forbidding and prone to mixups. It is unlikely that, in practice, judges would shift neatly between guidelines and "normal" decision modes. The result would be that judges would mix the two approaches in their minds and carry out neither one in practice.

The strategy adopted was to assign judges to an experimental guidelines group or to a control group that would handle bail in the normal way. The goal was to produce sufficiently large numbers of guidelines decisions and nonguidelines decisions that were comparable in all ways except for the mode of the decision. The decisions of sixteen judges over a period of approximately nine months were studied. Eight judges were randomly selected to employ guidelines. Another eight were randomly chosen to serve as controls, setting bail in the normal fashion. The eight judges who served as "guidelines" judges were not selected on the basis of their philosophical predispositions toward innovation whether in the name of court reform or in the interest of progressive research.

Data were collected prospectively during 1981 and 1982 using a sample stratified by judge and charge measures until 960 bail decisions had been produced for each of the experimental and control groups. (This approach yielded 120 bail decisions per judge, including twenty in each of the six charge categories.) The logistics of the experiment were demanding given the two versions of paperwork that had to be processed through the early stages of the system, the coordination and monitoring of several participants in the pretrial process, and the around-the-clock schedules of judges who decided bail.[13]

The experiment examined whether decisions under the new guidelines differed from "normal" decisions in a number of ways. It was

[13] For a discussion of the experiment and its logistics, see Goldkamp and Gottfredson (1985).

hypothesized, for example, that guidelines decisions would conform to the guidelines in a substantial majority of instances and that, when judges departed from the guidelines, they would note their reasons. It was hypothesized, therefore, that the visibility, rationality, equity, and effectiveness of the experimental judges' bail decisions would be enhanced in comparison with those of the control judges.

A full report of the results of the experiment is available elsewhere (see Goldkamp and Gottfredson 1984, 1985). Several findings led us to conclude that the voluntary guidelines had an impact on decision practices at the bail stage and that the approach has promise for bringing about policy reform in key areas of criminal justice decision making.

Perhaps the simplest and most important question asked was whether randomly "drafted" judges would use the bail guidelines as intended or would ignore or otherwise circumvent them. To measure this, bail decisions were compared for the experimental and control judges. A convincing majority of the decisions made by the guidelines judges—76 percent of all cases—fell within the presumptive decision ranges.

By contrast, only 57 percent of the nonguidelines judges' decisions fell within the guidelines' ranges. The difference, which was both statistically significant and substantial, demonstrated that the experimental judges followed the guidelines voluntarily in a large majority of the cases and that this represented a marked change in decision practice in the court.

A second important question was whether judges would give reasons when making decisions departing from those suggested by the guidelines. The judges were not accustomed to providing written reasons for many of their decisions in the criminal process and least of all for bail decisions. Again, however, the findings are reasonably encouraging. In 65 percent of the decisions that departed from the guidelines, the experimental judges checked off or noted reasons for their actions. In 35 percent of the cases reasons were not noted. Two judges conspicuously failed to give reasons. One appeared not to have understood the importance of the request to include reasons and therefore did not make the effort consistently; the other simply did not wish to provide reasons.

Two of the reasons most often given for departing decisions—the severity of the criminal charges and the defendant's history of failures to appear in court—were factors that were already taken into account in the guidelines. It seemed, therefore, that judges were confused or that they misunderstood the notion of making exceptions to the guidelines, though they were candid overall in expressing their reasons.

In discussing this finding with the judges, it turned out that the judges who indicated these reasons were not confused and had understood the aims of the guidelines quite well. They argued that charges were occasionally so serious—so violent or heinous—that extra weight beyond that provided by the guidelines ought to be given to the severity of charges. Similarly, it was pointed out that, in the risk scale, negative points were assigned for one or two or more prior failures to appear in court. One judge argued that extra weight ought to be given when a defendant had twelve prior absences in the last several years. (Most defendants charged with prostitution in the study had lengthy records of flight, often recording as many as twenty or more missed appearances in one year.) As a result, we concluded that the notation of reasons had worked reasonably and that efforts should be made to encourage all judges using guidelines to make the effort to note them.

Another important question asked was whether, under guidelines, bail decisions would be made more systematic, less disparate, and more equitable. A simple measure of equity in bail decisions was not readily available. Thus it was first necessary to decide on a definition of "similarly situated" at bail. It was reasoned that the definition of "similarly situated" must be tied to the goals of the bail decision and to the criteria deemed appropriate to accomplishing those goals. Two measures were adopted. First, the criteria defining the bail guidelines were used as the framework for comparing the similarity of decisions given similar classes of defendants. Charge seriousness was employed as another—if more questionable—framework for evaluating the equity of the experimental bail decisions. We concluded that the variability in bail decisions for given categories of defendants (whether defined by guidelines or by charge) was more than cut in half by use of the guidelines (Goldkamp and Gottfredson 1985).

On consideration of the findings of the experiment, the judges of Philadelphia's Municipal Court moved to adopt the guidelines for use by the full court in the spring of 1983. The use of bail guidelines continues there at the time of this writing. The court has revised the guidelines several times by taking advantage of the feedback-generating feature of guidelines, and an on-line computer-monitoring procedure has been developed and instituted.[14]

---

[14] At the time of this writing, some three years after the researchers departed from the site of the experiment, guidelines are still in use in the Philadelphia Municipal Court. The president judge of the municipal court, Joseph R. Glancey, premised on the use of guidelines, successfully sought legislation instituting a commissioner system to replace

Late in 1984, the National Institute of Justice funded the Bail Guidelines Project to test the bail-guidelines approach in three other jurisdictions. The aims of this research are to determine whether the findings from the Philadelphia experiment recur in locations with similarly serious concerns about pretrial release decision making but with notably different characteristics (such as court organization and laws governing bail and pretrial detention). Is the Philadelphia experience unique, explained perhaps by the quality of the leadership of the municipal court or by other particularly favorable aspects of the environment? Or can the voluntary guidelines approach effectively address bail-related issues in jurisdictions that are quite different?

The courts in Suffolk County (Boston Municipal Court and Suffolk County Superior Court), Massachusetts; Maricopa County (superior court), Arizona; and Dade County (circuit and county courts), Florida, were selected because of their interest in examining bail decision-making practices. In each of the locations, for example, jail overcrowding has had a long and particularly stubborn history, and the judiciaries have expressed concern about the effectiveness and equity of their bail decisions and their impact on the jails.

Since the beginning of the Bail Guidelines Project, the research staff has been working collaboratively with steering committees in each location and has reviewed empirical findings describing bail decisions and their consequences. The research is following a process similar to that in Philadelphia. Alternative models of decision guidelines based on empirical modeling of large samples of defendant data and policy discussion have been developed, and implementation of the guidelines is beginning so far in two of the three sites. In an evaluation phase, questions about the use of guidelines and their impact will be examined so that additional data relevant to assessment of the voluntary decision guidelines approach can be accumulated.

IV. Discrimination in Decision Modeling

A belief that traditional bail practices in the United States unfairly discriminated against the poor and minorities was one of the principal motivations for the bail reform movement of the 1960s (Foote 1954; Freed and Wald 1964). An important concern of critics of guidelines

---

judges at the bail stage. When commissioners make decisions departing from the guidelines, the district attorney and the public defender may appeal to a referee judge from the municipal court. The presumption is that decisions made within the guidelines will not be changed.

has been fear that reliance on empirical modeling may institutionalize discriminatory practices that were either unnoticed by the crafters of the guidelines or that were thought, erroneously, to have been corrected by them.[15] Given the potential importance of the discrimination question, this final section uses the experience and data from the Philadelphia bail experiment to assess its relevance.

In adopting a charge-severity dimension as one of the two defining axes of the decision grid, for example, the Philadelphia judges considered criticisms of that standard. Critics objected to its use in traditional bail practices as a surrogate measure of a defendant's potential dangerousness (the more serious the charge, the greater the danger posed), which, until recently, in most places was an illegitimate use of bail. But critics asserted also that the use of pretrial detention would be biased from an economic perspective: when cash bail was set strictly according to the seriousness of the charged offense, defendants who could afford the bail would be released, while those without financial resources would remain confined (Foote 1954, 1965; American Bar Association 1978).

These concerns notwithstanding, the Philadelphia judges adopted the severity dimension to counterbalance the risk dimension, expressing a wish to weigh the differential costs associated with the risks posed by different defendants. They reasoned, for instance, that a high-risk numbers runner posed a different potential cost to the decision maker than did a low-risk rapist should the release decision go awry.

The judges adopted an explicitly predictive approach. The individual items making up the classification dimension—which did not include such status variables as race or sex, for example—were fully discussed and, with the exception of the arrest item, were not found to be controversial.[16]

---

[15] Critics question how this problem has been addressed in recently developed guidelines, discuss how the effects of suspect status variables ought to be "purged" from descriptive guidelines models (Fisher and Kadane 1983; Sparks 1983), and emphasize the possibly serious implications for the justice process if the effects are not addressed (Rich et al. 1982; Blumstein et al. 1983).

[16] The predictive analysis found the record of a defendant's prior arrests to be more powerful than his record of prior convictions. The judges debated whether it was ethically proper to make use of arrest information, given that it could be used to rate the defendant negatively, increasing the odds of higher bail and possibly pretrial detention. The prevailing view was that the job at bail was essentially predictive and that, if an actuarial device were to be included in the guidelines, they would prefer to include the most powerful predictors. A similar argument developed over the telephone item. The classification ranked defendants with telephones as lower risks. When it was suggested that this might be economically discriminatory (on the assumption that poor defendants

Difficult questions about the discriminatory impact of criteria in the guidelines were avoided in Philadelphia when the judges chose the hybrid version of guidelines. Status-related issues had surfaced in the modeling of the ROR decision and in the construction of a descriptive version of guidelines that was seriously considered by the steering committee. The following discussion illustrates the potentially discriminatory effects of guidelines as they very nearly could have applied.

A. *The Effects of Gender and Employment*

Although ROR does not directly determine who will go to jail (detention is usually determined indirectly by the manipulation of cash bail by judges), in a large number of instances it determines who will not go to jail and therefore who among the criminally accused will be free pending trial without any form of constraint other than a personal promise to appear. Thus the modeling of the choice between ROR and cash bail had serious implications, particularly if the judges were to select a descriptive guidelines strategy.

As has been described in Goldkamp, Gottfredson, and Mitchell-Herzfeld (1981, app. D), a pool of candidate independent variables to be used in a model predicting ROR decisions was selected using three criteria: the correlates of ROR found in previous research (Roth and Wice 1978; Goldkamp 1979), factors expected theoretically to play a role in the decision (such as community ties, employment, and so on), and factors showing a minimal level of association with the criterion in the data. Using these criteria, forty-three independent variables were identified for further consideration. Further reduction was achieved by examining the relations of each of these variables with ROR within eight "slices" of the defendant sample defined by criminal charge.[17] Those variables displaying the largest number of relations across the eight charge subdivisions were determined to be the most broadly related and were selected for inclusion in multivariate analysis (see table 1).

Logit analysis, the multivariate method employed, postulates that

---

would not have a telephone), the counterargument was that being able to contact a defendant served the purpose of being able to guarantee the defendant's appearance in court, which was after all a major goal of bail.

[17] These "slices" should not be confused with the six categories based on felony-misdemeanor grading employed as a means of stratification in collecting the sample. Rather the "slices" were merely large categories of different types of crimes (not based on seriousness) within which the applicability of relations noted in the sample data overall could be tested in more detail.

TABLE 1

Relations between the ROR Decision and Various Independent Variables for Eight Types of Charges

Variables	Charge Category*								Number of Significant Relationships
	C62	C61	C53	C42	C32	C22	C12	C31	
Number of defendants	425	375	543	698	460	302	473	259	…
Percentage ROR	5	16	17	29	42	62	84	95	…
Victim characteristics:									
Number of person victims	N.S.	N.S.	N.S.	N.S.	N.S.	N.S.	+	+	0
Victim knows defendant	N.S.	N.S.	N.S.	N.S.	N.S.	N.S.	+	+	0
Spouse or child	N.S.	N.S.	S	N.S.	N.S.	N.S.	+	+	1
Family or relative	N.S.	N.S.	N.S.	N.S.	N.S.	N.S.	+	+	0
Friend	N.S.	N.S.	S	N.S.	N.S.	N.S.	+	+	1
Acquaintance	S	N.S.	N.S.	N.S.	N.S.	N.S.	+	+	1
Sex of victim	N.S.	N.S.	S	N.S.	N.S.	N.S.	+	+	1
Race of victim	N.S.	N.S.	S	N.S.	N.S.	N.S.	+	+	1
Seriousness of injury	N.S.	N.S.	N.S.	N.S.	N.S.	N.S.	+	+	0
Offense characteristics:									
Number of suspects	N.S.	N.S.	N.S.	N.S.	N.S.	N.S.	N.S.	N.S.	0
Number of municipal court numbers (transcripts)	N.S.	N.S.	N.S.	N.S.	N.S.	N.S.	N.S.	N.S.	0
Number of lower-level charges	S	N.S.	S	N.S.	N.S.	N.S.	N.S.	N.S.	2
Number of offenses charged	S	N.S.	S	N.S.	N.S.	N.S.	N.S.	N.S.	2
Community ties:									
Has a phone	N.S.	N.S.	N.S.	N.S.	N.S.	N.S.	N.S.	N.S.	0
Employment	N.S.	S	N.S.	S	S	N.S.	S	N.S.	4
Wages per week	S	S	N.S.	N.S.	N.S.	N.S.	N.S.	N.S.	2
On welfare	S	N.S.	N.S.	N.S.	S	S	N.S.	N.S.	3
Pays rent or mortgage or owns home	N.S.	S	N.S.	S	N.S.	N.S.	N.S.	N.S.	2
Owns a motor vehicle	S	S	S	N.S.	N.S.	S	S	S	3

132

Lives with spouse/child	N.S.	N.S.	S	N.S.	S	N.S.	N.S.	3
Marital status	S	N.S.	N.S.	N.S.	N.S.	N.S.	N.S.	1
Length of present residence	N.S.	N.S.	N.S.	N.S.	N.S.	N.S.	S	1
Probable surety: self	N.S.	N.S.	N.S.	N.S.	N.S.	N.S.	N.S.	0
Drug use	N.S.	S	N.S.	N.S.	S	N.S.	N.S.	2
Prior criminal history:								
Arrests	S	S	S	S	S	S	S	8
Recent arrests	S	S	S	S	S	N.S.	S	7
Serious personal arrests	S	S	S	S	S	S	S	8
Serious property arrests	N.S.	S	N.S.	S	S	S	S	6
Drug arrests	S	S	N.S.	S	S	S	S	7
Weapon arrests	S	S	N.S.	S	N.S.	S	S	6
Convictions	S	N.S.	S	S	S	S	S	8
Serious personal convictions	N.S.	S	S	N.S.	N.S.	N.S.	S	5
Serious property convictions	N.S.	S	S	S	N.S.	N.S.	S	4
Drug convictions	N.S.	N.S.	N.S.	S	S	S	S	5
Weapon convictions	S	S	N.S.	S	N.S.	N.S.	S	3
Felony convictions	S	S	S	S	N.S.	N.S.	S	7
Misdemeanor convictions	N.S.	S	N.S.	N.S.	N.S.	S	S	6
Prior FTAs	N.S.	S	N.S.	S	S	S	N.S.	4
Pending charges	N.S.	S	N.S.	S	S	S	N.S.	5
On parole, probation, or work release	N.S.	S	S	S	S	N.S.	S	6
Demographic characteristics:								
Race	S	S	N.S.	S	N.S.	N.S.	N.S.	3
Sex	S	S	S	S	S	S	S	6
Age	N.S.	S	N.S.	S	N.S.	N.S.	N.S.	2

SOURCE.—Goldkamp, Gottfredson, and Mitchell-Herzfeld (1981).

NOTE.—S = χ² significant at .05 level; N.S. = χ² not significant at .05 level.

* For a description of these charge categories, see Goldkamp, Gottfredson, and Mitchell-Herzfeld (1981, app. B).

† There were no victims for these crimes.

the probability of receiving ROR is a nonlinear function of the independent variables included in the model. The most parsimonious model adequately predicted the granting of ROR on the basis of knowledge of the following independent variables: seriousness of criminal charge, whether the defendant was living with spouse or child, prior arrests (none versus one or more), prior failures to appear in court (none versus one or more willful absences), felony convictions (none versus one or more), employment (employed or not in work force versus unemployed), and gender.[18]

Formula for the Probability of ROR under Descriptive Model 1.   The following formula summarized the logit model for prediction of ROR.

$$
\begin{aligned}
\text{ROR probability} = {} & -.515 - (2.38 \times \text{Charge1}) \\
& - (1.14 \times \text{Charge2}) - (3.16 \times \text{Charge3}) \\
& + (.41 \times \text{Charge4}) + (1.02 \times \text{Charge5}) \\
& - (1.77 \times \text{Felony Convictions}) \\
& - (.545 \times \text{Arrests}) \\
& - (.353 \times \text{Prior Failures to Appear}) \\
& - (.407 \times \text{Pending Charges}) \\
& + (1.66 \times \text{Living Arrangement}) \\
& - (.307 \times \text{Gender}) + (1.28 \times \text{Employment}).
\end{aligned}
$$

By inserting the appropriate values determined by each defendant's attributes, defendants may be assigned scores, ranging from approximately -10 to $+10$, that, when transformed, correspond to a probability that they would have received ROR. If this descriptive model were to be adopted unmodified for use as part of a prescriptive guidelines framework, a system for classifying defendants prior to their bail decisions would be derived from the formula in the fashion portrayed in table 2. By dividing the parameter estimates by a constant and rounding to the nearest whole number, a simplified point scale is obtained that prebail interviewers could employ to calculate an overall "ROR score" for the guidelines.

By selecting certain cutting scores, one possible if simplified guidelines classification might divide defendants into groups having low, medium, or high probabilities of receiving ROR.

Under such descriptive ROR guidelines, had they been in effect at the time the sample defendants had been entering the system, roughly 42 percent of the Philadelphia defendants would have been presumed

---

[18] The likelihood chi-square statistic ($2 \times$ observed $\times$ log[observed/expected]) for this model equaled 351.75 at 304 degrees of freedom and was significant at the .03 level.

TABLE 2

Parameters and Corresponding Points Estimated under the Logit Model Fitted to the ROR Decision

Variables	Parameter	Points
Add constant	−.515	−3
Charge category:*		
1 (most serious)	−2.38	−16
2	−1.14	−8
3	−.316	−2
4	.410	3
5	1.02	7
6 (least serious)	.00	
Felony convictions (1 or more)	−.177	−1
Prior arrests (1 or more)	−.545	−4
Pending charges (1 or more)	−.407	−3
Prior FTAs (1 or more)	−.353	−2
Living arrangement (lives with spouse or child)	.166	1
Gender:		
Male	−.307	−2
Employment	.128	1

NOTE.—For ease of application, points were calculated by dividing the parameters by a constant (.15) and rounding.

* For a description of the kinds of charges falling in each category, see Goldkamp, Gottfredson, and Mitchell-Herzfeld (1981, app. B).

to be granted outright ROR. Forty-five percent, on the other hand, would have been presumed not to be eligible for ROR. Thirteen percent would have fallen into the "no-presumption" (either ROR, ROR with conditions, or low-cash-bail) range.

This guidelines model (model 1) would build in gender and employment effects. Other factors being equal, female defendants and employed defendants would be more likely in future decisions under guidelines to receive ROR just as they were in the past. Whether this decision-making pattern originally stemmed from a view that women were better risks or from some other view, favoritism would continue to be shown to female defendants. Although an original goal of bail reform was to eliminate the practice of detaining persons merely because they were without financial resources, to the extent that employment indicates economic status these guidelines would continue to favor persons with financial resources.

Tables 3 and 4 display the distinct relation between this version of ROR guidelines and gender and employment. Roughly 69 percent of female defendants would be classified in the presumptive ROR cate-

TABLE 3

Classification of Philadelphia Defendants into Presumptive ROR Categories Based on Descriptive Logit Model of ROR (Model 1), by Gender

Gender	Presumed Cash Bail (Low ROR Probability)		ROR, Low-Cash Conditions (Medium ROR Probability)		Presumed ROR (High ROR Probability)		Total	
	Number	Percentage	Number	Percentage	Number	Percentage	Number	Percentage
Male	1,988	49.0	524	12.9	1,547	38.1	4,059	100.0
Female	126	21.0	62	10.3	412	68.7	600	100.0
Total*	2,114	45.4	586	12.6	1,959	42.0	4,659	100.0

NOTE.—Gamma = − .53; χ^2 = 208.9, df = 2; $p \leq .01$.
* Totals may vary due to the use of the employment variable in the logit model of ROR.

TABLE 4

Classification of Philadelphia Defendants into Presumptive ROR Categories Based on Descriptive Logit Model of ROR (Model 1), by Employment Status

Employment Status	Presumed Cash Bail (Low ROR Probability)		ROR, Low-Cash Conditions (Medium ROR Probability)		Presumed ROR (High ROR Probability)		Total	
	Number	Percentage	Number	Percentage	Number	Percentage	Number	Percentage
Not employed	1,339	55.9	280	11.7	775	32.4	2,394	100.0
Employed	775	34.2	306	13.5	1,184	52.3	2,265	100.0
Total*	2,114	45.4	586	12.6	1,959	42.0	4,659	100.0

NOTE.—Gamma = .38; χ^2 = 233.6, df = 2; $p \leq .01$.
* Totals may vary due to the use of the employment variable in the logit model of ROR.

137

gory compared with 38 percent of the male defendants. Fifty-two percent of defendants who were employed or not in the work force would
be classified in the presumptive ROR category compared with 32 percent of the unemployed defendants.

Not surprisingly, when confronted with these findings, the Philadelphia judges asked the research staff how the apparent biases against
male and unemployed defendants might be eliminated in a descriptive
guidelines format.

B. The "Wrong" Way to Purge the Effects of Status

Guidelines critics have noted instances when attempts were made to
eliminate the effects of status variables merely by dropping the obnox-
ious factors from the equation and then rerunning the new equation.
Fisher and Kadane (1983) and others have argued that the effects of the
status variables will not be removed in this fashion because the remaining predictors in the new equation will change their weights; in effect,
the weight of the purged variables will be redistributed among other,
seemingly neutral variables. Because the weights will be misspecified,
the overall ability of the model to predict ROR will suffer. And, because some of the criterion variance can be attributed to the status
variables, the predictor weights also will reflect this "unwarranted"
variation.

Had the Philadelphia judges wished to adopt a descriptive version of
guidelines for ROR, we could have attempted to remove the discriminatory effects of gender and employment in precisely this "wrong"
fashion.

*Formula for the Probability of ROR under Descriptive Model 2 (Dropping
Gender and Employment).*   For the purposes of this discussion, this approach was carried out and is represented in the following revised
formula.[19]

$$
\begin{aligned}
\text{ROR probability} = {} & -.727 - (2.42 \times \text{Charge1}) \\
& - (1.14 \times \text{Charge2}) - (.299 \times \text{Charge3}) \\
& + (.405 \times \text{Charge4}) + (1.05 \times \text{Charge5}) \\
& - (.217 \times \text{Felony Convictions}) \\
& - (.572 \times \text{Prior Arrests}) \\
& - (.36 \times \text{Prior Failures to Appear}) \\
& - (.409 \times \text{Pending Charges}) \\
& + (.23 \times \text{Living Arrangement}).
\end{aligned}
$$

---

[19] This model is also significant at the .001 level.

TABLE 5

Comparison of Parameters of Two Models of ROR

Independent Variables	ROR Model 1*	ROR Model 2†
Constant	−.515	−.727
Charge:		
1	−2.38	−2.42
2	−1.14	−1.14
3	−.316	−.299
4	.41	.405
5	1.02	1.05
Felony convictions	−.177	−.217
Arrests	−.545	−.572
Pending charges	−.407	−.409
Prior FTAs	−.353	−.360
Living arrangements	.166	.230

* Original descriptive model.
† Gender and employment status dropped.

The extent to which merely dropping the gender and employment variables has shifted the values of the parameters of the remaining factors (summarized in table 5) appears generally slight, though it is most noticeable in the weights of the living-arrangements and the felony-convictions variables.

When this formula is used to assign weights to the remaining criteria, defendants can be scored and, in a fashion similar to the procedure used for Model 1, grouped within a three-part classification according to their probabilities of receiving ROR.[20]

To discover what difference this approach would make if descriptive ROR guidelines were implemented, two questions can be asked. (1) To what extent have the new ROR guidelines reduced the relations between the guidelines classification and gender and employment status? (2) How differently would the new classification (model 2 guidelines) treat defendants compared with the original model unexpurgated of status effects?

To answer the first question, simple measures of association ("gamma coefficients") were calculated to measure the relations be-

[20] To make the procedures for constructing the three category classifications of defendants as similar as possible, the selection of cutting points was dictated by the distribution of defendants within the three categories. Use of the same cutting scores would have resulted in categories of ROR probabilities varying from model to model.

tween the status variables and the new classification for comparison with the original classification.[21] The gamma between the model 1 classification and gender, $-.53$, dropped to $-.34$ under the model 2 classification. The gamma between the ROR guidelines classification and employment status changed only slightly from model 1 to model 2, however, from .38 under the original model with the status effects fully included to .34 under the "wrongly" purged model. In short, the strategy of merely dropping the status variables from the equation reduced the gender effect of the ROR classification by 36 percent but the employment effect by only 11 percent.

Perhaps more to the point is a comparison of the ways in which the different classifications based on the two models of ROR categorize the same defendants. Overall, only 7 percent of the defendants changed categories from the first model to the second. Table 6 reveals that 96 percent of the defendants who were designated under the original descriptive model of ROR as presumed ROR releasees were also so designated by the classification based on dropping the status variables. However, 3 percent of the sample defendants presumed to be releaseable on ROR under model 1 fall within the borderline no-presumption category under the "purged" model. Of those classed in the no-presumption (or middle ROR) group under model 1 originally, only 67 percent are so grouped under model 2; 13 percent are now more liberally classified into the presumed ROR range under the second model, but 19 percent now are placed in the category presuming cash bail. Most of those classified as presumed cash bail defendants under model 1 were also grouped that way under the altered model; 2 percent were classified less restrictively into the no-presumption category under the second version of ROR guidelines.

C. The "Right" Way to Purge the Effects of Status

We might have sought to work with a model of ROR that retains the "correct" relations between the remaining independent variables and ROR (i.e., partialing out the effects of their interrelations with other variables). To do this it would be necessary to return to the original formula modeling the ROR decision. Several approaches to the problem of properly specifying an ROR model and trying to eliminate the

---

[21] Gamma coefficients, really a measure of relations between two ordinal-level variables, were employed for this purpose. Although gender and employment status are not ordinal measures, for simplicity of presentation they are treated as such. Other measures could have been used and would have produced the same results.

TABLE 6

Comparison of the Classification of Philadelphia Defendants under Models 1 and 2

Model 2	Model 1						Total	
	Presumed Cash Bail		ROR, Low-Cash Conditions		Presumed ROR			
	Number	Percentage	Number	Percentage	Number	Percentage	Number	Percentage
Presumed cash bail	2,063	97.6	113	19.3	7	.4	2,183	46.9
ROR, low-cash-bail conditions	51	2.4	395	67.4	65	3.3	511	11.0
Presumed ROR	0	.0	78	13.3	1,887	96.3	1,965	42.2
Total	2,114	100.0	586	100.0	1,959	100.0	4,659	100.1

NOTE.—Gamma = .99; χ^2 = 6,476.9, df = 4; $p \leq .01$. Percentages do not always total 100 due to rounding.

effects of the employment and gender factors would be available to the judges but would require a policy decision.

One method is to hold these variables constant in the formula by selecting one value to be fixed for each and then using the formula to reclassify defendants. The reason this amounts to a policy decision is that there are several combinations of values to be considered. In the ROR decision example, the judges could have decided to score all defendants in future cases under the guidelines in one of the following fashions: (1) as employed males, (2) as unemployed males, (3) as employed females, or (4) as unemployed females.

The implications of choosing one approach could be more than just theoretically important; other factors equal, female defendants have been more likely to receive ROR than have male defendants, and employed (or not in the work force) defendants have been more likely to receive ROR than have unemployed defendants. If the judges were to regard both status effects as perniciously discriminatory, they might decide, for example, to treat all defendants as females and as employed defendants have been treated in the past.[22] They would thus insert the values representing females and employed defendants in the original formula, with the following result.

Formula for the Probability of ROR under Descriptive Model 3.

$$
\begin{aligned}
\text{ROR probability} = -.515 \ &- (2.38 \times \text{Charge1}) \\
&- (1.14 \times \text{Charge2}) - (3.16 \times \text{Charge3}) \\
&+ (.41 \times \text{Charge4}) + (1.02 \times \text{Charge5}) \\
&- (.177 \times \text{Felony Convictions}) \\
&- (.545 \times \text{Arrests}) \\
&- (.353 \times \text{Prior Failures to Appear}) \\
&- (.407 \times \text{Pending Charges}) \\
&+ (.166 \times \text{Living Arrangement}) \\
&- (.307 \times \text{Gender, fixed at } -1, \text{ female}) \\
&+ (.128 \times \text{Employment, fixed at } 1, \text{employed value}).
\end{aligned}
$$

When Philadelphia defendants are classified using the weights from this formula into three categories of ROR presumptions, roughly 49 percent fall into the presumed cash grouping, 11 percent fall into the no-presumption range (which posits a choice of ROR, ROR with conditions, or low cash bail), and 41 percent fall into the presumed ROR category.

[22] In fact, the Philadelphia judges had decided that female defendants should be treated like male defendants.

Once again this ROR guidelines classification of defendants can be contrasted with the original model, which included the status effects without modification. The association between gender and the ROR classification shrinks notably from $-.53$ under model 1 to $-.28$ under model 3. The association with employment status and the ROR classification moved from .38 under model 1 to .34 under model 3. Thus "correct" specification had reduced the gender effect of descriptive ROR guidelines by 47 percent compared with the 36 percent reduction achieved by the "wrong" method represented by model 2. The "correct" approach had not achieved any greater reduction of the employment effect (about 11 percent), however, than had the model 2 method.

Table 7 displays the difference in the ways Philadelphia defendants would have been classified under models 1 and 3. Approximately 6 percent of the defendants would have been classified differently under model 3 overall. Five percent of the defendants placed in the presumed ROR category under model 1 would have moved to the no-presumption category (4 percent) and the presumed cash category (1 percent). Of the defendants placed in the no-presumption ROR category under model 1, 70 percent would be similarly classified under model 3, 24 percent would be moved to the presumed cash-bail category, and 6 percent would have been moved to the category presuming ROR release for defendants. Virtually all the defendants ranked as presumed cash-bail candidates under the model 1 guidelines classification were so placed under the model 3 version.

D. Discriminatory Practices and the Importance of Proper Specification of Guidelines Models: Conclusion

This section has examined the impact of issues raised by critics concerning the potential for institutionalizing discriminatory decision practices in the development of descriptive guidelines. Despite appearances, the central question is not technical but practical and ethical. To what extent are proper modeling procedures likely to improve the decision-making practices that are influenced by discriminatory factors, and to what extent are they likely to improve the situation compared with the application of the simpler (and statistically improper) methods? In the case of bail, how differently would defendants in Philadelphia at the time of the study have been treated as a result of adoption of either of the corrective models?

Clearly, it is not inappropriate for critics to be concerned about the

TABLE 7

Comparison of the Classification of Philadelphia Defendants under Models 1 and 3

| | Model 1 | | | | | | | |
| | Presumed Cash Bail | | ROR, Low-Cash Conditions | | Presumed ROR | | Total | |
Model 3	Number	Percentage	Number	Percentage	Number	Percentage	Number	Percentage
Presumed cash bail	2,105	99.6	141	24.1	20	1.0	2,266	48.6
ROR, low-cash-bail conditions	9	.4	410	70.0	70	3.6	489	10.5
Presumed ROR	0	.0	35	6.0	1,869	95.4	1,904	40.9
Total	2,114	100.0	586	100.1	1,959	100.0	4,659	100.0

NOTE.—Gamma = .99; χ^2 = 6,846.4, df = 4; $p \leq .01$. Percentages do not always total 100 due to rounding.

existence of discriminatory effects in decision practices. However, the debate over the magnitude of possible harmful effects of improper modeling procedures may have proved more important for theory than for practice.

Table 8 contrasts the classification generated by the "correctly" specified model 3 approach (based on insertion of fixed values for gender and employment status) with the classification based on the "wrongly" purged model 2. The difference is not great. Approximately 3 percent of the defendants would have been treated differently by the two models.[23]

Of equal interest are the two important findings. The "wrong" procedures reduced the role of the status variables (gender and employment status) nearly as much as the proper procedures did. Neither approach was able to eliminate their influence totally despite the use of sophisticated modeling procedures. The effects of employment status appeared especially difficult to minimize.

V. The Guidelines Concept versus the Guideline Criticism

Criticism of the guidelines approach has focused on empirical methods, challenged the capacity of the strategy to produce meaningful changes, and outlined technical issues likely to undermine the integrity of guidelines. The broad criticisms have questioned whether meaningful "implicit policies" can be identified by use of empirical research and statistical analyses, asserted that the approach is prone to institutionalize the status quo, and questioned whether empirically based guidelines are capable of altering decision patterns unless they are based on some form of enforcing legal authority.

The Philadelphia bail-guidelines experiment is germane to these debates for at least four reasons. The bail research followed the original conceptualization of the guidelines strategy; it was the first application of the guidelines approach to bail. The bail guidelines were evaluated by means of a rigorous experimental design—the first such design in any guidelines application. Appropriate statistical models were employed in their development.

The Philadelphia research shows that meaningful researcher/ decision-maker collaboration can produce both an informed examina-

---

[23] The gamma representing the correspondence between models 3 and 1 is .99. The gamma between models 3 and 2 is 1.00.

TABLE 8

Comparison of the Classification of Philadelphia Defendants under Models 2 and 3

Model 3	Model 2							
	Presumed Cash Bail		ROR, Low-Cash Conditions		Presumed ROR		Total	
	Number	Percentage	Number	Percentage	Number	Percentage	Number	Percentage
Presumed cash bail	2,259	100.0	84	15.9	0	.0	2,343	48.8
ROR, low-cash-bail conditions	0	.0	445	84.1	61	3.0	506	10.5
Presumed ROR	0	.0	0	.0	1,951	97.0	1,951	40.6
Total	2,259	100.0	529	100.0	2,012	100.0	4,800	99.9

NOTE.—Gamma = 1.0; χ^2 = 8,078.3, df = 4; $p \le .01$. Percentages do not always total 100 due to rounding.

tion of court policy and a thoughtful revision of decision practices. Although the findings have identified issues to be addressed in subsequent guidelines research, they also suggest that voluntary guidelines can be implemented and used and that they can produce change. They may provide a means by which the Philadelphia Municipal Court can manage and review its bail policies in the future and improve the quality of decision making.

Perhaps the evidence from Philadelphia will prevent overly hasty rejection of the potential of the guidelines strategy. The critical literature does, however, make an important point: the various technical tasks must be performed well, or the overall product will be suspect. Thus the performance of a host of research tasks, ranging from sample design and data collection and measurement to modeling the decisions under study, will determine the ultimate worth of the guidelines that result.

Even granting this observation as obvious, the critical literature runs the risk of condemning the guidelines approach too readily on the basis of narrow technical concerns. The technical points may or may not be important depending on the individual case and the overall picture.

Other concerns related to the likely impact of alternative models of guidelines are seldom discussed. For example, in classifying defendants or offenders in guidelines, the choice of a cutting point may be as critical as are other modeling questions (Gottfredson and Gottfredson 1986). A cutting point is simply the "score" or level of a measure that is chosen by the researcher to define the boundaries of a class, for example, the scores used to designate the "presumptive ROR" grouping under the descriptive models discussed above. Cutting-point selection may be important not only in translating the character of the original descriptive model into a guidelines format but also in defining how individuals with given attributes will be treated compared with others.

Although technical questions in any research enterprise are important, this focus in the debate about the ultimate value of guidelines misses what may be much larger questions about the methods relating to their implementation. To a great extent, the mixed results in evaluation of guidelines systems may be explained by varying degrees of attention to implementation issues.

Innovations may fail because researchers fail to work through practical, operational matters that may be crucial to decision makers who are considering how useful a particular innovation might be to them. The reasons for this may range from the relative inexperience of the researchers in dealing with implementation questions and the unrealistic expectations placed on research projects to attend to implementation issues when limited resources may barely provide the time or funding to accomplish basic research tasks to the resistance in the criminal justice agency to any innovation.

It may be axiomatic that the degree of resistance among decision makers toward an innovation varies directly with the lack of concern shown by the innovators to questions of implementation. If implementation questions are ignored and resistance is great (as is usual when decision makers are not consulted on impending reforms affecting them directly), then some may argue that nonvoluntary methods are the only recourse for bringing about change. However, criminal justice officials are skilled both at ignoring voluntary innovations and at circumventing nonvoluntary reforms imposed from the outside. Evaluations of nonvoluntary guidelines systems will thus certainly show the slippage that critics associate with the self-help guidelines approaches, if they have not already.

Because the original self-help, voluntary approach to guidelines emphasized implementation—the collaborative working relations between researchers and agency officials, the definition of the "problems" by the decision makers themselves, the examination of policy questions through problem solving and debate, and the use of research to provide feedback for policy analysis—it is difficult to accept the pessimism of critics who reject guidelines when such issues have not been addressed seriously. Of course guidelines that have never been implemented well or at all will not produce changes in decision patterns. As additional applications of guidelines are undertaken in the United States, therefore, a firm exploration of implementation questions that looks at both failures and successes should take priority.

REFERENCES

American Bar Association. 1978. *Standards Relating to the Administration of Criminal Justice: Pretrial Release.* 2d ed., tentative draft. Washington, D.C.: American Bar Association.

Blumstein, Alfred, Jacqueline Cohen, Susan Martin, and Michael Tonry, eds. 1983. *Research on Sentencing: The Search for Reform.* Vols. 1–2. Washington, D.C.: National Academy Press.

Carrow, Deborah M. 1984. "Judicial Sentencing Guidelines: Hazards of the Middle Ground." *Judicature* 68:161–71.

Carrow, Deborah M., Judith Feins, Beverly N. W. Lee, and Lois Olinger. 1985. *Guidelines without Force: An Evaluation of the Multijurisdiction Sentencing Guidelines Field Test.* Cambridge, Mass.: Abt Associates.

Cohen, Jacqueline. 1983. "Incapacitation as a Strategy for Crime Control: Possibilities and Pitfalls." In *Crime and Justice: An Annual Review of Research*, vol. 5, edited by Michael Tonry and Norval Morris. Chicago: University of Chicago Press.

Fisher, Franklin M., and Joseph B. Kadane. 1983. "Empirically Based Sentencing Guidelines and Ethical Considerations." In *Research on Sentencing: The Search for Reform*, vol. 2, edited by Alfred Blumstein, Jacqueline Cohen, Susan Martin, and Michael Tonry. Washington, D.C.: National Academy Press.

Foote, Caleb. 1954. "Compelling Appearance in Court: Administration of Bail in Philadelphia." *University of Pennsylvania Law Review* 102:1031–79.

———. 1965. "The Coming Crisis in Bail, Pt. 1." *University of Pennsylvania Law Review* 113:959–99.

Freed, Daniel, and Patricia Wald. 1964. "Bail in the United States: 1964." Working paper. Washington, D.C.: U.S. Department of Justice, National Conference on Bail and Criminal Justice, May.

Galegher, Jolene, and John S. Carroll. 1983. "Voluntary Sentencing Guidelines: Prescription for Justice or Patent Medicine?" *Law and Human Behavior* 7:361–400.

Goldkamp, John S. 1979. *Two Classes of Accused.* Cambridge, Mass.: Ballinger.

———. 1983. "Questioning the Practice of Pretrial Detention: Some Empirical Evidence from Philadelphia." *Journal of Criminal Law and Criminology* 74:1556–88.

———. 1985. "Danger and Detention: A Second Generation of Bail Reform." *Journal of Criminal Law and Criminology* 76:1–74.

Goldkamp, John S., and Michael R. Gottfredson. 1984. *Judicial Guidelines for Bail: The Philadelphia Experiment.* Washington, D.C.: National Institute of Justice.

———. 1985. *Policy Guidelines for Bail: An Experiment in Court Reform.* Philadelphia: Temple University Press.

Goldkamp, John S., Michael R. Gottfredson, and Susan Mitchell-Herzfeld. 1981. *Bail Decision Making: A Study of Policy Guidelines.* Washington, D.C.: National Institute of Corrections.

Gottfredson, Don M., Leslie T. Wilkins, and Peter B. Hoffman. 1978. *Guidelines for Parole and Sentencing.* Lexington, Mass.: Heath.

Gottfredson, Michael R., and Don M. Gottfredson. 1980. *Decision Making in Criminal Justice.* Cambridge, Mass.: Ballinger.

———. 1984. "Guidelines for Incarceration Decisions: A Partisan Review." *University of Illinois Law Review* 2:291–317.

Gottfredson, Stephen, and Don M. Gottfredson. 1979. *Screening for Risk: A Comparison of Methods.* Washington, D.C.: National Institute of Corrections.

———. 1986. "Accuracy of Prediction Models." In *Criminal Careers and "Career*

Criminals," edited by Alfred Blumstein, Jacqueline Cohen, Jeffrey Roth, and Christy Visher. Washington, D.C.: National Academy Press.

Knapp, Kay A. 1984*a*. *The Impact of the Minnesota Sentencing Guidelines—Three Year Evaluation.* St. Paul: Minnesota Sentencing Guidelines Commission.

———. 1984*b*. "What Sentencing Reform in Minnesota Has and Has Not Accomplished." *Judicature* 68:181–89.

Kress, Jack M. 1980. *Prescription for Justice: The Theory and Practice of Sentencing Guidelines.* Cambridge, Mass.: Ballinger.

Landes, William. 1974. "Legality and Reality: Some Evidence on Criminal Proceedings." *Journal of Legal Studies* 3:287–337.

Morris, Norval, and Marc Miller. 1985. "Predictions of Dangerousness." In *Crime and Justice: An Annual Review of Research,* vol. 6, edited by Michael Tonry and Norval Morris. Chicago: University of Chicago Press.

Petersilia, Joan, and Susan Turner. In this volume. "Guideline-based Justice: Prediction and Racial Minorities."

Rich, William L., Paul Sutton, Todd R. Clear, and Michael J. Saks. 1982. *Sentencing by Mathematics: An Evaluation of the Early Attempts to Develop and Implement Sentencing Guidelines.* Williamsburg, Va.: National Center for State Courts.

Roth, Jeffrey, and Paul Wice. 1978. "Pretrial Release and Misconduct in the District of Columbia." PROMIS Research Project Publication 16. Washington, D.C.: Institute for Law and Social Research.

Sparks, Richard. 1983. "The Construction of Sentencing Guidelines: A Methodological Critique." In *Research on Sentencing: The Search for Reform,* vol. 2, edited by Alfred Blumstein, Jacqueline Cohen, Susan Martin, and Michael Tonry. Washington, D.C.: National Academy Press.

von Hirsch, Andrew. 1982. "Constructing Guidelines for Sentencing: The Critical Choices for the Minnesota Sentencing Guidelines Commission." *Hamline Law Review* 5:164–215.

von Hirsch, Andrew, and Don M. Gottfredson. 1984. "Selective Incapacitation: Some Queries about Research Design." *New York University Review of Law and Social Change* 33:11–52.

Wilkins, Leslie T. 1981. *The Principles of Guidelines for Sentencing: Methodological and Philosophical Issues in Their Development.* Washington, D.C.: National Institute of Justice.

Wilkins, Leslie, Jack Kress, Don Gottfredson, Joseph Calpin, and Arthur Gelman. 1976. *Sentencing Guidelines: Structuring Judicial Discretion.* Albany, N.Y.: Criminal Justice Research Center.

Joan Petersilia and Susan Turner

Guideline-based Justice: Prediction and Racial Minorities

ABSTRACT

Although blacks compose only 12 percent of the national population, they account for almost 50 percent of the prison population. Many states have adopted the use of guidelines for sentencing, parole, and decisions concerning the level of probationer supervision. Some argue that use of certain factors in guidelines systematically adversely affects minority offenders. The extent to which commonly used guideline factors are correlated with race and recidivism was established using data on over 16,500 offenders convicted of felonies in California in 1980. Race and recidivism correlations were calculated for all convicted felons, for probationers, and for prisoners. When all factors in the data base were used, accuracy in predicting rearrests was seldom greater than a 20 percent improvement over chance. The use only of factors that were not racially correlated increased predictive accuracy from 3 to 9 percent above chance; including racially correlated factors increased predictive accuracy another 5–12 percent. When status factors related to race are excluded, the guidelines identify high-risk criminals about as well as they do now, but racially correlated factors that reflect seriousness of crimes cannot be omitted unless society is willing to treat serious offenders less severely because many of them are black.

Recent data from the U.S. Bureau of Justice Statistics indicate that, on any given day, more than 5 percent of all black males in their twenties

Joan Petersilia and Susan Turner are researchers in the criminal justice program at the Rand Corporation, Santa Monica, California. The authors would like to express their sincere appreciation to Allen Breed and Raymond Brown, the former and current directors of the National Institute of Corrections, for giving them the opportunity to conduct this research.

in the United States are in state prison. Over a lifetime, about 15 percent of all black males in this country can be expected to serve some time in an adult prison. By comparison, fewer than 0.5 percent of white males in their twenties are in prison on any one day, and only 2–3 percent of the white males will be imprisoned during their lifetime (Bureau of Justice Statistics 1985). This disparity has focused renewed attention on the issue of racial discrimination in the criminal justice system. Some contend that these numbers are further evidence that the system overtly discriminates against minority offenders, treating them more harshly than it does mature, white, middle-class offenders.

Critics of the system argue that sentencing reform can mitigate this apparent discrimination by limiting the customary discretion exercised by the courts and parole boards. Immune from review, judges and parole boards have had broad discretion in deciding who goes to prison and for how long. This discretion, the argument goes, has ultimately resulted in substantial race and class disparities. The establishment of well-articulated sentencing procedures, therefore, should result in more equitable treatment of all offenders, the elimination of racial discrimination in sentencing, and a better racial balance in prison populations.

A national commission on sentencing noted, "American sentencing laws and practices underwent more extensive changes in the 1975–1980 period than in any other 5-year period in American history" (Blumstein et al. 1983, p. 126). These changes have taken many forms. By 1985, at least fifteen states had enacted determinate sentencing statutes, ten states had abolished their parole boards, and thirty-five states had mandatory minimum-sentence laws. Of particular importance for the present study, many states and jurisdictions had established formal guidelines for sentencing decisions (e.g., prison vs. probation, length of sentence), for determining supervision levels for parolees and probationers, and for parole release. These guidelines are generally embodied in formal classification instruments that combine certain weighted criteria to achieve an overall offender-offense score, which is then linked to a specific, narrow range of sentences or dispositions. These scores are expected to help judges and other criminal justice practitioners make more consistent and uniform decisions and to guarantee equal treatment for all offenders, regardless of race.

However, many criminal justice researchers and practitioners doubt that sentencing reform alone can overcome racial disparities in sentencing, community supervision, and time served. The radical improvements in data collection and statistical analysis made possible by computer technology have enabled analysts to test more rigorously for racial effects at these and other decision points in the system. It has been shown that such factors as seriousness of crimes and prior criminal records explain much of the difference between black and white imprisonment rates. Indeed, several recent studies have observed that racial disparities in punishment result less from discrimination than from the disproportion of blacks committing more serious crimes. In a recently completed review of fifty-seven racial discrimination studies, Gary Kleck (1985, p. 285) concluded: "For the vast majority of offenses, jurisdictions, and judges, race exerted no statistically significant effect on adult criminal sentencing when legally relevant variables were controlled for, either for capital or noncapital crimes."

These results do not constitute an argument against guideline-based sentencing reform. However, they do implicitly challenge some of the basic assumptions behind the demand for such reforms, and they call for a reassessment of what this particular type of sentencing reform can, and should, be expected to accomplish.

To begin with, the rationale for sentencing reform begs an important question: Is the racial disparity in our prisons evidence of racial discrimination or of racial differences in crime and criminality? The distinction is important and is often missed in policy discussions. Racial *discrimination* occurs if system officials make ad hoc decisions based on race rather than on clearly defined objective standards. Thus strongly enforced guidelines could preclude purely discriminatory decisions. However, racial *disparity* occurs when such standards are applied but have different results for different racial groups. And sentencing reform may not be able to overcome this disparity.

The rationale for sentencing reform also begs another question: Does racial parity take precedence over other objectives of sentencing, probation, and parole decisions? As crime has worsened and public concern has risen, "just deserts" and "incapacitation" have become the major sentencing objectives. The courts are concerned with making the punishment fit the crime (and the criminal) and with protecting the public by incarcerating offenders who are most likely to reoffend when they return to the community. Given these objectives, sentencing and parole decisions have traditionally been based on criteria that not only weigh the relative deserts of an offender but also reflect the risk he poses to the community when released. Research has identified numerous criminal and noncriminal factors that correlate strongly with recidivism.

In developing guidelines, most jurisdictions have attempted to ensure fair and objective sentencing by including only factors that correlate with crime seriousness and recidivism. Therein lies the dilemma for reform: If, as research suggests, many of these factors also correlate strongly with race, using them is the functional equivalent of using race as a criterion. As one observer notes, "If we base sentencing decisions on various factors that correlate highly with race, it will have the same effect as using race itself as an indicator. That would undoubtedly be ethically inappropriate" (Coffee 1975, p. 1363). However, will eliminating racially correlated factors jeopardize the primary objectives of sentencing? Can the officials who are responsible for sentencing effectively weigh just deserts and predict recidivism without using such factors?

This dilemma forms the basis of the "equity versus accuracy" debate over sentencing reform. One theme in the debate has been the role played by so-called status factors—noncriminal factors such as education, employment, alcohol abuse, and so forth—in the decisions. Many of these factors apparently correlate with recidivism, and many of them also correlate highly with race. For example, long-term unemployment is generally thought to help predict recidivism, and it also happens to be higher in the black population. Thus when employment is considered in sentencing decisions, blacks are more likely than whites to be identified as high risks for release and are more likely to be given jail or prison sentences.[1]

Because status factors often do not reflect personal culpability, reformers have argued that these factors should not be considered, regardless of their correlation with recidivism. The appropriate alternative would seem to be to use factors that do represent personal culpability—that is, the seriousness of an offender's conviction crime(s) and his prior record—and that also identify offenders who present a high risk of returning to crime when they are released to the streets. Many states are making this shift. For example, Maryland has removed unemployment from its statewide sentencing guidelines in 1981, and education no longer appears in the Federal Parole Guidelines (Hoffman, Stone-Meierhoefer, and Beck 1978). Another viewpoint is that if any factor helps to assess an offender's threat to public safety, it should be used, regardless of racial correlation.

---

[1] For most factors, the distinction between criminal and status factors is clear; however, drug use is an exception. Drug use is under the control of the individual, easy to measure, and illegal. It is also highly correlated with recidivism and is routinely used in criminal justice decision making. On the other hand, drug use in itself is not dangerous criminal conduct. And some may argue that drug use is beyond the individual's control (Moore et al. 1984).

This equity versus accuracy debate accepts two assumptions that we believe should also be examined: first, that the system cannot eliminate racially correlated factors from sentencing and parole decisions without seriously jeopardizing the objectives of just deserts and public safety; and second, that factors found to correlate with recidivism predict recidivism accurately and that ignoring them would degrade the sentencing guidelines' predictive accuracy and their ability to achieve the sentencing objective of incapacitation.

This study examines (1) the factors that are actually included in sentencing, probation supervision, and parole guidelines across the country; (2) the degree of correlation between the commonly used factors and both race and recidivism for different subsets of the offender population; (3) the accuracy with which recidivism can be predicted using only factors that are not racially correlated; and (4) whether sentencing reform can overcome racial disparities without jeopardizing other objectives of the innovation.

In Section I we present a brief history of sentencing, probation, and parole guidelines; describe their form; and identify the criteria most often used in sentencing, community supervision, and parole decisions. In Section II we identify the criteria that correlate with race and demonstrate how removing them from the statistical models affects the prediction of recidivism. Finally, the conclusions and implications of the study are discussed in Section III.

I. The Development and Nature of Formal Guidelines

The appropriate use of discretion is one of the most troublesome issues for sentencing reform. Unguided discretion can produce arbitrary, unconsidered decisions that fail to achieve sentencing objectives and cause inequitable treatment of offenders. Yet, rigid and mechanical rules can also have unjust and inequitable results. Attempting to steer a reasonable middle course, many states have adopted empirically based guidelines or classification instruments. These guidelines are designed to curb discretion and ensure rational, consistent, and equitable decisions without preventing consideration of individual case factors. They generally specify the criteria to be used in sentencing, probation, or parole decisions and link them to a specific range of penalties.[2]

---

[2] For a detailed discussion of parole guidelines, see Gottfredson, Wilkins, and Hoffman (1978); sentencing guidelines are described in Kress (1980), Knapp (1982), and Rich et al. (1982); and Clear and O'Leary (1982) provide an overview of probation supervision guidelines.

In the past, many of these guidelines were simply "aids" to decision making. However, they are now being used in a more prescriptive fashion. Because they impose criteria and make criminal justice decisions more visible, their effects are being evaluated and are prompting changes in the rules regarding decisions. Consequently, it is important to look carefully at the potential effects of the various guidelines on the treatment of racial minorities.[3]

The use of classification instruments for sentencing, bail, and probation supervision has become widespread only since the 1970s, but parole classification has a long history. Parole guidelines were first developed by the U.S. Parole Commission. Such guidelines are now used in fourteen states, the District of Columbia, and the federal system. The U.S. Parole Commission's decision matrix, after which most of the other parole guidelines are modeled, is reproduced in Glaser (in this volume).

The matrix approach represented an important advance over earlier experience tables. First, a multidimensional parole classification scheme could take into account a variety of policy dimensions. Second, it allowed parole authorities to tailor their guidelines to their particular offender populations. The guidelines also could be tailored to the correctional population; that is, when prisons became full, the scores that would qualify an inmate for parole could be adjusted.

As the use of classification devices spread among parole boards, it became clear that the matrix approach was applicable not only to parole classification but also to decision making at a variety of other points in the criminal justice process. The matrix was versatile enough to incorporate the dimensions and variables associated with the particular decision to which it was applied.

The guidelines approach was next applied to sentencing, and many jurisdictions have developed sentencing guidelines at the state or at local levels. Most jurisdictions do not legally require judges to stay within the range specified by the guidelines; some leeway is usually allowed for cases in which special circumstances should be considered. However, some jurisdictions limit the range of deviation from the guidelines, and most require that judges state and justify (in writing) their reasons for departing from the guidelines.

---

[3] Although many bail and pretrial-release guidelines are in operation nationally, they are not examined here because we do not have a data base built on a population sufficient to test racial bias in the variables. However, the analysis of sentencing and parole guidelines is in many respects applicable to both bail and pretrial release, as well.

Four states—Minnesota, Pennsylvania, Utah, and Washington—have established statewide sentencing guidelines with specific recommendations on both the prison/probation decision and the length of prison terms. Six other states—Maryland, Massachusetts, Rhode Island, Vermont, Wisconsin, and New Jersey—have sentencing guidelines that currently apply to certain jurisdictions or to a limited range of offenses.

Classification instruments began to influence probation field services in the mid-1970s, when several probation departments became interested in trying to use "base expectancies" to assign probationers to different levels of supervision based on their "risk" of recidivism.

Probation departments' initial incentives to adopt formal classification procedures differed from those of other agencies. The probation departments were in serious need of an appropriate and systematic way to allocate their limited staff resources (Baird 1981). However, probation is primarily rehabilitation oriented, and probation officers were immediately uncomfortable making workload decisions based on recidivism predictors. They saw some of the more "hopeful" cases (i.e., first offenders) being singled out for "minimal" supervision, while the more hardened career criminals would be subjected to more intensive supervision. To develop a more balanced approach, they incorporated a "needs assessment" instrument in their classification process. Most probation classification instruments now use a combination of recidivism-prediction and needs-assessment scores to assign levels of community supervision.

Although probation agencies were late in jumping onto the "classification bandwagon," an explosion of classification systems is now occurring in probation. As Clear and Gallagher recently observed, "Ten years ago, a minority of probation agencies had formal classification systems; today the vast majority has some form of paper-driven offender classification" (Clear and Gallagher 1985, p. 424).

There can be little doubt that classification instruments are profoundly influencing criminal justice decision making, and their growth will almost certainly continue. Therefore, policymakers must begin to examine the impact of the use of such instruments on minority offenders. To address this issue in an informed light, we examined instruments now in use to identify and test the items they contain for their correlation with race.

Table 1 shows the criteria that were most commonly used in sentencing, probation supervision, and parole guidelines at the time of our

TABLE 1
Factors Included in Formal Guidelines or Classification Instruments

Factor	Sentencing	Community Supervision	Parole Release
Criminal record:			
No. of parole/probation revocations	‡	*	*
No. of adult and juvenile arrests		†	‡
Age at first arrest			
Nature of arrest crimes			
No. of adult and juvenile convictions	*	†	*
Age at first conviction		*	‡
Nature of prior convictions	†	‡	†
Repeat of conviction types	‡		‡
No. of previous felony sentences			†
No. of previous probation sentences		†	
No. of juvenile incarcerations			†
No. of jail terms served			†
No. of prison terms served			*
No. of incarcerations served	†		*
Age at first incarceration			†
Length of current term			‡
Total years incarcerated			‡
Commitment free period evidenced	‡	†	†
On probation/parole at arrest	†	†	†
Nature of current crime:			
Multiple conviction crimes	†		
Involves violence	*		*
Is property crime			‡
Weapon involved	‡		‡
Victim injured	*		†
Victim/offender forcible contact			‡
Social factors:			
Current age			†
Educational level		‡	‡
Employment history		†	‡
Mental health status		‡	
Family relationships		‡	
Living arrangements		‡	‡
Drug use		*	†
Juvenile use/abuse		†	
Alcohol use/abuse		†	‡
Companions		‡	
Address changes last year	†		
Attitude	†		
Financial status	‡		
Prison behavior:			
Infractions			†
Program participation			‡
Release plan formulated			‡
Escape history			‡

* 75 percent or more of those instruments identified used this factor.
† 50–74 percent of those instruments identified used this factor.
‡ 25–49 percent of those instruments identified used this factor.

study.[4] We must emphasize that new classification instruments are rapidly being developed and old ones are being modified, making it difficult to characterize them definitively. We have categorized the factors according to criminal record, nature of current crime, social factors, and prison behavior. The table also indicates how widely each criterion is used.

The information in table 1 was derived from a number of sources. Copies of sentencing and parole guidelines used by states were recently compiled by the National Council on Crime and Delinquency (NCCD). The NCCD information for 1983 was tallied in the Bureau of Justice Statistics (1983) bulletin, "Setting Prison Terms," and all the materials sent by the individual states were forwarded to Rand by the NCCD. Rand summarized this information, identifying the items that constituted each instrument. We updated the information in 1985 by contacting each state that had forwarded information to the NCCD, as well as states that we were told had implemented a formal classification instrument since 1983. Probation supervision guidelines were examined in a similar manner. Our original list of agencies that had implemented formal guidelines came from the American Justice Institute's project on "Classification Instruments for Criminal Justice Decisions." The American Justice Institute (1979) publication *Probation/Parole Level of Supervision Sourcebook* lists the twenty-three probation/parole agencies in the country that used instruments in 1979. We contacted these agencies, updated their department information, and asked them for information on other jurisdictions implementing such systems.

It is clear from table 1 that, as an offender moves through the system, the number of criteria used for decisions increases. Further, there are some interesting patterns across the guideline types. Only two of the criteria are used in more than 50 percent of the guidelines of all three types: number of adult and juvenile convictions and whether the offender was on parole or probation at the time of arrest. However,

---

[4] Sentencing guidelines reviewed included those from Rhode Island, Utah, Vermont, Washington, Wisconsin, Maryland, Massachusetts, Florida, Ohio, Arizona, Minnesota, West Virginia, California, Colorado, Pennsylvania, North Carolina, and New Mexico. Parole guidelines reviewed included those from the U.S. Parole Commission, Alabama, Alaska, Arkansas, Delaware, Idaho, Kansas, Kentucky, New York, Oklahoma, Oregon, Washington, Iowa, California Youth Authority (CYA), Georgia, Maryland, Michigan, Missouri, Pennsylvania, Utah, Florida, New York, Minnesota, Virginia, Wisconsin, Wyoming, District of Columbia, and Texas. Probation supervision guidelines include those from California, Illinois, Pennsylvania, Wisconsin, Connecticut, Georgia, Washington, D.C., Missouri, New York, Oregon, and Washington.

victim injury, violence, and the number of prior incarcerations figure
strongly in both sentencing and parole guidelines.

From the perspective of racial disparities, it is particularly significant
that none of the identified sentencing guidelines use social status criteria, although such items are used often in parole and community supervision guidelines. This suggests that concern about the influence that
social, or noncriminal, factors have on sentencing (at least as evidenced
in formal sentencing guidelines) may be overstated, while the effect of
such factors on parole and probation decisions may merit closer attention. It also seems to reflect the different emphasis at each decision
point: the primary objective of sentencing remains just deserts, while
probation and parole emphasize crime prevention through prediction of
recidivism.

II. Guideline Criteria and Racial Effects

Because the sentencing guidelines do not appear to rely heavily on
social status factors, one might conclude that they are less likely than
parole or probation guidelines to incorporate racial bias. If this were
correct, it might provide a rationale for eliminating such factors from all
guidelines. However, when we analyzed the frequently used guideline
criteria for correlations with race and recidivism, we found that the
issue was not so simple. Several of the prior record items (e.g., age at
first arrest) were significantly correlated with race and recidivism. If, as
is true in our California sample, black offenders are convicted of more
serious crimes and have more prior convictions, use of the guidelines
could well increase racial disproportionality in sentencing.

A. Establishing Correlations with Race and Recidivism

We have limited the analyses in this essay to the effects of guideline
criteria on blacks because the black/white differences have the greatest
relevance for the greatest number of states.[5]

To establish the extent to which variables correlated with both race
and recidivism, we needed data on a large sample of felons, both prisoners and probationers, who were convicted in the same year to determine whether the criteria that weighed most heavily in each guideline
correlated with race *for the particular offender population the guideline is
designed to affect*. This eliminates the possibility of bias in the sample

---

[5] Although the results are not presented here, we conducted the same types of analyses for Hispanics as well.

caused by characteristics that may differ between, say, probationers and imprisoned offenders. We know, for instance, that probationers and prisoners, on the whole, have different characteristics: probationers generally have committed less serious crimes and have fewer prior criminal convictions. Therefore, it is important to assess whether each guideline criterion is racially correlated for its intended population.

1. *Data and Methods*. We used data originally provided by the California Board of Prison Terms (CBPT), which collected detailed information on every person sentenced to state prison in California in 1980 and the same information for a sample of adult males who were sentenced to probation after conviction for certain (imprisonable) felonies. From this information, we selected for our data base information on approximately 16,500 males convicted in Superior Court in seventeen California counties of robbery, assault, burglary, larceny/theft, forgery, or drug possession/sale. These seventeen counties are among the most heavily populated in California and account for nearly 80 percent of the felony convictions in the state. Approximately 65 percent of the 16,500 offenders received probation; the remaining 35 percent received prison sentences. Approximately 40 percent were white, 32 percent were black, and 28 percent were Hispanic. The analyses reported here exclude Hispanics. These data were analyzed in an earlier study to investigate whether certain characteristics distinguish those who receive probation from those who receive prison sentences for the same crime (see Petersilia et al. [1985] for a description of these findings and the characteristics of the data base). Our statistical analyses indicated a significant correlation between receiving a prison sentence and having two or more current conviction counts, having two or more prior convictions, being on parole or probation when arrested, being a drug addict, being armed, using a weapon, and seriously injuring the victim.

The data base contains extensive information for each offender, in the following categories: (1) criminal history information and social status characteristics such as demographics, drug and alcohol use, and employment history; (2) important aspects of the case (e.g., number of conviction counts, weapon used, victim injured, accomplices, whether the victim was known by or related to the offender); (3) details describing the court's handling of the case (e.g., type of attorney, whether the offender obtained pretrial release, whether the case was settled by plea or trial); and (4) final outcome (type and length of sentence imposed).

We were unable to collect recidivism information for offenders in each of the seventeen counties due to budget constraints. We were limited to recidivism data for Los Angeles and Alameda counties. Hence our recidivism analysis relies on a subset of 511 sentenced probationers and 511 released prisoners. These offenders were tracked for an average of thirty-one months to determine their subsequent recidivism, defined here as any arrest during the follow-up period. A detailed description of the follow-up prisoner and probationer samples is given in Petersilia and Turner (1986). Briefly, the sample contained probationers and prisoners from Los Angeles and Alameda Counties who were comparable in terms of county of conviction, conviction offense, and factors shown to be associated with the decision to imprison (i.e., factors listed above). Approximately 45 percent of the follow-up sample was black, 28 percent was white, and 27 percent was Hispanic. Thus our complete data base includes very detailed offender and offense information for a seventeen-county statewide sample, and recidivism information on a two-county sample of persons convicted of serious crimes in California in 1980.[6]

To establish racial correlation, we used the seventeen-county data base to test the criteria used in *sentencing* guidelines on *all convicted offenders*, those used in *probation* guidelines on *probationers*, and those used in *parole* guidelines on *prisoners*.[7]

We looked at the degree to which specific items were related to race in two ways. First, we compared the means and proportions for the different races for probationers alone, for probationers combined with prisoners (i.e., all convicted felons), and for prisoners. The complete results of these tabulations for blacks and whites are presented in Appendix A. The following racial differences were the most pronounced for all three populations: (1) more blacks than whites have a juvenile

---

[6] The maximum follow-up period for a probationer extended from the time he was granted probation in 1980 until May 1, 1983 (when the data were sent to Rand). However, since 80 percent of the probationers spent some time in jail, we subtracted one-half of their imposed jail sentence (an estimate of jail time served) from the follow-up period. The resulting mean and median follow-up time for probationers was thirty-one months. The prisoners in our sample also had been sentenced in 1980. In August 1984, we received rap-sheet information for prisoners who had been released from their 1980 prison term for at least two years. The mean and median follow-up period for the prisoners was thirty-eight months. In order to have similar follow-up periods for both groups, we considered only arrests that occurred before January 15, 1984, thus creating an average follow-up period of thirty-one months for both probationers and prisoners.

[7] Some of the items identified in table 1 were not present in our data base, so we could not empirically test their racial correlation. For example, we could not test particular crime type of prior convictions or in-prison behavior.

conviction before age sixteen; (2) more blacks than whites have served time in a juvenile institution; (3) among probationers and all convicted felons, more blacks than whites are on probation or parole at the time of the current arrest; (4) whites tend to have a higher incidence of alcoholism and a slightly higher incidence of drug addiction than blacks; and (5) whites were more likely than blacks to have previously known their victims.

Second, to provide a more comprehensive picture of racial correlation with guideline variables, we then correlated each of the guideline variables with "being black" for each of the three offender populations. The race correlation coefficients are shown in columns 1, 3, and 5 of table 2.

We were particularly interested in identifying items that correlate with race but do not correlate strongly with recidivism. These items would be "suspect" since they would result in harsher treatment of minorities, without necessarily identifying offenders with a higher probability of rearrest. These items are underlined in table 2.

2. *Results.*   Although many of the correlations we found between items and race reach statistical significance, they are nevertheless small. The largest ones have a correlation coefficient of not more than 0.23, which explains less than 6 percent of the total variation between race and recidivism. Second, although some status factors are shown to be correlated with race, they are not among those most widely used (see table 1). The few "racially tainted" social status factors are outnumbered by criteria based on seriousness of the crime and prior record. Moreover, with the exception of employment, the other social status criteria that are racially correlated work to the disadvantage of white offenders. Among probationers, 8 percent of the whites were alcoholics, while only 3 percent of the blacks were; 4 percent of the whites were drug abusers, compared with only 2 percent of the blacks.

Third, while none of the formal sentencing guidelines we identified used social status factors, they still result in racial disparity for the population involved. Many of the criteria based on seriousness of the crime and prior record correlate with race for all convicted offenders. These findings are consistent with the results of our "means-and-proportions" analyses (see App. A). For example, 52 percent of the black offenders convicted of felonies in 1980 were on probation or parole when arrested, versus 41 percent of the white offenders; 20 percent of the black offenders had injured their victims, versus 12 percent of the whites; 28 percent of the black offenders' crimes involved

TABLE 2
Racial Correlations and Recidivism Predictions

Variables	Probationers		All Convicted Felons		Prisoners	
	Correlation with Black (1)	Correlation with Rearrest (2)	Correlation with Black (3)	Correlation with Rearrest (4)	Correlation with Black (5)	Correlation with Rearrest (6)
Prior criminal record:						
No. of juvenile convictions	.15	.23	.15	.20	.14	.16
No. of adult convictions	.11	.16	.07	.16	−.03	.16
Conviction before age 16?	.15	.16	.15	.16	.12	.14
No. of probation terms	.11	.16	.08	.13	.02*	.15
No. of juvenile incarcerations	.15	.15	.14	.16	.11	.15
No. of jail terms	.14	.16	.11	.16	.04	.18
No. of prison terms	.08	.13	.02	.16	−.06	.13
Incarceration before age 16?	.09	.11	.10	.12	.07	.12
No. of probation revocations	.07	.12	.04	.10	−.02*	.08*
On adult probation/parole?	.08	.20	.06	.18	−.04	.13
On juvenile probation/parole?	.10	.00*	.10	.06*	.10	.09
Out of incarceration 1 year or less?	.12	.23	.10	.22	.02*	.19

164

Current crime characteristics:					
No. of conviction counts	−.04	.02*	.02*	.00*	−.02*	−.03*
Violent offense?	.05	−.05*	.10	−.06	.10	−.07*
Property offense?	−.01*	.15	−.07	.16	−.10	.17
Weapon involved?	.05	−.06*	.07	−.08	.03	−.11
Injury involved?	.07	−.05*	.10	−.07	.12	−.11
Any accomplices?	.01*	.04*	.02	.01*	.03	−.01*
Know or related to victim?	−.08	−.11	−.09	−.07	−.09	−.01*
Drugs involved in offense?	−.05	−.10	−.05	−.10	−.04	−.09
Any victims vulnerable?	.05	−.02*	.06	−.02*	.06	−.03*
Status factors:					
High school graduate?	.01*	−.03*	.00*	−.07	−.02*	−.10
Employed?	−.04	−.11	−.03	−.10	.00*	−.08*
Married?	.02*	−.06*	.00*	−.10	−.05	−.12
Lives with spouse/children?	.01*	−.14	.00*	−.09	−.05	−.04*
Mental problems?	−.01*	.00*	−.02*	−.03*	−.03	−.07*
Drug addict?	−.04	.00*	−.05	.07	−.11	.13
Alcoholic?	−.09	−.05*	−.11	−.05*	−.13	−.03*
Age (older)	.01*	−.12	−.01*	−.09	−.09	−.05*

NOTE.—The racial correlations are based on a seventeen-county sample. Blacks were given a value of one, whites were given a value of zero, and the correlation between a race dummy and each variable was computed. The correlations with rearrest are based on a two-county recidivism sample. Any arrest was given a value of one, no arrest was given a value of zero, and the correlation between an arrest dummy and each variable was computed. Underlined entries (1) are correlated with race in such a way that they would negatively affect minorities and (2) do not correlate strongly with recidivism. These items would be "suspect" since they would result in harsher treatment of minorities without necessarily identifying offenders with a higher probability of arrest.

* Variable not correlated significantly with black/rearrest at least $p < .05$.

weapons, versus 22 percent of the white offenders' crimes. Thus some of the most widely used factors are in fact racially correlated, but they also relate to criminal behavior and not social status and are therefore regarded as "legitimate."

Fourth, we had expected to find fewer racially correlated criteria for prisoners than for probationers or all convicted felons. We reasoned that prison sentences implied that the offenders, regardless of race, would have lengthy prior records and serious conviction crimes. However, this was not the case. Of the racially correlated characteristics for prisoners, six were status-related factors, and, of those six, "drug addict," "mental problems," and "alcoholic" affected white prisoners adversely. The other racially correlated criteria were all based on criminal factors, and most of them were also racially correlated for all convicted offenders and probationers: prior juvenile convictions, current crime being violent, victim injured, weapon involved, having vulnerable victims, and being "on juvenile probation/parole at arrest."

These findings suggest that the concern over racial correlation and the use of social status factors in sentencing may be exaggerated. For probationers, only five of the fifteen most frequently used criteria reflect status factors. Of those, three are racially correlated, but only one (employment history) affects blacks adversely. For prisoners, only six of the thirty-two most frequently used criteria reflect status. In short, the most frequently used and racially correlated status criteria are drug abuse, alcohol abuse, and employment, and employment affects blacks adversely only when used in guidelines for community supervision and sentencing decisions, not for parole release. Consequently, dropping status factors from guidelines would do very little to reduce racial disparities in sentencing, probation supervision, and parole decisions. It might, in fact, increase them by removing criteria that make a greater number of white offenders look like bad risks.

Unfortunately, the racial correlation of other frequently used criteria appears to create a much more complex problem for sentencing reform. As table 2 shows, many of these racially correlated factors are also associated with recidivism—not only in this particular sample, but in other research as well.[8] Placing offenders with these criminal factors on

---

[8] Nearly all of our prior-record measures were correlated with being black: blacks possessed more serious and lengthy criminal histories. Prior record has consistently been shown to be the best predictor of future criminality.

probation under light supervision or on parole involves a high risk of recidivism. Nevertheless, these factors are racially correlated, and their expanded use may actually increase racial disparities in sentencing, probation supervision, and prison time served.[9]

B. Predicting Recidivism: Equity versus Predictive Accuracy

If, as the literature assumes, *factors strongly correlated with recidivism are strong predictors* of recidivism, the system faces a real dilemma. Can strong predictors of recidivism be omitted from guidelines—regardless of their racial "taint"—if the ultimate objective is "crime control" or identifying offenders with a high risk of recidivism? We addressed both the assumption and the dilemma by attempting to predict recidivism, using all the available factors, and examining how much predictive accuracy we would lose if we used only those factors that *do not correlate significantly with race* in our recidivism predictions.

1. *Methods.* We approached the analysis in two ways. First, we ordered all variables appearing in table 2 in terms of the absolute value of the race correlation coefficient (cols. 1, 3, and 5). "Tainted" variables are defined as those significantly correlated with race (at $p < .05$). We then "stepped in" each variable (using stepwise logistic regression), starting with the least racially correlated, and examined how much of the variance in subsequent rearrests we could explain. This allowed us to see if any particular variable added substantially to our ability to predict rearrest. We also compared the amount of variance explained

---

[9] Our analyses utilized the bivariate correlations between (1) items and race and (2) items and recidivism. We felt that this was the most direct way to examine how various items may affect blacks in sentencing, parole, and community supervision decisions. Our discussions assume that the shared variance between the items and race is predictive of recidivism. We see in table 2 that the number of juvenile convictions is correlated .15 with race and .23 with recidivism. From the numbers, we conclude that using the number of juvenile convictions for probation supervision decisions will adversely affect black offenders because they have, on the average, more juvenile convictions than white offenders. We also investigated a multivariate approach to assess the degree of shared predictive variance between the items and race. All twenty-nine items identified in table 2 are used to predict rearrest. A second model uses the same items plus "black" to predict rearrest. The extent to which the coefficients for individual items change from the first to the second model measures the shared predictive variance of the item and race. We compared these two models for our three samples. For all three groups, item coefficients changed from the first to the second model; however, the changes were relatively small. Standardized differences between coefficients (measured as the difference between the coefficients, divided by a pooled standard error) rarely exceeded .3. This analysis suggests that the items and race do share predictive variance—although it is relatively small, as we would expect based on the bivariate correlations seen in table 2.

by using only the nonracially correlated items with that obtained using all the variables.[10] These results are presented in Appendix B.[11] Overall, the adjusted R^2 for each of the three offender populations remains low even when all the available variables are considered. For the "all convicted felons" sample, the "untainted" factors account for about 1 percent of the variance; the addition of all the "tainted" factors raises the adjusted R^2 to 0.08. We see similar results when probationers and prisoners are considered separately. No individual factor in any case increases the adjusted R^2 by more than 3 percent. Knowing the offender is black does not increase the adjusted R^2 for probationers or all convicted felons. It does, however, increase the adjusted R^2 for prisoners by 2 percent.

This approach provides us with a measure of overall predictive ability but does not give us a clear picture of how accurately rearrest can be predicted using the "untainted" versus "tainted" factors.

Our second analysis directly assesses prediction accuracy. Our base rate for comparison is the accuracy percentage that would have resulted on the basis of "chance" (e.g., what would be predicted in the absence of any information).[12] We first considered the ability to accurately predict who would be arrested using only the few untainted variables for each population (those identified as not significantly correlated with black in table 2).

We measured the accuracy of our statistical predictions by adding the percentage of those actually arrested for whom we predicted an arrest and the percentage of those who did not get arrested for whom we predicted no new arrest. After determining our accuracy using the untainted items, we then included the tainted items (those significantly correlated with race), divided into five major groups: (1) crime characteristics, (2) prior-record characteristics, (3) other factors (e.g., drug and alcohol use), (4) demographics, and (5) race. We assessed the accu-

[10] For this analysis, we used the recidivism sample of all convicted felons, probationers, and prisoners. Each regression analysis was performed for each of the three offender populations.

[11] We used the LOGIST program written by Frank Harrell (1983), *SAS Supplemental User's Guide*, for these analyses. The values shown are analogous to the adjusted R^2 values in an ordinary least squares regression.

[12] The "by chance" percentages range from 53 to 60 percent. Chance is 50 percent only if the overall probability of the event occurring is actually 50 percent. The "percent accurate by chance" rate of arrests is calculated as (percent arrested × percent arrested) + (percent not arrested × percent not arrested).

racy of our predictions by successively adding the factors from each of the five groups.[13]

Crime characteristics include the number of conviction counts, whether the crime was a property offense, whether the crime was a violent offense (robbery or assault), whether the victim was known by or related to the offender, whether accomplices were involved, whether drugs were involved, whether any victims were vulnerable (e.g., elderly or handicapped), whether there was any injury involved, and whether a weapon was involved.

Prior-record factors include the number of prior prison terms, the number of probation revocations, whether the offender was on adult probation at the time of his 1980 arrest, whether the offender was on juvenile probation or parole at the time of his 1980 arrest, the number of prior adult convictions, the number of prior probation terms, the number of jail terms, whether the offender was incarcerated prior to age sixteen, whether the offender had been released from incarceration less than twelve months prior to his 1980 arrest, the number of prior juvenile convictions, and the number of prior juvenile incarcerations.

The "other factors" group included whether the offender had mental problems (measured by a summary variable), whether the offender was employed at the time of his 1980 arrest, whether the offender was a drug addict, and whether the offender was an alcoholic.

Demographics include whether the offender is married, whether he has a high school education, whether he lives with his spouse and/or children, and his age. Race is defined as whether the offender is black.

These groups are ordered in terms of the "sensitivity" of the factors. For example, if crime characteristics increase the accuracy of predicting subsequent recidivism, we may want to include them even if they were correlated with race because of the concept of just deserts. The inclusion of demographic factors correlated with race, however, would be more problematical, even if they help us predict rearrest.

2. *Results.*   Figure 1 presents the results of this analysis. These results challenge the assumption that a statistical model based on factors *associated with recidivism* will necessarily accurately *predict recidivism*. Using all the factors in our data base, many of which correlate signifi-

---

[13] Because only six or seven of the factors are untainted, for each offender group we measured their accuracy as a group rather than dividing them into crime characteristics, prior record characteristics, other factors, and demographics.

cantly with recidivism, our accuracy in *predicting* recidivism was seldom greater than 70 percent—about 20 percent greater than chance.

While these results are disappointing, they are not surprising. A growing body of research indicates that even sophisticated statistical methods and very detailed information have not significantly improved researchers' ability to predict future criminal behavior (see Moore et al. 1984). The best prediction instruments still produce three or four "false positives" (offenders predicted to recidivate who subsequently do not) for every "true positive," or correct prediction. As a result, many researchers have concluded that further research along these lines does not seem worthwhile to press.

The key issue for this study is, then, considering the inaccuracy of even the best predictions of recidivism today, how much would be lost by omitting the racially correlated factors from sentencing, probation, and parole supervision guidelines? The issue is not whether prediction guidelines could (or should) be used but the extent to which the state would be sacrificing predictive efficiency to promote racial equity if racially correlated factors were omitted.

Figure 1 shows that using only "untainted" items results in a predictive accuracy of rearrests for all convicted offenders of about 60 percent (3 percent above chance); for probationers, 61 percent (8 percent above chance); and for prisoners, 69 percent (9 percent above chance). The improvement in accuracy (above the level of chance) is statistically significant at $p < .05$.[14]

Such high accuracy rates may at first seem impressive. We must, however, consider what these accuracy rates really reflect. Sixty-three percent of the probationers were arrested during the follow-up period. If we knew nothing about the characteristics of the probationers, we could still make predictions about success. We could say that all of the probationers would be rearrested. In this case, our predictive accuracy would be 63 percent. Or we could say that no probationer would be arrested. In this case, we would be accurate only 37 percent of the time (the percentage who were actually arrest-free during the follow-up). A third approach would be to compare our accuracy with that predicted by chance. The percentage correctly classified by chance depends on the percentage of offenders who are actually arrested. If 50 percent of

---

[14] Chi squares from logistic regression models were chi square(6) = 17.84 for prisoners, chi square(7) = 22.23 for probationers, and chi square(6) = 17.76 for prisoners and probationers combined.

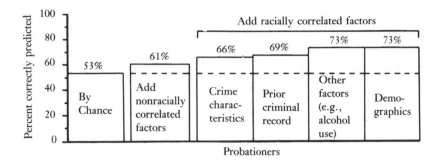

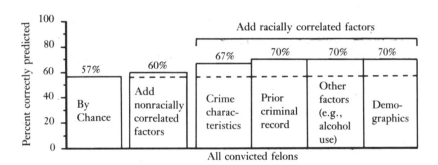

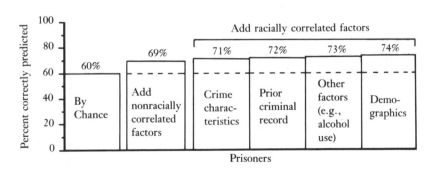

FIG. 1.—Ability to accurately predict rearrests. The area above the dashed line indicates the percentage correctly predicted above chance. The "demographics" category excludes race. Race does not increase the recidivism prediction for probationers. It does increase accuracy by at most 1 percent for all convicted felons and prisoners. In the sample, 63.1 percent of the probationers were actually rearrested, 68.2 percent of all convicted felons were rearrested, and 72.8 percent of prisoners were rearrested.

offenders are arrested, we would expect to be correct "by chance" 50 percent of the time. If 75 percent of the offenders are arrested, we would expect to be correct (.75 × .75 + .25 × .25) or 63 percent of the time. In our case, 63 percent of the offenders are arrested. We would expect, by chance, that 53 percent would be classified correctly. A 73 percent accuracy rate may sound impressive at first; however, it is only 20 percent better than chance for the probationers.

Accuracy continues to increase as additional sets of racially tainted factors are included. Adding tainted factors relating to crime character-istics, prior record, other factors, and demographics increases predic-tive accuracy to at most 74 percent. For probationers, tainted factors increase accuracy 12 percent over untainted factors alone; for all con-victed felons, these factors increase accuracy 10 percent; and for prison-ers, accuracy is increased less than 5 percent. For all three populations, the difference in accuracy when the tainted factors are added is statisti-cally significant.[15] In short, using only the untainted factors increased our predictive accuracy 3–9 percent above chance; including the tainted factors as well increased our predictive accuracy another 5–12 percent.

There are two ways of considering these figures. It could be argued that guidelines would improve equity by eliminating racial correlates, without greatly degrading the prediction of recidivism. Or it could be argued that, considering the possible consequences for public safety, it is vital to use whatever will improve prediction to any degree. Interpre-tation will depend heavily on how one views the objectives of sentenc-ing, probation, and parole and on expectations for reform efforts.

III. Conclusions and Implications

The criminal justice system is increasingly adopting decision-making guidelines as a means to make sentencing and parole decisions fair and consistent for all offenders. The inclusion of social status factors (such as education, employment, and alcohol abuse) in guidelines has been criticized because such factors more obviously introduce race and class distortions into the decisions. Further, they often have little to do with an offender's personal culpability or criminal seriousness.

However, our findings reveal that the concern over racially cor-

---

[15] Chi-squares differences for the logistic regression models containing untainted fac-tors alone and the models containing tainted and untainted factors were chi square(23) = 53.68 for prisoners, chi square(22) = 77.25 for probationers, and chi square(23) = 128.87 for all convicted felons.

related status factors may be exaggerated. Most sentencing guidelines now exclude them and rely on criteria associated with crime seriousness. This emphasis implies that sentencing and sentencing guidelines are more concerned with just deserts than with probable recidivism and are primarily based on the assumption that the most seriously criminal offenders should be incapacitated. In contrast, probation and parole guidelines often include noncriminal status factors, suggesting that these guidelines are more concerned with predicting an offender's likely behavior in the community than with just deserts. Although some of the commonly used status factors are racially correlated, some of them, in fact, work to the disadvantage of white offenders (e.g., white offenders in California are more likely than blacks to be alcoholics and drug abusers).

These findings do not mean that sentencing guidelines can be expected to result in less racial disparity, however. Although they are primarily based on factors related to conviction crime(s) and prior criminal record—factors that correlate significantly with recidivism—many of these factors are also correlated with race. If, as is true in our sample, black offenders are convicted of more serious crimes and have more prior convictions, use of the guidelines could well increase racial disproportion in sentencing. This may explain Minnesota's experience: after statewide sentencing guidelines were established, the minority population in prison increased significantly (Knapp 1984).

Our statistical analyses also bring into question the assumptions that factors *correlated* with recidivism can accurately *predict* recidivism and that omitting those that also correlate with race would seriously degrade predictive accuracy. Using all the factors available, we could not predict rearrests with much more than 70 percent accuracy—less than a 20 percent improvement over what would be predicted by chance. Omitting the factors that also correlated with race decreased accuracy by five to twelve percentage points. Deleting only the racially correlated, noncriminal status factors reduced accuracy by about 1 percent.

These findings suggest that, depending on the objectives of the guidelines, policymakers should no longer consider the problem of equity versus accuracy as an either-or dilemma. If ensuring public safety by predicting recidivism is the objective, guidelines could omit some racially correlated criteria without greatly reducing predictive accuracy. However, if just deserts is the objective, predicting recidivism is basically beside the point. The factors associated with serious criminality may indeed also correlate with recidivism, but the courts and the public are not concerned with that correlation when they judge that an offender is a serious criminal who should be given a severe sentence.

The debate over equity versus accuracy ignores a basic truth that must be acknowledged if progress is to be made in sentencing reform: *The guidelines may overcome discrimination, but they cannot be expected to overcome racial disparities in sentencing where serious criminality is disproportionately high in the black population.* Guidelines can omit status factors related to race and still identify high-risk criminals with nearly the degree of accuracy they now achieve, but they cannot omit racially correlated criteria that reflect crime seriousness unless society is willing to have all serious offenders treated less severely because many of them are black.[16]

Further, we believe that the issue of degrading predictive accuracy by omitting factors is, after a point, moot. There may be a natural ceiling on accuracy in criminological prediction. Using the most comprehensive data and advanced statistical techniques, research has not been able to predict recidivism with more than 70 percent accuracy. Given that criminal behavior is strongly influenced by opportunism, contextual factors, and offenders' emotional and psychological makeup, it may be that research along these lines is not worthwhile to press. Moreover, unless models can be developed that achieve complete accuracy, there will always be legal and ethical bars to using prediction for such purposes as selective incapacitation.

This does not mean that the courts should abandon incapacitation as an objective. The factors that identify serious criminality (e.g., juvenile record) also correlate with recidivism, so using them to establish just deserts also achieves the objective of incapacitation. This effect makes the debate over what factors can be included under a just deserts model versus an incapacitation model academic: regardless of which sentencing philosophy is being served, the factors used often overlap.

Although our analyses qualify some basic assumptions in the debate over sentencing reform, the issues remain highly complex and highly

---

[16] Some believe that the recording of factors relating to serious criminality may itself reflect racial discrimination. For example, it could be that, even though blacks and whites engaged in similar crimes, blacks have a higher probability of arrest. However, comparisons of self-reported crime commission rates with offenders' arrest records showed no racial differences in the probability of being arrested for *serious* crimes (Petersilia 1983). Hindelang (1978), comparing victimizations with arrests, found similar results.

charged, politically, ethically, and legally. Each state and jurisdiction will have to approach these issues in its own context, considering its own priorities and purposes, especially in light of its particular objectives for each kind of guideline.

Racial *discrimination* is clearly unacceptable. But whether the system chooses to tolerate racial *disparities* that result from imposing uniform, "legitimate" sentencing criteria is a local policy matter. We recommend that researchers and policymakers in each state discuss openly the objectives of their guidelines and establish the correlation of commonly used factors with both recidivism and race for their criminal populations. We believe this effort would be worthwhile because it would allow policymakers to assess how the guidelines they develop will affect sentencing objectives, public safety, and the racial composition of prisons. Further, it will cause the people responsible for these important decisions to address the equity issue in an informed light.

Appendix A

TABLE A1

Offender Characteristics in Seventeen-County California Sample: Means and Proportions

Variables	Probationers		All Convicted Felons		Prisoners	
	Black (N = 2,743)*	White (N = 4,113)*	Black (N = 4,862)*	White (N = 6,126)*	Black (N = 2,665)	White (N = 2,441)
No. of juvenile convictions	1.1	.6	1.2	.7	1.3	.8
No. of adult convictions	2.8	2.1	3.5	3.0	4.4	4.6
% with conviction before age 16	21.8	10.9	24.7	13.3	28.4	18.2
No. of probation terms	1.6	1.2	2.0	1.6	2.4	2.3
No. of juvenile incarcerations	.3	.1	.4	.2	.6	.4
No. of jail terms	1.5	.9	1.9	1.4	2.4	2.1
No. of prison terms	.3	.2	.4	.4	.6	.8
% with incarceration before age 16	5.3	2.0	8.2	3.7	11.8	7.5
No. of probation revocations	.2	.1	.2	.2	.2	.3
% on adult probation/parole	36.4	28.4	43.6	37.9	53.0	56.9
% on juvenile probation/parole	6.8	2.8	8.4	3.6	10.5	5.3
% out of incarceration 1 year or less	26.1	16.4	33.7	24.8	43.7	41.3
No. of conviction counts	1.1	1.1	1.4	1.3	1.8	1.8
% convicted of violent offense	16.7	12.8	29.4	20.6	46.3	36.9

% convicted of property offense	74.4	75.6	63.5	70.3	49.4	59.2
% with weapon involved in offense	17.5	14.0	28.4	22.4	43.1	40.1
% with injury involved	13.6	9.4	19.8	12.2	28.3	18.5
% with accomplices	45.9	45.3	48.3	46.0	51.1	47.8
% knowing or related to victim	15.3	21.7	13.5	20.2	11.4	17.3
% with drugs involved in offense	10.6	13.7	9.2	12.4	7.4	9.7
% with vulnerable victims	5.8	3.8	8.2	5.0	11.3	7.8
% high school graduates	47.2	46.4	48.2	48.4	49.6	52.0
% employed	36.6	40.6	35.1	38.2	33.4	33.4
% married	28.2	26.1	28.2	28.1	27.8	31.9
% living with spouse/children	17.9	17.0	18.6	19.0	19.0	22.7
% with mental problems	3.3	3.7	2.7	3.4	2.0	2.9
% drug addicts	2.2	3.8	5.2	7.7	9.0	16.0
% alcoholics	3.1	7.6	2.6	7.5	2.1	7.5
Mean age (years)	26.1	26.0	26.6	26.9	27.3	28.7

NOTE.—The white category includes whites, Indians, Chinese, Japanese, and other Asians. Offenders with unknown race were deleted from all table calculations. These seventeen counties account for approximately 80 percent of the state's felony convictions.

* Weighted sample sizes. (See Petersilia et al. [1985] for discussion of weighting scheme.) Because the seventeen-county data base contained only a sample of 1980 probationers but all prisoners, we weighted the "probationer" sample and the "all convicted felons" sample to reflect the true population proportion of prisoners and probationers. For analyses dealing with the seventeen-county "prisoners" only, we did not weight because we had a census of the prisoners.

177

TABLE B1

Ability to Predict Recidivism: Regression Results

Probationers		All Convicted Felons		Prisoners	
Variables	Cumulative Adjusted R^2	Variables	Cumulative Adjusted R^2	Variables	Cumulative Adjusted R^2
Any accomplices?	.00	Married?	.00	Employed?	.00
High school graduate?	.00	High school graduate?	.01	No. of probation revocations	.00
Age	.00	Lives with spouse/children?	.01	No. of probation terms	.00
Mental problems?	.00	Age	.01	No. of conviction counts	.01
Lives with spouse/children?	.01	No. of conviction counts	.01	High school graduate?	.01
Property offense?	.03	Mental problems?	.01	Out of incarceration 1 year or less	.02
Married?	.03	Any accomplices?	.01	Mental problems?	.03
Employed?	.03	No. of prison terms	.04	Weapon involved?	.04
No. of conviction counts	.02	Employed?	.04	Any accomplices?	.03
Drug addict?	.02	No. of probation revocations	.05	No. of adult convictions	.03
Drugs involved in offense?	.02	Drugs involved in offense?	.05	On adult probation/parole?	.02
Any victims vulnerable?	.01	Drug addict?	.05	Drugs involved in offense?	.02

178

Item	Value	Item	Value	Item	Value
Weapon involved?	.01	On adult probation/parole?	.06	Number of jail terms	.02
Violent offense?	.01	Any victims vulnerable?	.06	Married?	.03
Injury involved?	.00	No. of adult convictions	.07	Lives with spouse/children?	.02
No. of probation revocations	.03	Weapon involved?	.07	Number of prison terms	.02
No. of prison terms	.03	Property offense?	.07	Any victims vulnerable?	.03
Know or related to victim?	.05	No. of probation terms	.07	Incarceration before age 16?	.03
On adult probation/parole?	.07	Know or related to victim?	.07	Know or related to victim?	.03
Incarceration before age 16?	.06	Incarceration before age 16?	.07	Age	.03
Alcoholic?	.06	Out of incarceration 1 year or less	.07	Violent offense?	.03
On juvenile probation/parole?	.06	On juvenile probation/parole?	.07	On juvenile probation/parole?	.03
No. of probation terms	.06	Violent offense?	.07	Property offense?	.03
No. of adult convictions	.05	Injury involved?	.07	No. of juvenile incarcerations	.04
Out of incarceration 1 year or less	.05	Alcoholic?	.07	Drug addict?	.04
No. of jail terms	.05	No. of jail terms	.07	Injury involved?	.04
No. of juvenile incarcerations	.05	No. of juvenile incarcerations	.07	Conviction before age 16?	.04
No. of juvenile convictions	.07	Conviction before age 16?	.07	Alcoholic?	.03
Conviction before age 16?	.06	No. of juvenile convictions	.08	No. of juvenile convictions	.03
Black?	.06	Black?	.08	Black?	.05

NOTE.—The italicized items are racially correlated for their respective populations. The dependent variable in the logistic regression models was "any arrest" in the average thirty-one-month follow-up period. The recidivism models used the black and white offenders in the Los Angeles and Alameda County samples ($N = 738$).

REFERENCES

American Justice Institute. 1979. *Probation/Parole Level of Supervision Sourcebook.* Vol. 2. Washington, D.C.: National Institute of Corrections.

Baird, S. Christopher. 1981. "Probation and Parole Classification: The Wisconsin Model." *Corrections Today* 43:36–41.

Blumstein, Alfred W., Jacqueline Cohen, Susan Martin, and Michael Tonry, eds. 1983. *Research on Sentencing: The Search for Reform.* Washington, D.C.: National Academy Press.

Bureau of Justice Statistics. 1983. *Setting Prison Terms.* Washington, D.C.: U.S. Department of Justice.

———. 1985. *The Prevalence of Imprisonment.* Washington, D.C.: U.S. Department of Justice.

Clear, Todd R., and Kenneth W. Gallagher. 1985. "Probation and Parole Supervision: A Review of Current Classification Practices." *Crime and Delinquency* 31:423–43.

Clear, Todd R., and V. O'Leary. 1982. *Controlling the Offender in the Community.* Lexington, Mass.: Lexington.

Coffee, John C., Jr. 1975. "The Future of Sentencing Reform: Emerging Legal Issues in the Individualization of Justice." *Michigan Law Review* 73:1361–1462.

Glaser, Daniel. In this volume. "Classification for Risk."

Gottfredson, Don M., Leslie T. Wilkins, and Peter B. Hoffman. 1978. *Guidelines for Parole and Sentencing: A Policy Control Method.* Lexington, Mass.: Lexington.

Harrell, Frank. 1983. *SUGI Supplemental Library User's Guide.* Cary, N.C.: Statistical Analysis Systems Institute.

Hindelang, Michael. 1978. "Race and Involvement in Common Law Personal Crimes." *American Sociological Review* 43:93–109.

Hoffman, Peter, Barbara Stone-Meierhoefer, and James L. Beck. 1978. "Salient Factor Score and Releasee Behavior: Three Validation Samples." *Law and Human Behavior* 2:47–63.

Kleck, Gary. 1985. "Life Support for Ailing Hypotheses: Summarizing the Evidence on Racial Discrimination in Sentencing." *Law and Human Behavior* 9:271–85.

Knapp, Kay. 1982. "Impact of the Minnesota Sentencing Guidelines on Sentencing Practices." *Hamline Law Review* 5:237–56.

———. 1984. *Impact of the Minnesota Sentencing Guidelines: Three Year Evaluation.* St. Paul: Minnesota Sentencing Guidelines Commission.

Kress, Jack M. 1980. *Prescription for Justice: The Theory and Practice of Sentencing Guidelines.* Cambridge, Mass.: Ballinger.

Moore, Mark H., Susan Estrich, Daniel McGillis, and William Spelman. 1984. *Dangerous Offenders: The Elusive Target of Justice.* Cambridge, Mass.: Harvard University Press.

Petersilia, Joan. 1983. *Racial Disparities in the Criminal Justice System.* R-2947-NIC. Santa Monica, Calif.: Rand.

Petersilia, Joan, and Susan Turner. 1986. *Prison versus Probation: Implications for Crime and Offender Recidivism.* R-3323-NIJ. Santa Monica, Calif.: Rand.

Petersilia, Joan, Susan Turner, James Kahan, and Joyce Peterson. 1985. *Granting Felons Probation: Public Risks and Alternatives*. R-3186-NIJ. Santa Monica, Calif.: Rand.

Rich, William D., L. Paul Sutton, Todd D. Clear, and Michael J. Saks. 1982. *Sentencing by Mathematics: An Evaluation of the Early Attempts to Develop and Implement Sentencing Guidelines*. Williamsburg, Va.: National Center for State Courts.

Richard A. Berk

Causal Inference as a Prediction Problem

ABSTRACT

Impact assessments of criminal justice interventions depend on predictions of the "what-if" variety rather than on predictions of future events. They require "predictions" of what would have occurred if the experimental units that were exposed to the intervention had not been exposed. These predictions, when compared with the responses of treated units, form the basis for all evaluations of program impacts. The statistical concept of "strong ignorability" provides a framework for addressing the internal validity of all impact assessments. When use of strongly ignorable assignment mechanisms is not possible or practicable, strategies are available for achievement of assignments that are ignorable but not strongly ignorable. Strongly ignorable assignment mechanisms are clearly desirable; some might say mandatory.

Assessments of the impact of criminal justice programs are necessarily comparative. It is impossible to determine "what works" without at the same time specifying "compared to what?" Does incarceration deter repeat juvenile offenders? At the very least, that depends on the alternatives to which incarceration is compared. Does proactive police patrol discourage would-be burglars? That too depends on the alternatives with which proactive patrol is compared. Does selective incapacitation reduce property crime? Again, some kind of baseline is required. The point is that, even when no "control" condition is explicitly stated, an implicit comparison is made with what would have happened in the absence of the program.

Richard A. Berk is professor of sociology and statistics at the University of California, Santa Barbara. Sara Fenstermaker Berk and Phyllis J. Newton provided helpful comments on an earlier draft of this essay.

Within experimental traditions it is common to conceptualize such programs as "treatments," or "interventions." Then, drawing on Fisher (1951), Kempthorne (1952), and especially Rubin (1978), the causal effect of any intervention contrasts the outcome if a particular unit under study is exposed to the treatment with the outcome if the same unit under study is not exposed to the treatment. Two or more different treatments can also be contrasted. The units may be individuals, groups, organizations, or any other entity whose response to the intervention is of interest. But most important, the comparison involves the same unit under two or more conditions, which leads to serious practical problems: either it may be impossible to expose each unit to more than one condition or such multiple exposures may risk serious contamination across conditions. For example, how could a convicted murderer be exposed to both the death penalty and life imprisonment? Or how could a neighborhood be exposed to both police foot patrol and car patrol without the chance that the first treatment would affect responses to the second?

Rosenbaum and Rubin (1983) observe, therefore, that "inferences about the effects of treatments involve speculations about the effect that one treatment would have had on a unit which, in fact, received some other treatment" (p. 41). Another way of thinking about such speculations is that evaluations of program impact necessarily involve predictions. One is not predicting in the sense of forecasting some future event; thus, this essay is about a very different kind of prediction than are other essays in this volume. The prediction involves expectations about the likely result under two or more conditions; they are predictions of the what-if variety. A researcher might wonder, for instance, what would have happened had an executed murderer been imprisoned for life or what would have happened if a neighborhood under foot patrol had experienced car patrol instead. And as what-if predictions, they require inferences about comparisons that are virtually impossible to observe directly.

As a result, researchers interested in the impact of criminal justice programs must derive their conclusions from approximations of unobservable comparisons; all experimental and quasi-experimental designs can be viewed as efforts to make those approximations as accurate as possible.[1] In this essay I review some of the most popular methods by

---

[1] A true experiment conventionally requires that units being studied be assigned at random to experimental and control conditions. A quasi experiment requires that

which this is done, underscoring the what-if character of causal inferences.

Section I describes assignment mechanisms that are strongly ignorable. The internal validity of experimental designs and, hence, the statistical confidence placed on their outcomes requires that the condition of strong ignorability be satisfied. Section II discusses what can be done when assignment mechanisms are not ignorable, strongly or otherwise. One solution rests with the use of instrumental variable techniques. Section III reports on the kinds of research designs that make assignment mechanisms strongly ignorable. These include designs in which the researcher controls the process of assignment to both the experimental and the control conditions. When it is impossible to control every aspect of the assignment process, it is still possible, using quasi-experimental designs, to maintain strong internal validity. This is achieved with deterministic rules that are described in Section IV.

I. Strongly Ignorable Assignment Mechanisms

Since it is virtually impossible to contrast the results with a single unit under both experimental and control conditions, two kinds of comparisons are typically attempted. First, one can examine the response when the unit being studied is initially exposed to one of the conditions and then later to the other. Pretest/posttest quasi-experimental designs are an example; the pretest captures what happens in the absence of the treatment (i.e., "before"), and the posttest captures what happens in reaction to the treatment (i.e., "after").

To illustrate, a teenager's drug use might be measured before and after joining a "Just Say No" club. Such clubs, which make learning how to say "no" to illegal drug use the organizing theme, have recently received favorable publicity as social and recreational settings for teenagers. The prospects for an internally valid evaluation using a pretest/posttest design would be dramatically enhanced if nothing else affecting the outcome and related to the intervention changed between the pretest and the posttest (Cook and Campbell 1979, pp. 50–59).[2] In the case of a Just Say No club, this is unlikely. For example, the youth may have joined immediately after a brush with the law.

---

some units be assigned to the experimental condition and some to the control condition, but the assignment is not at random. In both cases the treatment is subject to manipulation.

[2] By "internally valid," one basically means that alternative explanations for an apparent treatment effect have been ruled out.

In addition, internally valid designs require that the treatment delivered to one unit "contaminates" no other unit (Cox 1958, pp. 19–21). For the pretest/posttest design, contamination can occur when, during the pretest period, subjects anticipate getting the treatment. Thus the teenager's drug use before joining a Just Say No club may be moderated by his expectation of joining.

For the second kind of comparison, the results can be examined when one unit is exposed to the treatment condition and another unit is exposed to the control condition. Internal validity is enormously enhanced for cross-sectional causal inferences when the two units are equivalent in all ways related to the intervention before the units are exposed to the treatment and the control conditions. To continue with the Just Say No illustration, comparing the drug use of a Just Say No member with that of nonmember teenagers in the same neighborhood risks comparing individuals who differ from one another in many ways besides club membership.

The logic just presented may be expanded and stated more formally. Internal validity requires that the process by which units are assigned to experimental and control conditions be "strongly ignorable." To be strongly ignorable an assignment system must satisfy three conditions. First, given some set of observable covariates, all variables related to both the response and the treatment assignment are included in that covariate set. Second, the treatment assigned to one unit in no way affects the response of any other unit. Third, for each possible configuration of levels of these covariates, there is a nonzero probability of units being assigned to both the experimental and the control conditions (Rosenbaum and Rubin 1983, p. 43).

The first criterion is central to what follows and is addressed in more depth shortly. The second criterion does not figure significantly in this discussion because, once it has been stated that contamination must be avoided, there is little to add. Finally, the third criterion is discussed below, where the distinction between "strong ignorability" and just plain "ignorability" is considered.[3]

It is also unreasonable to require that time 1–time 2 comparisons prohibit random (i.e., stochastic) fluctuations and, similarly, that the two distinct units not be allowed to vary randomly from one another.

---

[3] The term "ignorable," either by itself or when modified by "strongly," indicates that, once the X's are known, measured, and used to condition the treatment effect estimates, the assignment mechanism may be ignored. That is, the assignment mechanism does not have to be explicitly modeled.

For social phenomena at least, a deterministic world without chance forces is unrealistic. In the physical sciences it is often possible to minimize the impact of unsystematic "noise" by establishing near-comparable environments for the experimental and the control conditions. This is seldom possible in the social sciences without sacrifice of external validity, that is, without greatly weakening the inferences that can be drawn from what happened in the laboratory setting to what would happen in the real world.

As a result, comparisons in social science studies must rest on aggregate outcomes such as the mean, for which large samples virtually guarantee that random fluctuations on the average cancel out. What chance variation remains can be formally assessed through statistical inference (e.g., significance tests). Hence comparisons between the impact of experimental and control conditions are typically made between average outcomes.

The shift to aggregate responses allows one to state in statistical terms what strong ignorability produces. Internally valid designs permit causal inferences about the desired what-if comparison to be made in ways that on the average do not underestimate or overestimate the true treatment effect (i.e., a statistically unbiased estimate). As Rosenbaum and Rubin observe (1983, p. 42), this true effect is captured, therefore, by the difference in the expected (or mean) response to the experimental and control conditions (in the case of two conditions).

Under some circumstances, for example, those related to the kinds of statistical procedures used to estimate expected treatment effects, strong ignorability may also lead to estimates that on the average increasingly do not under- or overestimate the true treatment effect as the sample size gets large (i.e., an asymptotically unbiased estimate). In other words, while there is bias in small samples, the bias effectively disappears in large samples.

Figure 1 should help to make the concept of strong ignorability more concrete. The variable X is used to represent a number of covariates affecting the treatment assignment, T, and the response, R. For example, R might be the amount of illegal drug use, T might be whether teenagers join a Just Say No club, and X are all the things affecting both drug use and club membership (e.g., commitment to school, home life, prior arrests for drug use, and so on). Note that X includes all sources of systematic variation in treatment assignment; any remaining variation is a result of the stochastic disturbance term e_1 (assumed to represent chance, independent perturbations unrelated to X) and R. The letter R

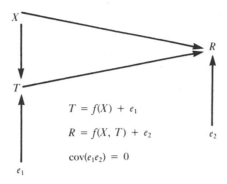

$$T = f(X) + e_1$$

$$R = f(X, T) + e_2$$

$$\text{cov}(e_1 e_2) = 0$$

FIG. 1.—An example of strong ignorability

is used to represent a consequence of X, T, and e_2, a second disturbance term assumed to represent chance, independent perturbations unrelated to X, T, or e_1.

Since X affects both T and R, any observed relation between T and R risks confounding the impact of X. Thus an apparent impact of club membership may really result from a more general motivation to stay out of trouble, which in turn fosters club membership and abstinence. However, because that confounding derives solely from X, and since X is in figure 1 observable, a researcher can in principle condition (or "partial") on X for the relation between T and R to extract an unbiased estimate of the true experimental effect.

Depending on the nature of a data set (especially R), a variety of statistical procedures may be used to condition on the X's. With a very large pool of units from which treatment and control groups may be drawn, it is often possible to match experimentals and controls on important confounding variables. In the Just Say No illustration, teenagers might be matched on such variables as age, sex, race, prior record, and school performance. Matching has the distinct advantage of requiring no assumptions about functional forms (see particularly Cochran 1983). It is not necessary to make any assumptions about the shape of the relations between X, T, and R (e.g., whether it is linear).

When a large pool of units is not available (which is typical in criminal justice evaluations), researchers may resort to one of several kinds of multivariate statistical procedures that adjust for preexisting differences between the experimental and the control groups. In contrast to matching, for which experimentals are paired with controls that are exactly the same on a set of covariates, statistical adjustments make the experimental and the comparison groups comparable on the average (i.e., the means of the X's are the same within chance fluctuations). If the assignment mechanism is strongly ignorable, unbiased estimates result with a much more efficient use of existing data. However, there is a price—functional forms must be assumed.

Perhaps the most popular form of multivariate adjustments is undertaken with the general linear model (i.e., analysis of variance, analysis of covariance, and multiple regression). Much of the time, however, the assumptions required by the general linear model are not compatible with the data, and alternative procedures are preferable. For example, if the response variable is binary (e.g., stopped using drugs or not), logit or probit procedures are most appropriate. If the response variable is bounded by some fixed number such as zero (e.g., the number of years in a prison term), Tobit techniques are often most useful. There are now at least two excellent texts in which such alternatives to the general linear model can be found (Maddala 1983; Amemiya 1985). To take another example, if the response variable is a count (e.g., the number of felony convictions), researchers may capitalize on statistical procedures based on the Poisson distribution (Cameron and Trivedi 1986). For example, Berk and Newton (1986) used Poisson regression techniques to evaluate the impacts of shelters for battered women, employing as a response variable the number of battery incidents during the posttest period. They found that shelters reduced the violence only for victims who had already begun taking steps toward greater independence from the offender. Women who fled to a shelter on an impulse were often subjected to retaliation when they returned home and were, therefore, worse off.

Unfortunately, the ability to condition on X properly, whether by matching or by statistical adjustments, will in practice depend on the degree to which there are experimental and control units for all configurations of X. For example, suppose that a functional form for the relation between X and R is not assumed and that, as a consequence, matching on X is employed. In other words, partialing is accomplished by looking at the responses to treatment and control conditions within configurations of X (e.g., male, 25 years of age, white, and so on). Clearly, if average treatment effects are to be calculated for a given configuration on X, there must be both experimental and control units having the same configuration on X. If either is missing, the expected response for the missing group must be imputed, and one is typically back to an assumed functional form for the relation between X and R.

That is, the researcher asserts that a particular functional form is appropriate and, using the data on hand, extrapolates or interpolates an imputed value for a missing expected response. For instance, if the functional form is linear, average responses are assumed to fall on a particular straight line, even average responses for unobserved units. Imputations are then easy to make.

If experimental and control units are observed for all configurations of X, a credible case for strong ignorability can be made (assuming one has all the X's). Unbiased or consistent estimates follow. If control or experimental units are missing for some configurations of X, claims of strong ignorability are sometimes dubious,[4] and internal validity depends on the plausibility of the functional form assumed for the relation between X and R. For example, if experimental and control units are available for most configurations of X, there is typically ample data to validate the assumed functional form. If most of the experimental units have some configurations and most of the control units have others, validation is very difficult.

To summarize, strong ignorability implies that, within chance fluctuations, there is an optimal approximation of the desired what-if predictive comparison. However, strong ignorability requires that all variables affecting T (treatment assignment) and R (response) be measured (prior to the application of the treatments) and that experimental and control units be available for each configuration of X (covariates affecting T and R). If the second condition is not met, one has an ignorable (but not strongly ignorable) assignment mechanism. Internal validity then depends on the credibility of the assumed functional form between X and R. If some of the variables in X are unknown or unmeasured, then the assignment process is not ignorable or strongly ignorable, and the usual conditioning (e.g., via multiple regression) will not produce valid inferences of the desired what-if predictive relation. This is perhaps the most common situation when criminal justice program evaluations are undertaken; the question is not whether the estimates of any treatment effect are unbiased (or even consistent) but, rather, what the nature of the biases is.

To illustrate, Bloom and Singer (1979) attempted to evaluate the impact of an innovative correctional facility for "defective delinquents." The comparison group included individuals who were diagnosed as

---

[4] The assignment mechanism may be strongly ignorable, but, through sampling variation, some of the cells may have no entries.

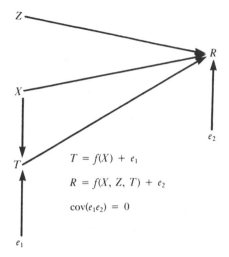

$$T = f(X) + e_1$$

$$R = f(X, Z, T) + e_2$$

$$\text{cov}(e_1 e_2) = 0$$

Fɪɢ. 2.—Inclusion of another set of variables, Z, in the strong-ignorability model

defective delinquents by the staff of the facility but who were not so defined by the courts and were therefore sent to a conventional prison. Although the response of rearrest was modeled in a sophisticated manner, the covariates used to condition the analysis included only age at release and the number of prior arrests for property crimes. Clearly, assignment to the special correctional facility was not strongly ignorable because there were a large number of neglected variables that could have affected the treatment assignment and the outcome. For example, there were no measures of performance in school, which could well affect both the incarceration decision and recidivism. Consequently, the finding that the special facility produced lower recidivism rates is not compelling.

Extending our formal discussion, consider the implications of another set of variables, Z, that affects R but not T. For example, in the Bloom and Singer study, race might affect R but not T; that is, there is no racial discrimination in the diagnosis. As figure 2 implies, Z can be safely ignored as long as the researcher is interested only in internal validity. In other words, the impact of Z is not confounded with the impact of T. More generally, it is not necessary to include all the causes of R; one does not have to model everything. However, if the researcher has measured Z, then Z can be included in any statistical analyses to improve the precision of treatment effect estimates. By including Z, estimates will be obtained that on the average are closer

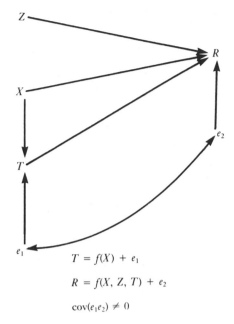

$$T = f(X) + e_1$$

$$R = f(X, Z, T) + e_2$$

$$\mathrm{cov}(e_1 e_2) \neq 0$$

Fig. 3.—Special case when assignment process is not strongly ignorable but inferences are internally valid.

to the true treatment effect. Greater statistical efficiency will be achieved.

II. What to Do If the Assignment Is Not Ignorable, Strongly or Otherwise

The requirement that X exhaust all possible sources of confounding is extremely demanding if the operation of the assignment process is not controlled by the researcher. In general, internal validity is seriously jeopardized. However, there is at least one special set of circumstances in which internally valid causal inferences can be credibly made when the assignment process is not strongly ignorable.

Consider figure 3. The two-headed arrow between the disturbance terms indicates that e_1 and e_2 are related. Since these disturbances are not observed covariates, and since they affect T and R, the assignment process cannot be strongly ignorable. However, as disturbance terms, the e's have certain convenient properties; in particular, they are unrelated to X. It is therefore possible to obtain statistically consistent (but biased) estimates of any treatment effects by using appropriate procedures. Basically, instrumental variable techniques that control for "selection bias" are employed (Heckman 1979; Barnow, Cain, and Goldberger 1980; Maddala 1983, pp. 257–67). Use of these techniques requires modeling the assignment process directly before trying to estimate any treatment effects. A separate equation representing the mechanism by which units have been assigned to treatments must be constructed; simply including X as a conditioning vector when treatment effects are estimated will not suffice. The results of the assignment equation are then used to construct an instrumental variable that is included in efforts to estimate the treatment impact. (For a thorough discussion of instrumental variable techniques, see Bowden and Turkington [1984].)

For example, Sherman and Berk (1984) report an evaluation of a program in Minneapolis to test the effectiveness of three police strategies in incidents of misdemeanor spousal violence: arresting the offender, ordering the offender off the premises for eight hours, and offering advice to the parties that could include mediation. While assignment to each of the treatments was designed to be random, allowance had to be made for situations in which the police had to make an arrest. For example, if the separation or advice treatments were assigned but the offender refused to cooperate, the police had to be permitted to make an arrest.

Sherman and Berk (1984) argue, in effect, that such processes could be represented by figure 3, with variables such as offender resistance among the covariate set X. They also argue for correlated disturbances, that is, chance perturbations uncorrelated with X but correlated with one another. Thus, if the offender was in a frame of mind that temporarily inclined him to assault a police officer, he may also have been more inclined to assault his wife at the next opportunity. Note that the correlated disturbances do not result from some new kind of X since the perturbations are not directly observable even in principle; all that is known are their implications (which may be observable). Using instrumental variable techniques, Sherman and Berk concluded that arrest was the most effective treatment for preventing new incidents of spousal violence.[5]

---

[5] Since the Minneapolis experiment relied on random assignment, and since for over 80 percent of the cases the randomization was properly implemented, the roles of the X and the correlated disturbances were small. The basic story was unchanged when the experiment was analyzed simply as a "proper" randomized experiment (i.e., without instrumental variable techniques).

III. Research Designs Making the Assignment
Strongly Ignorable

The likelihood of obtaining internally valid causal inferences of the what-if variety is often dramatically enhanced when the researcher can design and at least indirectly control the process by which units are assigned to experimental and control conditions. The researcher can produce a strongly ignorable assignment mechanism.

Consider figure 1 again. Suppose with no loss of generality that X is a single covariate and that within each of its levels cases are assigned to experimental or control conditions by the equivalent of a coin flip. Equal probabilities are not necessary, and the probabilities may vary across levels of X. The disturbance term has, therefore, a binomial distribution with a mean varying across levels of X while meeting all the assumptions listed earlier. That is, the disturbance term behaves much like a coin flip, with the probability of heads different for different values of X. For example, X might be whether an offender has a record of prior convictions for felonies, and for those with such records, individuals are randomly assigned 60/40 to experimental and control groups, respectively. Likewise, those without a prior record for felony convictions are randomly assigned 40/60 to experimental and control groups, respectively.[6]

Clearly, the assignment mechanism is strongly ignorable by construction (assuming no contamination across treatments), and an analysis that conditions on X will produce unbiased or consistent treatment effect estimates. In other words, it is necessary to control for X in the statistical analysis whether by matching or by statistical adjustments. Because the researcher controls the assignment process and measures the covariate X, all the necessary information about the assignment mechanism is known.

There is no need in practice to assign units within categories of X, although such "blocking" may be administratively convenient and may increase the precision of the estimated treatment effects. Indeed the classic "true experiment" based on random assignment does not require blocking. Note that in figure 4 there may well be a covariate vector X that affects R, but since X does not affect T (and therefore has the same status as Z), the assignment mechanism is strongly ignorable without taking X into account. In other words, it is possible to obtain unbiased

---

[6] Varying the assignment probabilities in this manner can often make the random assignment more palatable for policymakers by allowing the likelihood of receiving the treatment(s) to respond to "need."

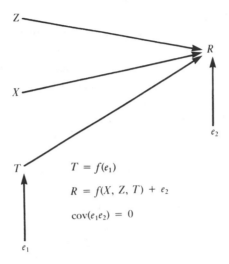

$$T = f(e_1)$$

$$R = f(X, Z, T) + e_2$$

$$\text{cov}(e_1 e_2) = 0$$

FIG. 4.—Example in which assignment mechanism is strongly ignorable without taking X into account.

or consistent estimates even if X is totally ignored. However, if any of the variables in X have been observed, they may be added to the statistical analysis to obtain more precise estimates of any treatment effects (just as in the case of Z).

To illustrate, Rossi, Berk, and Lenihan (1980) conducted an experiment with ex-offenders to determine the effect of eligibility for unemployment compensation on recidivism. Over 2,000 ex-offenders in Texas and Georgia were assigned at random to one of four experimental conditions or to one control condition on release from prison. These conditions varied by the number of weeks of eligibility and by the rate at which payments to ex-offenders would be reduced for each dollar earned in a legitimate job. The expectation was that the income would reduce the need for ex-offenders to resort to new income-producing crimes and, in addition, that the income would allow ex-offenders to look longer and more carefully for jobs with greater earning potential and security. The second expectation was confirmed but not the first.[7]

Translating the experiment into figure 4, T is the set of experimental

[7] Rossi, Berk, and Lenihan (1980) also report the results of a structural equation analysis in which the beneficial effects of the payments were undermined by the tendency of the payments to reduce labor force participation, and reduced labor force participation, in turn, increased recidivism. The positive and the negative effects of the payments effectively canceled each other out.

and control conditions. The X's are all the variables affecting recidivism that in the absence of random assignment would probably affect unemployment benefits eligibility: education, past work experience, family stability, and others. The Z's are variables affecting the outcome but not the eligibility, even in the absence of randomization (perhaps race, sex, and age). Response variables such as recidivism, labor market participation, and wages are represented by R. The basic message is that, because of randomization, the X's, which would ordinarily be related to eligibility, are uncorrelated with it on the average.

There are many other examples of randomized experiments in the evaluation of criminal justice programs (e.g., Kassebaum, Ward, and Wilner 1971; Lenihan 1977; Waldo and Chiricos 1977), and there is more generally a widespread consensus that random assignment is the best way by which to insure internal validity (e.g., Cook and Campbell 1979; Rossi and Freeman 1982; Farrington 1983). But sometimes random assignment is not feasible, and it is therefore reasonable to consider quasi-experimental alternatives that nevertheless have a substantial likelihood of strong internal validity.

IV. A Research Design That Produces Ignorable
(but Not Strongly Ignorable) Assignment

Perhaps the strongest quasi-experimental design producing ignorable (but not strongly ignorable) assignment is based on a deterministic rule by which units are assigned to treatments. Consider figure 5. A new term, A, has been added between X and T, while T's disturbances have been eliminated. The A is some assignment rule based on X. Typically, a cutoff point is defined on X, and units above (or below) that cutoff point are assigned to the treatment group and units below (or above) to the control group.[8] For example, prisoners above a certain level on measures of school achievement, X, might be assigned to a high school diploma equivalency program, while those below that level might be assigned to a program in remedial reading.

If units are really assigned on the basis of A (and only on the basis of A), treatment assignment is ignorable but not strongly ignorable; for each value of X, units have a probability either of 1.0 or of 0.0 of assignment to the experimental or the control group. Nevertheless, the confounded impact of X with the impact of T is fully mediated through A, so that, if X is used as a condition variable, internally valid infer-

---

[8] The design may be used when there are several treatment and control conditions.

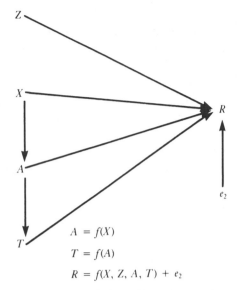

$$A = f(X)$$
$$T = f(A)$$
$$R = f(X, Z, A, T) + e_2$$

FIG. 5.—Ignorable (but not strongly ignorable) assignment in a quasi-experimental design.

ences about the impact of T may in principle be obtained. The role of Z may be completely ignored even if Z affects X, unless additional statistical precision is needed. Then Z may be added to the analysis (e.g., as variables in a regression equation).

Note that neither the covariate X nor the assignment rule have to make any substantive sense. One could, for instance, assign prisoners to a job-training program on the basis of their height or the number of letters they have received from home. Alternatively, X and A could be selected for substantive or practical reasons; it might well make sense to assign prisoners to a job-training program in auto mechanics on the basis of measures of mechanical aptitude. To produce ignorable assignment, however, the deterministic assignment rule must be fully followed.

Assignment through a deterministic rule leads to what is called a regression-discontinuity design, which may often be a viable alternative to randomized designs. There are, however, two important vulnerabilities. First, the requirement that X be included in any analyses of treatment effects reduces the precision of estimates compared with the efficiency produced by random assignment. This follows because X and T will be moderately correlated (since X affects T). Second, for reasons that need not trouble us greatly here (see, e.g., Trochim 1984), it is vital that the functional form of the relation between X and R be properly modeled.[9] If the incorrect functional form is used, internal validity is seriously compromised, and determining the proper functional form is often difficult.

To my knowledge, the only application of a true regression-discontinuity design in a criminal justice program evaluation is reported by Rauma and Berk (Berk and Rauma 1983; Rauma and Berk 1983). Their X was the number of hours worked in prison on a legitimate job. Individuals who worked more than 1,500 hours were eligible for unemployment benefits on their release from prison; those working less than 1,500 hours were not eligible. The cutoff point and assignment rule constituted their A. Using a dummy variable for membership in the treatment or the control group as the treatment indicator and the number of hours worked in prison as the sole conditioning variable, Rauma and Berk found that eligibility for the payments reduced recidivism over the first postprison year from roughly 30 percent to 20 percent.

Note that Rauma and Berk had to condition only on the hours worked (look again at fig. 5); unbiasedness did not require controlling for anything else. Note also that, while prospects of recidivism may well have differed between those who worked more than 1,500 hours and those who worked less, properly conditioning solely on the number of hours worked in prison made the experimental and the control groups comparable on the average for all the many variables on which they might otherwise have differed.

All evaluations of criminal justice program impacts are inherently comparative. However, the desired what-if comparisons are virtually impossible to obtain; one must be satisfied with causal inferences. For most applications these inferences are internally valid only if the assignment mechanism is strongly ignorable.

When the researcher has little or no control over the process by which units are assigned to treatment and control conditions, the likelihood of ignorability (strong or otherwise) is small. The researcher must be aware of and measure all the variables that systematically determine

---

[9] Basically, the functional form is crucial because, above (below) the cutoff, there are only experimental units, while below (above) there are only control units. This means that the responses for the experimentals and the controls must be extrapolated into the region occupied only by the other. Since these extrapolations require an assumed functional form, that form is central to all causal inferences. Deterministic assignment under regression-discontinuity designs is ignorable but not strongly ignorable.

both the assignment and the response, and a very large number of variables may be involved. The advantage of true experimental designs is that the assignment may be carried out in ways that are known to the researcher. This information leads to strong ignorability. Strongly ignorable assignment mechanisms are clearly desirable; some might say even mandatory.

REFERENCES

Amemiya, T. 1985. *Advanced Econometrics*. Cambridge, Mass.: Harvard University Press.

Barnow, B. S., G. G. Cain, and A. S. Goldberger. 1980. "Issues in the Analysis of Selectivity Bias." In *Evaluation Studies Review Annual*, edited by E. W. Stromsdorfer and G. Farkus. Beverly Hills, Calif.: Sage.

Berk, R. A., and P. Newton. 1986. "What a Difference a Day Makes: An Evaluation of the Impact of Shelters for Battered Women." *Journal of Marriage and the Family* 48:481–90.

Berk, R. A., and D. Rauma. 1983. "Capitalizing on Nonrandom Assignment to Treatments: A Regression-Discontinuity Evaluation of a Crime Control Program." *Journal of the American Statistical Association* 78:21–28.

Bloom, H. S., and N. M. Singer. 1979. "Determining the Cost-Effectiveness of Correctional Programs: The Case of Patuxent Institution." In *Evaluation Studies Review Annual*, edited by L. Sechrest. Beverly Hills, Calif.: Sage.

Bowden, J. R., and D. A. Turkington. 1984. *Instrumental Variables*. Cambridge: Cambridge University Press.

Cameron, A. C., and P. K. Trivedi. 1986. "Econometric Models Based on Count Data: Comparisons and Applications of Some Estimators and Tests." *Journal of Applied Econometrics* 1:29–53.

Cochran, W. G. 1983. *Planning and Analysis of Observational Studies*. New York: Wiley.

Cook, T. D., and D. T. Campbell. 1979. *Quasi-experimental Design Issues in Field Settings*. Skokie, Ill.: Rand McNally.

Cox, D. R. 1958. *Planning of Experiments*. New York: Wiley.

Farrington, D. P. 1983. "Randomized Experiments on Crime and Justice." In *Crime and Justice: An Annual Review of Research*, vol. 4, edited by Michael Tonry and Norval Morris. Chicago: University of Chicago Press.

Fisher, R. A. 1951. *The Design of Experiments*. New York: Hafner.

Heckman, J. J. 1979. "Sample Selection as a Specification Error." *Econometrics* 47:153–61.

Kassebaum, G., D. Ward, and D. Wilner. 1971. *Prison Treatment and Parole Survival*. New York: Wiley.

Kempthorne, O. 1952. *The Design of Experiments*. New York: Wiley.

Lenihan, K. J. 1977. *Unlocking the Second Gate*. Washington, D.C.: U.S. Government Printing Office.

Maddala, G. S. 1983. *Limited Dependent and Qualitative Variables in Econometrics*. Cambridge: Cambridge University Press.

Rauma, D., and R. A. Berk. 1983. "Crime and Poverty in California: Some Quasi-experimental Evidence." *Social Science Research* 11:318–51.

Rosenbaum, P. R., and D. B. Rubin. 1983. "The Central Role of the Propensity Score in Observational Studies of Causal Effects." *Biometrika* 70:41–55.

Rossi, P. H., R. A. Berk, and K. J. Lenihan. 1980. *Money, Work, and Crime: Empirical Evidence*. New York: Academic Press.

Rossi, P. H., and H. E. Freeman. 1982. *Evaluation: A Systematic Approach*. Beverly Hills, Calif.: Sage.

Rubin, D. B. 1978. "Bayesian Inference for Causal Effects: The Role of Randomization." *Annals of Statistics* 6:34–58.

Sherman, L. W., and R. A. Berk. 1984. "The Specific Deterrent Effects of Arrest for Domestic Assault." *American Sociological Review* 49:261–72.

Trochim, W. K. M. 1984. *Research Design for Program Evaluation: A Regression-Discontinuity Approach*. Beverly Hills, Calif.: Sage.

Waldo, G. P., and T. G. Chiricos. 1977. "Work Release and Recidivism: An Empirical Evaluation of a Social Policy." *Evaluation Quarterly* 1:87–110.

Tim Brennan

Classification: An Overview of Selected Methodological Issues

ABSTRACT

Classification methods have two fundamentally different but related goals.
The first is to build new classifications. The second is to assign unknown
cases to existing classifications. Many traditional offender criminological
classification systems are of questionable value, partly because of
confusion concerning purposes and roles of classification. The link
between purpose and method has recently become more important
because of the emergence of a vast range of quantitative methods. The
multidisciplinary origins of these methods have meant that some of their
embedded concepts and logic may be inconsistent with criminological
theory or data. No single method is best for all purposes. Used correctly,
new methods may dramatically upgrade the quality of our classifications.
A framework for creating and validating classifications in criminology is
urgently needed. The framework should include interacting stages for
choosing a content domain, constructing the classification, checking
internal validity, and establishing external validity.

The last decade has seen much turbulence over the methods of
classification used in criminology and criminal justice. Dissatisfaction
exists among researchers (Gibbons 1975) and practitioners (Eynon
1975). Some commentators oppose the use of classifications altogether
because of their negative social consequences and stigmatizing tendencies. Others advocate a return to the use of theoretical classification

Tim Brennan is instructor in statistics and policy analysis, Graduate School of Public
Affairs, University of Colorado.

because of limitations of empirical classifications (Hood and Sparks 1970).

The backlog of unassimilated information and the continual construction of new typologies have placed strong pressures on theoretical and practical classification methods. Useful findings for criminological classification are accumulating rapidly. Many traditional areas of criminal behavior are being rearranged according to new variables and methods (Chaiken and Chaiken 1984). Obviously, we do not yet possess a complete catalog of criminal types. We can expect continued controversy to surround classification as well as continued discovery of new criminal types.

The promise of taxonomic work in both theory and practice has not been realized. New typological findings have generally not been well assimilated either in theory or in practice. Many commentators have complained about the mass of disconnected typologies (e.g., Bottoms 1973; Solomon 1977). Numerous individual studies exhibit a lack of the cumulative development and integration that are crucial for both scientific progress and practical impact. Many researchers appear infatuated with classification techniques per se or with creating typologies as ends in themselves.

There are two distinct uses of the term "classification." The first is the creation of new classifications. The second is the assignment of individuals to preexisting classifications. Building new classifications in criminology has been the concern of researchers and theoreticians; assigning offenders to classes has been the concern of practitioners.

The two components of classification are interconnected. First, many methods of creating new classifications usually imply a logically appropriate or analogous "assignment" method. Second, conversely, if a preexisting classification system has low reliability or validity, the resulting assignment process is usually unreliable or meaningless.

Here is how this essay is organized. Section I examines various purposes of classification and illustrates how purposes and methods are intricately connected in classification studies. Section II provides a short history of classification methods in criminology. Section III reviews important properties and structures of classifications. Different kinds of classification are suitable for different purposes, and different classification structures are produced by different methods. Thus the methods, purposes, and structures of classifications are closely interrelated. Classification methods used by criminologists are reviewed in Section IV. Section V proposes a general strategy for classification research in criminology and discusses assignment problems. Conclusions and caveats about the use of classification methods are presented in Section VI.

I. The Purposes of Classification

Criminologists often appear vague about the purposes of classification. A classification cannot be expected to fulfill purposes for which it was not created (Opp 1973). Different purposes require different methods, and different data will usually produce different classifications. Minor changes in purpose can produce dramatically changed classifications of the same objects (e.g., Carroll 1980). Vagueness or confusion about research purposes may undermine the potential of recent methodological advances. Thus a clarification of purpose is important prior to the selection of methods.

A. Description

A major role of classification is the description of new or complex domains. Criminological phenomena are often complex and multidimensional, containing interrelations and hidden structures that require careful description and explication. Taxonomic description is used for such purposes in most scientific disciplines. There are repeated suggestions in the criminological literature that taxonomic description has been given short shrift and has been bypassed in the haste to develop explanatory classifications (Hood and Sparks 1970; Opp 1973). Social psychology has also recently been criticized for its neglect of descriptive tasks (Forgas 1979).

Simplification and summarization of complex data by means of classifications aim to achieve clarity of representation and description. In a discipline such as criminology, the diversity of criminal behavior and its causal factors are such that basic structures may remain shrouded in detail and remain unobserved. The grouping of similar objects into homogeneous classes is one way in which complex data can be progressively simplified to reveal underlying structures. Sokal (1974) comments that a paramount purpose of classification is the description and simplification of the structure of similarities among samples in such a way that general statements may be developed about classes of objects.

1. *Summarization and Cognitive Economy.*   A closely related purpose is the summarization of data into classes with minimum loss of salient information. Classification, whether created theoretically or empiri-

cally, is a major tool for summarization and offers a way to cope with information overload. To the degree that classes are homogeneous, the information provided by all members of the class can be summarized by a single central exemplar.

2. *Epidemiology and Descriptive Classification.* Another critical purpose of classification is the epidemiological study and enumeration of crime patterns (Glaser 1974). The need for clear definitions has usually meant that such classification systems use simple behavioral categories or tightly defined legal classifications. This structural requirement undermines the usefulness of such schemes for explanatory purposes to optimize accuracy of identification. Because accuracy and reliability are critical for enumeration purposes, more complex multidimensional classifications and fuzzy boundary systems are generally avoided.

B. Discovery of New Typologies

Classification is a way to discover new typologies of criminological phenomena (Ball 1970; Everitt 1974)—to discover "what the data have to say"—rather than to confirm or test null hypotheses (Green 1980). New criminal personality typologies by Megargee and Bohn (1979) and Carlson (1981) exemplify this use of classification. Shepard (1974), in an essay on the uses of multidimensional scaling, describes the discovery of hidden structures as possibly the greatest potential importance of such methods.

C. Prediction

Prediction is a major purpose of many classifications in both research and practice (Levinson 1982; Flanagan 1983). Classification is used to create groups with large differences on an external criterion. The problem of choosing a best method for predictive classification—given the same set of classification variables—has received much attention (e.g., Wilkins and MacNaughton-Smith 1964; Gottfredson and Gottfredson 1979).

Predictive classification can be differentiated from descriptive classification in terms of both purpose and methodology. Predictive classification does not aim to describe a domain realistically, nor is it always aimed at developing causal or explanatory insights. Predictive classifications can have high predictive utility yet be almost irrelevant in terms of explanation, treatment, or description. The prediction is based strictly on group separation and within-group homogeneity on a particular criterion variable.

1. *Predictive Classification and Criminal Justice Decisions.*   Predictive classifications have been developed for innumerable specific decisions and behaviors. They have been directed at such behaviors as escape, recidivism, violence, and suicide. Many criminal justice decisions— such as sentencing, pretrial incarceration, parole, probation supervision levels, and custody and security levels—are based on the prediction of various risks (Levinson 1982). For example, there is currently much public debate over the use of predictive classifications in sentencing (e.g., Greenwood and Abrahamse 1982). Both ethical and methodological issues are implicated in this use of classification.

2. *Differential Predictive Accuracy.*   Separate classes may have different levels of predictive accuracy. The unique predictability of each class is based largely on the within-class homogeneity on the chosen criterion variable. Offender classes can be ranked according to their homogeneity levels regardless of their mean scores. Donovon (1977) demonstrated this feature of differential predictability in a study of delinquent behavior that showed that the high delinquent types had the highest variances in delinquent behavior; that is, the highest predictive accuracy was found in the least delinquent classes. Sampson (1974) demonstrated the same kind of phenomenon in studying probation prediction.

D. Creating New Analytical Entities or "Ideal Types"

The act of classification, whether done empirically or conceptually, inevitably creates new analytical entities that can be further described, studied, compared, or explained or that can be used within an experimental context. When such analytical entities are created using theoretical inferences, they have been referred to as theoretical concepts, ideal types, or conceptual categories. Empirical, qualitative, impressionistic, or statistical approaches to classification can also create new entities.

The importance of precise specification of the "event to be explained" is too often overlooked. This may have hindered the development of criminology (Gibbons 1975) because researchers and theoreticians have attempted to develop explanations for ill-defined classes of events. Meehan (1968) notes that the maxim "no phenomenon, no explanation" is often violated, especially by those wishing to develop general explanations. Vagueness in specifying the chosen event can devastate causal or explanatory studies since the researcher may misconstrue the event being explained. For example, legalistic classifications are widely criticized for not providing sufficient causal homogeneity for useful explanatory research. The behaviors falling within legal classes may simply be too diverse for explanatory analysis. This is shown dramatically in the recent work of Donovon and Marlatt (1982) in their classification of arrested drunk drivers. The use of unseparated mixtures of criminal types impedes efforts to develop explanations. Preliminary classification of such mixtures into homogeneous criminal types may be needed to study etiology, course, duration, or treatment.

E. Theory Confirmation and Model Testing

Classification is also used to test hypotheses and models and to confirm theoretical systems. For example, Blackburn (1971) examined Megargee's proposal of overcontrolled and undercontrolled homicidal types; Blackburn confirmed the two broad types but found that they split into four subtypes. Hindelang and Weis (1972) tested aspects of Eysenck's personality theory of criminal types using cluster analysis. Butler and Adams (1966) exemplify the use of inverse factor analysis in trying to confirm the I-level typology.[1] Unfortunately, the types that emerged from their analysis had no clear relation to the original I-level types. Koller and Williams (1974) specified a number of hypotheses relating early parental deprivation to delinquency and tested these using multivariate ordination and classification techniques.

There are many problems in the statistical confirmation or validation of theoretical typologies (including problems of cluster validity) and of statistical tests of significance when using multivariate clustering. Detailed reviews of these issues can be found in Jardine and Sibson (1971), Dubes and Jain (1979), and Blashfield, Aldenderfer, and Morey (1982).

Classification also has a role in causal and explanatory work by unraveling causally heterogeneous mixtures of criminal types. This reiterates the need to clarify the "event to be explained." Gibbs (1960) emphasized the importance of causal homogeneity as a basis for hypothesis development and testing by arguing that even specific offenses such as rape, robbery, and assault are hazardous as a basis for causal analysis since they may not be unitary in causation. Many studies using various classification methods have supported Gibbs's argument by identifying diverse causal patterns within specific behavior such as homicides, drunk driving, and delinquent running away (e.g., Blackburn 1971; Brennan, Huizinga, and Elliott 1978; Donovon and Marlatt 1982).

---

[1] The I-level typology is a system of classification based on a domain of interpersonal maturity levels. It has had wide use in the treatment and diagnosis of delinquent youth (Warren 1966).

F. Classification and Nomenclature

Classification shapes the development of a nomenclature for criminal types. Every discipline shares a professional dictionary of terms, names, and concepts. The quality of a nomenclature is critical for ease of communication, storage and retrieval of information, avoiding unnecessary misunderstandings, and so on. Taxonomic systems and classifications representing vast amounts of information can be summarized by a naming system.

1. *The Proliferation of Type Names.*   Many of the originators of traditional criminal classifications coined useful names that have gained broad popularity and use. Warren and her colleagues, in offering the I-level system, coined highly effective names for types of offenders: "asocial aggressive," "cultural conformist," "situational emotional reactor," and so on. These terms graphically captured the social psychology posited for the offenders they describe. Much of the popularity of this system may be due to this clarity of communication, the ease of learning, and the explanatory framework used to understand youthful offenders. This system beautifully illustrates one aspect of naming—the need to convey the central features or process of a class in a few graphic terms. Similarly, Merton's classification of adaptations to social structural conditions used a graphic set of names such as the "retreatist," the "ritualist," and the "innovator."

Names for types of criminals come from diverse sources. Schrag (1959) discovered that inmates had recognized and named certain types: the "square john," the "right guy," the "con politician," and the "outlaw." Interestingly, sociologists of deviance had identified similar types and had named them "prosocial," "antisocial," "pseudosocial," and "asocial." The names given to types are efforts to communicate and to describe a core process or feature. In academic circles the central themes, features, or processes that are the basis of names are often based on behavioral, sociological, psychopathological, or psychological data.

Behavioral classifications, for example, and those based on criminal careers tend to use behaviorally oriented naming systems (e.g., Roebuck 1971; Glaser 1972; Gibbons 1973). There is a confusing, overlapping mass of behavioral types in the literature. For example, a limited sampling of violent criminal types reveals the terms "subcultural assaulters," "quasi-insane assaulters," "psychopathic assaultists," "violent sex offenders," "addictive supporting predators," "undercontrolled homicides," "overcontrolled homicides," "one-time losers," "professional heavy criminals," "vocational predators," "mixed-pattern," "jacks-of-all-trades," and so on. This list is almost endless (Solomon 1977) and has yielded confusion rather than clarity. Each main domain of criminological behavior offers a similarly ebullient but confusing list of names.

The lack of stability and consensus in criminal classification has produced much name changing over the years. The above listings suggest the overlap, ambiguity, and lack of integration in these classifications (Gibbons 1975; Solomon 1977). Perhaps there is a right time for coining new names, but this must be based on a convergence of description, corroboration by other researchers, and a basic understanding of the causal processes or central features involved. Nomenclature can be undermined by ambiguity of class definitions, unreliability of techniques for assigning cases to classes, instability of the reference classifications, partial coverage of the population being classified, vagueness of the population being classified, and within-class heterogeneity.

2. *Recent Trends in Nomenclature.*   Criminological taxonomists are now showing more hesitance about coining new names. Many of the more recent offender classifications avoid the use of names or use acronyms that do not imply a specific core process and that can be more easily modified when stability and validity are demonstrated. Megargee and Bohn (1979) used such terms as "Able," "Baker," and "Charlie." Others totally avoid new names and give short descriptive profiles of the prototype of each class (e.g., Donovon and Marlatt 1982).

At the earliest stages of taxonomic description, where stability and convergence of classifications are a distant goal and when greater clarification of the causal and theoretical aspects of a classification is necessary, it may be unwise to finalize nomenclature. Yet we cannot avoid naming for use in communication, information storage, and retrieval purposes. With the advent of computer techniques for handling information, some kind of coding system is necessary. A more exact scientific system of numerical codes may eventually coexist with a more graphic nomenclature to provide a dictionary covering the multiplicity of offender types.

II. A Historical Overview of Classification Methods in Criminology and Criminal Justice

The history of criminological classification is extensive and turbulent. The methods and kinds of classifications in vogue have undergone major changes. A review of taxonomic methodologies used by criminologists suggests a parallelism with other sciences in that three general stages are found (Cattell 1965; Boulding 1980). A literary and impressionistic stage is followed by a clinical theorizing stage that is finally complemented by a quantitative stage. These stages are characterized by different methods of creating and evaluating classifications and by different kinds of classifications. Implicit in this progression are trends toward increased objectivity, increased precision, and increased information content. Each methodological change seeks to bring about some improvement in the scientific quality of criminological classification.

We are now embroiled in the incorporation of quantitative multivariate methods into theoretical and practical classification systems. Profound methodological developments are occurring, and criminologists are struggling to learn exactly what the new quantitative multivariate methods offer and how they can best be used. Much of the current criminological literature has now entered the third, quantitative phase. Many practitioners and scholars of offender classification remain caught up in methods and typologies of earlier stages.

A. The Literary/Impressionistic Stage

In this stage the investigator arrives at a classification intuitively and illustrates it with a few positive instances. The classifications are personal, subjective, and often highly creative. Classifying criminals was a favorite pastime of philosophers, scholars, and authors over the centuries, and a massive literature was produced. Observation and data collection were seldom systematic; many of the principles of scientific classification were violated and a confusing mass of competing, unreliable, and nonoperational systems offered. The classifications produced at this stage have been of limited scientific usefulness.

B. The Clinical/Theoretical Stage

This stage is also largely nonquantitative. However, it involves higher levels of systematic observation and theoretical speculation. Many clinical theories have been offered to explain and classify criminals, especially from psychology, psychiatry, and sociology. This stage also produced numerous theoretical typologies with little consensus among their proponents. Many of these typologies attempted to explain and subsume all forms of criminal behavior.

While this stage was theoretically exciting, by 1975 the general evaluation of its merit was negative, and a deep pessimism was voiced regarding the value of taxonomic research. The criticisms were leveled at both the methods and the products of earlier stages.

1. *Poor Operational Measurement.*   Criticisms focused on the weakness of operational measurement. Many theoretical and clinical systems were based on abstract theoretical concepts that were not easily measurable. If the basic concepts are not measurable, the resulting typological systems can be neither proved nor disproved. Some have referred to this body of theoretically based classification systems as a massive facade of "pseudo-knowledge" (Cattell 1965).[2] In criminology, the taxonomic products of this stage appear weighty, impressive, and of great theoretical importance, but researchers were unable to validate them, nor could correctional practitioners discover their practical importance (Eynon 1975; Gibbons 1975). To this day many of the most prominent theoretical systems have never been empirically validated.

2. *Inadequate Assignment Procedures.*   Theoretical and clinical typologies may be crippled by inadequate, cumbersome, or unreliable assignment procedures. Assignment techniques are critical in practice for the correct placement of new inmates, but these techniques were often missing, vague, and ambiguous or required extensive clinical training. Even with the most rigorous attempts to train practitioners, unreliability of assignment remained a serious problem (Beker and Hyman 1972).

3. *Poor Predictive Validity.*   Virtually all uses of classification in criminal justice systems depend on predictive validity. Reviewers were almost unanimous in criticizing the available theoretical typologies for inadequate predictive validity (Hood and Sparks 1970; Bottoms 1973; Gibbons 1975).

4. *Poor Reliability and Replication.*   In reviewing twenty years of work, Gibbons (1975) acknowledged that virtually all attempts to replicate the traditional clinical and theoretical classifications empirically had failed. Replication studies simply could not find these "types." This led to charges that they were simply theoretical artifacts with no basis in reality.

5. *Nonconvergence and Theoretical Confusion.*   The existence of numerous theoretical systems created conflict and confusion for both practitioners and researchers. The competing systems were difficult to inte-

---

[2] Similar critiques are found in other disciplines during this time. For example, in reviewing biological classification Sokal (1964) described much of the earlier nonquantitative work in that field as taxonomic "mythology."

grate (Kinch 1962; Warren 1971) and often had diverging implications for decision making and intervention (Solomon 1977). Many reviewers noted the confusion among practitioners regarding classification and how it could be effectively implemented (D. M. Gottfredson 1975).

6. *Inadequate Power for Interventions and Control.* The "power" of a classification is based jointly on the presence of good predictions and a good level of explanatory coherence. The latter is important in developing appropriate interventions. None of the available classification systems had this combination. The theoretical classifications had little predictive validity, and the empirical classifications had little predictive or explanatory power. Thus criminal justice personnel were given only a minimal basis for intervention and control (Hood and Sparks 1970; Eynon 1975).

7. *Oversimplification and Reductionism.* The empirical classifications of this time in general were usually based on the cross classification of a few broad variables. Hood and Sparks (1970) and other reviewers criticized this approach for reductionism and oversimplification, claiming that it reduced explanatory power, predictive power, and descriptive accuracy.

C. A Transition Phase of Pessimism, Rejection, and Search for New Approaches

Criminal justice practitioners reacted to the above deficiencies in predictable ways. Many became dissatisfied and cynical. Others simply ignored the official classification systems of their agencies and continued to classify offenders largely on impressionistic personal grounds. Official classification systems in jails and prisons were often subverted by line staff who preferred to rely on personal discretion. This response remains common in bureacratic situations in which strict supervision is difficult or impossible, as in custodial and security classifications in crowded jails and prisons.

Subjective assignment was often the only reasonable option to a line classification officer. The complexity of real-life decisions, coupled with the inadequacy of formal bureaucratic classification systems, was such that most classification officers or committees continued to rely largely on subjective criteria and intuition (D. M. Gottfredson 1975; Daudistel, Sanders, and Luckenbill 1979). As recently as 1979, a majority of jails conducted most of their security and custody classifications on the basis of discretion and subjective classification (Bohnstedt and Geiser 1979).

By the mid-1970s there was a mixture of extreme pessimism and confusion regarding classification among many criminologists. Most of the major theoretical classification systems (such as the I-level classification and the juvenile typology of Cloward and Ohlin [1969]) had come under fire for poor reliability and validity (Beker and Hyman 1972). None had clearly survived empirical validation. Reviews by European criminologists were also pessimistic (Bottoms 1973; Opp 1973). The spirit of this time of transition is captured by Eynon (1975): "Until we begin serious scientific research on classification and treatment, we will have to content ourselves with inflicting our ignorance upon the hapless offenders who have fallen into our clutches" (p. 73).

The implication was that criminal classification could no longer rely mainly on theoretical speculation or poorly constructed empirical systems and that attention had to be given to upgrading the scientific quality of classification systems.

D. The Stage of Multivariate Quantitative Classification

Critics sought a breakthrough in methodological sophistication. Fortunately, such a development had been under way in other disciplines since the late 1950s, and a new methodology was emerging under the general label of "numerical taxonomy" (Sokal and Sneath 1963; Jardine and Sibson 1971; Sneath and Sokal 1973). The development of taxometric methods of classification continues unabated and has been so prolific that a new interdisciplinary journal, *Journal of Classification*, was started in 1984.

Many of the earlier critics sensed the potential of multivariate quantitative methods for classification (Hood and Sparks 1970; Gibbons 1975). Hindelang and Weis (1972) suggest that the availability of new classification methods in the social sciences has allowed "the analysis of new problems of a kind and magnitude which were formerly difficult, if not impossible to research, and makes possible more precise and rigorous investigations of old problems" (p. 268).

At this stage a number of themes were evident. First, many reviewers were optimistic about the potential advantages and possibilities of quantitative multivariate methods. Second, some urged caution, asserting that these methods were not a panacea and would be useful only if their assumptions were properly understood and if they were carefully handled (Hood and Sparks 1970; Bottoms 1973). Third, experimentation with new methods occurred in some early application studies. Many of these studies were intended to demonstrate and evaluate the new methods (Ballard and Gottfredson 1963; Wilkins and MacNaughton-Smith 1964; Fildes and Gottfredson 1973); others were serious attempts to tackle old substantive problems (Blackburn 1971).

What were the expected advantages of these new methods? Obviously, quantification might produce higher levels of precision, consistency, and reliability. The multivariate approach also allows empirical classifications to be constructed with far higher information content than was previously possible. The overall hope was to produce classifications of higher scientific quality than those achieved in the earlier stages (Skinner and Blashfield 1982). The presumed advantages of quantitative classification techniques included higher objectivity, greater precision of measurement, higher information content, and a general improvement in descriptive, predictive, and theoretical validity. Whether such improvements will be achieved is still questionable. The methods are complex, and the challenge of learning how to use them in a criminological context remains a critical issue. As of the mid-1970s there was a growing number of published taxometric classifications in criminology, and the incorporation of taxometric methods had been in progress for about ten to fifteen years.

In the last decade, quantitative classification has employed two main strategies. The first is to continue the traditional approach of simple bivariate cross classification. The second is characterized by the use of multivariate taxometric methods.

Much of the classification research prior to 1970 used the bivariate cross-classification approach. Hood and Sparks (1970) criticized this approach for its restriction to a "few broad variables" and for oversimplification. This approach creates simple monothetic classes of low information content, which usually places severe limitations on both theoretical and predictive power.[3] An even simpler early quantitative approach created "polar" types by imposing cutoffs on some unidimensional scale (Hood and Sparks 1970). Such univariate and bivariate approaches to classification are still often found in the criminological literature. For example, Dunford and Elliott (1984) create a classification of delinquents by imposing cutoffs on two scales of seriousness and frequency of self-reported delinquent acts. Similarly, the current inmate classification models of the Bureau of Prisons

---

[3] Monothetic classes are created by means of logical and successive divisions of a population using selected variables. The term is discussed in Sneath and Sokal (1973) and also in a later section of this essay.

and of the National Institute of Corrections rely on simple thresholds imposed across a single additive risk scale. Similar "risk classifications" are currently used in jails and prisons throughout the country (Bohnstedt and Geiser 1979).

The more contemporary methodological trend is the use of multivariate taxometric methods. Perhaps the most influential early paper introducing these methods to criminology was that of Wilkins and MacNaughton-Smith (1964), who advocated a number of divisive monothetic methods for predictive classification. These and other multivariate methods of classification were soon being used widely. To date, only a few attempts have been made to develop and validate new substantive classification systems (e.g., Brennan, Huizinga, and Elliott 1978; Megargee and Bohn 1979).

The multivariate taxonomic study of the behavioral, psychological, and social domains of criminal populations remains at an early stage. Three final points regarding the current situation may be noteworthy. First, there is no slackening of proposed new typological systems; new systems are appearing in virtually every line of criminological inquiry (e.g., Mrad, Kabacoff, and Duckro 1983; Chaiken and Chaiken 1984). Second, there is no consensus among the advocates of rival classification systems, and all current classifications in criminology are highly provisional. Conflicts and disagreements exist regarding both research classifications (Johnson, Simmons, and Gordon 1983; Zager 1983) and applied classifications. Skepticism among criminal justice personnel regarding all current offender classifications is a serious problem. Third, the methodologies used to create these classification systems remain highly varied.

III. Some Important Structures and Qualities of Classification Systems

This section turns attention to the structural features of classification systems. This may give some perspective on qualities to be considered when asking, What is a good classification system? One response is, Good for what? Some have asserted that the goodness or value of a classification system is basically a nonmathematical question (Kozelka 1982) and that the main issue is whether the classification makes sense in terms of substantive purposes. Purpose, in fact, guides the selection of classification structures as well as evaluative criteria.

Classification structure has received little attention in criminological work. There has usually been a statement of preference for certain qualities, such as reliability, validity, ease of use, minimization of a "nonclassifiable" category, and so on. The discussion has seldom addressed the "structural form" of a class or how this fits with the purposes of classification or with criminological theory. This raises new questions, many of which have not been resolved. For example, criminologists have yet to clarify the structural form of a "class" appropriate for different purposes—for causal etiological typologies, for descriptive typologies, or for predictive classifications.

A. Monothetic versus Polythetic Classifications

Monothetic and polythetic class structures are two distinct kinds of classifications. Both are used by criminologists in a fairly ad hoc manner, with few guidelines being followed for selection of the appropriate structure.

Monothetic classes are defined by "boundary" conditions and are created by means of the repeated subdivision of a sample on successive variables. Divisive classification progressively splits a population into smaller monothetic groups. This is basically the Aristotelian approach of logical classification. Many theoretical systems in criminology use monothetic division to define classes using cutoff scores, or boundaries, on a few theoretical variables. "Types" are exactly defined by boundary conditions on the key discriminating variables. The classes produced are always disjoint and nonoverlapping. Every member of a monothetic class by definition possesses the full set of defining variables. The membership criteria are exact. The outstanding advantage of monothetic classification is the simplicity and clarity of class definitions. New individuals can be easily and unambiguously assigned to an existing classification. Also, theory is explicitly used in both the selection of variables and the cutoff scores. Many of the early quantitative classifications in criminology used monothetic divisive techniques such as association analysis and predictive attribute analysis (Gottfredson, Ballard, and Lane 1963; Wilkins and MacNaughton-Smith 1964). These methods are described in Section IV.

Polythetic classes are constructed by the simultaneous use of all classification variables to assess overall similarity among members. Classes are built from the ground up in an agglomerative manner. The process begins at the interindividual level. Cases are grouped together on the basis of high mutual similarity. Classes are based on high internal cohesion and similarity rather than on boundary conditions. All agglomerative hierarchical clustering techniques will produce polythetic classifications. The recent typologies of Megargee and Bohn (1979) and Carlson (1981) show the use of agglomerative clustering to create polythetic classes of offenders.

The advantages of polythetic classification stem from the use of over-all resemblance. Classes usually have higher within-class homogeneity and higher information content and may be regarded as more "natural" since they emerge from the basic similarity structure within the sample. Boundaries are less likely to be arbitrary. The "central exemplar" of each polythetic class is usually an excellent representative of the class. A main goal in polythetic classification is to describe the profile of a central exemplar. Paradoxically, this renders the highly contemporary polythetic approach very similar to traditional subjective classifications in criminology since the latter also appear to be based on the recognition of central exemplars, or prototypes (Mischel 1979).

B. Natural versus Artificial Classifications

Much classification in criminology has the aim of avoiding "artificiality" and cleaving as much as possible to the "reality" of the cases being classified. Thus the "boundaries" between classes should reflect some important natural difference. This distinction between natural and artificial classifications relates to the above polythetic/monothetic distinction but goes beyond it. Classifications place objects into classes using logical rules. Two broad kinds of rules can be delineated—intrinsic and extrinsic. The former try to discover the inherent, or "natural," structure of data; the latter impose logically defined classes on data (Williams and Dale 1964). To illustrate, books can be intrinsically grouped by similarity of information content or extrinsically classified by using authors' names. The latter classification, while useful for storage and retrieval, has no relation to the former. Natural classification tries to emphasize natural as opposed to artificial boundaries.

However, this distinction has been attacked in a controversial debate among classification theorists (Enc 1976). The distinction between "natural" and "artificial" classifications is weakened by noting that all classifications are abstract, purposeful, and, to some extent, artificial. The debate has forced the empirical taxonomists to acknowledge the theoretical assumptions implicit in their methods. The distinction alerts us to two broad styles exhibited by criminologists in their taxonomic work. The first creates classifications using conceptualization and extrinsic classification rules. The second emphasizes the descriptive and exploratory roles of discovering intrinsic structure in criminological data.

C. The Scope, Coverage, or Range of a Classification

The scope of a classification is the range of phenomena to which it applies. For example, Megargee and Bohn's (1979) classification of criminals based on the Minnesota Multiphasic Personality Inventory has broad scope and covers virtually all criminals. Other systems focus on a narrower range of criminal behavior, for example, Blackburn's (1971) classification of homicides. The risk classification systems used in jails and prisons for custody and security decisions have broad scope and try to classify all incoming offenders and most offense types. Most of the traditional typologies were broad in scope, as they attempted to explain many forms of criminality in a single general theoretical perspective (Solomon 1977). Classifications were often seen as better if they included a maximum number of offenders within their descriptive or explanatory range.

1. *Disadvantages of Broad Coverage.*   In attempting to "explain everything," such systems may also lose descriptive accuracy and become less relevant to any particular offense. Disadvantages include a loss of predictive power and increased ambiguity. Evaluation criteria of classification can be inversely related; that is, scope is negatively related to predictive validity. Criminal justice practitioners may be better served by narrow classifications that may achieve greater predictive accuracy and that retain high relevance to particular offenses or decisions.

2. *Matching Scope with Purpose.*   A more general goal is to match the classification's scope to its purposes. Predictive classifications of recidivism may be improved by narrowing their scope to particular kinds or classes of offenses. In this way, predictor variables can be chosen to be most salient to the behavior in question. The drunk-driver classification by Donovon and Marlatt (1982) offers a useful example of a focused, "narrow range" classification.

D. Precision

Precision of measurement and of class definitions varies widely among criminological classifications. Precision includes accuracy of measurement, the presence of explicit diagnostic criteria for each class, and the clarity of "meaning" or conceptualization of the classes. Poor precision implies that the classes are vaguely defined and that recognition criteria are unavailable, nonoperational, or unreliable. The diagnostic process of assigning unknown cases into a classification is undermined when recognition criteria are poor. Diagnostic work in the related fields of medical and psychiatric classifications was hindered for centuries by imprecise measurement and conceptualization. Many of the classification systems currently used in jails and prisons exhibit low precision (Bohnstedt and Geiser 1979). This feature requires subjective judgments from line staff to make such classifications workable.

Precision usually increases with information content. Thus precision is higher at the lower levels of a hierarchical classification, where the types are more concrete, particular, and narrow. Classes at higher levels are more general, more abstract, and their meanings less precise. This loss of precision results when too much information is deleted and when more diverse cases are forced into broader classes. The many sociological, psychological, and psychiatric classifications in criminology illustrate the common structure of low precision of measurement coupled with broad, abstract classes. Applied classifications require high precision since these must deal unambiguously, reliably, and efficiently with large numbers of cases. Systems that lack precision usually produce confusion and dissatisfaction at the line level in most correctional agencies and ultimately are rejected when the workers revert to subjective judgment (Lipsky 1980).

E. The Level of Abstraction of Classifications: The Vertical Structure

Many classifications are structured hierarchically from broad, general classes at the top to narrow subclasses at the bottom. Subclasses are "nested" beneath more inclusive classes. Both theoretical and empirical classifications can be structured hierarchically.

1. *Confusion in Criminology over the Level of Abstraction.*   Various levels of abstraction have differing advantages and disadvantages (Hood and Sparks 1970). The requirements of criminal justice practitioners for simplicity and ease of use demand a few general classes; yet the simultaneous need for predictive validity and precision demands narrower classes with high information content.

Most criminological classifications have used only a single level of abstraction and a few broad types. The need for simplicity and parsimony is probably responsible. Many past reviews of typological work in criminology focused on the advantages of such simplicity. Yet the well-known I-level system (Warren 1966), in which three broad classes (levels 2, 3, and 4) each contain nested subtypes, illustrates nesting at various levels of inclusiveness. For instance, the I-2 level contains the subclasses "asocial aggressive" and "asocial passive," while the I-4 level contains the four subclasses "neurotic acting out," "neurotic anxious," "situational emotional reactor," and "cultural identifier." Some of the more recent classification that works with cluster-analytic methods offers nested classifications at varying hierarchical levels (Donovon and Marlatt 1982).

2. *What Is the Best Level of Abstraction?*   Not all levels of abstraction are equally good or useful. Some levels are simply too global and abstract, while others are too refined. The guiding criteria again must be the purpose of the classification. Overly refined distinctions simply produce confusion. Rosch (1978) argues that most hierarchical classifications have a "basic level" of abstraction that is optimal for using, thinking about, naming, and communicating. This particular level retains a maximum amount of useful information in the fewest classes; it maximizes the ratio of parsimony to information content within the context of a particular purpose. Information increases moving down a hierarchical classification toward the basic level, and little is gained in moving beyond it.

Criminologists have disagreed regarding the right level of abstraction for classification. Most offender typologies contain between four and ten classes (Hood and Sparks 1970). Such broad classes may not capture the full diversity of criminal behavior. A more particularized and less abstract level is offered by Gibbons (1973), who classified criminal careers into fifteen types, for example, semiprofessional property offenders, property offender "one-time losers," and auto-thief joyriders. His system contains three main classes of sex offenders with many subtypes. Gibbons draws important distinctions between all fifteen classes and suggests that much information would be lost at a higher level of abstraction. Many of the more recent empirical research studies are forcing us toward more specific distinctions, and the trend is toward more particularized classifications within circumscribed domains of criminal behavior.

There are, however, disadvantages at more particularized levels of classification. Subordinate levels—although they have precision, rich detail, and high homogeneity—gradually incur much overlap and redundancy among subclasses. They may be unsuitable for highlighting differences among criminal types in comparative studies. Also, there is a larger cognitive load in remembering many subtypes and the subtle differences among them. More abstract levels are easier to understand and remember, so the "basic level" of a hierarchy is generally preferable for most purposes.

The level of abstraction of a classification system is also critically relevant for treatment. A common response to the problem of abstraction in classification is to ask for individualized treatment. In many criminological contexts this is neither practically nor theoretically feasible. The financial and personnel resources of correctional systems could not cope with the development and implementation of totally individualized programming. No bureacratic organization can deal with an infinite variety of offender behaviors; all institutions require classification of some sort. Prottas (1979) and Lipsky (1980) have demonstrated that in virtually all person-processing institutions classification at some degree of abstraction is necessary for client processing to begin.

Such an infinite variety of individualized treatment classifications may be contrasted with the idea of "requisite variety," which asserts that any attempt to describe, control, or explain a phenomenon must match the phenomenon in terms of complexity and variety (Ashby 1956). What is critical is whether the classification falls significantly below the complexity of offender behavior in terms of salient information and distinctions as defined by the user's purpose. Thus a particular distinction may be salient to a warden's purpose but not to that of the courts. The balancing of these purposes will determine the level of abstraction used in any particular situation.

F. The Horizontal Structure of a Classification

A number of critical structures are subsumed by the concept of the horizontal structure. Two important structures for criminological research are the internal homogeneity of classes and the boundary conditions, or separations, between classes.

1. *Internal Cohesion and Homogeneity.*   Cohesion can vary from tight, compact classes in which all members have high mutual similarity to classes with low internal connectedness. Various classification methods are suited to creating or detecting either kind of class. Criminologists have often demanded high internal cohesion or high homogeneity in their studies of criminal typologies (Hood and Sparks 1970). Yet it is clear that homogeneity does not necessarily have to extend over all classificatory variables. The demand for complete or high homogeneity across all variables will almost always result in the failure to find any classes that meet this structural requirement. This perhaps explains the dismal failure of many early studies to identify the "criminal specialist" since most early studies used methods that sought complete class homogeneity (Hood and Sparks 1970). Polythetic methods that can relax the internal homogeneity requirement within criminal classes are probably appropriate in addressing this question.

Diverse clustering methods now exist that are differentially geared for discovering classes with differing internal cohesion levels (see Sec. IV). Homogeneity can be assessed in many ways, for example, by computing the within-class variances on all relevant variables. Classes can be compared on these variances and ranked according to levels of homogeneity (Tryon and Bailey 1970). Another approach is to examine the average interobject similarity levels using any of the many similarity coefficients that are available (Hudson 1982).

2. *Separation between Classes and Boundary Conditions.*   Classes can be well separated or they can be only marginally separated by vague, blurred, or overlapping boundaries. Ordination techniques such as principal coordinates analysis or multidimensional scaling can be used in conjunction with classification methods to give a graphical mapping of the classes to illustrate boundary conditions and the relations between classes (Roberts, Williams, and Poole 1982). With much criminological data the boundaries between classes are not clear-cut and are filled with intermediate cases. Thus classification methods that are overly sensitive to these intermediate cases may fail through the problem of "chaining," that is, when classes collapse, or "chain," into one another because of the presence of the intermediate cases. In effect the boundary conditions are such that the analytical method is unable to keep the two adjacent classes separate (Wishart 1969).

IV. Methods for Constructing Classifications

Many approaches are used for creating classifications. Some of the more frequently used traditional, as well as the more recent quantitative, methods are described here. Comments on the general design and the advantages or disadvantages of each approach are provided.

A. Some Traditional Approaches to Constructing Classifications

Some traditional approaches to constructing classifications are included here since they are still widely used. Furthermore, there is as yet no strong evidence that newer quantitative methods provide any great advantage over traditional approaches (van Alstyne and Gottfredson 1978; Gottfredson and Gottfredson 1979).

1. *Subjective Classification.*   Most traditional criminal typologies emerged from a subjective "pattern-recognition" process, in which recurrent patterns of features are recognized on the basis of close observation of criminals. Occasionally, such clinical observation and description is augmented with inferential reasoning (Garside and Roth 1978) and a new type then described and named. Prior to the development of

statistical methods, this approach dominated all fields of classification, including medical nosology, psychiatric types, and plant and species taxonomy. It has had a long and successful history with an almost total absence of formal statistical methods. The great value of this approach is the richness of clinical description, the high face validity, and the impressive production of theoretical typologies. The critical skills required to create classes are careful observation and insightful recognition of recurring and distinctive features.

The "expert" does not start with a data matrix that correlates everything with everything but with observations or conjectures regarding criminal types. There may be no knowledge of causality or prognosis but, rather, simply the recognition of a pattern. Meehl (1979) suggests that this typification process may occur when a clinician notices individual cases exhibiting a recurrent or striking configuration and then describes and names the pattern. Experienced jail and prison staff as well as inmates often indulge in such intuitive or subjective categorizing. The "square john" and "con politician" of Schrag's (1959) inmate study as well as many other criminal types described in the literature emerge from this process.

The problems of this approach relate to validity, reliability, the projection of personal bias, and imaginative but fictional constructions. In warning of the drawbacks of intuitive categorization, Green (1980) has noted that "students of perception know that anyone who stares long and hard enough at nothing will eventually see something" (p. 814).

Subjective classification has produced a huge literature on criminal typologies. As noted elsewhere, this is characterized by conflict and confusion rather than by convergence. Different names were often coined for similar types. The experts may have emphasized different features that often were of the same configuration and then argued over whether the types were really distinct. Operational measurement was a recurrent problem. While the originator of a typology claimed the ability to identify types, the ordinary jailer often was not given clear diagnostic criteria and was generally unable to identify these types in practice. Although subjective typologies were useful for theorizing and for clinical work, many were impractical because of the absence of measurable diagnostic criteria.

2. *Enumeration of Frequencies of Configurations: The "Cartet Count."* In this traditional approach, the classifier specifies all possible combinations of selected criminal attributes and counts the number of cases fitting each pattern. This has long been known as the "cartet-count"

method (Cattell and Coulter 1966). It is still frequently used by criminologists.

Recently, Chaiken and Chaiken (1984) developed a criminal classification using this method. They simplify criminal behavior into eight dimensions: assault, robbery, burglary, drug deals, theft, auto theft, fraud, and forgery or credit card swindles. By dichotomizing each inmate's response on each of these eight behaviors strictly to a "yes/no" option, they create a total of 256 possible configurations. After counting the frequencies of inmates fitting each separate configuration and allowing cases with "uninteresting" distinctions to be classified together, they found ten configurations that accounted for 59 percent of the inmates.

This method has strengths and weaknesses. It is well grounded in empirical data and is objective and easily operationalized. It has been involved, at least partially, in the development of many well-known criminal typologies (Roebuck 1971). However, it is appropriate only if there are few classificatory variables and if these can be realistically dichotomized. With n variables scored as dichotomies, the number of configurations is 2^n. If scores are trichotomized, this figure is 3^n. The number of configurations quickly becomes impractical. In the Chaiken and Chaiken study, for example, trichotomization would generate 6,561 configurations.

The cartet count is a limited method in that it is usually restricted to few variables, dichotomized scoring, and a restrictive disjoint definition of a type requiring either/or boundaries and a highly compact homogeneous form of a class. These are structural requirements and may not fit the purposes of many typological studies. The Chaikens, for example, had to relax this structure by allowing cases with "uninteresting differences" to enter some of their main classes. Thus their classes have somewhat higher diversity than would be produced by the strict classification rules of the method. The method is often used to give a rough starting classification for refinement by other methods, for example, in the well-known BCTry system (Tryon and Baily 1970). Similarly, Wishart (1969) uses a modified version of the cartet count to give starting "types" for his mode-seeking clustering method.

3. *Theoretical or Conceptual Classification.* The use of theory to build classifications has long been preferred by many criminologists. Classifications are produced a priori by means of conceptual categories that operate as extrinsic classification rules. In the usual approach, the researcher uses a theory to justify the variables, cutoff scores or bound-

aries to separate high- and low-scoring classes, and the particular cross classifications or theoretical interactions that define the classes. The dichotomized or trichotomized variables and the selected cross-classifications produce logical monothetic "boxes" into which offenders are categorized. Such classifications have disjoint boundaries and are usually limited to two or three main variables. Each class has a simple profile of high/low scores on each variable. In the univariate case this produces what used to be known as "polar" types—the chosen cutoffs isolate high and low poles on a single attribute. For example, the "extrovert" and "introvert" are polar extremes on a single personality distribution.

Many well-known typologies in criminology use this general approach. Illustrative examples can be found in each of the main theoretical disciplines feeding into social deviance and criminology. Sociologists are especially fond of conceptual typologies. Merton's (1964) typology of modes of adaptations to social structure is a monothetic classification that is developed from social theory and that uses two broad social variables and a two-way cross classification. The first variable is acceptance or rejection of cultural goals; the second is acceptance or rejection of prescribed means to achieve these goals. The types are defined by various score combinations, and a useful set of names was coined—"conformists," "retreatists," "ritualists," "rebels," and "innovators." This classification inspired much speculative and empirical work to confirm, elaborate, and compare the hypothesized types.

A recent illustrative example of conceptual classification in criminal behavior studies is that of Dunford and Elliott (1984). The aim was to build a classification of delinquents on the basis of self-reported delinquent behaviors. They selected the dimensions of "seriousness" and "frequency" of delinquent behaviors over time to develop a delinquent typology. Cutoffs on each dimension were chosen conceptually. The typology is based on a cross classification of the two variables, each being dichotomized to give boundary conditions. Four delinquency types are defined:

1. Nondelinquents—fewer than four offenses and no UCR Part I offenses during any given calendar year.

2. Exploratory delinquents—four to eleven self-reported delinquent behaviors and no more than one UCR Part I offense in any given year.

3. Nonserious-patterned delinquents—twelve or more self-reported delinquent behaviors and no more than two UCR Part I offenses in any given year.

4. Serious-patterned delinquents—youth committing at least three Part I UCR offenses in a given year regardless of frequency of any other delinquent offenses.

A validation study was then conducted using numerous between-type comparisons on other variables linked to delinquency theory. Many comparisons were statistically significant, suggesting that the typology may be valid. One might question the meaning of validity in this approach. The boundaries were logically chosen to separate low-frequency/low-seriousness from high-frequency/high-seriousness delinquents. The selection of different cutoff points virtually anywhere on the two dimensions would probably produce alternative typologies with similar significant differences. However, irrespective of the validity issue this study is interesting in that it illustrates the current use of a fairly traditional approach.

The main dangers of conceptual classifications are artificiality, oversimplification, and, in many early systems, poor measurement and vague definition of abstract variables. First, conceptual monothetic classes may be artifacts with no relation to the actual structure of the data. The chosen cutting points may violate continuous distributions or may diverge from natural boundaries in the data. The cross classification and cutoffs simply force individuals into predefined boundaries. Artificiality may also extend to the selection of the typology's level of abstraction. Why should the number of types be strictly defined by the number of cells in a contingency table? Should the number of types always be an even number? Is it not possible that there may be three, five, or seven classes in a typological system?

Second, the restriction of the cross-classification approach to only a few broad variables may violate the complexity of the domain by forcing the deletion of many salient variables. In a related study, Elliott, Dunford, and Huizinga (1985) acknowledge the problem: "Although the inclusion of only two behavioral dimensions in the identification of career offenders is probably overly simplistic, it is a more complex definition than that employed by most researchers attempting to select or identify career offenders."

This implies not only that their own typology may be oversimplistic but that this problem has pervaded most prior work on criminal career typologies. Such oversimplification is a direct result of the classification methodology used in this field of study, that is, the conceptual method of cross classifications on a few selected variables. Furthermore, many of these studies are restricted to a single behavioral dimension of frequency (e.g., Wolfgang, Figlio, and Sellin 1972; Shannon 1981). The two broad measures of "seriousness" or "frequency" often used in this type of research require the compression of many specific frequency and seriousness scores for diverse offenses into two single scores. There may be much important information contained in the specific offenses that is lost by this process.

Finally, many theoretically generated typologies use abstract variables that are often only vaguely conceptualized and poorly measured (Ferdinand 1966; Schafer 1969; Solomon 1977). This was a major criticism of Merton's system (Opp 1973).

B. Recent Quantitative Approaches: Taxometric Methods

Criminology is now adding taxometric methods to its arsenal of techniques for constructing classifications. A huge multidisciplinary literature now exists on taxometric methods, and an in-depth technical review would be outside the scope of this essay. Technical descriptions are available (Jardine and Sibson 1971; Everitt 1974; Hartigan 1975; Hudson 1982; Lorr 1983). The intention here is to examine a few major methods and comment on some critical features of importance to criminologists.

There is no single "best" method; rather, different data and problems require different classification strategies. The problem is to select a method that best fits the research data and purpose (Williams 1971; Lorr 1983).

1. *Hierarchical Agglomerative Clustering.* These were among the earliest clustering methods developed and were quickly adopted by criminologists (Baer 1970). Many recent papers illustrate their use in developing offender classifications (Blackburn 1971; McGurk 1978; Megargee and Bohn 1979; Donovon and Marlatt 1982). Although there are many forms of agglomerative clustering, they all embody the following series of steps. (1) Assess all objects over a common set of attributes. (2) Compute the similarity between each object and every other object. (3) Initiate clustering by joining the closest pair of objects into a cluster. (4) Join the next-closest pair (this may include joining a single object to a previously created group). (5) Continue this joining until all objects are grouped together in a single cluster (this requires a procedure for joining, or fusing, clusters).

The result of an agglomerative clustering is a hierarchical tree structure called a "dendrogram," which illustrates graphically all fusions at successive similarity levels. Highly similar cases are joined at the earliest levels of fusion, while at the later levels the degree of mutual similarity diminishes. Once fusions occur, they are irrevocable. This distinguishes these methods from iterative relocation clustering, in which cases can be shuffled around to find a best fit. Since a full hierarchy is produced, the researcher must decide on the optimal vertical level of the hierarchy that fits his purposes. Thus the researcher must choose a level of abstraction (i.e., the number of classes).

The many variations in agglomerative hierarchical clustering stem from the different ways of linking cases and clusters together. The following overview of linkage strategies may be pertinent to criminologists since they each produce classifications with quite diverse structural characteristics.

"Single linkage" is sometimes called "nearest-neighbor" clustering or the "minimum-linkage" method (Johnson 1967). The linkage rule is that an object can join a cluster if it is more similar to "at least one member" of that cluster than to any member of any other cluster. Thus it need be linked to only one member of a cluster to gain membership. Two clusters can fuse together simply on the basis of their two closest members. Fusion, or joining, is very easy. Clusters grow rapidly and readily fuse together, creating loose, sprawling agglomerations.

The classes produced by this method are characterized more by the property of segregation from other classes than by high internal homogeneity (Cattell and Coulter 1966). The method has usually performed poorly in comparative studies of cluster methods and often fails to recover known structure from data (Milligan 1980). If intermediate or hybrid cases exist in a data set, they cause clusters to collapse easily into one another. This tendency of "chaining" is a major problem for single-link clustering. Given the noisy nature of much criminological data, this method may not be suitable for research in this field.

"Complete linkage" means that a case can join a cluster only if it is linked to "all existing members" of the cluster. This is a very stringent condition and forces the emerging clusters to be highly compact and homogeneous. Two clusters can join together only if all points in both clusters are linked together at the required similarity level. The most remote pair of points in the two clusters must be linked. Thus it is sometimes known as the "furthest-neighbor" method.

While single link is the weakest joining strategy, complete linkage is the most stringent. Criminologists seeking highly homogeneous, "compact" clusters in their data may find this method appropriate. For example, in the cartet-count approach used by Chaiken and Chaiken

(1984), the concept of class that is used by these researchers is similar to the complete-linkage approach. It would appear to be a useful alternative to the method used by Chaiken and Chaiken.

"Average linkage" is a strategy that is midway between the above two strategies in stringency. Conceptually, each cluster member must have a greater "average similarity" to the other members of that class than to all members of any other class. The distance between two clusters is defined as the average of the distances between all pairs of individuals in the two groups. The method may be important for criminologists since it seems to avoid some of the problems of single- and complete-linkage methods and has performed well in various comparative studies of clustering methods (Brennan 1980; Milligan 1980). It has been criticized, however, for imposing a spherical shape on clusters irrespective of their natural shape (Wishart 1969).

Ward's "minimum-variance method" joins cases and clusters on the basis of the loss of information resulting from their fusion (Everitt 1974). Ward (1963) proposed that the loss of information resulting from classifying cases together could be measured as the total sum of squared deviations of every point to the cluster in which it belongs. Fusions are thus selected between objects or clusters that produce the lowest increase in this error function. This method is important in that it has already had successful use in this field (Megargee and Bohn 1979) and has performed well in terms of recovery of known structure in many of the available Monte Carlo studies (Edelbrock 1979; Milligan 1980).[4] However, it has also been criticized for imposing a spherical structure, for insensitivity to natural boundaries between clusters, and for breaking up large clusters.

Other hierarchical clustering methods are available (e.g., McQuitty 1966). New methods originate frequently in other disciplines, but most remain untested on criminological problems. They require careful analysis to ascertain that their implicit definitions of "class" and "similarity" are consistent with criminological conceptions. They also require empirical evaluation and comparison against standard methods.

2. *Iterative Relocation Clustering: Partitioning Methods.* This family of methods offers an alternative to hierarchical clustering when data sets are large, as is often the case in criminological studies. A second advan-

---

[4] Monte Carlo studies are studies in which artificial or simulated data of a known structure are used for studying the performance and properties of a quantitative data analysis technique. Milligan (1980) provides a review of Monte Carlo studies used to evaluate and compare various cluster-analytic methods.

tage is that the initial placement of an object into a class can be corrected later if the early assignment is poor. Thus the method can correct its mistakes. The basic steps are as follows. (1) A set of trial cluster centers is chosen. (2) Each case in the sample is compared to these centers and assigned to the closest (most similar) center. (3) The centroids, or "central profiles," of the new classes are calculated and used as new cluster centers. (4) The similarity of each case to the new cluster centers is recomputed and cases reassigned to the nearest center. (5) This process is repeated until it converges on a partition where there are no further reassignments or where there is no further improvement in an algebraic function of the quality of the classification. A typical function indicating the quality of the achieved classification is the sum of squares from each point to its cluster center. Variations of this method stem from the many ways to choose the starting "trial" centers, the variety of algebraic functions that can be used to indicate good partitioning, and the treatment of nonclassifiable cases. Detailed treatments can be found in Anderberg (1973), Everitt (1974), and Hartigan (1975).

Many criminologists have used the well-known BCTry system of clustering (Tryon and Bailey 1970). This system contains an iterative clustering approach that uses a cartet-count method for selecting initial cluster partitions. Criminological illustrations are given by Hindelang and Weis (1972) in studying Eysenck's personality theory of criminality and in various typological studies of delinquency (Stein, Gough, and Sarbin 1966; Donovon 1977).

Iterative clustering has advantages and disadvantages. A major issue is that its conception of a "cluster" can be expected to impose specific shapes on data as it tries to minimize its clustering function. Most clustering functions impose shape constraints on clusters. These constraints may or may not be consistent with structures in the data or with preconceptions in the mind of the criminologist. There is no consensus regarding which algebraic function is most appropriate for behavioral classification studies (Everitt 1974). Another serious problem is that the method can "converge" on a "local minimum" solution. If new starting points are chosen, the method may converge on a new and different solution. Thus repeated trials with different starting points are usually prudent. However, the method fares well in comparative Monte Carlo studies against other clustering methods (Brennan 1980; Milligan 1980), particularly when realistic starting solutions are given to the method.

3. *Monothetic Division Methods.*   This class of methods uses repeated division of a sample to produce hierarchical monothetic classes. The most commonly used of these techniques in criminology have been predictive attribute analysis (PRED) and association analysis (Mac-Naughton-Smith 1965). Another well-known divisive method is the automatic interaction detector (AID). These create monothetic classes not known in advance that emerge from the structure of the data. Most monothetic methods are deliberately predictive in intent and may be regarded as useful substitutes for predictive methods such as multiple regression (Hartigan 1975). They have been intermittently used in criminology since the early papers by Ballard and Gottfredson (1963) and Wilkins and MacNaughton-Smith (1964). A recent example is provided by Flanagan (1983) in creating a classification to predict inmate misconduct within correctional institutions.

Advantages of monothetic divisive techniques are their sensitivity to complex interactions between variables, their avoidance of additive linear assumptions, and their simplicity. The a priori specification of complex interactions within multivariate data is often extremely difficult. Thus such methods appear to have much to offer by giving a systematic search for relevant interactions.

In monothetic division, classes are constructed by splitting a total sample using variables taken one at a time. The variable selected for splitting is that with the strongest relation to the criterion variable. In PRED this process involves the selection of the attribute with the largest chi-square or phi-coefficient with the criterion. In the AID, by contrast, the splitting rule aims to find the largest reduction in unexplained variance of the external criterion. It examines all attributes and many splitting points and finds the best combination of attribute and splitting point in terms of predicting the external criterion. Thus it avoids the rigid dichotomization of continuous variables at the mean or median used by PRED and is clearly a refinement of the latter method. In both methods the basic splitting logic is successively applied to give a divisive tree. All these methods have stopping rules to terminate the divisive process when the groups become too small or when no further significant associations are found with the criterion.

These methods are criticized for unreliability and instability of the divisive trees, overfitting to particular data sets, and fragmentation. For example, there may be many candidate variables for the first split with no clear differences in their degrees of association to the criterion variable. Yet one of them must be chosen, thus concealing other potentially important splits. Such arbitrariness can occur at any splitting point. Minor differences in data sets can thus produce quite different trees, for example, as between an initial and a cross-validation sample. The problem of "fragmentation" occurs when minor fragments of a class are repeatedly shaved off from the extremes of a large class. These may simply be outliers, or errors, yet they add confusion. Also, there are many different algebraic functions that can define the association between the predictors and the criterion variable. There is no consensus on which function or measure is best under which circumstances (Everitt 1974).

Some studies have compared the predictive power of divisive monothetic methods against standard techniques such as multiple regression and multidimensional contingency table analysis (Brennan and Huizinga 1975; van Alstyne and Gottfredson 1978; Gottfredson and Gottfredson 1979). The results suggest that divisive classification techniques do not have a clear advantage over conventional linear additive approaches. This is not surprising in the case of association analysis, which is basically a descriptive technique and was not developed as a predictive method. What is more surprising is the failure of methods such as PRED to outperform linear regression methods (Gottfredson and Gottfredson 1979). The AID, which is arguably the most advanced of the divisive methods, has seldom been used in these comparison studies. In the one study in which it was used, it performed somewhat better than did multiple regression methods (Brennan and Huizinga 1975).

4. *Ordination and Multidimensional Scaling Techniques.* Ordination and scaling techniques offer an alternative that is occasionally used to provide a dimensional mapping of criminological data. Ordinations do not create a classification but rather provide a dimensional space in which to view and map a sample. This may allow any clustering structure in the data to be eyeballed. An additional advantage is that they do not assume that clusters exist in the data. They provide a useful complement to methods that assume cluster structure. Gower's technique of principal coordinates, for example, has been used with success in criminology. Koller and Williams (1974) developed a delinquent typology and mapped this into a two-dimensional space using Gower's technique to illustrate the relations between the clusters. Sampson (1974) used the same technique to map prisoners into a two-dimensional space. Other forms of multidimensional scaling have been used for exploratory mapping of complex criminological domains to examine both dimensional and typological structures (Forgas 1979).

V. Toward a Strategic Framework for Quantitative
Classification in Criminology

The emergence of quantitative methods can upgrade the scientific quality of criminological classification. However, the risk of misuse or misinterpretation of these methods is high. The necessity of careful thought prior to conducting a classification study has been emphasized repeatedly (Cormack 1971; Skinner and Blashfield 1982). There is a compelling need for a research strategy to help ensure the productive use of the new techniques.

As yet there are few guidelines for the strategic use of multivariate classification methods in a criminological context. To minimize the production of spurious findings and poor-quality studies, some researchers have tried to articulate strategies to improve the quality of classification studies (e.g., Ball 1970; Anderberg 1973; Skinner 1981; Skinner and Blashfield 1982). This section attempts to incorporate these ideas into the criminological context and to make a start toward such a strategy for this discipline. The framework includes four main stages, each involving some subsidiary issues (see fig. 1).

This framework represents four interacting stages in creating a new classification system. Many studies simply apply one specific classification technique to one set of data and do little else. This is unsuitable for most research purposes since little reliability or validity can be claimed for the resulting classes. Several useful reviews of specific validation and consistency approaches are available (Blashfield and Draguns 1976; Dubes and Jain 1979; Skinner 1981; Blashfield, Aldenderfer, and Morey 1982).

A. Stage 1: The Attribute Space Problem: Choosing a Content Domain

The first step is to select a content domain of classificatory variables. This can influence the quality of the resulting classification as much as can any subsequent decision. Changes in variables can dramatically alter the typological structures.

1. *Theoretical Clarity versus Incoherence.* The "content domain" of variables can be theoretically coherent or simply an ad hoc mixture of variables. Many early offender classifications incoherently mixed behavior, social factors, demographic features, personality factors, and other variables (Roebuck 1971; Solomon 1977). Unfortunately, this approach has serious problems: variables are selected on a hunch or by intuition, and boundaries of the domain are delimited in a vague, atheoretical fashion. Also, diverse behavioral, social, and psychological

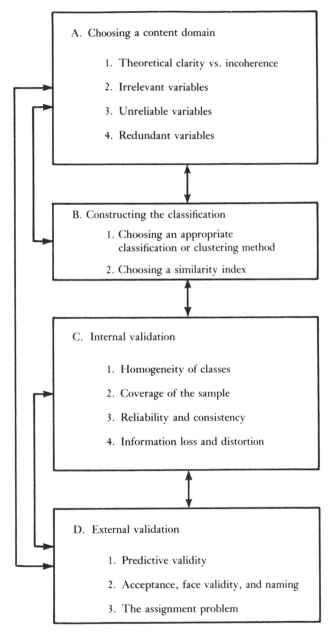

FIG. 1.—A procedural framework for classification research showing linkages between selection of method and interaction with substantive/theoretical context.

data may be lumped into a confusing mixture, and the resulting classification may have no clear focus.

The tendency to base typological studies on atheoretical and often incoherent mixtures of variables continues. This approach has problems other than incoherence, including a high likelihood of spurious findings, an endless stream of exploratory studies, and difficulty in relating one study to another. Innumerable classifications can be produced since an almost infinite number of classification variables can be specified. Confusion is also produced when numerous overlapping or alternate typologies are created by using different "mixes" of variables.

Some theoretical focus and delimitation or a specific purpose is required to select variables and limit boundaries. In this way, theory infuses and guides empirical classification. Both Toulmin (1953) and Enc (1976), in examining the mutual interaction between classifications and theory, emphasize the importance of selecting content domains by explicit reference to theoretical positions. We need a well-reasoned framework for integrating variables into content domains in a defensible manner. One possibility is the development of multiaxial classification (Mezzich 1979). A second may be a criminological analogue of the biopsychosocial framework offered by Engel (1977) for psychiatric and medical classification. New quantitative methods may improve the quality of our classifications, or the opportunity may be sabotaged by a morass of incoherent empirical classifications.

2. *Irrelevant Variables.* A related problem is that of irrelevant variables. Such variables are likely when using the above ad hoc approach. They can be devastating to classification work since they add "noise" and confusion and can "blur" boundaries between classes and thus obscure the presence of classes (Ball 1970; Milligan 1980). It appears that the recognition of classes in multivariate data is more difficult when discriminating variables are swamped by irrelevant variables. Unfortunately, the solution involves the paradox that one cannot obtain a good classification until one has good discriminating variables yet that one cannot assess discriminating power until the classification is available. Thus the building of a content domain is often a dynamic process that involves "bootstrapping," in which trial classifications are repeatedly evaluated to ascertain the discriminating power of variables (see Cattell and Coulter 1966; Friedman and Rubin 1968; and Hand 1981).

3. *Unreliable Variables.* Unreliable variables can also introduce errors that may blur boundaries and disguise or distort underlying

classes. Some quantitative methods are very susceptible to measurement error (Baker 1974; Brennan 1980; Milligan 1980). Single-link clustering methods perform less well than do complete-link methods with noisy data (Baker 1974). This is a serious issue since it is widely known that criminal justice data are not always reliable.

4. *Redundant Variables.* The inclusion of redundant or highly correlated variables in classification may overweight a single factor and introduce bias. For example, inmate security classifications often jointly include length of sentence, seriousness of offense, and expected time served among other variables. However, these are all logically and empirically correlated, and their joint inclusion will overweight the "current offense," which is triple weighted in the resulting classification. In a security context this overweighting may be sensible. However, such redundancy introduces implicit and often unknown bias.

The issue of redundancy and correlated variables has a long history in the classification literature (Cronbach and Gleser 1953). One solution is a preliminary factor analysis of the domain and the use of factors in the clustering analysis (Friedman and Rubin 1968). This clarifies the terms of reference of the domain and explicates underlying redundancy. It is useful in exploratory work when large numbers of variables are used. However, it must be acknowledged that there is no standard approach to this problem (Anderberg 1973).

B. Stage 2: Constructing the Classification

After the content domain has been selected, the next stage involves constructing the classification. Two issues need to be addressed, namely, deciding which method of classification should be selected and choosing a similarity index.

1. *Choosing an Appropriate Classification or Clustering Method.* The first critical decision is the selection of a method for categorizing cases. This is tantamount to deciding on the structural form of a "class" for empirical classifications. Each classification method contains a structural definition of a "type" embedded in its mathematics and in its algorithm. Decisions must be made to choose between full hierarchical agglomerative models, partitioning models, monothetic devisive models, and ordination techniques. The choice can be very difficult. The chosen method and class structure must be consistent with implications of criminological theory and with the form of data being used. For example, what form of "class" is appropriate when searching for typologies of criminal behavior? How much internal homogeneity should

be expected? Does current explanatory theory suggest very compact classes, or loose, diverse criminal tendencies, or both? Does current theory suggest overlapping membership in types? Does theory suggest that boundaries between types are disjoint or fuzzy? Few of these questions have yet been addressed.

Criminological theory must be examined for its implications regarding such questions. Theoretical guidance is critically required in selecting appropriate classification methods as well as in selecting variables. However, the analysis of criminological theory to clarify its implications for classification has hardly begun. This has caused havoc in criminological research, particularly in studies of crime specialization and career criminal research. Meehl (1979) recently discussed this problem in the area of psychiatric classification and noted that clustering algorithms ought not to be "arbitrarily concocted but should reflect our conjectures, however primitive, about the underlying causal structure" (p. 572). Criminology has neglected this challenge and has paid the consequences. Currently, there are few guidelines for choosing appropriate definitions of "class" or "type." If compact homogeneous classes are implied by causal theory, then techniques sensitive to such structures must be used. If theory implies loose orientations, then methods that can recover these structures are more appropriate. The selected method must be consistent with both theory and data. A method such as Ward's (1963) minimum-variance technique may be quite useful in recovering spherical minimum-variance classes, but it is completely incapable of recovering straggly modal or overlapping clusters. The requirement of some consistency between the structural form of a "class" that is embedded in the method, that is, contained in the data, and the form that is implied by theory is important. If a classification method uses an embedded concept of a "type" that has no relation to that implied by theory or that is at odds with that implied by the theory, there will be much waste of time and manpower.

2. *Choosing a Similarity Index.* Assessments of similarity can be a critical building step in classification. In criminological research to date, only two similarity coefficients have received substantial use. These are the Euclidean distance coefficient and the correlation coefficient. Yet an enormous number of alternative coefficients exist, each with different properties and with different ways of emphasizing the various components of similarity (Cronbach and Gleser 1953; Everitt 1974; Fox 1982).

The issue of appropriateness of different similarity coefficients has virtually been ignored in criminology. Yet the selected similarity approach must also be consistent with the assumptions of theory and the nature of the data. One of the few studies of similarity within a criminological context demonstrated that a change in the similarity coefficient could dramatically alter the results of a classification even though the same data and the same method of clustering were used (Brennan 1980). This is consistent with findings of researchers in other disciplines (Jardine and Sibson 1971; Fox 1982).

An important distinction should be drawn between a "pattern of criminality" (which may be described by the shape of an offender's profile of scores) and the "severity" of the profile of scores (which may be described by the general elevation of the scores of the individual). Two offenders may have the same "pattern" (e.g., both drug dealing and theft), yet one may indulge only a few times per year, while the other may indulge hundreds of times per year. The correlation coefficient emphasizes pattern and would not distinguish between these, while the distance coefficient is sensitive to both pattern and elevation and would probably separate these cases into subtypes (Cronbach and Gleser 1953; Brennan 1980; Skinner 1981). Thus the use of the correlation coefficient in classification studies may be hazardous if severity is an important issue. Criminological classification must be sensitive to the elements of similarity that are being emphasized. This requires guidance from our theories and a clear articulation of the purpose of the analysis.

C. Stage 3: Internal Validation

Once a classification has been developed, evidence of certain important internal properties is needed. The following structural properties should be examined as a routine part of an internal validation of a new classification.

1. *Homogeneity of Classes.* This is strongly influenced by the kind of classification technique used. Single-linkage methods produce weak, loosely linked classes, while complete-linkage methods can produce only tight, compact classes. Evidence should be presented on the levels of internal cohesion of each class across all classificatory variables.

2. *Coverage of the Sample.* What proportion of the sample is left unclassified? When loose heterogeneous classes are allowed, a larger proportion of the sample will be classified, and vice versa. Coverage is to some extent a function of the classification method. For example, an approach such as complete linkage will often leave a large proportion of

cases unclassified because the classes cannot meet the stringent joining criteria. As joining criteria are relaxed, coverage will increase.

3. *Reliability and Consistency.* Some test of reliability is a necessary component of internal validation. Do the same types emerge when a sample of similar individuals is used? One frequent approach to this question is to conduct split-sample studies in which both halves of the sample are separately classified and the resulting solutions compared. Another question is whether minor changes in the method will produce the same classification structure. For example, in the iterative relocation method it is usually wise to repeat an analysis using different initial starting solutions and to test whether the same classes emerge (Ball 1970; Everitt 1974). A large literature exists on coefficients to express the stability of classifications emerging either from the same data set or from separate samples using the same variables (Milligan 1980).

4. *Information Loss and Distortion.* All classification involves the deletion of selected information about unique cases. Various coefficients have been developed to assess the loss of information that results from a particular classification, that is, the difference between the total information contained in the raw data and the information retained by the classification. A useful evaluation approach is to assess this distortion with one of the many coefficients available (Blashfield, Aldenderfer, and Morey 1982).

D. Stage 4: External Validation

The next stage involves establishing the external validity of the classification. This is accomplished by assessing the relation between the classification and other variables that were not used in its construction. Such variables may be related to long-term outcomes of treatment programs, recidivism rates, effects of punishments, or differential treatment effects. Thus external validation is critically related to the prognostic uses of a classification, its decision-making utility, and its general practical and predictive usefulness.

1. *Predictive Validity.* Most uses of classification within the criminal justice system demand a strong relation between a classification and those particular behaviors that it purports to predict (escape, suicide, and treatment outcomes). A related aspect of predictive validity is the ability of the classification to suggest how a particular offender may react to different treatment modalities. A serious challenge to classification in criminology is that predictive validity has consistently been lacking in many areas of application (Hood and Sparks 1970; Monahan

1981). However, since most early work used inadequate classification methods, poor predictive validity would be expected.

2. *Acceptance, Face Validity, and Naming.*   An important problem for classification research is its acceptance by practitioners. Predictive validity will help in achieving acceptance by practitioners. Yet acceptance is contingent also on the presence of coherent interpretations of the classes and a clear nomenclature, on the face validity of the system, on its consistency with the intuitive experience of the practitioner, and on effective decision-making implications of the classification for the practitioner. Much of this responsibility is on the original developer of a new classification. Yet such tasks are frequently given only cursory attention.

3. *The Assignment Problem.*   When criminological classification remained at the level of subjective, abstract systems, assignments could not be made objectively. Misclassification of offenders into inappropriate classes could easily occur on the basis of bias, inadequate information, and so forth. Objective classifications give a foundation on which objective assignment techniques can be developed. This essay has emphasized methods to achieve improved empirical classifications since these are obviously a preliminary requirement. Yet misclassification can easily occur at the assignment stage even with very good objective classifications being used as the reference system. Important issues when considering the assignment problem are (1) increased information content, (2) the need for diagnostic criteria, and (3) the use of computerized and quantitative assignment methods.

First, if classifications consist of a few variables and simple cutoff scores to designate membership, the assignment task is simple. The monothetic divisive trees represent an easy assignment task since few variables are involved and assignment rules are few and explicit. However, with the increased information content of polythetic classification, assignment is much more complex and may require computerized methods: it is well known that human beings have a limited ability to process a large amount of information. With the more recent multivariate classifications such as those of Megargee and Bohn (1979), there may be great advantage in using quantitative assignment methods. For classification with high information content, continued reliance on subjective assignment would, in all likelihood, introduce serious inconsistency and higher misclassification rates as well as being impractical.

Second, efficient assignment requires clear, reliably measured, and valid criteria for assigning new cases. Without such criteria, assignment is virtually impossible. It is amazing that many of those offering new classification systems in criminology could ignore this requirement for so long.[5]

Since the direction of criminological classification is toward more complexity, more information, and more refined subdivisions, much more attention needs to be paid to the provision of very well validated diagnostic criteria.

A large literature exists regarding computerized and quantitative assignment methods, that is, discriminant methods and nearest-neighbor methods for identifying the "true" membership of an unknown case within an existing objective classification (Lachenbruch 1975; Hand 1981). However, much of this work has been done in other disciplines. These methods can use the data and dimensions of an existing empirical classification to give mathematical assignment rules for assigning unknown cases into the classification.

A review and evaluation of these methods for use in criminological classification has recently been published (Brennan and Camilli 1982). It demonstrated that, given an accurate, well-defined initial classification, standard techniques (e.g., linear discriminant or the K-nearest-neighbor methods) can be accurate and robust. A majority of new cases can be correctly assigned. However, accuracy of assignment breaks down rapidly as the quality of the reference classification is diminished through unreliable variables, poor class separation, or progressive violation of the assumptions of the assignment methods. This is a critical finding since an examination of many of the new empirical classifications being developed by criminologists (McGurk 1978; Donovon and Marlatt 1982) will indicate that they are generally characterized by such inadequate structures. Thus perfectly accurate assignment using quantitative methods may remain elusive. More basic research needs to be directed at the problem of using such quantitative assignment methods within the context of real-world, nonoptimal classification structures used in criminal justice settings.

Shortcomings in the reference classifications may continue to frustrate quantitative assignment techniques even though steady improvements are occurring. Technological breakthroughs in quantitative as-

[5] Criminology is not alone in overlooking this critical task. Medical classification left much of the international classification of disease in "shambles" because of inconsistency in the use of criteria and nomenclature. Medical diagnoses were improved by the eventual introduction of well-defined diagnostic criteria.

signment do not seem to be necessary. Available techniques can be effective if there is a reliable and valid objective classification to work with. The major area in which improvement seems to be urgent is in the initial development of improved objective classifications.

VI. Conclusion

The literature on classification methodology has increased substantially in the last decade. Most of these developments did not originate in criminology and are not frequently used or well understood by most criminologists. However, these developments are clearly entering into criminal justice research and practice (Megargee and Bohn 1979; Gottfredson and Gottfredson 1979).

Cross-disciplinary transfer of methodological concepts can be hazardous. The production of spurious and misleading results is a serious danger. In conducting classification research, an analyst must make many methodological choices. These include such things as the choice of input variables, transformations, similarity coefficients, and a clustering or classification method. Guidance in making many of these decisions is often lacking. For example, there are now over 100 new cluster-analytic techniques available, and there remain many unsolved problems in their use. The critical concepts of "cluster" and "similarity" embedded in these methods have yet to be clearly related to a criminological context. There is no agreement on the best criteria of optimality for clustering or ordination to represent patterns of similarity between objects in a sample with a minimum of distortion. Problems persist in regard to tests of significance for clusters. Yet applied reseachers in most fields have not waited for theoretical and mathematical answers to these problems and have aggressively used these techniques. A critical challenge, therefore, is to learn how to incorporate these powerful quantitative techniques into criminology in a manner that solves rather than creates problems.

A danger is that the easy availability of computer algorithms may encourage thoughtless or inappropriate use of complex classification methods to produce a confusing mass of nonconverging and perhaps artificial empirical typologies. Skinner (1981) notes that too often an available clustering algorithm is thoughtlessly applied to a convenient data set as an end in itself. Earlier, Cormack (1971) condemned the growing tendency to regard numerical taxonomy as a "satisfactory alternative to clear thinking." The results of this approach could be disastrous for criminological research. The fragmented and confusing production of numerous theoretically generated typological systems has already created much disorder in this field (Ferdinand 1966), and this should not be repeated with quantitative classifications. Fortunately, researchers are becoming more wary of the blind use of classification techniques. The danger of spurious findings and the results of many of the Monte Carlo studies have demonstrated the difficult problems faced by the user in applied situations.

Only a few criminological researchers have actively conducted comparative evaluative study of some of these new methods on the problems and data of criminology (van Alstyne and Gottfredson 1978; Gottfredson and Gottfredson 1979; Brennan 1980). We remain, unfortunately, in a situation where there is a need for comparative evaluative studies using a greater variety of classification techniques and data types. For example, the extensive studies of Gottfredson and Gottfredson (1979), which evaluated various divisive monothetic classification methods in a context of parole-success prediction, did not include the AID method of Sonquist and Morgan (1963), which is arguably the most powerful of the monothetic predictive techniques. Fortunately, many workers in a number of closely related disciplines (including psychiatry, medicine, and business and marketing) are also conducting comparative studies of new classification methods on a variety of data types and are thus aiding this evaluative task (e.g., Golden and Meehl 1980; Milligan 1980). Such studies have given useful guidelines on the qualities and performance of the different methods. Yet we still have insufficient comparative data and theoretical guidance to say with certainty which method is best for which particular classification problem. Until such guidance is available, applied researchers must pay special attention to reliability and stability problems and may be advised to conduct cross-method and split-sample reliability studies. Milligan (1980) has recently suggested that the relative success of certain clustering algorithms (e.g., Ward's minimum-variance method and the group-average method) may make them useful candidates for inclusion in comparative studies of methods since they have shown relatively good cluster recovery in several evaluations and may provide standards for comparison.

To upgrade the scientific quality of criminological classification, a methodological framework for classification studies is urgently required. The latter part of this essay has outlined the features of such a framework that would encourage much more attention to be paid to validation and reliability studies in new classification research.

REFERENCES

Anderberg, M. R. 1973. *Cluster Analysis for Applications*. New York: Academic Press.

Ashby, W. R. 1956. "Self-Regulation and Requisite Variety." In *Systems Thinking*, pt. 2, edited by F. E. Emery. London: Penguin.

Baer, Daniel J. 1970. "Taxonomic Classification of Male Delinquents from Autobiographical Data and Subsequent Recidivism." *Journal of Psychology* 76:27–31.

Baker, F. B. 1974. "Stability of Two Hierarchical Grouping Techniques: Case 1: Sensitivity to Data Errors." *Journal of the American Statistical Association* 69:440–45.

Ball, G. H. 1970. *Classification Analysis*. Menlo Park, Calif.: Stanford Research Institute.

Ballard, K. B., and D. M. Gottfredson. 1963. *Predictive Attribute Analysis and Prediction of Parole Performance*. Vacaville: California Medical Facility.

Beker, J., and D. S. Hyman. 1972. "A Critical Appraisal of the California Differential Treatment Typology of Adolescent Offenders." *Criminology* 10:1–59.

Blackburn, R. 1971. "Personality Types among Abnormal Homicides." *British Journal of Criminology* 11:14–31.

Blashfield, R. K., M. S. Aldenderfer, and L. C. Morey. 1982. "Validating a Cluster Analytic Solution." In *Classifying Social Data*, edited by H. C. Hudson and Associates. San Francisco: Jossey-Bass.

Blashfield, R. K., and J. G. Draguns. 1976. "Evaluative Criteria for Psychiatric Classification." *Journal of Abnormal Psychology* 85:140–50.

Bohnstedt, M., and S. Geiser. 1979. *Classification Instruments for Criminal Justice Decisions*. Washington, D.C.: National Institute of Corrections.

Bottoms, A. E. 1973. "Methodological Aspects of Classification in Criminology." In *Collected Studies in Criminological Research: Methodological Aspects of Classification in Criminology*. Vol. 10. Strasbourg: Council of Europe.

Boulding, K. E. 1980. "Science: Our Common Heritage." *Science* 207:831–36.

Brennan, T. 1980. *Multivariate Taxonomic Classification for Criminal Justice Research*. Report prepared for the National Institute of Justice. Washington, D.C.: U.S. Government Printing Office.

Brennan, T., and G. Camilli. 1982. *Evaluation of Objective Assignment Techniques for Criminal Justice Classification*. Report prepared for the National Institute of Justice. Washington, D.C.: U.S. Government Printing Office.

Brennan, T., and D. Huizinga. 1975. *Theory Validation and Aggregate National Data*. Vol. 12. Final report to the Office of Youth Development. Boulder, Colo.: Behavioral Research Institute.

Brennan, T., D. Huizinga, and D. S. Elliott. 1978. *The Social Psychology of Runaways*. Lexington, Mass.: Lexington.

Butler, E. W., and S. W. Adams. 1966. "Typologies of Delinquent Girls: Some Alternative Approaches." *Social Forces* 44:401–7.

Carlson, K. A. 1981. "A Modern Personality Test for Offenders." *Criminal Justice and Behavior* 8:185–200.

244   Tim Brennan

Carroll, J. M. 1980. "'Purpose' in a Cognitive Theory of Reference." *Bulletin of the Psychonomic Society* 16:37–40.

Cattell, R. B. 1965. *The Scientific Analysis of Personality*. Baltimore: Penguin.

Cattell, R. B., and M. A. Coulter. 1966. "Principles of Behavioral Taxonomy and the Mathematical Basis of the Taxonome Computer Program." *British Journal of Mathematical and Statistical Psychology* 19:237–69.

Chaiken, M. R., and J. M. Chaiken. 1984. "Offender Types and Public Policy." *Crime and Delinquency* 30:195–226.

Cloward, R. C., and L. E. Ohlin. 1969. "Types of Delinquent Sub-cultures." In *Juvenile Delinquency*, edited by Ruth Cavan. Philadelphia: Lippincott.

Cormack, R. M. 1971. "A Review of Classification." *Journal of the Royal Statistical Society* 134:321–67.

Cronbach, L. J., and G. Gleser. 1953. "Assessing Similarity between Profiles." *Psychological Bulletin* 50:456–73.

Daudistel, H. C., W. B. Sanders, and D. F. Luckenbill. 1979. *Criminal Justice: Situations and Decisions*. New York: Holt, Rinehart & Winston.

Donovan, J. E. 1977. "A Typological Study of Self-reported Deviance in a National Sample." Ph.D. dissertation, University of Colorado, Department of Psychology.

Donovon, D. M., and A. Marlatt. 1982. "Personality Sub-types among Driving-while-intoxicated Offenders." *Journal of Consulting and Clinical Psychology* 50:241–49.

Dubes, R., and A. K. Jain. 1979. "Validity Studies in Clustering Methodologies." *Pattern Recognition* 11:235–54.

Dunford, F. W., and D. S. Elliott. 1984. "Identifying Career Offenders Using Self-reported Data." *Journal of Research in Crime and Delinquency* 21:57–86.

Edelbrock, C. 1979. "Mixture Model Tests of Hierarchical Clustering: The Problem of Classifying Everybody." *Multivariate Behavioral Research* 14:367–84.

Elliott, D. S., F. W. Dunford, and D. Huizinga. 1985. "The Identification of Career Offenders Utilizing Self-reported and Official Data." In *Prevention of Antisocial and Delinquent Behavior*, edited by J. D. Burchard and S. N. Burchard. Washington, D.C.: U.S. Government Printing Office.

Enc, B. 1976. "Spiral Dependence between Theories and Taxonomy." *Inquiry* 19:41–71.

Engel, G. L. 1977. "The Need for a New Medical Model: A Challenge for Biomedicine." *Science* 196:129–96.

Everitt, B. S. 1974. *Cluster Analysis*. London: Heinemann.

Eynon, T. G. 1975. "New Roles of Research in Classification and Treatment." In *Correctional Classification and Treatment: A Reader*, edited by the W. H. Anderson Company. Cincinnati: W. H. Anderson Co.

Ferdinand, T. N. 1966. *Typologies of Delinquency: A Critical Analysis*. New York: Random House.

Fildes, R., and D. M. Gottfredson. 1973. "Cluster Analysis in a Parole Sample." *Journal of Research in Crime and Delinquency* 9:2–11.

Flanagan, T. J. 1983. "Correlates of Institutional Misconduct among State Prisoners." *Criminology* 21:29–39.

Forgas, J. P. 1979. "Multidimensional Scaling: A Discovery Method in Social Psychology." In *Emerging Strategies in Social Psychology*, edited by G. P. Ginsberg. London: Wiley.

Fox, J. 1982. "Selected Aspects of Measuring Resemblance for Taxonomy." In *Classifying Social Data*, edited by H. C. Hudson and Associates. San Francisco: Jossey-Bass.

Friedman, H. P., and J. Rubin. 1968. "Logic of Statistical Procedures." In *The Borderline Syndrome*, edited by R. R. Grinker. New York: Basic.

Garside, R. F., and M. Roth. 1978. "Multivariate Statistical Methods and Problems of Classification in Psychiatry." *British Journal of Psychiatry* 133:53–67.

Gibbons, D. C. 1973. *Society, Crime and Criminal Careers*. Englewood Cliffs, N.J.: Prentice-Hall.

———. 1975. "Offender Typologies—Two Decades Later." *British Journal of Criminology* 15:140–56.

Gibbs, J. P. 1960. "Needed: Analytic Typologies in Criminology." *Southwestern Social Science Quarterly* 40:321–29.

Glaser, D. 1972. *Adult Crime and Social Policy*. Englewood Cliffs, N.J.: Prentice-Hall.

———. 1974. "The Classification of Offenses and Offenders." In *Handbook of Criminology*, edited by D. Glaser. Chicago: Rand McNally.

Golden, R. R., and P. E. Meehl. 1980. "Detection of Biological Sex: An Empirical Test of Cluster Methods." *Multivariate Behavioral Research* 15:475–96.

Gottfredson, D. M. 1975. "Diagnosis, Classification and Prediction." In *Decision-Making in the Criminal Justice System*, edited by D. M. Gottfredson. Washington D.C.: U.S. Government Printing Office.

Gottfredson, D. M., K. B. Ballard, and L. Lane. 1963. *Association Analysis in a Prison Sample and Prediction of Parole Performance*. Vacaville, Calif.: Institute for the Study of Crime and Delinquency.

Gottfredson, G. D. 1975. "Organizing Crime: A Classificatory Scheme Based on Offense Transitions." *Journal of Criminal Justice* 3:321–32.

Gottfredson, S. D., and D. M. Gottfredson. 1979. *Screening for Risk: A Comparison of Methods*. Washington, D.C.: National Institute of Corrections.

Green, B. F. 1980. "Three Decades of Quantitative Methods in Psychology." *American Behavioral Scientist* 23:811–34.

Greenwood, P. W., with A. Abrahamse. 1982. *Selective Incapacitation*. Report no. R-2815-NIJ. Santa Monica, Calif.: Rand.

Hand, D. J. 1981. *Discrimination and Classification*. New York: Wiley.

Hartigan, J. A. 1975. *Clustering Algorithms*. New York: Wiley.

Hindelang, M. J., and J. G. Weis. 1972. "The BCTry Cluster and Factor Analysis System: Personality and Self-reported Delinquency." *Criminology* 10:286–94.

Hood, R., and R. F. Sparks. 1970. *Key Issues in Criminology*. New York: McGraw-Hill.

Hudson, H. C. 1982. *Classifying Social Data*. San Francisco: Jossey-Bass.

Jardine, N., and R. Sibson. 1971. *Mathematical Taxonomy*. London: Wiley.

Johnson, D. L., J. G. Simmons, and B. C. Gordon. 1983. "Temporal Consistency of the Meyer-Megargee Inmate Typology." *Criminal Justice and Behavior* 10:262–68.

Johnson, S. C. 1967. "Hierarchical Clustering Schemes." *Psychometrika* 32:241–54.

Kinch, J. W. 1962. "Continuities in the Study of Delinquent Types." *Journal of Criminal Law, Criminology and Police Science* 53:323–28.

Koller, K. M., and W. T. Williams. 1974. "Early Parental Deprivation and Later Behavioral Outcomes: Cluster Analysis Study of Normal and Abnormal Groups." *Australian and New Zealand Journal of Psychiatry* 8:89–96.

Kozelka, R. M. 1982. "How to Work through a Clustering Problem." In *Classifying Social Data*, edited by H. C. Hudson and Associates. San Francisco: Jossey-Bass.

Lachenbruch, P. A. 1975. *Discriminant Analysis*. New York: Haffner Press.

Levinson, R. B. 1982. "A Clarification of Classification." *Criminal Justice and Behavior* 9:133–42.

Lipsky, M. 1980. *Street-Level Bureaucracy*. New York: Russell Sage.

Lorr, M. 1983. *Cluster Analysis for Social Scientists: Analysing and Simplifying Complex Blocks of Data*. San Francisco: Jossey-Bass.

McGurk, B. J. 1978. "Personality Types among 'Normal' Homicides." *British Journal of Criminology* 18:146–63.

MacNaughton-Smith, P. 1965. *Some Statistical and Other Numerical Techniques for Classifying Individuals*. London: H.M. Stationery Office.

McQuitty, L. L. 1966. "Similarity Analysis by Reciprocal Pairs for Discrete and Continuous Data." *Educational and Psychological Measurement* 26:825–31.

Meehan, E. J. 1968. *Explanation in Social Science: A System Paradigm*. Homewood, Ill.: Dorsey Press.

Meehl, P. E. 1979. "A Funny Thing Happened to Us on the Way to the Latent Entities." *Journal of Personality Assessment* 43:564–77.

Megargee, E. I., and M. J. Bohn. 1979. *Classifying Criminal Offenders*. Beverly Hills, Calif.: Sage.

Merton, R. K. 1964. *Social Theory and Social Structure*. New York: Free Press.

Mezzich, J. E. 1979. "Patterns and Issues in Multiaxial Psychiatric Diagnosis." *Psychological Medicine* 9:125–37.

Milligan, G. W. 1980. "An Examination of the Effect of Six Types of Error Perturbation on Fifteen Clustering Algorithms." *Psychometrika* 45:325–41.

Mischel, W. 1979. "On the Interface between Cognition and Personality." *American Psychologist* 34:740–54.

Monahan, J. 1981. *Predicting Violent Behavior: An Assessment of Clinical Techniques*. Beverly Hills, Calif.: Sage.

Mrad, D. F., R. Kabacoff, and P. Duckro. 1983. "Validation of the Megargee Typology in a Halfway House Setting." *Criminal Justice and Behavior* 10:252–62.

Opp, K. D. 1973. "Problems of Classification in Criminology." In *Collected Studies in Criminological Research: Methodological Aspects of Classification in Criminology*, edited by the Council of Europe. Strasbourg: Council of Europe.

Prottas, J. M. 1979. *People-Processing*. Lexington, Mass.: Lexington.

Roberts, J. M., M. D. Williams, and G. C. Poole. 1982. "Used Car Domain: An Ethnographic Application of Clustering and Multidimensional Scaling." In *Classifying Social Data*, edited by H. C. Hudson and Associates. San Francisco: Jossey-Bass.

Roebuck, J. B. 1971. *Criminal Typology*. Springfield, Ill.: Thomas.

Rosch, E. 1978. "Principles of Categorization." In *Cognition and Categorization*, edited by E. Rosch and B. B. Lloyd. Hillsdale, N.J.: Erlbaum.

Sampson, A. 1974. "Post-prison Success Prediction." *Criminology* 12:155–73.

Schafer, S. 1969. *Theories of Criminology*. New York: Random House.

Schrag, C. C. 1959. "Preliminary Criminal Typology." Paper presented at the meeting of the American Sociological Association, Chicago, September.

Shannon, L. 1981. *Assessing the Relationship of Adult Criminal Careers to Juvenile Delinquency: A Study of Three Birth Cohorts*. Iowa City: University of Iowa, Iowa Urban Community Research Center.

Shepard, R. N. 1974. "Representation of Structure in Similarity Data: Problems and Prospects." *Psychometrika* 39:373–421.

Skinner, H. A. 1981. "Towards the Integration of Classification Theory and Methods." *Journal of Abnormal Psychology* 90:68–71.

Skinner, H., and R. K. Blashfield. 1982. "Increasing the Impact of Cluster Analysis Research: The Case of Psychiatric Classification." *Journal of Consulting and Clinical Psychology* 50:727–35.

Sneath, P. H. A., and R. R. Sokal. 1973. *Numerical Taxonomy*. San Francisco: W. H. Freeman.

Sokal, R. R. 1964. "The Future Systematics." In *Taxonomic Biochemistry and Serology*, edited by C. A. Leone. New York: Ronald.

———. 1974. "Classification: Purposes, Principles, Progress, Prospects." *Science* 185:1115–23.

Sokal, R. R., and P. H. A. Sneath. 1963. *Principles of Numerical Taxonomy*. San Francisco: W. H. Freeman.

Solomon, H. M. 1977. *Crime and Delinquency: Typologies*. Washington, D.C.: University Press of America.

Sonquist, J. A., and J. N. Morgan. 1963. "The Problems in the Analysis of Survey Data, and a Proposal." In *The Detection of Interaction Effects*, edited by J. Sonquist. Ann Arbor: University of Michigan Press.

Stein, K. B., H. G. Gough, and T. R. Sarbin. 1966. "The Dimensionality of the CPI Socialization Scale and an Empirically Derived Typology among Delinquent and Non-delinquent Boys." *Multivariate Behavioral Research* 1:197–208.

Toulmin, S. 1953. *The Philosophy of Science*. New York: Harper & Row.

Tryon, R. C., and D. E. Bailey. 1970. *Cluster Analysis*. New York: McGraw-Hill.

van Alstyne, D., and M. Gottfredson. 1978. "A Multidimensional Contingency Table Analysis of Parole Outcome." *Journal of Research in Crime and Delinquency* 15:172–93.

Ward, J. H., Jr. 1963. "Hierarchical Grouping to Optimize an Objective Function." *Journal of the American Statistical Association* 58:236–44.

Warren, M. Q. 1966. *Interpersonal Maturity Level Classification*. Sacramento: California Youth Authority, Community Treatment Project.

———. 1971. "Classification of Offenders as an Aid to Efficient Management and Effective Treatment." *Journal of Criminal Law, Criminology and Police Science* 62:239–68.

Wilkins, L. T., and P. MacNaughton-Smith. 1964. "New Prediction and Classification Methods in Criminology." *Journal of Research in Crime and Delinquency* 1:19–33.

Williams, W. T. 1971. "Principles of Clustering." *Annual Review of Ecology and Systematics* 2:303.

Williams, W. T., and M. B. Dale. 1964. "Fundamental Problems in Numerical Taxonomy." *Advances in Botanical Research* 2:35–68.

Wishart, D. 1969. "A Numerical Classification Method for Deriving Natural Classes." *Science* 221:97–98.

Wolfgang, M. E., R. M. Figlio, and T. Sellin. 1972. *Delinquency in a Birth Cohort*. Chicago: University of Chicago Press.

Zager, L. D. 1983. "Conclusions about the MMPI-based Classification System's Stability Are Premature." *Criminal Justice and Behavior* 10:310–15.

Daniel Glaser

Classification for Risk

ABSTRACT

Officials assessing the risks to be taken with alleged or convicted offenders have traditionally been guided only by their subjective deliberations on each case. Subcultural norms shape such risk determinations, and psychological processes result in the decision makers judging carelessly or in a biased fashion but being overconfident about the wisdom of their decisions. Statistical tabulations that provided ways of identifying relative risk from past experience were extolled at first as remedies for the defects of subjective risk assessment. They were not much used in criminal justice agencies, however, until they were developed collaboratively by researchers and officials, and they dealt not only with risk assessment but also with other central concerns in the decisions for which they were employed. They now have very diverse forms and applications but are not used nearly as much or as well as they could be.

Criminal justice officials make innumerable types of decisions that determine the fates of individuals. Important examples include the decisions to arrest, book, charge, prosecute, release on recognizance, convict, grant probation, incarcerate, place in a less-than-maximum-security prison, parole, and, for those on probation or parole, supervise very closely. One factor in most of these decisions is an assessment of the risk that the suspected, accused, or convicted person will commit new offenses or otherwise misbehave. Officially, risk considerations are not supposed to enter into some of these judgments such as that to convict, but in the informal practices of our overloaded and plea bar-

Daniel Glaser is professor of sociology and senior research associate of the Social Science Research Institute of the University of Southern California. Lawrence Bennett, Leslie T. Wilkins, Norman Holt, James Beck, and the editors of this volume helped to improve this essay.

gain–directed justice system, there is virtually no type of decision that assessments of risk do not sometimes affect.

Repeatedly for centuries, the process of evaluating risks in dealing with alleged or convicted offenders has come under much scrutiny. This attention is usually a reaction to violent crimes by a releasee, but it may also be evoked by evidence of excessive restraint imposed on persons who were patently not dangerous. Increasingly in recent decades, social scientists have systematically studied how risk is assessed in practice and have proposed new ways of estimating relative dangerousness. These suggestions have been followed in many places but sometimes in a manner quite different from what social scientists endorse.

In this essay, Section I discusses the traditional process of risk assessment in criminal justice agencies and its problems. Section II describes efforts to improve this process by various types of formal devices and procedures (now usually called decision guidelines) and analyzes some of the issues that they raise. Section III examines applications of guidelines in granting release on recognizance, in deciding whom to prosecute or to prosecute with extra resources, in sentencing, in classifying prisoners for custodial security, in parole, in community supervision decisions, and in evaluation research. Section IV concludes with a discussion of prospects and possibilities for decision guidelines in criminal justice.

I. Traditional Subjective Decision Making

Most of the types of decisions listed in the opening paragraph of this essay are made subjectively, in the sense that they involve no overt listing of pros and cons and no explicit formula in weighting these factors. This is sometimes called intuitive, or clinical, decision making. The person who must decide simply mulls over the factors that seem relevant, including those pertinent to assessing risk, and reaches a decision.

In subjective assessments of risk, deliberation is often protracted, for example, when the choice among alternative possible actions seems important but difficult and when there is no rush. Yet it may be brief or almost instantaneous if the problem seems routine or if immediate action is necessary. If any thought is involved at all, however, the process of decision making is amenable to psychological and sociological analysis that can be useful both for understanding its limitations and for improving it.

A. The Process of Deliberation on Risks

Deliberation sometimes seems to be an overt process that is observable by others. This occurs, for example, whenever there is a protracted but calm and thorough discussion that clearly produces an interchange of ideas and of reactions to them by different people but that culminates in their collectively developing consensus on one shared idea, judgment, or decision. Such separate yet shared thinking is evident when a committee or other deliberative group seems to be "highly productive" as it reaches complete agreement or when an individual decision maker seems to benefit from consulting with others before making up his or her mind.

These decisive conversations seem to involve "collective" thinking. Yet a major school of social psychology, symbolic interactionism, conceives of individual thought also as a process of conversation. Thinking, from this perspective, is a process of covert—that is, imaginary—conversing with oneself and with specific or generalized other persons (Mead 1934; Stryker 1980). From this perspective, which the author shares, unless a decision is purely a reflex action, it is always the terminating stage of a subjective conversation in the mind of one person. This internal discourse occurs when deliberating, whether as a member of a group that reaches consensus, as part of a group with differences of opinion, or as someone who is acting completely alone. Sometimes, private thought is even audible to others, as when persons are overheard talking to themselves and they explain that they were "just thinking aloud."

Risk assessments always involve case classification since the person about whom a judgment must be made is implicitly or explicitly equated with others in a more or less clearly conceived group who are categorized as relatively safe or dangerous individuals. This process becomes audible and observable in discussions among police, court, or correctional officials about what risks to take with someone.

Of course, considerations other than risk also enter into most criminal justice agency decisions. These considerations may include the time or cost of alternative actions, probable public reactions, and abstract notions of just deserts for a particular offense. Yet risks of future danger from the decision that must be made are almost always considered also.

What is the process of deliberation involved in assessing risks when making subjective decisions on the separate cases of a criminal justice agency? What are its problems and pitfalls? Are there alternative ways of assessing risks that may alleviate these problems?

B. Subcultures in Routine Risk Classification

In an article that has become a classic to sociologists of law, David Sudnow (1965) described how attorneys in a public defender's office acquire—and share with the prosecutors and judges with whom they negotiate pleas—a consensus about the risks in various types of sentence for what they call "normal crimes." Thus, as a normal crime in the court that he studied, "*burglary* is seen as involving regular violators, no weapons, low-priced items, little property damage, lower-class establishments, largely Negro defendants, independent operators, and a non-professional orientation to the crime." "*Child molesting* is seen as typically entailing middle-aged strangers or lower-class middle-aged fathers (few women), no actual physical penetration or severe tissue damage, mild fondling, petting and stimulation, bad marriage circumstances, multiple offenders with the same offense repeatedly committed, a child complainant, via the mother" (p. 260). The consensus among these lawyers included notions of the risks typically involved with each of the normal types of offense. Negotiation on every separate case usually begins with arguments as to whether it is a normal type of the particular offense or whether it involves a defendant who is a better or worse risk than most others charged with this crime. Usually, the guilt of the accused is assumed.

As Sudnow points out, these risk-classification norms vary between courts and are probably different for private rather than public criminal defense lawyers. Attorneys new to the process have to learn the local norms before they can efficiently resolve cases to the general satisfaction of their coworkers and with a minimum investment of time and effort per case. Comparative studies of the operations of criminal courts in different locations have found that a "courthouse subculture" develops in each, giving each court somewhat different norms as to the risks involved in alternative dispositions for particular types of cases (see, e.g., Eisenstein and Jacob 1977; Levin 1977; Littrell 1979).

Risk-assessment norms probably also vary from one collective workplace to another not only for courts but also for other types of criminal justice agencies. Thus the criteria for evaluating risk are likely to be somewhat diverse among different police stations where decisions to arrest and to book are made, penal institutions where prospects of escape or violence must be judged in allocating housing and work assignments to inmates, parole boards that have release discretion, and probation or parole supervision offices that must decide which releasees should get the most surveillance or other kinds of controls.

These normative variations reflect a basic principle of sociology and anthropology that I call the law of sociocultural relativity: social separation fosters cultural differentiation. Cultures are acquired by communication and tend to be continuously changing. When people in different workplaces do not interact with each other, their subcultures are likely to diverge.

The influence of local subcultural norms in risk assessment is objectionable from at least two standpoints. First, their variation conflicts with the ideal of maintaining uniform justice practices throughout a jurisdiction. Second, local norms may generate quite inaccurate judgments of risks. The inaccuracies of risk-assessment norms, however, probably reflect psychological principles that affect human thought in all types of settings.

C. Some Individual Mental Factors in Risk Assessment

Reaching a difficult decision that may have important consequences is an anxiety-producing experience. There is usually much relief when the decision is made, especially if there is confidence that the correct choice was made. The gratification from such anxiety reduction tends to reinforce overconfidence in the wisdom of one's past judgments by the process that Leon Festinger (1964) conceptualized as minimizing cognitive dissonance. He asserts that "the greater the conflict before the decision, the greater the dissonance afterward. Hence the more difficulty the person had in making the decision, the greater would be his tendency to justify that decision (reduce the dissonance) afterward. The decision can be justified by increasing the attractiveness of the chosen alternative and decreasing the attractiveness of the rejected alternative, and one would expect a post-decision cognitive process to occur that accomplishes this spreading apart of the attractiveness of the alternatives" (pp. 4–5).

The reduction of anxiety once a choice is made and overconfidence afterward in the wisdom of their decisions tend to make persons act prematurely, that is, before they have adequately considered all relevant facts and arguments. Herbert Simon, the Nobel laureate in economics, gained distinction by pointing out that business and government administrators usually make any decision that satisfices—that seems good enough—instead of maximizing the utility of their actions as classical economics assumes.

This pattern of insufficient effort in making decisions is also fostered by additional psychological mechanisms, well catalogued in Robin

Hogarth's *Judgment and Choice* (1980), as biases in the mental processing of information. These are often evident in the subjective decision making of criminal justice officials.

One source of bias that Hogarth calls "availability" is the tendency to attach undue importance to easily recalled information, such as highly publicized cases, when assessing the risks with a particular case. This bias impedes systematically looking at the record for the majority of similar cases. Another source of bias is "selective perception," which is the tendency to seek information consistent with one's prior views and to disregard or to downplay conflicting evidence. Among the many others are what he calls "order effects," which is the tendency to be disproportionately influenced in one's decision by the first case of the type that one encountered or by the most recent case rather than by a cross section of all cases. Also, to reduce mental effort in routine decisions, we develop "rules of thumb," he points out, without adequate knowledge of their long-run consequences.

Another common source of bias in risk assessment by criminal justice officials is an excess conservatism that comes from statistically biased feedback. Police officers who release juveniles with mere warnings, judges who grant probation, prison officials who place inmates in a minimum security setting, and parole board members who release prisoners before the maximum sentence is served are informed much more regularly and vehemently of those released offenders who use this increased freedom to commit new crimes than of the majority, in most settings, who behave properly.

The more officials are "burned," as they say, by learning of their bad assessments of risk, the more cautious they are likely to be the next time. This long prior experience of senior officials with biased feedback probably explains why diversion programs such as those providing supervision and assistance to offenders in the community, which are intended to reduce the number who are incarcerated, are typically used instead to "broaden the net" of the justice system by receiving offenders who would normally be released without supervision (see Klein 1979).

Confronted with evidence of poor risk assessments in subjective decision making, officials typically call for more staff and better staff training. They may also take the precaution of requiring that decisions be reviewed more by higher officials or be approved by a committee before they are carried out. Although two or more heads may make decisions with more protracted deliberation than those made by one official alone, expansion of the subjective decision-making process by making it include discussions with others frequently only imposes the more conservative biases of the senior officials on the judgments of their juniors. An alternative approach is to change risk assessment to a more objective procedure.

II. Statistical Guidelines in Classification for Risk

The subjective process of assessing risks in particular decisions for specific offenders consists of classifying each case into a category of others about whom one has assumptions of dangerousness. The objective method is to compile statistics that show the risks of danger for various categories of offenders. In American criminal justice systems this objective approach was pioneered shortly after World War I but was not widely accepted until its objectives and methods were reconceptualized after World War II.

A. *Proposing Prediction as a Panacea*

Using sixty-seven categories of information available to the parole board, Sam B. Warner (1923) compared 300 inmates who had been successful on parole from the Massachusetts Reformatory with 300 who had failed on parole. He concluded that the only difference between the two groups that was large enough to provide useful guidance to the board was the subjective classification of the inmate by the board's advisory physician (then called an "alienist") as an accidental, recidivist, or feeble-minded offender. Shortly thereafter, however, sociologist Hornell Hart (1923, p. 405) asserted "that the percentage of violations of paroles among men paroled from the Massachusetts Reformatory could be reduced one-half through scientific utilization of data already being collected . . . is the conclusion which should have been reached . . . in a recent study. This conclusion, however, is quite at variance with those found by Professor Warner." Hart calculated that thirty-five of the differences found by Warner probably could not be explained by chance and that fifteen were significant at the .01 level. He suggested that these items be given a weighting based on "the intercorrelations between the various items . . . as well as their correlations with parole violation" (p. 411) and added, "On the basis of such scores it would be possible to make reports to the Board in a form somewhat like the following: Jim Jones has a prognostic score of 93 points. In the past experience of the Board among men with prognostic scores in the neighborhood of 93 points, only 19 percent have violated parole. . . . Will Smith has a prognostic score of 21 points. In the experience of the Board among men with diagnostic scores close to 21 points, 80 percent have violated their paroles" (p. 411).

The first development of such a weighting system was reported in 1928 by Professor Ernest W. Burgess of the University of Chicago. He compiled statistics from the records of the last 1,000 men paroled from each of the state's three prisons before a date two-and-a-half years earlier. The records revealed that, in the period since their release, 25.7 percent of these 3,000 releasees had been declared parole violators. He also classified these men on various items of information that were recorded in their prison files before their release and found that twenty-one of these items had categories with violation rates significantly above or below the 25.7 percent overall rate. Thus violation rates were markedly lower for first offenders than for recidivists, for murderers or sex offenders than for burglars or forgers, for those with regular work records than for those with no or irregular work records, for those with no disciplinary punishments in prison than for those with many or serious punishments, and for those with average than for those with very low or very high intelligence-test scores. Burgess took twenty-one such differentiating factors and gave each parolee one point for every one of these factors on which he was classified in a category with a violation rate below 25.7. Of those who by this system had sixteen to twenty-one points, only 1.5 percent had violated parole, but of those with four or fewer points, 76 percent had violated.

These findings seemed to exceed even Hart's optimistic expectations. Burgess (1928) proposed that prediction methods be adopted to guide all types of social work, observing that

> the practical value of an expectancy rate should be as useful in
> parole administration as similar rates have proved to be in
> insurance. . . . Not only will these rates be valuable to the Parole
> Board, but they will be equally valuable in organizing the work of
> supervision. For if the probabilities of violation are even it does
> not necessarily mean that the prisoner would be confined to the
> penitentiary until his maximum was served, but that unusual
> precautions would be taken in placing him and in supervising his
> conduct. Less of the attention of the parole officers need in the
> future be directed toward those who will succeed without
> attention and more may be given to those in need of assistance.
> [P. 248]

During the same period, but quite independently, Harvard criminal law professor Sheldon Glueck and his wife, Eleanor, were completing the first of their series of follow-up studies at five-year intervals of a group of inmates paroled from the Massachusetts Reformatory whose paroles expired in 1921–23. In this and in studies with other samples later they not only relied on official records but located, investigated, and interviewed most of the subjects in the community. Their post-parole criterion of reformation was whether, by their standards, the ex-prisoner was pursuing a constructive and law-abiding life. Although only 20 percent had been declared parole violators by the state, they deemed 80 percent to have been failures.

The Gluecks found that seven preparole factors sharply differentiated between successes and failures as they defined these contrasting outcomes. They then gave each individual a "failure score," which was the sum of the percentage of failures in his categories on each of the seven factors (e.g., 60 on the factor "mental abnormality" if "none" but 87 if "psychotic"), so that the lowest total failure score that anyone could have from the seven factors was 274 and the highest 499 (1930, pp. 281–86). In the prediction table that they developed, failure rates by their standards varied from 95 percent for those with the highest failure scores to 29 percent for those with the lowest scores.

Glueck (1946), who raised what then seemed like immense funds from private foundations to support over three decades of extensive research, was an ebullient salesman. On the prospects for application of his failure scores he proclaimed,

> Suppose . . . that a judge had before him separate prognostic
> tables based on fines, on imprisonment in a penitentiary, on
> imprisonment in a reformatory, on probation, or even more
> discriminately on results obtained by different probation officers.
> And suppose that the judge, on consultation of the prognostic
> tables, found that Prisoner X according to past experience with
> other prisoners who in certain pertinent particulars resembled X,
> had say nine out of ten chances of continuing in crime if sent to
> a prison, seven out of ten if sent to a reformatory, five out of ten
> if placed on probation, and only two out of ten if placed on
> probation under Supervisor Y. Clearly, the judge . . . using
> objectified and organized experience . . . based on hundreds of
> similar cases . . . would greatly improve his exercise of discretion
> in imposing sentence. [Pp. 68–69]

Despite Glueck's eloquence, his rhetoric had no immediate impact on government practice. In Illinois, however, the board of parole created the position of sociologist-actuary at each of the state's prisons. These appointees applied the Burgess point system to every prisoner on the board's docket for parole consideration, producing a report that indicated the individual inmate's favorable or unfavorable classification on each of the twenty-one factors as well as a conclusion in the following form. This individual has a total of x factors favorable to success on parole and y factors unfavorable. In past experience, prisoners with these totals had a parole violation rate of z percent, of whom w percent had major violations and $(z - w)$ percent minor violations.

A variety of analogous parole or probation prediction studies were made in various states and some other nations during the next thirty years, gradually becoming more sophisticated methodologically (see Schuessler 1954; Simon 1971). Illinois, however, was the only state that routinely applied its tables to every prospective parolee. Yet it was doubtful if these tables greatly influenced decisions even in this state. Their failure to become panaceas—as Hart, Burgess, and the Gluecks expected—results from methodological problems in all prediction and from the context in which the tables were applied.

B. Methodological Issues in Risk Prediction

Statistical prediction tables classify current cases into categories that follow-up studies of past cases show had diverse percentages of whatever behavior the tables are used to predict. Because they are based on past cases, some writers prefer to call them "experience tables." Let us suppose that a study of 1,000 persons released from prison over five years ago might be able to classify them, by information known before their release, into five categories—A, B, C, D, and E—each of which had a different percentage who committed new crimes within five years after their release. Several problems would arise in using this information for making risk assessments of current prisoners in order to make decisions on how long to confine them.

1. *Stability.* Suppose that the percentages of prison releasees in categories A, B, C, D, and E who were not convicted of any new offenses within five years after they got out were, respectively, 70, 60, 50, 40, and 30 percent. Using this knowledge to make sentencing or parole decisions requires the assumption that these percentages would be the same for all future offenders classifiable into these five categories. If the factors affecting the category into which a prisoner is classified include performance in tests of vocational skills when in prison, it might be that the above rates of postrelease success would be higher in

prosperity than in periods of economic recession. In Illinois, after the pioneering research by Burgess, the tables were revised several times on the basis of new research to test the stability of the predictors over long periods and thus to reduce the original twenty-one-factor tables by eliminating those factors for which parole violation rates fluctuated. By such studies, Ohlin (1951) produced a twelve-factor table for Joliet and Menard prisons using a follow-up of all parolees released from 1930 through 1950, and Glaser (1954) produced a seven-factor table for Pontiac Prison using a follow-up of all parolees released from 1940 through 1950.

2. *Accuracy.* Suppose that the hypothetical findings presented above were found to be quite stable, so that one confidently predicted that 30 percent of all prisoners classifiable in category A would be convicted of new offenses within five years. The tables, however, would not indicate which individuals in category A would be in this 30 percent who will be convicted of new crimes and which would be in the 70 percent who will not.

If one defines "accuracy" as the number of errors that would result from making decisions from an experience table, one could minimize errors by predicting that category A prisoners would not commit new felonies, although this would mean that 30 percent of the predictions would be in error. The alternative, that is, to predict that category A prisoners would commit new felonies, would make 70 percent of one's case predictions erroneous. For category D, in which 60 percent had committed new felonies, the least-error prediction would be that category D prisoners would commit new crimes, and the same prediction would be made for category E prisoners.

3. *Base Rates and Prediction Efficiency.* In prediction research, the outcome that is being predicted is called the "criterion." For example, the criterion may be committing a new felony, succeeding on parole, violating probation, being regularly employed, or failing to show up in court after release on recognizance. The "base rate" is the percentage of all persons with whom one is concerned who in the past exhibited this criterion. "Efficiency," which is expressed as a percentage, is the extent to which a prediction table permits one to improve on the prediction that everyone in a group will have the group's base rate of the criterion.

In the absence of any research that justifies diverse predictions for different members of a group, the most accurate forecast one can make is that everyone in the group will behave as most have in the past. If the base rate is 40 percent, the least-error prediction is that none will have the criterion, but if the base rate is 55 percent, the most accurate prediction is that everyone will have the criterion. The objective of efficiency in prediction is to improve on base-rate outcomes by identifying categories of subjects who will have rates of the criterion much different from the base rate.

The closer the base rate for everyone studied is to 100 percent, the more difficult it is to identify a category of subjects with a rate of less than 50 percent of the criterion, so that one can make a prediction for them that will have fewer errors than saying that everyone will have the criterion outcome. Conversely, the closer the base rate is to zero, the harder it is to find a category with a rate of over 50 percent for which one would minimize errors by predicting that all in that category would have the criterion. For example, because about 90 percent of all income tax law violators who are adult first offenders succeed on probation, it is very difficult to find an appreciable category of them, identifiable by prerelease information, in which less than 50 percent succeed, so that the most accurate prediction for that category would be failure (Ohlin and Duncan 1949; Reiss 1951). If the base rate is near 50 percent, it is easiest to classify cases into categories with markedly more or less than 50 percent criterion rates.

Much of the failure of some prediction tables to improve on the efficiency of case decisions occurs because they are applied to groups with criterion base rates close to either zero or 100 percent. It is usually difficult to identify in advance a category of persons most of whom will experience what is a rare event for their total group or to identify a category most of whom will not have what is a very common experience in the group from which one wishes to differentiate them (Meehl and Rosen 1955).

Base rates also affect the ability of experts to make accurate subjective predictions. If trying to identify in advance those prisoners who will be convicted of violent felonies on parole, one usually has to improve on a base rate of less than 10 percent. Of course, such predictions are frequently made by parole board members or by the psychiatrists whom they enlist as consultants, and, because of the psychological sources of overconfidence already discussed, they are likely to be very certain about the accuracy of their predictions. Usually, no one can check on their accuracy, however, because those whom they designate as likely to commit new violent felonies are not released. Nevertheless, on a few occasions when legally improper commitment procedures resulted in appellate court orders for the release of hundreds of persons confined as criminally insane because psychiatrists said that they were dangerous, the postrelease violent-crime rates of the releasees proved to be negligible (Steadman and Cocozza 1974; Thornberry and Jacoby 1979).

4. *Interaction of Prediction Factors.* The early prediction studies treated all significant factors as additive and of equal weight, so that a subject was assigned one point for each factor in which he was classified in a category that had more than the base rate of their criterion. Therefore, the earliest Illinois prediction tables were based on twenty-one to twenty-seven factors, each factor potentially contributing one point to a subject's total prediction score.

The Gluecks and others gave greater weights to those factors most markedly related to the criterion. They also used fewer factors, partly because they found that each additional factor used in a total factor score had less effect on the contrast in percentages between score categories.

These diminishing benefits from adding more information reflect the intercorrelation of factors. For example, number of prior felony convictions, number of prior incarcerations, age at first arrest, drug addiction, and longest job ever held in the community are five factors that, taken separately, differentiate offenders into categories with contrasting recidivism rates. However, obtaining Burgess-type total scores by applying all five will not improve predictive accuracy fivefold, partly because persons with three or more prior felony convictions comprise a disproportionate number of those with one or more prior incarcerations, those first arrested before age sixteen, those who were drug addicts, and those never employed at one job for more than a year.

Multivariate statistical regression analysis—difficult to do in the pre-computer age, when the early studies were made—facilitates the calculation of optimum prediction scores using several factors simultaneously. This produces scoring in which a few factors contribute larger weights to the total score than do the others and in which the total number of factors used for the best possible predictions is relatively small.

An alternative way of taking intercorrelations into account is to use what has been called a "configuration table," or a "decision tree," rather than a numerical scoring system. As is usually done, all the past cases studied are divided into categories by every available type of prerelease information on them to determine which factor dichotomizes them into categories with the most statistically significant contrast in percentages of the criterion (for discussions of statistical methods used in classification and prediction, see Brennan [in this volume]; Gottfredson [in this volume]). The cases in each of the categories of the most significant dichotomy are then dichotomized by all the remaining variables to determine which make the most statistically significant further contrast in their percentages of the criterion. This may often result in a different combination of factors being used in the successive dichotomizations that determine the final risk classifications. It also reveals immediately the factor categories determining the ultimate risk assessment for any individual, which permits a decision maker to consider the validity of the information in the particular case or its unique features.

The features of configuration analysis described above are well illustrated by figure 1. In a Massachusetts Department of Corrections analysis of recidivism by prisoners in their first year of release, with a base rate of 25 percent the most statistically significant dichotomy was between those with twelve or more prior court appearances, who had a recidivism rate (RR) of 29 percent, and those with eleven or fewer prior court appearances, whose RR was 20 percent. For those with twelve or more prior court appearances, the further dichotomy with the most significant contrast in RR was between those twenty-seven or younger at release, who had an RR of 48 percent, and those twenty-eight or older, whose RR was 23 percent. For the releasees with eleven or fewer prior court appearances, however, the most significant further split was by a different age at release—those twenty-five or younger had an RR of 24 percent, and those twenty-six or older had an RR of only 6 percent. Further significant dichotomization was achieved only for the category with eleven or fewer prior court appearances who were twenty-five or younger at time of release. Those in this group who at the court proceedings that resulted in their imprisonment had seven or more charges had an RR of 32 percent, but those with six or fewer charges had an RR of 14 percent.

Officials and others often reject the best prediction tables as taking too little information into account because they do not appreciate the significance of intercorrelation of predictive factors. For example, the Massachusetts configuration in figure 1 uses only three distinct factors—prior court appearances, age at release, and number of charges—and only the first two for most cases. The Salient Factor Score of the U.S. Parole Commission (1985) uses only seven kinds of prerelease data to calculate prediction scores. Critics point out that the files from which

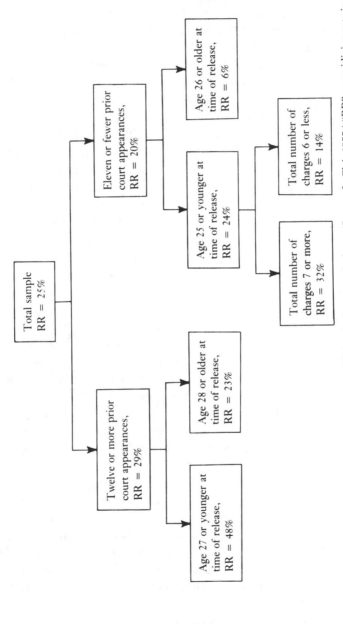

FIG. 1.—Decision tree for risk classification of offender recidivism in first year of release. (Source: LeClair 1977.) "RR" = recidivism rate in first year of release.

subjective risk assessments are made include many more types of information on most cases, including personal letters from people who have worked with the individual and detailed accounts of crimes. They overlook that most prediction-table research starts with fifty to 100 or more separate factors but that interaction effects result in only a few factors making the most stable and significant predictions.

Actually, it has been demonstrated in various contexts that presumed experts make more accurate subjective predictions if given only a half-dozen or fewer of the most predictive types of information on each case than if given these plus a large dossier of additional material (Wilkins 1965; Bartlett and Green 1966, app. 4). This brings up that most persistent issue: Do statistical tables really predict human conduct better than does a good subjective appraiser of case study information, especially one who has interviewed and perhaps observed at length the individual on whom a risk classification must be made?

5. *Case Study versus Statistical Predictions.*   Parole board members, judges, and others are often skeptical about claims that statistical tables produce more accurate risk classifications than they could make by subjective assessment. They point out that the information on which unfavorable assessments are made statistically, such as an extensive prior criminal record or a poor employment history, would also lead them to consider an offender a poor risk for release and that the favorable factors, such as older age at release or a good conduct record in prison, are items that they regard favorably. They stress that, for many cases falling into a similar risk classification in the prediction tables, they have unique information of great importance for their decisions, such as their impression that there exists an exceptionally good relation between the offender and a former employer who appeared before them or the offender's expression when they interviewed him of what seemed to be sincere remorse.

Such debates have long pervaded many fields where important decisions must be based, at least in part, on the prediction of human conduct. The landmark case for preferring risk classifications from relevant statistical tables to those derived from case study assessments was made in psychologist Paul Meehl's *Clinical vs. Statistical Prediction* (1954). He summarized twenty empirical tests of one method against the other in predictions of human conduct made by both methods for large samples of cases that were followed up to see which prediction was correct. The studies were very diverse and included predicting psychiatric disorders in mental patients, performance of armed-forces personnel receiving various types of technical training, and the recidivism of prisoners. In sixteen of these tests the statistical predictions proved correct much more often than did the predictions made from case studies, in three somewhat more often, and in one less often, but the evidence in this one case was somewhat ambiguous. Although some outstanding clinicians surely can make risk classifications more accurately than can those of a poorly developed statistical prediction table, Meehl's evidence that statistical methods were much more likely to be superior was not easily disputed.

Published studies in the criminal justice field have, to my knowledge, always found statistical predictions more accurate than case study predictions for the same samples of cases (e.g., Mannheim and Wilkins 1955; Gottfredson 1961; Glaser 1962; Holland, Holt, and Brewer 1978; Holland and Holt 1980; Carroll et al. 1982). Yet the routine use of predictive statistics for making case decisions in criminal justice agencies has always required their presentation to officials with forms and procedures that make it clear that action is unlikely to be taken on the basis of statistical predictions alone.

6. *Selectivity*.   Statistical predictions from actuarial tables guide risk classifications by insurance companies and by some banks and loan firms. Why was it that—despite their initial development in the 1920s, their repeated improvement by researchers in subsequent decades, and the evidence of their superiority to case study assessments—until around 1970 statistical predictions were used routinely only by one agency in the criminal justice system, namely, the Illinois parole board? Furthermore, when that board used them, it consisted of part-time members who were political appointees. It also collected two or more narrative case reports and recommendations on each case, hastily interviewed the prisoners on whom it made decisions as well as others, and inspected a large dossier of additional material provided by the prison. No one had any clear idea how much weight the actuarial prediction had in this board's decisions on granting or denying parole. My impression from being employed as one of its sociologist-actuaries in the prisons in 1950–54 was that this board's persistent collection of prediction reports was by then mostly a consequence of bureaucratic inertia.

Members of many parole boards, other criminal justice officials, and diverse additional commentators objected to the proposals by prediction-table developers that fateful decisions on the denial or the granting of liberty to offenders be based solely on statistical studies. They described the use of these tables as "treating people like numbers" and as "not taking into account the personal factors in each case." They pointed out also that risk estimations are far from the only considerations influencing their sentence or parole rulings and that they have such additional concerns as minimizing disparity in penalties for similar offenses and guessing at the amount of risk that the public will tolerate with different offenders.

If one recognizes that a prediction table used for risk classification is relevant to only one of many considerations in the decisions of criminal justice officials and that minimizing errors of prediction is not their only concern, then the utility of statistics on past experience can be assessed from a standpoint other than efficiency in making accurate predictions.

"Selectivity" refers to how well a prediction table's categories rank cases with respect to the probability of their having the criterion outcome. An experience table that divided cases into categories with diverse outcomes and that yielded stable predictions for future cases could be very useful for risk assessment even if the base rate was not close to 50 percent and no category had a least-error prediction that improved on the base rate.

One of the complaints of those trying to use prediction tables is that the tables tend to distribute cases into a bell-shaped curve, with most falling in the middle-risk categories for which predictions are close to the base rate and very few falling in the extremely low or high risk categories that make decisions most certain.

The "mean cost rating" (MCR) is a statistical index of selectivity developed by Duncan et al. (1953) that has in recent years been increasingly used. It is mathematically identical with the Gini coefficient much used in economics and sociology (Duncan and Duncan 1955). A table has an MCR of 1.0 if it dichotomizes cases into one category with none, and into one with all, having the criterion, but its MCR is zero if all categories have the base rate. Its MCR is between these extremes if it separates cases into categories with different rates of the criterion. The size of the MCR indicates the extent to which its classification of risks approaches a perfect split into all and none categories. The MCR for the Massachusetts configuration in figure 1 is 0.47.

C. Collaboratively Developed Decision Guidelines

An accelerating rate of acceptance of statistical tables for risk classification has occurred during the 1970s and 1980s because of a change in stance by researchers. They began to present their prediction tables as purely advisory information and in many cases designed tables to deal with other problems besides classification for risk. But most important for the acceptance of these tables, the officials who would use them were involved in designing the tables.

The beginnings of this change of stance occurred around 1960, when Don Gottfredson and Kelly Ballard, researchers for the California Department of Corrections, developed statistical tables for California's parole board to advise them on which prisoners would be paroled if the board were consistent with its past practices rather than on the probable violation rates of different categories of prisoners. This analysis was of much interest to board members.

Further collaboration of researchers with parole board members was fostered by National Parole Institutes, a program conducted by the National Council on Crime and Delinquency with federal grants, which three or four times a year brought about twenty members of different parole boards together for a week of intensive discussions on decision making generally and on parole prediction specifically.

The fourteen one-week institutes in about four years eventually involved members of the federal and of nearly every state parole board in the country. One of their standard features was at least a half a day during which board members compared their predictions with those of statistical tables for a set of hypothetical cases.

Growing out of these institutes was the Uniform Parole Reports Program, which helped members of different parole boards reach consensus on procedures to compile uniform statistics and to submit them to the council for compilation and publication. All fifty states and the United States Board of Parole participated in this program with the council into the 1970s, and these compilations are now continued as a federal service by the Bureau of Justice Statistics of the U.S. Department of Justice.

Early in the 1970s, Don Gottfredson and statistician Leslie T. Wilkins worked with members of the U.S. Board of Parole (now called the U.S. Parole Commission) to develop a new type of statistical table to aid case decisions. This action was prompted by a federal court decision that ordered the board to articulate its policies for granting parole (*Childs v. United States Board of Parole*, 371 F. Supp. 1246 [D.D.C. 1973], *modified*, 511 F.2d 1270 [D.C. Cir. 1974]). The board's *Parole Guidelines*, of which the 1985 version is shown in table 1, are designed to cope simultaneously with the board's interest in the imposi-

TABLE 1

U.S. Parole Commission's Guidelines for Decision Making

	Parole Prognosis*			
Offense Severity	Very Good (10–8)	Good (7–6)	Fair (5–4)	Poor (3–0)
Category 1 (e.g., theft or fraud under $2,000)	≤4	≤8	8–12	12–16
Category 2 (e.g., unlawful entry to United States as an alien)	≤6	≤10	12–16	16–22
Category 3 (e.g., theft or fraud, $2,000–$20,000)	≤10	12–16	18–24	24–32
Category 4 (e.g., theft or fraud, $20,000–$100,000)	12–18	20–26	26–34	34–44
Category 5 (e.g., theft or fraud, $100,000–$500,000)	24–36	36–48	48–60	60–72
Category 6 (e.g., theft or fraud, over $500,000)	40–52	52–64	64–78	78–100
Category 7 (e.g., forcible rape)	52–80	64–92	78–110	100–148
Category 8 (e.g., aircraft piracy)	100+	120+	150+	180+

SOURCE.—U.S. Parole Commission (1985, p. 10).

* Salient factor scores for 1981 are in parentheses. Data in table are guideline ranges and are in months.

tion of consistent penalties for similar crimes and its concern for risk classification. The "offense severity" categories rank all the several hundred federal offenses in one of seven categories on the basis of the board's judgment of their seriousness, which is reviewed annually. The columns classify offenders by the risk of their violating parole using a statistical prediction table's categories called the Salient Factor Score. The entries in the body of the table show the range of confinement terms imposed by the board in past years on 80 percent of the prisoners with each of the combinations of offense severity and parole risk indicated.

These guidelines do not dictate exactly which term of confinement a prisoner should serve, but they do show which terms of confinement would be consistent with most of their prior decisions for similar cases. The parole decision makers are free to impose any lawful term of confinement, but, if they depart from the period indicated in the guidelines, they must provide written reasons. Every six months the commission meets to review a compilation of their decisions in the previous half year, including the reasons recorded for overriding the guidelines. From this review the board can decide to alter the guidelines, changing the severity that they assign to a particular offense or the confinement duration range with which they wish to guide their future decisions. The board's staff also have repeatedly examined the validity of the Salient Factor Scores, which have proven to be extremely stable predictors for federal prisoners.

The federal parole guidelines were a turning point. During the 1970s and the 1980s they were followed by the adoption of a wide variety of decision guidelines by many types of criminal justice agencies. The distinctive feature of all guidelines that have become firmly institutionalized in organization practices is that they were developed collaboratively by researchers and agency officials. In some settings, however, the research was much more thorough and influential than in others, and officials have varied greatly in the extent to which they attend to the guidelines in making their decisions.

III. The Varieties of Guidance in Risk Classification

There is now a rapid rate of change in the design and use of decision guidelines for risk classification in criminal justice agencies. Any survey would probably be incomplete and out of date before it was done, or soon thereafter. The effort here, therefore, is not to be exhaustive but to illustrate the variations of recent practice in diverse fields.

A. Pretrial Release

In the twentieth-century United States, persons charged with crimes who were released pending trial have either paid bail or arranged for a bail bondsman to pledge money bail for them in exchange for a nonreturnable fee of 5–10 percent of the bail. This, of course, made pretrial confinement mostly a consequence of the poverty of the accused. Although judges almost everywhere have authority to release persons pretrial on recognizance with no bail, this was uncommon in American courts until well past mid-century.

The turning point in this history was a crude experiment in decision guidance early in the 1960s, when some New York City judges permitted the Vera Foundation to make recommendations to them on granting "release on recognizance" to randomly selected pretrial detainees while a control group went through traditional procedures. The researchers consulted successful bondsmen on the factors that they considered in deciding whether a person was likely to skip bail and on this basis developed a scoring system for predicting who would abscond. The four factors included were stability of residence in the community, family ties, current and prior employment, and absence of a prior criminal record.

Law-student volunteers interviewed the pretrial detainees in jail on score items and checked the validity of responses by appropriate telephone calls. The 40 percent whose scores exceeded a cutoff point were recommended for release on recognizance, and 55 percent of these received it from the judge. About 98 percent of the recognizance cases showed up for trial, which is as high as the percentage from the control group cases who posted bail.

The U.S. Department of Justice gave much publicity to the Vera experiment and joined a number of private foundations to promote bail reform nationally. A survey of this effort through 1971, covering a national sample of twenty jurisdictions, concluded that the percentage of defendants jailed pretrial declined by about one-third for those with felony charges and by one-quarter for those with misdemeanor charges, with use of recognizance increasing from 5 to 23 percent for felony defendants and from 10 to 30 percent for misdemeanants (Thomas 1976, pp. 37, 39, 65, 72).

The Vera point system was not derived from actual collection of statistics on the correlates of failure to appear in court; indeed, tests find this scale weak for predicting either the failure to appear or the commission of new offenses while released (Gottfredson 1974; Goldkamp 1979). However, court officials seem to be satisfied with the consistency, efficiency, and apparent reasonableness that such numerical guideline systems give to pretrial release decisions (Bohnstedt and Geiser 1979, vol. 1).

Statistical factor analyses have identified four quite independent complex variables as best predicting appearance in court. These are social maturation—indicated most strongly by being married, living with a spouse, age, and, less consistently, by owning one's own home and having utilities in one's own name; employment—in which being currently employed and the time employed on this or the last job are about equal as predictors; prior arrests; and residential ties—indicated mainly by length of time at the current address but also by having a telephone at this residence (Ozanne, Wilson, and Gedney 1980). These findings mainly support the Vera scoring system but also suggest ways of improving it.

In practice, judges seem also to consider other factors in reaching their decisions on the conditions for pretrial release. One study found that the defendant's demeanor in court, defined in terms of respectfulness shown toward the judge, was the only factor of many studied that significantly predicted the judge's granting recognizance or lowering bail (Frazier, Bock, and Henretta 1980). Several studies claim that the seriousness of the offense and the prior criminal record are the only factors, and these have traditionally been the basis for announcement of the normal bail charges in some courts, subject to alteration in response to aggravating or mitigating arguments by prosecution and defense (e.g., Ebbeson and Konecni 1975).

Gottfredson, Wilkins, and Hoffman (1978, chap. 8) recommended that a grid be developed collaboratively with judges for guiding pretrial release decisions. One dimension would have a ranking of offenses by seriousness, and the other dimension would be a scale of points empirically demonstrated to provide the best statistical prediction of appearance at trial. The body of the table would indicate judicial consensus on a policy of either refusing bail, imposing a specified range of bail, or granting recognizance for most cases with each combination of offense severity and risk of not appearing at trial.

One limitation of research on the risks of failure to appear in court is that it can be based only on those who were released. If many offenders are confined who have a high probability of appearing for trial if released, this cannot be known, as there is no experience with their release. However, because courts in different jurisdictions are highly diverse in their pretrial release policies (Thomas 1976), researchers can select several that are quite inconsistent then can pool their data to have a more optimum sample than any single jurisdiction could provide for development of a good prediction table on risk of failure to appear.

Recent experimental evidence supports the conclusion that bail-reform guidelines can play an effective, nondiscriminatory role in judicial decision making. Goldkamp and Gottfredson (1985; Goldkamp, in this volume) collected information from a stratified sample of judges and charges on 4,800 bail decisions made between 1977 and 1979. These data were used to produce a model of bail guidelines that incorporated both a charge-severity dimension and a risk-classification dimension.

The guidelines were implemented and evaluated with the cooperation of sixteen Philadelphia municipal court judges in 1981 and 1982. Eight randomly selected judges agreed to use the guidelines or to record their reasons for noncompliance. Another eight randomly selected judges continued to set bail in the normal fashion. Of those judges using the guidelines, 75.7 percent of their decisions fell within the recommended guidelines' ranges (Goldkamp and Gottfredson 1985, p. 141). Fifty-seven percent of the control judges' decisions fell within the guidelines' ranges. When the two bail-decision samples were compared, it was determined that equity of bail practices was greatly improved with the guidelines (Goldkamp and Gottfredson 1985, chap. 9). In 1983, Philadelphia's municipal court judges moved to adopt the guidelines that are still in use today.

B. Risk Classification in Selecting Cases for Prosecution

Public prosecutors have enormous influence in American criminal justice systems. Whom to prosecute, what to charge, and how to prosecute or to negotiate a plea bargain are largely at their discretion, and their recommendations greatly influence sentencing. Such influential decisions are often made by their junior staff, acting hastily and without checking facts carefully, on the basis of their subjective impressions of each case and influenced by workload pressures. Typically, the decision to prosecute is made by a screening attorney who receives documents and possibly conducts some interviews. About half of those whom the police feel merit prosecution are likely to be dropped by the prosecutors, most of them in the screening and others in the course of later proceedings. The subsequent prosecution decisions are often made during off-the-record plea negotiation, although practices and conventions vary greatly from court to court. There is a risk that these practices lead to inadequate prosecution of some dangerous offenders and to excessive effort in prosecution of nondangerous persons.

During the 1970s, to increase the rate of conviction and the penalties for career criminals, the U.S. Department of Justice subsidized programs for prosecutors to designate priority cases through a quantitative scoring system applied by clerks and to assign the cases with the highest scores to special "vertical prosecution" teams of attorneys (Wolfgang 1980). Each of these "career criminal bureaus" developed its own scoring system for defining its targets, some giving more points to particular types of offenses or offenders than others. There has been some effort to evaluate the selection of cases for vertical prosecution from a cost-benefit standpoint since the greater attorney time that this procedure demands reduces the total number of cases that a jurisdiction can prosecute (Weimer 1980). However, there remains a great need for development of statistical guidelines to make prosecution decisions more consistent and more cost-effective in attaining whatever are defined as their goals.

Prosecutors in the Netherlands have been experimenting with guidelines since the 1970s, beginning with the objective of making severity of penalties for drunken driving in different communities more consistently related to blood-alcohol content. Although evaded at first in some localities, by 1980 they had created a lower but more consistent use of unconditional confinement penalties in all jurisdictions than had existed six years earlier (van der Werff 1981; van Dijk 1983).

From stepwise regression of later findings on factors in prosecution of property cases, van Dijk (1983) developed a point system for the decision to prosecute on the basis of prosecutions in preceding years and intended to increase consistency of practices. Items weighted included total value of items stolen, number of charges, and age of offender (with both the very old and the very young weighted less). When forty prosecutors tried it during a test period, they were instructed to record their reasons whenever they decided not to follow it. Except for one new prosecutor, who was fearful of dismissing any charges, they followed it exactly in 78 percent of their cases, with deviations generally involving slightly different weighting of some items for particular cases. Somewhat revised guidelines evoked complete conformity in 74 percent of the cases.

When these guidelines were presented to a conference of prosecutors in The Hague, they added a point for drug addiction. Van Dijk, emphasizing the desirability of such collaboration of researchers with users, asserts that "guidelines should not be derived directly from empirical data on existing practices. They should always be based upon a normative assessment of such data by the prosecutors themselves. The calculation of the scores will be made by legal clerks. If a prosecutor decides to deviate from the decision as suggested by this score he will write down his reasons for doing so on a short form" (1983, p. 14). These forms were to be periodically analyzed by research staff, who would discuss their findings with the prosecutors.

After detailing the negative consequences of unchecked prosecutorial power, Vorenberg (1981) called for prosecutorial guidelines, records of charging and bargaining decisions, and court review of these, asserting, "Given guidelines and post hoc reporting by prosecutors, courts could determine whether particular charging or bargaining decisions were consistent with the prosecutor's general pattern, fell within specific, previously announced exceptions, or were instances of prosecutorial thoughtlessness or vindictiveness" (p. 1570). Although large prosecution offices develop some rules and supervision for their staff attorneys (e.g., Kuh 1975), nothing like standard guidelines or their enforcement as Vorenberg suggests prevails in the United States.

C. Sentencing Guidelines

Using the same method of collaboration between researchers and users that they had pioneered with the U.S. parole guidelines, Gottfredson and Wilkins undertook a project to develop guidelines for sentencing, which is recounted in Kress (1980). Sentencing decisions are somewhat more complex than are parole decisions. Sentencing guidelines of various types have been developed or implemented in many jurisdictions (for a summary, see Goldkamp [in this volume]). The initial sentencing guidelines developed by Gottfredson and his colleagues were said to be voluntary in two senses. First, they were developed voluntarily by the courts; they were not mandated by legislation. Second, compliance with them by judges was voluntary; judges retained full discretion to ignore the guidelines and to impose any lawful sentence.

Although voluntary sentencing guidelines were developed in many jurisdictions, most have since been abandoned. Two major evaluations of voluntary guidelines have been completed, one concerning local systems in Denver, Chicago, Newark, and Philadelphia (Rich et al. 1982) and the other concerning statewide guidelines in Maryland and Florida (Carrow et al. 1985). Both evaluations concluded that the guidelines had little apparent impact on reduction of sentencing disparities and that they did not significantly change patterns of judicial sentencing decisions. Both evaluations blamed the guidelines' lack of impact on their voluntariness (in the second sense noted above) and recommended that future sentencing guidelines be given legal force, so that judges were required either to follow them or to give reasons for not doing so.

A next generation of "presumptive" sentencing guidelines has been developed in Minnesota, Pennsylvania, and Washington that research shows have reduced sentencing disparity (Knapp 1984; Kramer and Lubitz 1985; Washington State Sentencing Guidelines Commission 1986). Similar devices are under development in the federal system by the newly created U.S. Commission on Sentencing. In format, presumptive sentencing guidelines resemble their voluntary predecessors, but they give judges narrower ranges of choice in length of imprisonment to impose, are more specific in stating which mitigating or aggravating circumstances justify the use of this discretion, and permit appellate courts to review this use (Martin 1984; Knapp 1985).

Sentencing guidelines were conceived as improving justice by making explicit the basis for court penalties, by reducing disparity of punishment for similar offenders convicted of the same type of offense, and by making explicit the reasons for any ostensible disparities by asking judges to record the reasons for any deviations from the guidelines (Gottfredson, Wilkins, and Hoffman 1978).

The major barrier to achievement of such effects in American courts has been the plea-bargain system. In the cultures of most courthouses, an agreement on a mutually acceptable penalty is reached informally by prosecution and defense in the course of pretrial negotiations. In jurisdictions in which judges have little discretion in determining terms of confinement, charges can be altered—usually by dropping some of those that were most serious—to make the agreed-on penalty result from the defendant's plea of guilty; the crime is made to fit the punishment rather than vice versa. Where the judge has greater discretion in fixing terms of confinement, the penalty is heavily influenced by the prosecutor's recommendation to the judge (Rich et al. 1982).

D. Custodial Risk-Classification Guidelines

A maximum security prison now may cost over $100,000 per cell to construct and over $20,000 per inmate annually to operate. Minimum security prison facilities include camps with barracks or even tents that cost as little as $1,000 per occupant to construct and only a few thousand dollars per inmate for annual operations. Furthermore, prisoners in minimally secure facilities can be employed full-time at a variety of tasks, and, especially when paid the usually low inmate wage rate, the value of their work to the administration can contribute to the cost of their care.

Correctional institutions thus have an economic interest in classifying inmates efficiently. However, the public rarely notices if an institution is orderly and has no escapes, but nothing jeopardizes a jail or prison official's career as much as does blame for escapes or riots. Consequently, institution supervisors have always tried to assess the risk of a prisoner escaping or being disorderly and have tended to make their assessments conservatively.

Correctional officials usually classified inmates on the basis of subjective impressions but were remarkably astute. They influenced prisoners' behavior by making them earn by conformity the small comforts in housing, job assignment, food, or freedom of movement that were valued tremendously in the inmate community. However, officials quickly punished misconduct and cultivated inmate informers to learn of serious rule violations or of escape plans.

More recently, prisons have become more bureaucratized, and risk classification has been conceived as a clinical task. Caseworkers interviewed, tested, and corresponded on newly received inmates for about a month, then prepared a narrative initial classification report that recommended a particular custody level for the prisoner.

Actually, these clinical classifications often had little impact. A committee of representatives from all major segments of prison staff, usually dominated by a custodially oriented officer, reviewed classification reports and decided on custodial risks to be taken. A California study found that these committees tended to place inmates where there was need for them on the inmate work force and where housing was available regardless of the caseworker's advice (Klempner 1976). Wardens also tended to hoard safe and skilled inmates but to transfer elsewhere if possible those who were risky or otherwise an administrative problem. In another California study, classification caseworkers were asked to rate 293 minimum security prisoners for the probability of their having serious disciplinary reports or trying to escape, but their ratings had little relation to the subsequent conduct of these inmates and added nothing to the greater predictive power of objective information available on each inmate (Holland and Holt 1980).

In the late 1970s several prison systems developed statistical guidelines for custodial risk classification. California Department of Corrections researchers Holt, Ducat, and Eakles (1981) met repeatedly with prison caseworkers and administrators to obtain their views on optimum classification principles. This revealed surprisingly little consensus among the caseworkers but showed that employee concerns were related mainly to their work roles. A scoring system to predict disciplinary problems and escape attempts was developed by multivariate statistical analysis of objective information in inmate records and was used to classify prisoners into four custody levels of increasingly higher security risk. Also the institutions, and separate units of some of them, were classified into four levels by the custodial control that they provided (Gettinger 1982).

The California "point system" assigns unfavorable points to an inmate for length of sentence, prior misconduct or escapes at any institution, and prior criminal record and multiple points for prior assaults on staff or for deliberately causing serious injury to anyone while confined; it deducts points for months of good behavior and for above-average performance at work or school in the last year of incarceration.

In 1980, when the point system was introduced at Folsom Prison, a Level IV, or maximum security, establishment, only 37 percent of the inmates had Level IV scores, and 19 percent were Level I, which qualified them for the lowest-security camps. Fifteen months later, 76 percent of the Folsom inmates were Level IV and only 3 percent Level I. Some lower-level inmates are permitted at each prison for less securely controlled work assignments, and caseworkers are allowed to override the score-system recommendations in their classification of some inmates if they write out their reasons and obtain approval from the classification supervision office in Sacramento.

Before the point system was initiated, there were vacancies at the low-security facilities despite crowding elsewhere, for cautious officials did not designate enough inmates as eligible for minimum custody; soon after the system was adopted, the Level I inmates were on waiting lists for space at Level I institutions. Prisoners generally liked the point system because it made the reasons for their custody classification explicit instead of being an inexplicable clinical judgment of staff.

In 1984 California's point system had been in operation for four years, during which time the prisoner population had increased by 66 percent, from 23,511 to 39,105, but the escape rate per year per thousand of the average daily population declined by 36 percent. Inmate deaths by violence also declined, and such serious inmate disorder as occurred was largely confined to the Level IV institutions, where it could most readily be controlled (Holt and Glaser 1985).

More or less similar procedures for inmate classification have also been adopted in the federal system and in over thirty state systems. Most widely used is an additive point system developed for the National Institute of Corrections from a survey of correctional officials on the factors and relative weights they recommend. The federal system defers especially to the type of caseworker complaint still frequent in California, which asserts that rigid reliance on statistical tables for custodial risk classification demeans the professional training and pride of the staff. Therefore, many of its points are determined by the staff's subjective assessment of prisoners. A trial application of the California, National Institute of Corrections, and federal point systems to 2,000 Nevada prisoners found that differences in the three resulting sets of inmate custodial classifications were not very great (California Department of Corrections 1986; Baird and Austin, n.d.).

One California official complained to a reporter that, instead of adopting the point system because caseworkers were not classifying appropriately, they should have fired the incompetent caseworkers; the official did not realize, of course, that the deficiencies of prior classification were not due to unqualified caseworkers but rather to inherent limitations in subjective risk classification by anyone for most cases.

Point systems for custodial risk classification have also been adopted by the nation's largest jail—Los Angeles County—which now holds 15,000 inmates, which is more than most state prison systems. They are also employed in other county jails (Bohnstedt and Geiser 1979, vol. 3).

E. Parole Guidelines

The collaborative development of the U.S. Parole Commission's guidelines has already been described. The Bohnstedt and Geiser (1979) survey found that most parole boards now use some form of guidelines, many of them simply taking the Salient Factor Score system without testing its predictive qualities for their prisoners but ranking the crimes with which they deal by seriousness and reaching consensus on the range of confinement terms they would try to maintain for most cases with each combination of offense and offender scores. It also found that some states also made up their own offender scoring systems without prediction research. However, many researchers working in different jurisdictions have devised very sophisticated parole prediction tables and innovative statistical methodologies for them (Gottfredson, Wilkins, and Hoffman 1978; Wainer and Morgan 1982).

The Michigan Department of Corrections has developed two well-tested configuration tables for predicting the postrelease behavior of its prisoners, one for assaultive risks and one for property-crime risks. The assaultive-risk classification is used to guide decisions on transfer of inmates to a halfway house or to work or study release and for granting home furloughs as well as for other reductions in custody. The property-crime-risk table was developed later and applied only to prisoners with no history of assaultive crimes. Being in a high property-crime-risk category reduces eligibility for work release or furloughs, but not as much as does being in a high assaultive-risk category, and both tables influence parole decisions (Murphy 1980).

F. Risk Classification for Probation and Parole Supervision

The United States in recent years has had about 1.25 million persons on probation and .25 million on parole compared with half a million confined in prisons and jails.

Supervision of conditionally released offenders provides a combination of assistance and control by a limited number of persons, most of whom have the additional task of preparing presentence reports, an aspect of their work to which they give the highest priority. Because parole officials usually are assigned large caseloads, they cannot closely watch or assist most of those whom they supervise.

These officials necessarily make subjective risk classifications, giving more attention to persons under their supervision about whom they worry and less to others. Although some subcultural norms have developed to guide such distinctions (McCleary 1978, chap. 4), these are neither rigorously validated nor standardly applied.

The most influential change in this situation was initiated in the late 1970s by the Wisconsin Department of Corrections. To develop scoring systems and forms to standardize the classification of cases for different amounts of staff attention, department researchers held extensive meetings with the most experienced agents. Out of these discussions and a series of studies and trials evolved two standard forms that were cleverly designed to replace existing administrative record forms so as not to increase the total amount of paperwork involved in supervision. Indeed, the standardized forms on which most items can simply be checked require less work from agents and secretaries than do the traditional, largely narrative reports that they replaced.

Wisconsin's "assessment of client risk" form applies risk-score factors derived from stepwise multivariate regression analysis of past experience in that state that account for 58 percent of the variance in criminal behavior by probationers and parolees while under supervision. The total risk scores were found highly selective in differentiating Wisconsin probationers and parolees by the prospects of their release being revoked. Revocations varied from only 1 percent for the one-eighth of cases having the lowest scores to 39 percent for the one-eleventh of cases having the highest scores in a population with a base rate of only 11.3 percent revocations (Baird, Heinz, and Bemus 1979, table 1).

Wisconsin's total risk scores were also found to be quite predictive of revocation rates for probationers in Los Angeles County and for parolees in the California Youth Authority as well as for releasees elsewhere. In a more rigorous test with New York City probationers, however, it was found less useful; a more valid risk-assessment-scoring system was devised there that changed some of the Wisconsin factors and that altered the weights for others (Wright, Clear, and Dickson 1984).

The Wisconsin researchers also developed a "reassessment of risk" form to be applied every six months after supervision begins. It changes some of the included information items to cover only the preceding six months on probation or parole and replaces other items with scores on behaviors related to personal adjustment. It also changes weights on some items retained, but its main distinction is that it adds more items that depend on the professional judgments of the agents. Thus it cannot readily be tested from records in another situation, such as New York City, but trials by supervisory staff elsewhere are desirable.

The Wisconsin system also uses an initial "needs assessment" form and, every six months, a "needs reassessment" form, which are derived not from statistics on past experience but from a consensus of agents on the relative importance of various types of assistance that their clients require. They score each client on eleven needs: employment, educational or vocational training, financial management, family relationships, companions, emotional stability, alcohol usage, other drug usage, mental ability, health, and sexual behavior, with higher scores for a category indicating greater assistance needs on it. They add more points for the agent's overall assessment of the client's needs. The needs score showed moderate reliability but virtually no utility for predicting revocation of probation or parole.

The primary purpose of this widely copied Wisconsin system is to standardize time allocations in the supervisor's job, with more time to be given to clients with high risk or need scores and less to those with minimum scores. Traditionally, Wisconsin agents were required to have at least one face-to-face contact with each client per month, but in a quasi experiment officers in one area were asked to have at least two such contracts per month with maximum risk or need clients and only one contact every two months with those that had low ratings on both forms. A time study showed that the actual contrast in time and contacts for differently scored clients was much greater than the required contact ratios. A follow-up of these cases and of those in a similar area with the traditional monthly minimum of one contact for all clients indicated that the increased contacts markedly reduced revocations of maximum risk or need cases, but there was no difference in revocation rates for those with medium or minimum scores (Baird, Heinz, and Bemus 1979).

Other types of rigorous evaluations of these guidelines may be desirable. One would be an investigation of whether revocation criteria differ in practice for maximum, medium, and minimum supervision categories and whether this might explain the diverse success rates in the Wisconsin quasi experiment. Another would be a long-run follow-up of experimental and control or comparison cases in maximum, medium, and minimum supervision categories to infer whether there are long-run crime-reduction benefits from varying the intensity of surveillance and assistance on the basis of these supervision guidelines.

Numerous other scoring systems for standardized guidance of probation or parole supervision have been devised in various locations, some relying more exclusively on objective data and some requiring more subjective assessments of each case (Bohnstedt and Geiser 1979, vol. 2). The Wisconsin system, which has been most widely copied, reflects much collaboration of users with researchers in development and considerable reliance on ratings based on subjective impressions of the users. In its reassessment forms especially, it assumes that the client is capable of improving, and it is in these forms that especially great emphasis is given to eliciting the supervisor's assessment of change in the client.

G. Risk Classification for Quasi-experimental Evaluation

It is generally agreed that the ideal way to test causal theories and treatment technologies is by random experiments. As David Farrington (1983) shows, this research method is much more feasible in the criminal justice system than is usually assumed. Nevertheless, administrative inertia, legal or ethical barriers, and other problems generally make random experiments difficult or impossible to conduct. Sometimes they are feasible only under such unusual conditions or restraints that their conclusions would not be generalizable to more typical circumstances or cases. Therefore, a variety of quasi-experimental evaluation methods have been developed as less perfect alternatives to random experiments (Cook and Campbell 1979).

One such alternative, initiated by Leslie T. Wilkins in the late 1950s in Britain and during the 1960s in California, is to use risk classification as a substitute for randomization in assuring that persons who had a program that is to be evaluated are comparable to those who did not have it. The "base-expectancy" tables that he proposed are outcome-prediction tables based on factors that can be known before the subjects are exposed to the program that is to be assessed. Thus, to evaluate the effects of different prison conditions, base-expectancy tables would predict postrelease recidivism using as prediction factors such pre-prison factors as prior criminal record, current offense, age at admission, preadmission educational attainment, work record, or alcohol and drug use. Research has generally shown that such preconfinement information is much more predictive of postconfinement conduct than are observations of performance in prison.

Base-expectancy tables classify subjects into preprogram risk groups. This compensates for selection effects, that is, the possibility that differences between the subsequent conduct of those in a program and those not in it are due to those in it having much different prospects than the others to begin with. If vocational training classes get better-than-average prisoners, we would expect their students to have better-than-average postrelease conduct even if the classes were of no value. Conversely, if they get atypically high-risk cases, then we do not know the extent to which their subsequent record is due to the classes or to the selection of students for them.

The base-expectancy method can be used in two ways for program evaluation. The first method is to calculate expected outcome rates for everyone in the program. For example, the percentage likely to be convicted of a new felony within one year after release can be estimated using a prediction table that classified all prisoners in the recent past into contrasting risk groups and that used only information knowable at admission rather than information on programs or conduct during imprisonment. Of course, if the program to be evaluated is for probationers or for pretrial releasees, the base-expectancy table must be able to predict their subsequent conduct and must be based on information available at their admission to probation or pretrial status, respectively. Programs are then evaluated by whether the subjects have actual outcome rates that are better or worse than their expected rates.

The Massachusetts Department of Corrections has been perhaps the most regular user of base-expectancy methods of evaluation in recent years. With configuration tables such as that presented here as table 1, its researchers first evaluated special counseling programs for inmates (Carney 1967, 1969) and in recent years evaluated a large variety of "reintegration programs" for prisoners, including prerelease home furloughs, work and school release, halfway houses, liberal visiting privileges, and coed institutions (LeClair 1978, 1981). The counseling programs had different effects on different risk groups, but the reintegration programs were all followed by lower-than-expected recidivism rates for the inmates selected to receive them.

The second way of using base-expectancy tables is to compare program effects for different risk groups. Thus several evaluations of halfway houses find that they produce the greatest difference between expected and actual failure rates for groups who have the highest failure rates with or without halfway houses, such as youthful recidivist offenders, especially those who are auto thieves (Hall, Milazzo, and Posner 1966; Beha 1977; Beck 1979). This finding may be partially due to the worst risk groups having a more easily improved base rate than the others, but they were not always the closest to a 50 percent outcome rate, the easiest on which to achieve a statistically significant improvement.

IV. Prospects and Possibilities

Decision guidelines have been differentiated on two dimensions, namely (1) whether conformance of officials to them is legally presumptive or voluntary and (2) whether they are mainly descriptive, in being "designed largely to articulate and codify past . . . practices," or prescriptive, in being "focused primarily on developing new . . . policies" (Blumstein et al. 1983, p. 135). Although these distinctions were originally applied only to sentencing guidelines, they are appropriate for all the instruments for risk classification that are discussed in this essay. What are the prospects and possibilities for devices that are more presumptive and prescriptive in their influence on decision makers? Would such devices be a boon or a bane to our criminal justice system?

Descriptive bail-reform guidelines that were quite voluntary, this essay pointed out, became more presumptive in Philadelphia after they were shown to make pretrial release decisions by different judges more consistent. This is a sufficient contribution to the achievement of a government "of laws, not men" to make it probable that such guidelines will also be developed and adopted in other jurisdictions. Whether the guidelines will also become more prescriptive, however, depends on whether statistical prediction of new offenses and of failure to appear on pretrial release improves greatly. Prospects of such improvement are limited by the low base rates for failure to appear, but research that samples jurisdictions with a variety of pretrial release policies and that then focuses on the highest risk categories might make appreciable advances. Its findings could be the basis for experimental variation of the mode of release for marginal risk types of offenders, for example, to assess how much risk reduction can result from release under special constraining conditions, with surveillance in the community or with paid work programs that are less costly than jailing.

The demand for prosecution guidelines is likely to grow with the spread of sentencing guidelines because the latter can so readily be evaded through plea bargaining that ignores the "real offense," thus causing the judge to impose the presumptive penalty for an inappropriate charge (Coffee and Tonry 1983). Discussing this problem in Minnesota, Michael and Don Gottfredson assert that "if the commission is to continue to fix presumptive imprisonment sentences for the same groups, the commission must either modify the guidelines in relation to the impact of the criminal history score, or have a program to develop guidelines for prosecutorial decisions that are congruent with the state sentencing policy" (1984, pp. 310–11).

Sentencing guidelines tend to be prescriptive not so much by introduction of new principles for penalty decisions but by reverting to classical limitations on the objectives that can be considered when sentencing. Thus Minnesota's guidelines, increasingly taken as a model because they are so presumptive, determine penalties solely on the basis of the severity of the offense and of the prior criminal record, in conformity to the just-desert movement that has produced extreme overcrowding of American prisons in recent decades. This movement was a reaction to disparity in punishments produced by the subjective decision making of prosecutors, judges, and parole boards.

Yet sentencing guidelines of the Minnesota variety confirm Emerson's claim that "a foolish consistency is the hobgoblin of little minds." If classification for risk in sentencing and corrections is best to serve the public's interests, it should, by the preponderance of statistical evidence, determine which alternative to the most severe penalties justifiable on the basis of just desert can most cost-effectively reduce long-run risks to the public. For example, employment history should surely be considered in determining the penalties for some types of offenders for whom it can be demonstrated that this factor greatly affects the prospect that suspended sentences, fines, or community service will reduce recidivism rates, be less punitive on their families, and be much more cost-effective for society than is imprisonment. Progress in making sentences of net benefit to society requires guidelines that are more complicated than the Minnesota variety; they should assess just deserts for the offense and criminal history primarily to fix

upper and lower limits for acceptable penalties. But in making presumptive sentence recommendations they should consider statistical
data on the recidivism rates of specific kinds of offenders with alternative types of sentences.

As has been detailed elsewhere (Glaser 1984), the just-desert focus
is based on illusions as to the fairness that it provides if it also prevents
or impedes focusing on economy, noncriminalization, crime-spree
interruption, incapacitation, differential association, and retraining
objectives that can make sentences more cost-effective. Such multiple objectives could be considered in research to develop sentencing
guidelines that indicate probable reformation and control by day fines,
house arrest, community service, and other alternatives to traditional
incarceration. A Maryland poll by Stephen Gottfredson and Ralph
Taylor (1984) shows that the public is much less punitive than were the
Minnesota and other state and federal legislators in the 1970s and 1980s
who declared that punishment is the only purpose of sentencing.

Parole guidelines are becoming obsolete because states that impose
determinate sentences eliminate or greatly curtail parole, especially
when they adopt sentencing guidelines. The typical parole board's
practice of reviewing sentences to reduce disparities in the penalties
imposed by different courts may be accomplished more effectively by
presumptive sentencing guidelines that apply to all courts in a state or
the federal system, especially if the guidelines include the possibility of
appellate review as in Minnesota. The parole board's practice of considering an inmate's prison conduct in determining the release date need
also not be missed, for this review can be better accomplished by well-
tested prisoner classification systems. These can now lead gradually to
minimum custody housing, work furloughs, transfer to halfway
houses, or other conditional release.

Inmate-classification guidelines should also be developed to improve
on the erratic decisions of officials not only in deciding on the appropriate custody levels for different prisoners but also in determining which
kinds of treatment or training programs, housing, and other conditions
of confinement should be provided for different types of inmates.
These judgments could be guided by statistical evidence of their probable contribution to behavior change. A parallel development can be
improvements in the community supervision guidelines discussed
above both for probationers and for those whom prisoner-classification
guidelines authorize various types of conditional release. This would
give more research-based direction to the types of assistance and sur-

veillance provided in the community for different types of conditionally released offenders.

Finally, base-expectancy tables can provide quasi-experimental evaluations of any criminal justice policies that currently are diverse—in police, courts, and corrections. These assessments may not be as rigorous scientifically as are classical controlled experiments, but they are much more feasible. Also, because they require little or no disruption of prevailing conditions, it may well be that their conclusions can be generalized to other settings more successfully than can those of "unnatural" experimental arrangements.

Continued growth is highly probable in statistical evaluations of policies and programs and in the use and improvement of objective guidelines for case decisions. This prediction is confidently asserted here because these developments reflect a pervasive trend in modern history that the great social scientist Max Weber (1978) called "rationalization." It is a trend now accelerating in almost every field of human activity due to the advancement and proliferation of computers, the growth of science, and the upgrading of average levels of education. Because of the defects of subjective decision making, this trend can be a net benefit to criminal justice systems. However, experience indicates that risk-classification tables will be used most if they are developed by researchers in close collaboration with policymakers and administrators and if they address not only risk classification but also other problems of concern to the officials who use them.

REFERENCES

Baird, S. Christopher, and James Austin. N.d. *Current State of the Art in Prison Classification Models.* San Francisco: National Council on Crime and Delinquency.
Baird, S. Christopher, Richard C. Heinz, and Brian J. Bemus. 1979. *The Wisconsin Case Classification/Staff Deployment Project.* Project Report no. 14. Madison, Wis.: Department of Health and Social Services, Division of Corrections.
Bartlett, C. J., and Calvin C. Green. 1966. "Clinical Prediction: Does One Sometimes Know Too Much?" *Journal of Counseling Psychology* 13:267–70.
Beck, James L. 1979. "An Evaluation of Federal Community Treatment Centers." *Federal Probation* 43:36–39.
Beha, James A., II. 1977. "Innovation at a County House of Correction and Its

Effects upon Patterns of Recidivism." *Journal of Research in Crime and Delinquency* 14:88–106.

Blumstein, Alfred, Jacqueline Cohen, Susan E. Martin, and Michael H. Tonry. 1983. *Research on Sentencing: The Search for Reform.* Washington, D.C.: National Academy Press.

Bohnstedt, Marvin, and Saul Geiser. 1979. *Classification Instruments for Criminal Justice Decisions.* 5 vols. Washington, D.C.: National Institute of Corrections.

Brennan, Tim. In this volume. "Classification: An Overview of Selected Methodological Issues."

Burgess, Ernest W. 1928. "Factors Determining Successes or Failure on Parole." Part 4 of *The Workings of the Indeterminate-Sentence Law and the Parole System in Illinois,* by Andrew W. Bruce, Ernest W. Burgess, and Albert J. Harno. Springfield: Illinois Board of Parole.

California Department of Corrections. 1986. *Inmate Classification System Study: Final Report.* Sacramento: California Department of Corrections.

Carney, Francis J. 1967. "Predicting Recidivism in a Medium Security Correctional Institution." *Journal of Criminal Law, Criminology, and Police Science* 58:338–48.

———. 1969. "Correctional Research and Correctional Decision-Making: Some Problems and Prospects." *Journal of Research in Crime and Delinquency* 6:110–22.

Carroll, John S., Richard L. Wiener, Dan Coates, Jolene Galegher, and James J. Alibrio. 1982. "Evaluation, Diagnosis, and Prediction in Parole Decision Making." *Law and Society Review* 17:199–228.

Carrow, Deborah M., Judith Feins, Beverly N. W. Lee, and Lois Olinger. 1985. *Guidelines without Force: An Evaluation of the Multi-jurisdictional Sentencing Guidelines Field Test.* Cambridge, Mass.: Abt.

Coffee, John C., Jr., and Michael Tonry. 1983. "Hard Choices: Critical Tradeoffs in the Implementation of Sentencing Reform through Guidelines." In *Reform and Punishment,* edited by Michael Tonry and Franklin E. Zimring. Chicago: University of Chicago Press.

Cook, Thomas D., and Donald T. Campbell. 1979. *Quasi-Experimentation.* Chicago: Rand McNally.

Duncan, Otis D., and Beverly Duncan. 1955. "A Methodological Analysis of Segregation Indexes." *American Sociological Review* 20:210–17.

Duncan, Otis D., Lloyd E. Ohlin, Albert J. Reiss, Jr., and H. R. Stanton. 1953. "Formal Devices for Making Selection Decisions." *American Journal of Sociology* 58:573–84.

Ebbeson, Ebbe B., and Vladimir J. Konecni. 1975. "Decision Making and Information Integration in the Courts: The Setting of Bail." *Journal of Personality and Social Psychology* 32:805–21.

Eisenstein, James, and Herbert Jacob. 1977. *Felony Justice: An Organizational Analysis of Criminal Courts.* Boston: Little, Brown.

Farrington, David P. 1983. "Randomized Experiments on Crime and Justice." In *Crime and Justice: An Annual Review of Research,* vol. 4, edited by Michael Tonry and Norval Morris. Chicago: University of Chicago Press.

Festinger, Leon. 1964. *Conflict, Decision and Dissonance*. Stanford, Calif.: Stanford University Press.

Frazier, Charles E., W. Wilbur Bock, and John C. Henretta. 1980. "Pretrial Release and Bail Decisions: The Effects of Legal, Community and Personal Variables." *Criminology* 18:161–81.

Gettinger, Stephen. 1982. "Objective Classification: Catalyst for Change." *Corrections Magazine* 8:24–37.

Glaser, Daniel. 1954. "A Reconsideration of Some Parole Prediction Factors." *American Sociological Review* 19:335–41.

———. 1962. "Prediction Tables as Accounting Devices for Judges and Parole Boards." *Crime and Delinquency* 8:239–58.

———. 1984. "Six Principles and One Precaution for Efficient Sentencing and Correction." *Federal Probation* 48:22–28.

Glueck, Sheldon, and Eleanor T. Glueck. 1930. *500 Criminal Careers*. New York: Knopf.

———. 1946. *After-Conduct of Discharged Offenders*. New York: Macmillan.

Goldkamp, John S. 1979. *Two Classes of Accused: A Study of Bail and Detention in American Justice*. Cambridge, Mass.: Ballinger.

———. In this volume. "Prediction in Criminal Justice Policy Development."

Goldkamp, John S., and Michael R. Gottfredson. 1985. *Policy Guidelines for Bail: An Experiment in Court Reform*. Philadelphia: Temple University Press.

Gottfredson, Don M. 1961. "Comparing and Combining Subjective and Objective Parole Predictions." *Research Newsletter* 3:11–17.

Gottfredson, Don M., Leslie T. Wilkins, and Peter B. Hoffman. 1978. *Guidelines for Parole and Sentencing*. Lexington, Mass.: Heath.

Gottfredson, Michael. 1974. "An Empirical Analysis of Pretrial Release Decisions." *Journal of Criminal Justice* 2:287–304.

Gottfredson, Michael R., and Don M. Gottfredson. 1984. "Guidelines for Incarceration Decisions: A Partisan Review." *University of Illinois Law Review*, pp. 291–317.

Gottfredson, Stephen D. In this volume. "Prediction: An Overview of Selected Methodological Issues."

Gottfredson, Stephen, and Ralph B. Taylor. 1984. "Public Policy and Prison Populations: Measuring Opinions about Reform." *Judicature* 68:190–201.

Hall, Reis H., Mildred Milazzo, and Judy Posner. 1966. *A Descriptive and Comparative Study of Recidivism in Pre-release Guidance Center Releases*. Washington, D.C.: U.S. Department of Justice, Bureau of Prisons.

Hart, Hornell. 1923. "Predicting Parole Success." *Journal of Criminal Law, Criminology, and Police Science* 14:403–12.

Hogarth, Robin. 1980. *Judgment and Choice*. New York: Wiley.

Holland, Terril R., and Norman Holt. 1980. "Correctional Classification and the Prediction of Institutional Adjustment." *Criminal Justice and Behavior* 7:51–60.

Holland, Terril R., Norman Holt, and David L. Brewer. 1978. "Social Roles and Information Utilization in Parole Decision-Making." *Journal of Social Psychology* 106:111–20.

Holt, Norman, Gary Ducat, and Gene Eakles. 1981. "California's New Inmate Classification System." *Corrections Today* 43:24–35.

Holt, Norman, and Daniel Glaser. 1985. "Statistical Guidelines for Custodial Classification Decisions." In *Correctional Institutions*, edited by Robert M. Carter, Daniel Glaser, and Leslie T. Wilkins. 3d ed. New York: Harper & Row.

Klein, Malcolm W. 1979. "Deinstitutionalization and Diversion of Juvenile Offenders: A Litany of Impediments." In *Crime and Justice: An Annual Review of Research*, vol. 1, edited by Norval Morris and Michael Tonry. Chicago: University of Chicago Press.

Klempner, Jack. 1976. "Decision Making in a State Prison Reception and Guidance Center." Ph.D. dissertation, University of Southern California.

Knapp, Kay. 1984. *The Impact of the Minnesota Sentencing Guidelines —Three Year Evaluation*. St. Paul: Minnesota Sentencing Guidelines Commission.

———. 1985. *Minnesota Sentencing Guidelines and Commentary Annotated*. St. Paul: Minnesota CLE Press.

Kramer, John H., and Robin L. Lubitz. 1985. "Pennsylvania's Sentencing Reform: The Impact of Commission-established Guidelines." *Crime and Delinquency* 31:481–500.

Kress, Jack M. 1980. *Prescription for Justice*. Cambridge, Mass.: Ballinger.

Kuh, Richard H. 1975. "Plea Bargaining: Guidelines for the Manhattan District Attorney's Office." *Criminal Law Bulletin* 11:48–66.

LeClair, Daniel P. 1977. *Development of Base Expectancy Prediction Tables for Treatment and Control Groups in Correctional Research*. Publication no. 9875-37-250-8/77-CR. Boston: Massachusetts Department of Corrections.

———. 1978. "Home Furlough Program Effects on Rates of Recidivism." *Criminal Justice and Behavior* 5:249–58.

———. 1981. *Community Reintegration of Prison Releases: Results of the Massachusetts Experience*. Publication no. 12335. Boston: Massachusetts Department of Corrections.

Levin, Martin A. 1977. *Urban Politics and the Criminal Courts*. Chicago: University of Chicago Press.

Littrell, W. Boyd. 1979. *Bureaucratic Justice*. Beverly Hills, Calif.: Sage.

McCleary, Richard. 1978. *Dangerous Men: The Sociology of Parole*. Beverly Hills, Calif.: Sage.

Martin, Susan E. 1984. "Interests and Politics in Sentencing Reform: The Development of Sentencing Guidelines in Minnesota and Pennsylvania." *Villanova Law Review* 29:21–113.

Mannheim, Hermann, and Leslie T. Wilkins. 1955. *Prediction Methods in Relation to Borstal Training*. London: H.M. Stationery Office.

Mead, George H. 1934. *Mind, Self, and Society*. Chicago: University of Chicago Press.

Meehl, Paul E. 1954. *Clinical vs. Statistical Prediction*. Minneapolis: University of Minnesota Press.

Meehl, Paul E., and Albert Rosen. 1955. "Antecedent Probability and the Efficiency of Psychometric Signs, Patterns or Cutting Scores." *Psychological Bulletin* 52:194–215.

Murphy, Terence H. 1980. *Michigan Risk Prediction: A Replication Study.* Final Report no. AP-O. Lansing: Michigan Department of Corrections, Program Bureau.

Ohlin, Lloyd E. 1951. *Selection for Parole.* New York: Russell Sage.

Ohlin, Lloyd E., and Otis D. Duncan. 1949. "The Efficiency of Prediction in Criminology." *American Journal of Sociology* 54:441–52.

Ozanne, Marq R., Robert A. Wilson, and Dewaine L. Gedney, Jr. 1980. "Towards a Theory of Bail Risk." *Criminology* 18:147–61.

Reiss, Albert J., Jr. 1951. "The Accuracy, Efficiency and Validity of a Prediction Instrument." *American Journal of Sociology* 56:552–61.

Rich, William D., L. Paul Sutton, Todd R. Clear, and Michael J. Saks. 1982. *Sentencing by Mathematics: An Evaluation of the Early Attempts to Develop and Implement Sentencing Guidelines.* Publication no. R-071. Williamsburg, Va.: National Center for State Courts.

Schuessler, Karl F. 1954. "Parole Prediction: Its History and Status." *Journal of Criminal Law, Criminology, and Police Science* 45:425–31.

Simon, Frances H. 1971. *Prediction Methods in Criminology.* London: H.M. Stationery Office.

Steadman, Henry J., and Joseph J. Cocozza. 1974. *Careers of the Criminally Insane.* Lexington, Mass.: Heath.

Stryker, Sheldon. 1980. *Symbolic Interactionism: A Social Structural Version.* Menlo Park, Calif.: Benjamin Cummings.

Sudnow, David. 1965. "Normal Crimes: Sociological Features of the Penal Code in a Public Defender's Office." *Social Problems* 12:255–76.

Thomas, Wayne H., Jr. 1976. *Bail Reform in America.* Berkeley: University of California Press.

Thornberry, Terence P., and Joseph E. Jacoby. 1979. *The Criminally Insane: A Community Follow-up of Mentally Ill Offenders.* Chicago: University of Chicago Press.

U.S. Parole Commission. 1985. *Parole Commission Rules.* Chevy Chase, Md.: U.S. Parole Commission.

van der Werff, Cornelia. 1981. *Penalties Sought and Imposed for Driving under the Influence of Alcohol and Drugs—1978.* Research Bulletin of the Ministry of Justice. The Hague: Ministry of Justice.

van Dijk, Jan J. M. 1983. *The Use of Guidelines by Prosecutors in the Netherlands.* The Hague: Ministry of Justice.

Vorenberg, James. 1981. "Decent Restraint of Prosecutorial Power." *Harvard Law Review* 94:1521–69.

Wainer, Howard, and Ann M. B. Morgan. 1982. "Robust Estimation of Parole Outcome." *Journal of Research in Crime and Delinquency* 19:84–109.

Warner, Sam B. 1923. "Factors Determining Parole from the Massachusetts Reformatory." *Journal of Criminal Law, Criminology, and Police Science* 14:172–207.

Washington State Sentencing Guidelines Commission. 1986. *Report to the Legislature—January 1, 1986.* Olympia: Washington State Sentencing Guidelines Commission.

Weber, Max. 1978. *Economy and Society: An Outline of Interpretive Sociology.*

Edited by Guenther Roth and Claus Wittich. Berkeley: University of California Press. (Originally published 1921.)

Weimer, David L. 1980. "Vertical Prosecution and Career Criminal Bureaus: How Many and Who?" *Journal of Criminal Justice* 8:369–78.

Wilkins, Leslie T. 1965. *Social Deviance*. Englewood Cliffs, N.J.: Prentice-Hall.

Wolfgang, Marvin E., ed. 1980. "Symposium on the Career Criminal Program." *Journal of Criminal Law and Criminology* 71:83–123.

Wright, Kevin N., Todd R. Clear, and Paul Dickson. 1984. "Universal Applicability of Probation Risk-Assessment Instruments: A Critique." *Criminology* 33:113–34.

Lee Sechrest

Classification for Treatment

ABSTRACT

Treatment classifications for prisoner rehabilitation generally lack
theoretical coherence. They tend to assign individuals to descriptive
classes that possess little or no direct relation to treatment programs. The
mismatch between classification systems and treatment programs can only
serve to undermine achievement of rehabilitative goals. There are two
kinds of treatment programs: those that offer services as a package and
those from which services are selected from a menu of possible options.
Much additional research is needed on the relation between offender
needs, including postrelease needs, and treatment programs before the
goal of rehabilitation can be realized.

Classification is the allocation of persons to classes in such a way that
persons in each class are similar. Or, in a more formal, statistical sense,
classification has occurred whenever people are grouped in such a way
that the variance within groups is less than the total variance. The
problem, of course, is that the definition is neutral with respect either
to the basis of classification or to the variable or variables in which
similarity is produced (or variance reduced). Grouping criminal offenders by sex, a common practice, certainly results in variance within
groups on many other variables that is less than the total variance, but
such a classification may or may not be useful for particular purposes.

Unfortunately, the term "classification" has become blurred in usage
so that one cannot always be exactly sure what is meant by it. In its
older and more nearly literal sense the term refers to a process by which
objects, in this case criminal offenders, are put into discrete categories
or classes. The eighteenth-century Linnaean system of classifying

Lee Sechrest is professor of psychology, University of Arizona.

plants is the prototype. In a pure classification system, there are no degrees; a plant, after all, is either a geranium or it is not. Ordinarily, classes are assumed to be mutually exclusive, although Gottfredson (1983) has suggested the term "clump" to refer to classes that overlap.

An alternative use of the term classification in the criminal justice system, however, regards it as the entire process involved in planning for the future of an offender. Flynn (1982), for example, says that "classification is now defined as the process by which a correctional system assesses an individual offender's needs, strengths, and weaknesses and determines differential handling and assignment of offenders in the system" (p. 58). When the term is used in this way, I am reminded of the assertion of my mentor, George A. Kelly (1955): "Diagnosis . . . is the planning stage of treatment" (p. 1190).

The term classification has little specific value if it is used to refer to the interrelated processes of study, analysis, and decision making about the disposition of criminal offenders. Hence, in this essay, I use the term to denote a process by which offenders are placed into groups assumed to be like for decision-making purposes. Any number of dimensions—or discrete characteristics—may enter into a classification system. For example, one might classify prisoners according to intelligence, personal stability, and prior work history. Ultimately, however, in a classification system, dimensions have to be reduced to categories. The aim of classification is, in any case, to produce similar groups within the usually extraordinarily heterogeneous set of persons, juveniles or adults, who come to get themselves labeled as criminal offenders (Quay 1987).

Levinson (1984) has noted four uses of the term classification: (1) procedures for assigning prisoners to facilities at appropriate security levels, (2) procedures for assigning inmates to living quarters within institutions, (3) procedures for assigning inmates to a custody level, and (4) procedures for assigning prisoners to program activities on an individualized basis. The same distinctions could, of course, be applied to offenders being considered for probation, release, or parole.

Levinson's first three uses of the term classification have to do with management of prisoners in relation to the safety of the public, institutional staff, and the inmates themselves (Rans and Fowler 1981). These purposes of classification are not directly relevant to the concerns of this essay, but typical examples of such classification systems and work on them are Baird, Heinz, and Bemus (1979); Eaglin and Lombard (1981); Austin (1983); and Hanson et al. (1983). Classification for management is certainly not irrelevant to treatment concerns, however. Criminal offenders may not be available for treatment or may not be amenable to treatment if they are poorly managed. Poor management may even subvert treatment, as when a prisoner who may benefit from treatment programs is enticed by more misguided companions to attempt escape or to engage in gang behavior.

This essay focuses on issues related to classification of prisoners for purposes of rehabilitation. Regardless of which classification system is used or what range of variables is adopted, the very idea of classification for treatment assumes the acceptance of rehabilitation as a correctional goal. That assumption does not necessarily imply complete credulity concerning the prospects for rehabilitation, for, in my opinion, we still know remarkably little about how to reduce criminal propensities and replace them with more accepted ways of life. Still, without the assumption of some likelihood of rehabilitative success, there is little rationale for treatment at all, let alone classification in its service. One of the arguments to be advanced in this essay is that better classification for treatment will improve the outcomes of that treatment and give hope for eventual realization, even if partial, of the ideal of rehabilitation (Sechrest, White, and Brown 1979).

Section I reviews several classifications that have implications for treatment programs. It is argued that most of these systems do not adequately match classification goals with treatment objectives and that most lack theoretical justification for the approach taken to classifying offenders. Section II discusses the general characteristics of treatment classifications. Emphasis is placed on ways in which they are developed and on what features are desirable to make them implementable, dependable, and stable. Section III describes how offenders, once classified, are matched with appropriate treatment packages. Section IV deals with the advantages of using problem-oriented classification systems. This approach offers flexibility for coping with the changing needs of offenders throughout their incarceration. The final section concludes that we are still far from integrating classification systems and treatment programs. Much additional research is required before effective integration is likely to be achieved.

I. Systems of Classification of Criminal Offenders
Many ways of classifying criminal offenders exist, but only a few of the possibilities have actually been exploited. Warren (1971) describes six types of offender classification systems that have been employed:

"prior-problem orientation," "reference-group typologies," "behavioral classifications," "psychiatry oriented," "social perception and interaction," and "empirical-statistical." She observes that type of offense has also sometimes been incorporated into classification schemes. What is remarkable about these bases for classification is that, with the possible exception of empirical-statistical approaches and reference group typologies, they are so simple and so nearly one-dimensional. Offenders have been classified on the basis of prior problems *or* behavioral manifestations *or* psychiatric diagnosis, and, within any one approach, the categories have generally been mutually exclusive so that offenders end up in one category or another. The implications of such classifications for treatment are almost bound to be very limited.

Austin and Lipsky (1982) list the classification categories used in a jail system: medical needs, psychiatric needs, aged, young appearance, sex offender, escape risk, gang affiliation, known informer, violent behavior, and inmate rearrests. These categories have no coherence as a system and are much more oriented toward management than toward treatment. They do not, however, constitute mutually exclusive categories; one could have multicategory classifications, for example, young-appearing, psychiatrically disturbed, sex offenders, and some of those classifications might have important implications for treatment.

Warren (1971) looked at sixteen different approaches to classifying juvenile offenders and discerned six commonly identified types of offenders: neurotic, subcultural identifier, asocial, conformist, antisocial manipulator, and situational. These six types appear to be derived primarily from considerations about factors determining initial involvement in criminal activity; whether they are useful and implementable in making decisions about treatment requires independent demonstration. Again, however, they reflect only limited aspects of individuals as total cases, and they seem somewhat simplistic in the scant consideration they give to the complex circumstances that underlie delinquent activity. Given that serious and repeated delinquency is, fortunately, rare, certainly rarer than "neurosis" or than belonging to the subculture from which many delinquents come, not much insight is afforded by labeling it as "neurotic," "subcultural," or "conformist."

A. Examples of Offender Classification Systems

It is useful to consider several of the previous and current approaches to classifying offenders. Most classification schemes bear little obvious relationship to treatment, and no attempt is made here to be exhaustive.

Some examples are chosen solely for illustrative purposes. No classification system appears to have been meant to apply to both adult and juvenile offenders; each focuses on one or the other group.

1. *Offense Behavior.*   Many writers have made distinctions among offenders based on the particular type or pattern of criminal behavior characteristic of the person. Illustrative are the attempts by Gibbons to classify juvenile (1970) and adult (1973) offenders. Juvenile offenders are classified as predatory delinquents, conflict gang delinquents, casual gang delinquents, casual delinquents, auto thieves, drug users, overly aggressive delinquents, "behavior problem" delinquents, and female delinquents. Adult offenders are classified as professional thieves, professional "heavy" offenders, semiprofessional property offenders, property offender "one-time losers," auto-thief joyriders, naive check forgers, white-collar criminals, professional fringe violators, embezzlers, personal offender "one-time losers," "psychopathic" assaultists, violent sex offenders, nonviolent rapists, nonviolent statutory rapists, and narcotics addicts. These categories are undoubtedly meant to be fairly exhaustive of the types of offenders in the criminal justice system, but as systems they lack coherence and have uncertain implications for treatment at best. Some of the categories imply etiology (behavior problems, psychopathic), some involve the conditions of offense (white-collar crime, gang involvement), and some mystify (female).

2. *Psychiatric/Psychodynamic.*   For many years at least some criminologists have been persuaded that crime is to be understood in terms of the psychodynamics of its etiology. The most influential theoretical position has been that of the Freudians. One of the earliest efforts at classifying criminal offenders from a psychodynamic perspective was provided by Alexander and Staub (1956). They began, however, by noting that some criminal behavior has its origins in organic or toxic factors, which is more of a medico-psychiatric than a dynamic category. The remaining categories of offenders were those in which the behaviors involved compulsion or were symptomatic of intrapsychic conflicts, those that could be regarded as representing normal ego and superego development (criminal subculture), and those labeled "genuine" criminals, that is, lacking altogether in superego. Alexander and Staub identified two additional categories of "casual" criminal behavior: "mistaken," meaning that the behavior resulted from severe strain, and "situational," resulting from the undermining of the superego by temporary circumstances, such as intoxication. These categories do presumably entail different types of treatment.

Jenkins and Hewitt (1944) and Hewitt and Jenkins (1946) applied Freudian theory in setting forth a classification scheme for juvenile offenders. They distinguished among overinhibited, underinhibited, and pseudosocial offenders. These categories correspond fairly well to the neurotic (plus symptomatic), genuine, and normal categories of Alexander and Staub. Hewitt and Jenkins believed that the over-inhibited offender must be provided with relief through a socially acceptable way of expressing repressed impulses, that the underinhibited offender needs to be helped to synthesize a superego by a strong authority, and that the pseudosocial offender needs to be helped to enlarge his concept of in-group and build new loyalties. The pseudosocial offender is likely to be helped most by a strong masculine personality with a capacity for warmth, fairness, and fixity of purpose.

There appear to have been no systematic attempts to provide evidence for the reliability with which the psychodynamic classifications can be implemented nor for their usefulness in formulating and carrying out treatment programs.

3. *I-Level Classification.*   One of the most influential and widely cited classification systems for juveniles has been the I-level system, originally proposed by Sullivan, Grant, and Grant (1957). I-level classification was said to be an ego-development theory more general than its application to delinquent behavior would suggest. Warren (1983) has stated that it has origins in child development research and theory, psychoanalysis, Lewinian theory, phenomenological psychology, and social perception. The strongest single influence, however, was that of H. S. Sullivan and his emphasis on interpersonal interaction. In the theory, each I-level represents a stage at which a crucial interpersonal problem must be mastered, and each stage represents a possible level of fixation if the problem is not mastered. Seven different levels of interpersonal maturity have been described, but only three occur commonly among delinquents.

According to I-level theory, all individuals have a relatively consistent way of looking at the world and at themselves in relation to it. The major dimension is perceptual differentiation: how many and what kinds of distinctions are made in describing the world. Increasing I-levels reflect increasing capacities to look at the world in complex, abstract ways. The lowest I-level, I-1, is that of the infant, and to grow beyond it, the infant must develop the crucial self/nonself distinction. Without that discrimination, an individual would be capable of little in the way of planful and, hence, delinquent behavior.

The I-2 level is associated with a view of reality as related to the individual's own needs, and a person at that level would be preoccupied with satisfying his or her own needs without regard to the interests of others. At I-3, the individual is governed by a few, usually strong, rigid, rules or formulas and applies the same standards to others. At I-4, the person has become aware of the expectations of others and has internalized many of the values of others. Such a person is capable of a global identification with others around him. At levels I-5 through I-7, the person develops an increasing differentiated view of the world and of himself. According to the findings of Warren and her associates, few delinquents are found at I-5 (less than 1 percent) and, presumably, none at higher levels.

The I-level theory is augmented by distinctions made within levels derived from experience (with just what reliance on formal empirical data is uncertain). The 4 percent or so of I-2-level delinquents are divided into those that are asocial aggressive and asocial passive. Around 30 percent are at I-3, and they fall into the categories of the passive conformist, the cultural conformist, and the antisocial manipulator. At level I-4, representing the remaining 60+ percent of delinquents, are found the neurotic acting out, the neurotic anxious, the situational emotional reaction, and the cultural identifier. Several of the I-level distinctions bear obvious resemblance to categories proposed by psychodynamic theorists.

Jesness (1974; Jesness and Wedge 1985) has devised an objective questionnaire method for doing I-level assessment, thus obviating some of the serious problems associated with the need for interviews and their subjective element. In line with the view that I-level assessment is appropriate for nondelinquent as well as delinquent youth, and in order to reduce some of the opprobrium associated with the conventional labels for categories, Jesness has suggested alternative terminology, such as undersocialized for unsocialized, pragmatist for manipulator, and introspective for neurotic anxious.

The various I-level types are said to benefit most from somewhat different types of treatment, although some of the distinctions are minimal (e.g., Lerman 1975). For example, I-2s should respond best in group or foster homes presenting simple and concrete demands with only gradual insistence on conformity. They require external orientation and need structure and support rather than insight counseling. No distinction is made by Lerman (1975), however, between the needs of the asocial aggressives and the asocial passives. Similarly, the I-4s are said to require warm, supportive, trusting relationships with internally oriented specialists in group and individual therapy, but distinctions between the needs of the four subtypes are minimal.

Palmer (1983) points out that the I-level system is to be distinguished from classifications that result in no more than a binary categorization of offenders as "amenable" or "not amenable" to intervention generally without specifying any particular form of intervention. For example, Chaiken, Chaiken, and Peterson (1982) recommend that efforts be concentrated on active but "less serious" offenders, and von Hilsheimer (1982) believes that the system must focus on inmates "most likely to benefit" from treatment.

Palmer (1974) himself at one point suggested that only three wider subcategories of I-level classified delinquents might need to be considered distinct and as candidates for differential treatment. Specifically, he indicated the desirability of distinguishing the "passive conformist," the "power oriented," and the "neurotic" as separate types. This simpler configuration is merited in part, according to Palmer, by the fact that nearly all (88 percent) of delinquents can be encompassed by these three types. As will be evident, these three types bear a strong resemblance to types distinguished by Hewitt and Jenkins (1946) and Quay and Parsons (1971).

Palmer is probably the most insistent proponent of I-level classification and its effectiveness. For example, he made a vociferous reply (1975, 1978) to the allegation that "nothing works" in rehabilitation of delinquents. Palmer's case is difficult to make. The problem is that there is no clear-cut test of I-level classification and treatment, and the approaches that have been tried have yielded equivocal and, to this writer, unpersuasive results. The lack of any clear-cut test stems from failure in some tests of I-level classification to use strong, that is, randomized designs and in all instances from incomplete realization of the treatment requirements. In every instance, compromises had to be made in type of placement, the training of staff, and so on (e.g., Jesness 1971a, 1971b, 1975; Lerman 1975; Palmer 1978). Thus failure to find the effects that were expected or desired might be attributable to weak treatment (Sechrest and Redner 1979).

Unfortunately, however, the findings that have emerged concerning I-level classification in relation to treatment do not add up to a persuasive case for the system. A major shortcoming in the tests that have been made is that researchers—proponents of I-level theory—seem not to have formulated any specific hypotheses in advance of the tests; at least the published articles do not set forth such hypotheses. In the main, the hypotheses were limited to expectations that outcomes would be different for different groups in different treatments. The methods of statistical analysis almost always have permitted multiple tests looking for differences. The differences, when found, are usually not large, are not necessarily consistent across studies, and are not necessarily entailed by the theory. For example, Jesness (1971a) compared responses to twenty-bed and fifty-bed living units of boys classified in a way similar to I-level and found that "neurotic" boys appeared to do better in the small units, with no differences in the large units. No rationale for expecting any particular results, other than the obvious expectation that the small units would be better, was given. For some reason results in the small units were somewhat better for black than for white youth, but not for Mexican-American youth.

Jesness (1975) also compared responses to a school providing emphasis on transactional analysis to one emphasizing behavior modification and found some significant differences among an unknown, but presumably large, number of statistical tests. Again, however, the results were neither predicted in advance nor entailed by the theory. For example, the transactional analysis program was found to be better for I-3 boys and the behavior modification program better for the I-4 boys in producing gains on achievement tests.

Palmer (1978) reported better response of "conflicted" youth to special placements in the California Treatment Program than in regular dispositions, but the results were not better in CTP for power-oriented youth; in fact, there was some reversal in the latter group. All in all, the findings concerning I-level classification have to be regarded as, perhaps, intriguing but scarcely as affording a dependable basis for classification and treatment of delinquent youth (Sechrest, White, and Brown 1979).

4. *Quay Classification System.*   Another system for classifying juvenile offenders has been developed and tested over the years by Quay (see, e.g., Quay and Parsons 1971). The Quay system is based on responses of youth to a questionnaire, and the types were established by multivariate statistical analyses. Quay's analyses, as well as those conducted by independent investigators, have consistently produced four different categories of delinquents, although these types refer to "dimensions" of the scale. The four types are Undersocialized Aggression, Socialized Aggression, Attention Deficit, and Anxiety-Withdrawal-Dysphoria. Undersocialized Aggression is much related to

what has often been called the "psychopath" and was originally identified as one type by Hewitt and Jenkins (1946). Socialized Aggression is closely related to the "subcultural delinquent" pattern, also previously and repeatedly identified (Hewitt and Jenkins 1946). The Attention Deficit dimension is one identified by Quay and previously called "immature." Finally, the Anxiety-Withdrawal-Dysphoria dimension was labeled "overinhibited" by Hewitt and Jenkins (1946) and resembles the "neurotic" I-level types.

Quay's typology has been the subject of considerable research, probably more than any other typology, in part because from the beginning it was based in a relatively easy to administer, objective measure. The psychometric properties of the Quay scales have been well established, and it has also been the focus of a wide range of related attempts to establish the construct validity and correlates of the scales (Quay 1987). Like I-level, however, its value in relation to differential treatment remains to be established. Quay and Parsons (1971) speculated, however, that the immature (Attention Deficit) type would respond best to Transactional Analysis (unlikely, in my opinion, particularly in view of the better current understanding of the dimension), the neurotic (Anxiety-Withdrawal-Dysphoria) to individual counseling, the unsocialized psychopath (Unsocialized Aggressive) to behavior modification, and the subcultural (Socialized Aggressive) to reality therapy.

5. *Megargee Classification.*   The Minnesota Multiphasic Personality Inventory (MMPI) is one of the oldest and most widely used instruments in psychology. The MMPI consists of 550 items in true-false format. It was developed empirically to assess psychopathology, and in its original form it yielded scores on eight "clinical" scales representing various aspects of psychopathology, a masculinity-femininity scale, and some validity scales to detect response biases. The item pool has proven widely useful for other purposes, however, and Megargee and his associates (Megargee and Bohn 1979) analyzed the responses to the items by various groups of youthful offenders to determine whether empirically different types might be discerned.

Predictably with such a large item pool, dependence on purely statistical procedures for identifying types, and both sample and population differences, completely consistent results have not been obtained from various attempts to replicate Megargee's work. Nonetheless, the ten types that he proposed have been found with some consistency across nineteen attempts at cross-validation (Zager 1980). Megargee chose to use neutral labels for the offender types in order to avoid connotative meanings that labels often convey. Thus it is not easy to summarize his types, but they may be roughly described as follows: (1) well-adjusted, (2) well-adjusted underachievers, (3) depressed, (4) extroverted psychopath, (5) submissive anxious, (6) hedonistic manipulator, (7) introverted impulsive, (8) immature hostile, (9) suspicious aggressive, and (10) unstable disturbed. Although Megargee and others believe that these classifications have implications for treatment, those implications appear not to have been spelled out in any detail and certainly have not been tested. It seems likely that the Megargee approach will produce more categories of offenders than we have treatments. The uses of the system thus far have seemingly been limited to management rather than to treatment of inmates (see Zager 1980).

6. *Quay's Adult Typology.* More recently, Quay (1984) has reported on a system for classification of adult offenders based on a set of ratings to be made by observers and ratings based on life history information, called the Correctional Adjustment Checklist and the Correctional Adjustment Life History. The system itself is called the Adult Internal Management System (AIMS). Inmates are classified by the system into five groups, designated by numerals in hopes of avoiding unwanted negative connotations. The five groups correspond roughly, however, to Aggressive Psychopath, Manipulative, Situational, Inadequate-Dependent, and Neurotic-Anxious. Although Quay's adult system was probably intended more for management than for treatment purposes, its stated aim does include assignment to programs. The AIMS approach appears to have very good psychometric properties. Its relevance to differential treatment remains to be demonstrated.

It is difficult to know to what extent any of these classification systems is being implemented for treatment or other purposes. The Megargee system has been implemented in the Federal Correctional Institute in Tallahassee, where he does his research, and Quay's systems for both juveniles and adults have been widely promoted. The I-level classification is reportedly (Jesness, personal communication 1986) being used in a number of institutional settings in several states, but the manner in which and the purposes for which it is used are unknown. I have not been able to discover any current use being made of a systematic psychiatric classification system for criminal offenders, although psychiatric diagnoses are widely made in individual cases consequent to consultation.

B. Range of Variables Employed in Offender Classification Systems

A notable fact about most efforts at classification, and particularly about the most heavily promoted system, I-level, is that the classification criteria are restricted to personal characteristics of the individual offender, for example, maturity and anxiety. Such an approach to classification can have implications for only a narrow range of treatment approaches—either those directed at correcting or those capitalizing on the personal characteristics at issue. For example, the I-level system takes no account of abilities, family situation, or temporal point of intervention. Warren (1966) did, however, take the explicit position that no truly comprehensive theory of delinquency is possible and that the intent of the I-level system was to concentrate on the individual's responsibility for his or her own behavior.

Thus the range of variables employed in classification efforts directed at treatment has been generally narrow: certain personality characteristics, psychopathology, aggressive behaviors, educational level, vocational skills, and a few others. Even the personality characteristics that have been incorporated into treatment have been few and narrow in range: anxiety, impulsivity, social sensitivity, and self-esteem. Perhaps the range of variables tapped in classifying offenders for treatment is only characteristic of the field of intervention more generally. There is not much evidence of better classification for treatment in other areas of human malfunctioning. Still, one wonders why such personality variables as the needs for achievement, power, and affiliation; locus of control; stimulus seeking; and the like—all found interesting and useful in other contexts—have not been considered in any evident way in classifying offenders for treatment. One wonders why such important variables as availability of family and other social support, stability of home neighborhood, likely availability of postrelease economic support, and so on are seemingly so little reflected in classification systems. Even such a critical variable as the amount of time a prisoner has left to serve has not generally been included in classifying offenders for treatment. For an offender with at least five years to serve, as an example, one needs to find a prison vocation that will carry him through the first three or four years, but then there should be a shift toward vocational planning for the release. An offender who comes in with a drug or alcohol problem needs help, but the kind of help needed is likely to be quite different from the help that will be needed when that same offender is in the last several months of a five-year stretch.

Implementation of I-level classification and treatment actually seems to require classification of the *treaters;* that is, the personnel are the treatment (e.g., Palmer 1967, 1973; Warren 1983). Lerman (1975) suggests that I-2 treatment agents require "extreme patience," that I-3 treaters must be "strict, but fair, with an impersonal approach," and that I-4 personnel should be "warm, supportive, trusting" and specialists in individual and group therapy. It seems unlikely that any one person could shift back and forth between such roles as are implied. Warren (1983) has noted that treatment settings and treaters must be considered along with treatment modalities in planning interventions. Presumably, classification of treaters would prove no more tractable a problem than classification of offenders, perhaps even less so. In the case of treaters, more than with offenders, one might have to deal with the dynamics between persons. That is, one would have to take into account not only the relationship between offender and treater but between offender and multiple treaters and between treaters. The problems begin to grow by orders of magnitude. A more realistic approach may require greater emphasis on techniques and technologies so as to bring more personal variables into a range within which we may deal with them.

II. Characteristics of Classifications for Treatment

In this section, I examine classification systems for treatment with respect to their development, requirements, and dependability and stability. Each of these characteristics has important implications for creating and evaluating the usefulness of treatment classifications.

A. *Development of Classification Systems*

Classifications for treatment may be developed in three ways: theoretical, empirical, and pragmatic. (Solomon [1977] cites only the first two.) Theoretical classification systems begin with some assumptions about criminal behavior, its origins, and its treatment and then derive a set of categories from those assumptions. The I-level system, said to be based on personality theory broader than that pertaining solely to criminal behavior (Sullivan, Grant, and Grant 1957), is the best example of a theoretical classification system. Psychiatrically oriented systems provide other examples. Theoretical systems may be derived without respect to data on frequencies of types, possible measurement difficulties, empirically overlapping categories, and feasibility of implementation.

Empirical classification systems begin without many explicit assumptions but focus on the search for groups of offenders sharing characteristics of interest. Empirical systems must, however, begin with at least some assumptions about which characteristics will be included in the set of measures obtained. Ethnicity, physical appearance, or birth order are not among characteristics usually included in attempts to find useful ways of classifying offenders. One does find personality and behavioral characteristics (Megargee and Bohn 1979; Quay 1984). Having defined characteristics of interest and obtained measures of them, empirical approaches proceed by statistical methods for locating commonalities (such as factor analysis and cluster analysis; see Brennan, in this volume). Once the empirical types have been defined, the task of determining relevance for treatment begins. Although the promise of import for treatment is sometimes made, that promise has not often been realized.

Other classification systems are developed pragmatically, the term "system" usually being an exaggeration. Offenders are classified according to immediate problems such as their need for medical attention, according to their "escape potential," or according to obvious behavioral characteristics, such as substance-abuse problems. These pragmatic classifications are often related to management problems but also often to treatment; the treatments are usually specific and limited in nature and are meant to resolve the problem that triggered classification. Longer-term rehabilitative goals seldom play an important role.

B. Requirements for a Classification System

One can specify a number of desiderata for a classification system to be employed in implementing treatment strategies. The classification scheme should be based in theory and be theoretically consistent. It might be thought that an empirically derived classification system would be as satisfactory as a theoretical system, but that is not so. An empirical system provides no guidance for the improvement of the classification system or for the choices that are left when initial treatment decisions prove ineffective. Whatever its deficiencies, an advantage of the I-level system is that it is theoretically based. Moreover, it may have an additional advantage in being based in a general theory of personality development and not one limited to criminal offenders; consequently, it can benefit from whatever advances are made in the more general theory.

A desirable classification system should be efficient, reliable, and pertinent to a large majority of offenders. A system will not be optimal if it is expensive to implement or if it requires an inordinate amount of time for decision making. Obviously, a classification system will also lack value if it cannot be reliably implemented. Lack of reliability could stem either from difficult judgments required or from reliance on unstable characteristics of the offender or his situation. Criticisms have been directed at the I-level classification system extensively used in California because the system depends on clinical interviews and because extensive training is required in order to produce dependable performance by raters (Beker and Heyman 1972). That criticism is somewhat mitigated, however, by the existence of the Jesness (1974) instrument. A classification system that depended on extended observations of incarcerated offenders might similarly be criticized as being impractical. A good classification system should provide for positive classification and treatment prescriptions for a large majority of those offenders examined. A system that, for example, singled out 3 percent of offenders as good prospects for psychoanalytic treatment and that did not differentiate among the other 97 percent would not be greatly useful.

The link between classification and treatment should be direct, distinct, and theoretically consistent. One problem with empirical methods of classification is that it is often not clear just what treatment approaches would be entailed by the classifications achieved. For example, Stein, Sarbin, and Kulik (1971) describe seven types of antisocial delinquents derived from empirical analyses, but the implications for treatment are most unclear. What, as an instance, ought one to do with a "nonparentally defiant" type? (Obviously, a classification system might be of interest for more purely theoretical reasons; the context here is treatment.) Similarly, although the MMPI-based system proposed by Megargee and his associates (Megargee and Bohn 1979) was apparently meant to direct treatment, the implications for treatment are obscure and have never been spelled out. One needs to be certain how to move from class to treatment. It does not help much to know merely that treaters should be attentive to characteristics of persons in the class. Moreover, if the classification system is to be of real value, treatment distinctions between classes must be fairly sharp. The classification system will be of limited value if treatment distinctions are limited or blurred, as seems sometimes the case for I-level classification (see Lerman 1975).

Finally, an obvious requirement of a good classification system is that it lead to treatments that are both effective and differentially effective. It is not much help to know that a particular class of offenders *should* do better in, let us say, highly structured rather than unstructured environments if they do not in fact do better in such environments. It is no more help to know that they should do better in such environments if, in fact, nearly all offenders really do better in those environments. A well-validated classification system will be supported by evidence indicating that offenders assigned to treatments in accord with their classifications actually do markedly better than those offenders not so assigned. Palmer (1978), for example, has produced some evidence suggesting that delinquents assigned to treatments on the basis of I-level categories do better than controls not so assigned.

From a public safety perspective, it is important that differential treatment effects persist after treatment, for example, after release from prison; otherwise the effects may be regarded as restricted to management concerns. As an instance, Bohn (1981) reports that implementation of the Megargee classification scheme results in reduced violence in a penal institution, and there are reports of similar findings with respect to the use of the Quay system (Quay 1984), but in neither case was there any evidence of effects on behavior of released inmates.

Jesness (1971a, 1971b, 1984) reported on the application of I-level classification and pointed to evidence for effects on both behavioral and psychological measures in incarcerated delinquents; postrelease parole violations, however, were not different across groups. These results and others that are similar cannot be taken as indicating more than that some types of classification and, subsequently, differential treatment are useful in management of inmates. These results should not be taken as indicating that classification is useful for treatment.

C. Dependability and Stability of Classification

A satisfactory classification system must be dependable, regardless of who does the classification, under what immediate circumstances, and when. The outcome should be the same no matter who does it. It should be the same whether there are six persons waiting to be classified or only one, whether the classification is done in a receiving unit or in a diagnostic center, and so on. And the classification should be the same if it is repeated at some later time.

A good classification system should be able to reflect real changes in an offender but should not be so unstable that it changes without apparent reason. How much constancy one should expect probably depends greatly on the nature of the classification system employed.

Megargee's system, for example, is based on MMPI responses and presumably reflects basic dispositions that ought not to change readily. Thus the complaint directed at Megargee's system, that only a quarter of retested inmates retained their original classification with a lapse of time averaging about ten months, is probably warranted (Simmons et al. 1981). One would not suppose that either I-level or Quay (immature, aggressive, normal) classifications should change very much without extensive intervention. By contrast, classifications incorporating situational variables and life circumstances might change substantially over relatively short periods of time—as inmates approach release dates, as their spouses become more or less supportive, and so on.

Some writers argue that classification must be dynamic and reflect changes over time (e.g., Baird 1981; Clements 1981; Flynn 1982). Schnur (1982) writes that classification must be a continuous process. That view is more compatible with the idea of diagnosis than classification, but the idea that classification is not a one-time act, whether for management or treatment, is critical.

A particularly intriguing observation, fraught with difficulties for the classification process, is that classification is likely to be affected by placement. For example, offenders assigned to units according to the Quay classification system varied according to whether they were assigned to homogeneous or heterogeneous program units, with behavior true to type being more likely on the homogeneous units. That phenomenon makes classification truly dynamic and the process demanding.

III. Matching Offenders to Treatments

Wide agreement exists that offenders should in some manner be matched to treatments (National Institute of Corrections 1981; Rans and Fowler 1981; Smith and Berlin 1981; Palmer 1983; Warren 1983) and that this is the purpose of classification (e.g., Fox 1982). Just how that matching should occur, however, is specified less often. There are problems on both sides of the equation: we do not have good ways of classifying offenders, and we do not have good ways of classifying services.

The notion of efficiency in allocation of resources is fundamental to propositions about classification for treatment. Correctional resources are limited, and they ought, therefore, to be applied to the greatest advantage (Chaiken, Chaiken, and Peterson 1982; Rans and Joyce 1982;

von Hilsheimer 1982). Appropriate classification is assumed to result in both more effective allocation of resources and in their better management (Rans and Joyce 1982). Presumably, better classification leads to better decisions about which offenders get what services. Specific suggestions, though, have often focused on selecting out those offenders who are amenable to change (Chaiken, Chaiken, and Peterson 1982; von Hilsheimer 1982). The resulting two-category classification of offenders as good and poor prospects is not likely to produce optimal use of resources because provision is not made for differential treatment among the good prospects.

Current classification systems are at best insufficient (Gottfredson 1983). We lack the theoretical sophistication to develop useful classifications, and the methodologies used in developing empirical systems have been generally inadequate (Brennan 1980). The National Institute of Corrections (1981) is probably quite right in asserting that most agencies have done little on their own to improve their classification systems. The reports relevant to classification produced by diagnostic centers are not often used to provide treatment (Gettinger 1982). Unfortunately, one of the reasons for failures of classification systems may be a lack of resources for the services that are involved (e.g., Austin and Lipsky 1982).

Classification may be related to treatment by two basic plans. These plans are portrayed in figure 1. They differ only with respect to the service provisions. In Plan A, treatments are "packaged" according to the presumed requirements of persons within each class. The packages need not necessarily be totally dissimilar, but it is implied that the packages are coherent and integral, with various aspects of the overall service package closely linked to each other.

Plan B allows for an array of services that are delivered as discrete units. Different sets of services are selected for each class from the overall service "menu," and overlap between classes is assumed. Such a plan would not be so likely to require segregation of inmates according to class. A category constituted of younger, brighter, conflicted offenders without good work skills might share with a category of older offenders with marketable skills a need for counseling and substance-abuse programs but have a special need for vocational training; the older group might, however, require special family service interventions.

A variant classification system would permit multiple class memberships, and that variant could be accommodated under either Plan A

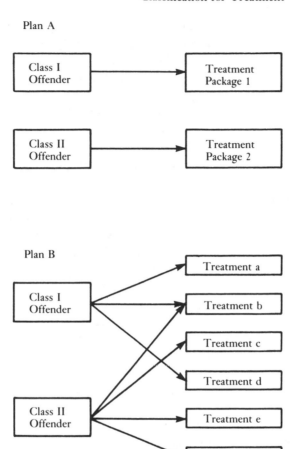

FIG. 1.—Two plans for relating offender classification to treatment

or Plan B. Thus, for example, one might have a treatment package designed for all inmates categorized as "newly admitted substance abuser," and that would not keep an inmate from belonging to another category of "youthful, poorly educated, lacking in basic work skills." The more sets of classifications there are, however, the greater the difficulties in administering the system and the greater the loss of efficiency from classification. If the number of different "cross-cuts" becomes too large, then one does not have a classification system at all but some version of individual service planning.

The only alternative plan would seem to abandon attempts at classification and try to plan an array of services according to the individual needs of each person, a process more akin to *diagnosis* than to classification. Otherwise, services are provided on a basis that is haphazard with respect to characteristics of individuals, a state of affairs that probably resembles too much what happens now.

IV. Problem-oriented Classification

Kaufman (Kaufman and English 1979) argues against using the word "need" as a verb in the sense "he needs a job" or "he needs more self-control." Using "need" as a verb tends to foreclose solutions to problems that are represented by "need" used as a noun. As a noun, need refers to a discrepancy between things as they are and things as they ought to be. Thus "he cannot meet expenses that are required for survival" or "he has no meaningful way to occupy his time." To reduce either of these discrepant states, a job might be helpful. But in the first instance, so might a direct cash subsidy, a winning lottery ticket, or a beneficent relative. In the second case, money is not the issue; an absorbing avocation might serve as well as a job. Similarly, "he has difficulty controlling his impulses." Therefore, some form of behavioral training might be in order, but so might closer supervision or placement in a less complex environment. The task is to determine what the "real versus ideal" discrepant states are, the real needs, and then to determine the possible and feasible ways of reducing those discrepancies.

A useful offender classification system might well begin with a determination of the common "needs" of offenders expressed in terms of discrepancies between things as they are and as they ought to be. Even before that beginning, however, or perhaps as a part of it, account must be taken of the status of the offender with respect to any sentence that must be served. A prisoner with a minimum of eight years to serve is likely to have as a primary need a strategy for survival reflecting the discrepancy between conditions outside and inside prison. That the offender was unemployed and lacks useful job skills or that he committed a homicide in the course of a robbery may be quite irrelevant to his needs. If that offender is within two years of release, the likelihood that he will have no means of support upon release becomes critical.

Short-time prisoners should almost certainly be classified in terms of their economic prospects upon release. To simplify matters, one might classify them as poor prospects or good prospects. Good prospects might reflect useful work skills, a good relation with an employed spouse, a supportive and financially sound family, or substantial savings. Prisoners classified as having poor prospects might become eligible for a treatment package designed to reduce their financial needs and thereby to reduce the discrepancy between their actual economic status and that deemed desirable. The package might be diverse with respect to types of interventions, and the particular elements of it to which each individual would be exposed would depend on individual diagnosis. For example, though, one part of the package might be designed to enhance vocational skills, another part to improve social skills required to acquire and keep a job, and another part to improve relations with family members who could be helpful during a transitional period. Since postrelease financial problems for some prisoners may be greatly exacerbated by their unrealistic expectations about how much money they ought to earn, still another part of the treatment package might be an intervention designed to reduce expectations to realistic levels—not that we necessarily know how to do all these things.

Another classification variable would probably have something to do with adequacy of interpersonal functioning. Inmates classified as having such problems would, again, be exposed to a treatment package whose elements would be employed according to the problems manifested by the individual, as established by diagnostic study. Elements in the package might include intervention to help control aggression, assertiveness training, stress management, enhancement of family relationships, and so on.

The important feature of such a classification system would be that it identifies a problem area and a cluster of relevant interventions. An offender would not be assigned to an intervention program without the problem for which the assignment was made having been identified.

Classification might be much more effective if it were based on problems rather than solutions. Training a prisoner to be a computer technician only makes sense if it is also likely that he could make enough money in that way to come close to meeting his expectations. If not, then either a more lucrative job must be envisioned or a way of reducing expectations must be found.

What the specific needs are that might form the basis for a treatment-oriented classification system is difficult to say without knowing the offender population and facility involved. With juvenile offenders, for example, one important basis for classification would be the nature of the offender's home and family situation. It ought to matter whether an anxious twelve-year-old offender must go back to a chaotic home situation or to a stable one. For inmates facing long incarceration, an important classification feature would be the likely "hardiness" of the offender, his ability to endure prison life. The important aspect of classification should be that it is directed toward identification of problems to be dealt with and away from characteristics of the individual.

It is difficult to see how an adequate system of classification for treatment could be planned without a great deal more knowledge than we now possess about treatments and their effectiveness. We need to know more about the nature of each of our treatments, the needs they address, the effects that can be expected, and any limiting conditions that may exist. In effect, we need a classification system for treatments before we can effectively classify for purposes of treatment. To be more concrete, counseling is frequently mentioned as a desirable intervention for criminal offenders, although rarely, I think, in the context of any particular problem for which counseling might be thought a specific treatment or treatment of choice. Just what is counseling, and what is it supposed to do? The truth is that there is no prescription for counseling; one thinks more in terms of nostrum than therapy. When one considers further how counseling is likely actually to be implemented in a correctional facility, the futility of classifying inmates so that they will get some of it becomes laughable—or perhaps worth crying over. Before the days of antimicrobial drugs, there was not much value in diagnosing patients as suffering from infectious disease except for management purposes, to keep them away from other persons. Once the specific therapy was discovered, however, the diagnosis became of utmost importance. Until we have reasonably specific treatments for the problems of criminal offenders, classifying prisoners for treatment seems pointless.

If we knew that counseling of a particular variety could be counted on to increase self-esteem, then we could determine those larger problems to whose solution an improvement in self-esteem might make a contribution, and we could with confidence recommend counseling for inmates determined to have such problems and low self-esteem. Similarly, if we knew just what effects vocational training produces within a prison system, we could relate those effects to problems and their alleviation. Vocational training may keep inmates out of trouble, may enhance their postrelease economic prospects, may help to instill a sense of personal pride, or may teach work habits of value if they are able to get a job at all. Different kinds of vocational training experiences might have different effects. If we knew what the effects were, we could better relate that form of intervention to types of problems.

We do not have a way of classifying treatments that makes much sense. In their review of interventions, Lipton, Martinson, and Wilks (1975) used ad hoc categories reflecting arbitrarily variant aspects of the interventions. Their categories included educational and vocational interventions, group psychotherapy and individual psychotherapy, milieu, and "other." These labels not only do not reveal much about the nature of the interventions, but they have almost nothing to do with either the problems toward which they are directed or with the outcomes that might be achieved. Consider educational interventions as an instance. What problems are supposed to be remedied by providing education to offenders? If the aim is to increase employability, then the intervention should be classed as economically directed, with education as a specific part of the package. On the other hand, education could be part of a general esteem-enhancing package, or it could be part of a package designed to keep inmates out of further trouble stemming from idleness. Or it could be other things.

A major advantage in a classification system that reflects problems to be dealt with is that such a system may reveal starkly the deficiencies in our ability to intervene. A system that categorizes offenders according to presumed underlying psychopathology may suggest little more than that treatment should deal with that pathology, as by psychotherapy. A system that categorizes offenders as economic risks or as deficient in ability to manage interpersonal relations points to much more specific methods for intervention, particularly if the system is elaborated by attention to more refined estimates of the problem and potentials for dealing with it. If the system results finally in the conclusion that an offender does not handle stress very well, then the implication is inescapable that a method for improving that deficiency should be provided.

Differential treatments suggested by classification schemes, however strongly indicated, may not be implementable, which may make the classification system itself pointless. One reason treatments cannot be implemented is cost; the suggested differential treatments are not affordable. A second reason may be logistical; the suggested differential treatments may not be administratively possible within the strictures of a secure institution. A third reason is that suggested treatments may not be maintainable. Jesness (1971b, 1984), for example, reported an experiment involving six cottages with different staff orientations; assembling and maintaining the right staff with the right orientation might be well beyond the capabilities of any institution over any period of time and might be only possible with the impetus of a highly motivated research staff. Palmer (1967), one of the principals involved in application of the I-level system, admitted that it would be very difficult to implement. Whatever their initial promise and success, I-level treatment centers are not prominent in the field of juvenile delinquency today. Since some of the findings, although equivocal, are at least promising in an otherwise dismal sea of results, the approach probably deserves continuing investigation.

Still other limitations on implementability of differential treatments may stem from legal and ethical concerns. Suppose a classification system, even a validated one, indicates that one class of offenders should be treated quite gently and another class rather harshly. Henn, Bardwell, and Jenkins (1980) explored differences between "socialized" and "undersocialized" delinquents and found that the former group is a good bit less likely to be involved in postrelease offenses. Would such findings justify early release and community treatment of the socialized group? Greenwood (1982) proposed something of that sort of a distinction for adult criminal offenders and has come under scathing attack on grounds that such differential disposition of "like" cases is unethical and unconstitutional. For example, Greenwood's classification system employed such variables as employment history and prior drug use, and such variables were vigorously attacked as surrogates for race and class. How would inmates be classified as "likely to benefit from treatment" or "not likely to change" (as von Hilsheimer [1982] suggests) without employing similar "status" variables that are only surrogates for race and class?

Classification is not without its hazards, the potential effects of labeling being among them. Clements (1981) suggests that the effects of labeling may sometimes be severe, although he appears to have reference to problems stemming from misclassification that might result from sending an inmate to an inappropriately restrictive facility. Other observers believe, however, that labeling can produce the very behavior that the label, and the classification underlying it, seek to ameliorate. Labeling may also produce stigmatizing effects, even in prisons, when some inmates are "labeled" as "dummies" or "crazies." Whether the classification is correct or not, the labeling effect may be detrimental. Given, however, that prison cultures have their own informal classification systems and that prisoners are labeled anyway, one cannot be sure that there is an incremental bad effect from a formal system. Whether a problem-oriented classification system might result in labeling effects is not known. I would assume the risk to be relatively lower than when inmates are classified solely on personal characteristics.

V. Conclusion

If we do not intend to treat all offenders alike and do not intend to behave haphazardly toward them, then some form of classification for treatment is necessary. I argue that efforts to date have been too little grounded in theory, too simplistic, and too much focused on individual, personal characteristics of offenders. Although a good many schemes or systems of classification have been proposed and used over the years, their impact has been limited. We have at best only glimmerings of any possible utility. The situation is much the same for juveniles and adults, but more emphasis has been placed on classification of juvenile offenders for treatment.

At the root of classification problems is the lack of any dependable means of treatment or intervention for offenders, again whether for juveniles or adults. Classification systems for offenders have been derived or developed with virtually no regard for treatment; relevance to treatment has been something to be searched for rather than something forming part of the structure of the classification system. It is difficult, however, to determine which comes first, inadequate classification or inadequate treatment. We need to strive toward the development of a classification/treatment system.

My own view is that our best prospects for improvement will come from better theory and its application to identifying the basic problems that keep criminal offenders from leading law-abiding lives and then to determining the kinds of interventions that will ameliorate those situations. Such an enterprise will require a multifaceted classification system that will consider the totality of an offender's status at any given time and in any given circumstances. The system will take into account the life situation of the offender along with the offender's own characteristics, and it will be dynamic, reflecting changes as they occur. No hint of such a system is in the offing.

Remarkably, the classification systems that have been proposed and used to date seem to have been limited to identified offenders, and for the most part they appear to be focused on offenders as they enter the criminal justice system. Ideally, a classification system should help us to know how to deal with offenders not yet identified. For example, how might we intervene with an unsocialized aggressive youngster to keep him from becoming an identified offender? Although it is perhaps trite to say so, prevention is the best form of treatment. At the other end, however, we also need to have a classification system that enables us to deal with those who have been processed through the criminal justice system and are about to leave it. No attempts at all appear to have been made to classify offenders for purposes of postrelease intervention. What are we to do with an inadequate-immature youth who is leaving a detention facility in that condition?

One of the tritest conclusions, often to the point of being vacuous, that a reviewer of some problem can reach is that "we need more research." Trite and vacuous or not, that conclusion is inescapable. Quay (1975) reviewed the literature on I-level and his own classification systems, the two most widely used in delinquency, and the entire bibliography came to only thirty-five items. That body of literature has grown only marginally in the succeeding years, mostly in the form of commentary and not research. Moreover, a paltry portion of that research has to do with treatment; most is on the methodology. By contrast, the literature on smoking cessation, weight control, treatment of enuresis, reduction in test anxiety, and countless other topics numbers in the hundreds of articles per topic. The call for more research may be trite, but it is justifiable.

Lamentably, I conclude that we do not know very much about the classification of criminal offenders for treatment. We do not know the appropriate bases on which classification might best take place; efforts to date have not been impressive. A major part of the problem results from the limited importance of classification systems in a world in which we do not know how to provide effective treatments. We probably treat offenders too much alike, but we do not know enough about how to treat them differently. Well over a decade ago, Quay (1975) reached a conclusion with which I currently concur: "This question of the match between offender characteristics and treatment modalities, i.e., differential classification and treatment, remains perhaps the most important problem for research in applied corrections" (p. 412).

REFERENCES

Alexander, F., and H. Staub. 1956. *The Criminal, the Judge, and the Public.* Glencoe, Ill.: Free Press. (Originally published 1931.)

Austin, J. 1983. "Assessing the New Generation of Prison Classification Models." *Crime and Delinquency* 29:561–76.

Austin, J., and P. Lipsky. 1982. "Promises and Realities of Jail Classification." *Federal Probation* 45:58–67.

Baird, S. C. 1981. "Probation and Parole Classification: The Wisconsin Model." *Corrections Today* 43:36–41.

Baird, S. C., R. C. Heinz, and B. J. Bemus. 1979. *The Wisconsin Case Classification/Staff Deployment Project.* Project Report no. 14. Madison, Wis.: Department of Health and Social Services, Division of Corrections.

Beker, J., and D. S. Heyman. 1972. "A Critical Appraisal of the California Differential Treatment Typology of Adolescent Offenders." *Criminology* 10:3–59.

Bohn, M. J., Jr. 1981. "Inmate Classification and the Reduction of Institution Violence." *Corrections Today,* vol. 42, no. 4.

Brennan, T. 1980. "Multivariate Taxonomic Classification for Criminal Justice Research." Report prepared for the National Institute of Justice, Washington, D.C.

———. In this volume. "Classification: An Overview of Selected Methodological Issues."

Chaiken, J., M. R. Chaiken, and J. E. Peterson. 1982. *Varieties of Criminal Behavior: Summary and Policy Implications.* Santa Monica, Calif.: Rand.

Clements, C. B. 1981. "The Future of Offender Classification: Some Cautions and Prospects." *Criminal Justice and Behavior* 8:15–38.

Eaglin, J. B., and P. A. Lombard. 1981. "Statistical Risk Prediction as an Aid to Caseload Classification." *Federal Probation Quarterly* 45:25–32.

Flynn, E. E. 1982. "Classification Systems: Community and Institution." In *Holistic Approaches to Offender Rehabilitation,* edited by L. Hippchen. Springfield, Ill.: Thomas.

Fox, V. B. 1982. "History of Offender Classification." In *Holistic Approaches to Offender Rehabilitation,* edited by L. Hippchen. Springfield, Ill.: Thomas.

Gettinger, S. 1982. "Diagnostic Centers: Are They the 'Edsels' of Corrections?" *Corrections Magazine,* vol. 8, no. 5.

Gibbons, D. C. 1970. *Delinquent Behavior.* Englewood Cliffs, N.J.: Prentice-Hall.

———. 1973. *Society, Crime, and Criminal Careers.* Englewood Cliffs, N.J.: Prentice-Hall.

Gottfredson, D. M. 1983. "Diagnosis, Classification, and Prediction in the Criminal Justice System." In *Criminological Diagnosis: An International Perspective,* edited by F. Ferracuti and M. E. Wolfgang. Lexington, Mass.: Lexington.

Greenwood, P. 1982. *Selective Incapacitation.* Santa Monica, Calif.: Rand.

Hanson, R. W., C. S. Moss, R. E. Hosford, and M. E. Johnson. 1983. "Predicting Inmate Penitentiary Adjustment: An Assessment of Four Classificatory Methods." *Criminal Justice and Behavior* 10:293–309.

Henn, F. A., R. Bardwell, and R. L. Jenkins. 1980. "Juvenile Delinquents Revisited: Adult Criminal Activity." *Archives of General Psychiatry* 37:1160–63.

Hewitt, L. E., and R. L. Jenkins. 1946. *Fundamental Patterns of Maladjustment: The Dynamics of Their Origin*. Springfield, Ill.: Illinois State Printer.

Jenkins, R. L., and L. E. Hewitt. 1944. "Types of Personality Structure Encountered in Child Guidance Clinics." *American Journal of Orthopsychiatry* 14:84–94.

Jesness, C. F. 1971*a*. "Comparative Effectiveness of Two Institutional Treatment Programs for Delinquents." *Child Care Quarterly* 1:119–30.

———. 1971*b*. "The Preston Typology Study: An Experiment with Differential Treatment in an Institution." *Journal of Research in Crime and Delinquency* 8:38–52.

———. 1974. *Classifying Juvenile Offenders: Sequential I-Level Classification Manual*. Palo Alto, Calif.: Consulting Psychologists Press.

———. 1975. "Comparative Effectiveness of Behavior Modification and Transactional Analysis Programs for Delinquents." *Journal of Consulting and Clinical Psychology* 43:758–79.

———. 1984. "The Preston Typology Study: An Experiment with Differential Treatment in an Institution." In *Psychological Approaches to Crime and Its Correction: Theory, Research, and Practice*, edited by I. Jacks and S. G. Cox. Chicago: Nelson-Hall.

Jesness, C. F., and R. F. Wedge. 1985. *Jesness Inventory Classification System: A Supplement to the Manuals for the Sequential I-Level Classification System and the Jesness Inventory*. Palo Alto, Calif.: Consulting Psychologists Press.

Kaufman, R., and F. W. English. 1979. *Needs Assessment: Concepts and Application*. Englewood Cliffs, N.J.: Educational Technology Publications.

Kelly, G. A. 1955. *The Psychology of Personal Constructs*. New York: Norton.

Lerman, P. 1975. *Community Treatment and Social Control: A Critical Analysis of Juvenile Correctional Policy*. Chicago: University of Chicago Press.

Levinson, R. B. 1984. "Differential Treatment: An Adult Typology." In *Psychological Approaches to Crime and Its Correction: Theory, Research, and Practice*, edited by I. Jacks and S. G. Cox. Chicago: Nelson-Hall.

Lipton, D., R. Martinson, and J. Wilks. 1975. *The Effectiveness of Correctional Treatment: A Survey of Treatment Evaluation Studies*. New York: Praeger.

Megargee, E. I., and M. J. Bohn. 1979. *Classifying Criminal Offenders: A New System Based on the MMPI*. Beverly Hills, Calif.: Sage.

National Institute of Corrections. 1981. *Prison Classification: A Model Systems Approach*. Washington, D.C.: U.S. Government Printing Office.

Palmer, T. 1967. "Personality Characteristics and Professional Orientations of Five Groups of Community Treatment Project Workers: A Preliminary Report on Differences among Treaters." CTP Report Series no. 1. Sacramento: California Youth Authority.

———. 1973. "Matching Worker and Client in Corrections." *Social Work* 18:95–103.

———. 1974. "The California Youth Authority Treatment Project." *Federal Probation* 38:3–14.

———. 1975. "Martinson Revisited." *Journal of Research in Crime and Delinquency* 12:133–52.

————. 1978. *Correctional Intervention and Research*. Lexington, Mass.: Lexington.

————. 1983. "The 'Effectiveness' Issue Today: An Overview." *Federal Probation* 46:3-10.

Quay, H. C. 1975. "Classification in the Treatment of Delinquency and Antisocial Behavior." In *Issues in the Classification of Children*, vol. 1. San Francisco: Jossey-Bass.

————. 1984. *The Differential Behavioral Classification of the Adult Male Offender*. Technical report prepared for the U.S. Department of Justice Bureau of Prisons, contract J-1C-22, 253. Philadelphia: Temple University.

————. 1987. "Patterns of Delinquent Behavior." In *Handbook of Juvenile Delinquency*, edited by H. C. Quay. New York: Wiley (in press).

Quay, H. C., and L. B. Parsons. 1971. *The Differential Behavioral Classification of the Juvenile Offender*. Washington, D.C.: U.S. Bureau of Prisons.

Rans, L. L., and L. T. Fowler. 1981. *Classification: Key to Correctional Development? A Framework for Agencies and Practitioners*. Paper presented at the 1981 annual meeting of the American Society of Criminology, Washington, D.C.

Rans, L. L., and N. M. Joyce. 1982. "Adult Institution Classification: Design and Validity Report." Springfield: Illinois Department of Corrections, Bureau of Policy Development.

Schnur, A. C. 1982. "Initial and Reclassification Procedures." In *Holistic Approaches to Offender Rehabilitation*, edited by L. Hippchen. Springfield, Ill.: Thomas.

Sechrest, L., and R. Redner. 1979. "Strength and Integrity of Treatments in Evaluation Studies." In *How Well Does It Work?* Washington, D.C.: National Institute of Law Enforcement and Criminal Justice.

Sechrest, L., S. O. White, and E. D. Brown, eds. 1979. *The Rehabilitation of Criminal Offenders: Problems and Prospects*. Washington, D.C.: National Academy of Sciences.

Simmons, J. G., D. L. Johnson, W. D. Gouvier, and M. J. Muzyczka. 1981. "The Meyer-Megargee Inmate Typology: Dynamic or Unstable?" *Criminal Justice and Behavior* 8:49–54.

Smith, A. B., and L. Berlin. 1981. *Treating the Criminal Offender*. Englewood Cliffs, N.J.: Prentice-Hall.

Solomon, H. M. 1977. *Crime and Delinquency Typologies*. Washington, D.C.: University Press of America.

Stein, K. B., T. R. Sarbin, and J. A. Kulik. 1971. "Further Validity of Antisocial Personality Types." *Journal of Consulting and Clinical Psychology* 36:177–82.

Sullivan, C., M. Q. Grant, and J. D. Grant. 1957. "The Development of Interpersonal Maturity: Applications to Delinquency." *Psychiatry* 23:73–385.

von Hilsheimer, G. 1982. "The Team Approach to Diagnosis." In *Holistic Approaches to Offender Rehabilitation*, edited by L. Hippchen. Springfield, Ill.: Thomas.

Warren, M. Q. 1966. "Classification of Offenders as an Aid to Efficient Management and Effective Treatment." Prepared for the President's Commission on Law Enforcement and the Administration of Justice, Task Force on Corrections.

———. 1971. "Classification of Offenders." *Journal of Criminal Law, Crime, and Social Policy* 62:239–58.

———. 1983. "Applications of Interpersonal-Maturity Theory to Offender Populations." In *Personality Theory, Moral Development, and Criminal Behavior*, edited by W. S. Laufer and J. M. Day. Lexington, Mass.: Lexington.

Zager, L. D. 1980. "The MMPI-based Classification System: A Critical Review of Derivation Procedures and Recent Investigations of Its Generalizability and Dynamic Feature." Unpublished manuscript. Tallahassee: Florida State University, Department of Psychology.

Tim Brennan

Classification for Control in Jails and Prisons

ABSTRACT

Classification systems provide means for maintaining institutional safety and order, for providing inmates protection and services, and for managing and allocating personnel and resources. A traditional "judgmental" approach is being largely displaced by objective data-based procedures. The two basic components of institutional classification are the selection of risk factors and the formulation of decision rules. Risk factors in use include consensus-based models, equity-based models, and selections based on empirical prediction and psychometric testing. Decision rules in use or under consideration include linear additive point scales, decision trees, matrix classifications, and attempts to integrate the objective and judgmental aspects of classification. Jail and prison classifications differ procedurally and substantively. Because their populations, resources, policy orientations, and architectures differ, no one standardized classification can fit both kinds of institutions. Weaknesses in management, methodology, and application characterize most correctional classifications; however, the overall move toward use of objective methods has facilitated cumulative scientific evaluation and improvement through "bootstrapping."

Achievement of virtually all jail and prison objectives requires use of classifications. The pressures of overcrowding, scarce fiscal resources, and legal challenges have contributed to a renewed focus on classification. Litigation has forced an examination of the costs of classification errors to inmates and staff and to the public. The high costs of new construction have caused concern over wasteful use of high security resources and excessive restrictiveness. Concern with public and in-

Tim Brennan is instructor in statistics and policy analysis, Graduate School of Public Affairs, University of Colorado.

stitutional safety has also forced a reexamination of classification errors (Solomon and Baird 1982).

Although classification is increasingly seen as critical for jail and prison operation, its link to various institutional policies and operations remains confused (Flynn 1982). Fowler and Rans (1982) suggest that much of the failure in jails and prisons stems from administrative confusion over its role. The issue is complex since classification serves several purposes, some of which are not immediately obvious or may be secondary to others, while some purposes may conflict. Confusion is shown in widespread administrative failure to provide clear guidelines for classification (Fowler and Rans 1982).

Policy orientations and choices of classification systems interact. Changes of policy often require changes in classification, and vice versa (Brennan, in this volume). As Fowler and Rans (1982) note: "value issues interact with technological issues in the design and implementation of classification systems. In many ways, values determine technologies and their potential outcomes" (p. 19). Thus restrictive policies produce restrictive classification, while liberal or inmate-oriented policies lead to less restrictive forms of classification.

Classification is linked to numerous goals, as the following quotation from a 1970 judicial opinion demonstrates: "Classification is essential to the operation of an orderly and safe prison. It is a prerequisite for the rational allocation of whatever program opportunities exist within the institution. It enables the institution to gauge the proper custody level of an inmate, to identify the inmate's educational, vocational, and psychological needs, and to separate nonviolent inmates from the more predatory. Classification is also indispensable for any coherent future planning" (Gettinger 1982, p. 27).

Any single classification decision may implicate multiple goals. For example, placing inmates into maximum security can simultaneously involve the goals of containment, punishment, rehabilitation, and deterrence. There is no general consensus regarding how these goals should be prioritized. A classification system generally must balance conflicting goals against each other and pursue all of them at some minimally acceptable level. This is a difficult balancing act. Optimizing inmates' rights may demand compromises in, for example, public safety, deterrence, and other goals. One solution is to have separate classification systems for each goal—security, custody, treatment and rehabilitation, and reentry classifications are separated. Each classification system is designed for the specific goal involved and used sequentially and independently. However, such sequential separation is not always feasible.

Containment and security usually receive priority in jails and prisons (Alexander 1982), and administrative and management goals are often emphasized more than inmates' rights (Flynn 1982). Thus efficient processing, public safety and security, and expedient decision making are usually prioritized over fairness, equity, least restrictive custody, and comparable objectives (Solomon and Baird 1982).

Section I presents an overview of the roles of institutional classification. Changing methods for jail and prison classifications are described in Section II. This section begins by documenting traditional approaches to classification. It then examines forces that cause reform and concludes with a description of current approaches. Section III considers recent research on risk factors for custody and security classifications. The diversity of jail and prison institutional classifications is described in Section IV by first considering the reasons for such variation and then reviewing selected jail and prison classification systems. Section V provides a brief overview of why institutional classification systems fail. A summary and conclusions are presented in Section VI.

I. The Roles of Institutional Classification

Classification is a key process in solving many of the problems of jails and prisons. This section describes various primary and subsidiary roles performed by control classification systems in jails and prisons.

A. *Inmate, Staff, and Public Safety*

A high priority goal for jails and prisons is to provide a safe environment for all inmates and staff. This necessitates the valid identification and classification of violent offenders and their separation from likely victims. Both inmate and staff safety are linked to identification, classification, and supervision of dangerous inmates. Alexander (1982) indicates that this goal has first-order priority in most institutional classification approaches. Failure to separate predators from victims is likely to result in victimization and an unsafe, anxiety-provoking environment. Identification and separation of these types is coupled with higher supervision of the dangerous or high-risk offenders. Suicide screening procedures similarly attempt to identify prisoners having a high risk for suicide and highlight their need for appropriate surveillance and treatment.

Public safety also depends on valid classification of levels of dangerousness. Such classifications are coupled with security constraints and release recommendations to minimize escape, erroneous community placements, and serious recidivism. Classification decisions that release apparently high-risk inmates to the community often become a focus of public controversy (Bottoms 1973). Discretionary release into the community of persons who then commit serious offenses can produce intense media attention, public scorn, and strong criticism of the classification procedures used in jails and prisons.

B. Classification for Rehabilitation and Reintegration

Reintegration of inmates often is pursued by placing them into educational or vocational programs in the communities near the institution. In this instance, classification must balance public safety with the goals of offender rehabilitation and reintegration. Correct classification aims to protect the prisoner's rights to avoid deterioration of social skills, to have access to rehabilitation programs, and to be placed in the least restrictive environment. This minimizes the isolation of inmates from the outside community while simultaneously achieving the often opposing goal of public protection. A good classification system will provide a rational basis for balancing such objectives. Mistakenly classifying offenders as high risk may restrict an inmate's participation in rehabilitative programs and thereby undermine the goals of rehabilitation and treatment.

C. Equity, Fairness, and Consistency

These classification goals are important to both inmates and corrections staff. Poor classification can undermine all three of these goals. The goal of consistency requires classification methods that attempt to minimize subjectivity and bias and use reliable data. Newer objective classification approaches aim to constrain or limit the extremes of subjective discretion, bias, and prejudice.

D. Provision of Appropriate Service

Classification is a basic mechanism for identifying the various vocational, educational, physical, and mental health needs of inmates. This identification helps protect offenders from "deliberate indifference" to certain treatment needs (e.g., medical, drug and alcohol, and psychiatric problems) and protect their right to receive minimally adequate treatment (National Institute of Corrections 1981). The courts have seen classification as a means of ensuring consistent and equitable allocation of housing and program resources. Valid classification is a primary buttress to the right to be reasonably protected from violent assault or the fear of violence. Neither inmates nor staff want the anxiety of "surprises." Thus classification has a critical role in reducing anxiety by creating an orderly, predictable, and controlled environment.

E. Efficiency and Rationality in Resource Utilization

Correct classification is crucial for avoiding waste. Correct "matching" of inmates with agency resources is the foundation of efficient resource allocation. For example, erroneous overclassification of inmates into inappropriately high security or custody levels constitutes systematic waste of assets. Similarly, when needed services are withheld from an eligible inmate, the results may be violence, escape failure to rehabilitate, or lawsuits. Thus both positive and negative errors can produce waste, extra costs, and reduced efficiency.

Valid classification becomes even more crucially important when there are severe resource shortages. A recent National Institute of Corrections (1984) report asserts, "the increasing demand for both security and program resources, coupled with the probability that the availability of both will decrease, calls for an especially efficient and effective classification decision that will make the most advantageous use of physical, financial and human resources" (p. 9).

F. Management Planning

Classification is a tool for coherent planning of budgets, staffing, programs, and physical space requirements (Fowler and Rans 1982). Planning in jails and prisons is generally based on enumeration of inmate population characteristics, sizes, and trends. Glaser (1974) has described the use of classification for enumeration and accurate estimation of population structures and trends. By providing more accurate planning data than do global population estimations, classification systems can forecast differentiated levels of need for various resources and services and can provide more accurate and detailed estimations of resource requirements.

In virtually all instances where jails and prisons have introduced objective classification systems, the new systems showed that planning for new construction was based on erroneous assumptions. Enormous financial savings resulted because planners had consistently overestimated the need for expensive maximum security cells and underestimated the need for minimum security space (Levinson 1982; Austin 1983).

G. Social Control and Discipline

Classification serves several social control functions that are not immediately obvious (Hobbs 1975). It is intricately involved in maintaining the stability and order of the institution through consistent and appropriate processing decisions. It governs distribution of various rewards and punishments. It is critical in minimizing discord, maintaining orderliness, and generating consistent inmate expectations and predictions that help allay the anxiety generated by the presence of many deviant individuals.

Social control concerns will usually prioritize community and institutional goals above the concerns of inmates. Control classifications identify and label threatening individuals and impose constraints or barriers on them. Such restraints not only separate but may stigmatize certain individuals.

Classification is strongly linked to the control and management of inmates' behavior since it governs access to rewards and may circumscribe privileges. For example, misbehavior is often "punished" by reclassifying the person to a less privileged level, while good behavior is rewarded by reclassification into custody levels having greater privileges.

The line classification officer plays a critical role in regulating inmate behavior (Prottas 1979). Institutional expectations for good or bad behavior are conveyed and enforced via the classification process. If subjective discretion is allowed, the authority and power of the lineworker is enhanced. Officers may informally escalate the degree of harshness resulting from classification decisions in order to manage difficult or ambiguous situations. Such discretionary escalation is more easily imposed when procedures are traditional, subjective, and informal. Under these circumstances, classification is used, in effect, as a tool to achieve discipline and control.

H. Institutional Order

Institutions deal with "classes of clients" since bureaucratic responses must always be standardized. Prisons and jails cannot plan for, provide responses to, or cope easily with innumerable individualized distinctions and cannot deal with all possible contingencies (Prottas 1979; Lipsky 1980). Classification is a main mechanism for creating simplicity and order out of the diversity of most inmate populations. Such simplification is a preliminary step to the planning, selection, and design of standardized institutional responses.

Until individuals are classified, bureaucracies are unable to deal with them (Prottas 1979; Lipsky 1980). All bureaucratic actions or decisions require that the new "inmate" be defined. In jails and prisons the initial classification transforms "citizens" into "inmates," who are then eligible for appropriate institutional housing, treatment intervention, and program placement.

Classification contributes to bureaucratic orderliness by making inmate movement, rehousing, and transfers predictable and consistent. Alexander (1982) has noted that unpredictability and disorganization tend to undermine personal relations and trust, which undermines most of the other goals of corrections. Classification aims to reduce disorder and uncertainty by eliminating arbitrariness, vagueness, unclear criteria, bias, subjectivity, and prejudice from most inmate processing and movement decisions.

I. Communication

Both staff and inmates require accurate understanding of the various labels used to describe inmates. When these names are vague or inconsistent, communication can break down, expectations and predictions do not hold up, and institutions lapse into disorganization. Anxiety rises with inability to communicate justifications for classification decisions. Valid and rational classification decisions help to provide a sense of predictability, which in turn allays anxiety. Meaningless labels and unpredictable decisions come from unclear criteria, unclear decision rules, informal discretion, and high heterogeneity among "classes" of inmates that are presumed to be homogeneous.

J. Monitoring and Accountability

Classification has recently been recognized to be fundamental for monitoring goal achievement. Fowler and Rans (1982, p. 23) suggest that classification systems and data they produce can indicate whether goals and policy objectives are being achieved.

Effective monitoring depends on whether appropriate data are designed, collected, and used. Information that indicates achievement of the various policy goals of a jail or prison can, in theory, be routinely and accurately collected. Top managers have responsibility for the design, support, and monitoring of such data collection. Yet such accountability procedures have often been undermined by both poor management skills and the prevalence of classification that is subjective, informal, and undocumented. If data are available that indicate the extent to which each major policy is achieved, accountability becomes possible. This function of classification can be threatening to both line and administrative staff and may therefore provoke resistance and sabotage at both levels (Prottas 1979).

K. Protection from Liability

Many jail and prison personnel are starting to realize that good classification is a means of avoiding public embarrassment, maintaining good public relations, and avoiding costly litigation. Errors can devastate the public image of a facility. Valid classification is a main instrument in avoiding such errors. In addition, objective classification provides documentation and justification for decisions. Thus it provides more protection against litigation than informal approaches that are deficient in both documentation and justifications—the basic prerequisites for protection in legal disputes.

If a jail or prison, however, has introduced objective classification and then does not properly implement it or fails to follow established procedures, it becomes in fact more vulnerable to litigation. This is because it then becomes easier to demonstrate that agency personnel failed to follow official procedures. Thus it behooves institutional personnel to be adequately trained and to follow established procedures carefully.

In summary, there are a variety of roles of institutional classifications that can support the needs of inmates, staff, institutions, and the public. Objective classification systems offer advantages over more traditional systems in fulfilling most of these goals. The next section examines the differences between these two approaches.

II. An Overview of Changing Methods for Jail and Prison Control Classification

This section examines some current trends in approaches to institutional security and custody classification. The traditional "judgment" approach is gradually being abandoned and objective numerical procedures have emerged. Various forces of change have channeled and motivated these trends.

A. The Traditional Approach to Classification

The traditional "judgmental" model of classification used neither standardized risk factors nor explicit logical decision rules but emphasized subjective expertise and clinical assessment. Risk factors were diverse, usually unwritten, and seldom quantified. The traditional approach, particularly in prisons, was often leisurely. Inmates were given a battery of social, psychological, and medical tests over a few weeks to determine their initial classification. Counselors and professional staff would then make recommendations regarding custody, treatment, and security. A similar extended approach was impracticable in jails due to high inmate turnover and the unavailability of professional staff. Consequently, the jail classification process was extremely simplified and largely subjective.

The subjective approach is slowly being abandoned. More formalized classification methods are being used in both jails and prisons. Glaser (1982) notes an interesting connection between changing institutional authority structures and the emergence of more formalized classification. He indicates that where "patrimonial" authority is exercised—where power is delegated on the basis of personal relations and trust rather than on expertise, skills, or training—classification is usually informal, casual, and discretionary, with minimal record keeping. As this patrimonial authority gives way to a more bureaucratized authority structure, the demands for efficiency, accountability, and management control produce a more formalized systematic classification approach. Glaser (1982) suggests that the traditional approach was the norm until well into the 1950s. A review of the nation's jail classification by Bohnstedt and Geiser (1979) suggests that many of these facilities still used this traditional approach in the late 1970s.

B. Forces Causing Reform of Jail and Prison Traditional Classification

Various weaknesses in the traditional approach have produced strong pressures on jails and prisons to improve their classification practices. These criticisms helped establish a set of criteria that institutional classification must try to meet.

First, the courts have been active in forcing correctional facilities to change their classification practices. Courts have demanded that classification employ coherent methods that can be objectively applied and rationally explained. The courts repeatedly stress that classification criteria must be applied consistently.

Traditional subjective classification systems have been criticized for being based on unvalidated assumptions. The courts have demanded at least some level of predictive validity for custodial and security classifications. This implies that risk factors and decision methods should be validated. Such requirements pose problems for subjective procedures since it is often difficult to test the validity and rationality of an entirely subjective classification procedure.

A second powerful source of pressure to change classification systems emerges from standard-setting bodies and professional organizations such as the American Correctional Association (ACA). The National Institute of Corrections, for example, has formulated fourteen guidelines for classification, which have influenced the development of many jail and prison approaches. These are consistent with both ACA accreditation standards and court decisions. Since these National Institute of Corrections principles have been highly influential, they are briefly reviewed below.

1. *Clear Definition of Goals and Objectives.*   Many traditional systems of classification did not explicitly state their goals, purposes, or priorities. The absence of such policy guidelines can create havoc in the design and implementation of classification systems (Fowler and Rans 1982).

2. *Written Policy and Procedures.*   Many jails and prisons avoided written procedures or provided only inadequate policy and procedure manuals. Classification manuals should be written clearly and concisely; they should be understood by the staff, and they should be periodically revised and updated. This guideline also emphasizes that each policy must be linked to an explicit classification procedure.

3. *Collection of Complete High-Quality, Verified, and Standardized Data.* Traditional systems offered few guidelines to staff regarding collection of inmate data. Yet accurate standardized information is critical for correct classification (Austin 1983). Missing or ambiguous data, redundancies, and errors undermine the validity of any classification system. This guideline emphasizes the importance of verified and standardized data.

4. *Valid, Reliable, and Objective Instruments.*   This guideline parallels legal decisions and emphasizes that classification factors can often be discriminatory, biased, or invalid. It emphasizes the need for high-quality objective instruments.

5. *Limiting and Structuring Discretionary Power.*   Bias and subjectivity can often enter classification through staff discretion. Traditional subjective approaches allowed almost total discretionary latitude in decision making. This guideline thus aims to control and structure discretion.

6. *Identify Inmates Who Are Management Problems.*   This guideline emphasizes the need for procedures to identify prisoners with special

needs (e.g., medical, mental health, or protective custody needs) and to provide appropriate services for these individuals.

7. *Matching Offenders with Programs.* Classification in jails and prisons often omit this "matching process" (Holt, Ducat, and Eakles 1982). Recent research suggests that large proportions of eligible inmates do not receive the services for which they qualify (Austin and Lipsky 1980). "Matching" requires correct identification of offender needs and systematic referral to appropriate programs. Explicit matching also helps indicate gaps in the institution's resources.

8. *Least Restrictive Custody Level.* This principle requires that inmates be placed in the lowest custody level appropriate for their safety and that of the community. However, traditional subjective classifications tend to systematic overclassification. The newer objective systems perform better but may still commit this error.

9. *Prisoner Involvement.* Traditional classification was often a "black box" not only to the inmate but to many jail and prison staff as well. The adoption of objective systems helps make the classification procedure explicit, coherent, and understandable. These features will facilitate appropriate levels of prisoner involvement.

10. *Systematic Reclassification.* Jails and prisons vary in the timing and frequency of reclassification. Arguably, reclassification is more critical in prisons because of longer sentences. In jails, where a high proportion of inmates are released within days, the necessity for elaborate reclassification procedures is sometimes questioned. However, many jails have a substantial proportion of inmates who may stay up to a year. For those inmates reclassification is crucial.

11. *Efficiency and Ease of Use.* Classification procedures will fail if they are cumbersome, unwieldy, or difficult to learn. Staff understanding and acceptance is also critical for successful and efficient implementation.

12. *Ongoing Evaluation Development.* Regular evaluation and periodic monitoring are recommended to identify weaknesses that can then provide a basis for modifications and improvements. Without continuous evaluation it is impossible to determine whether the system is achieving its specified goals.

13. *Constitutionality.* Many jail and prison systems, when developing new procedures, routinely conduct a legal review. This guideline suggests that forms, procedures, risk factors, and so forth, should receive legal scrutiny to assess adherence with the current state or constitutional requirements.

14. *Input from Staff during System Development.* Staff involvement in

the design and implementation of any new institutional classification is seen as highly advisable. Studies on the implementation of new classifications suggest that it is perilous to ignore or prohibit staff input.

These principles and guidelines have gained broad currency in professional training programs and in the correctional literature (Solomon 1980; Gettinger 1982; National Institute of Corrections 1982). They represent an attempt by national and professional organizations to provide leadership to jails and prisons in this area.

Third, the media often selectively focus on errors of underclassification while systematically ignoring errors of overclassification. Thus the public may assume that "serious criminals" are frequently released and that classification decisions are excessively liberal; this can produce a popular demand for harsher sentences and more restrictive classification.

Elected sheriffs and judges are sensitive to these pressures and often adopt highly restrictive classification policies. In contrast, the correctional and professional bodies strongly emphasize the principle of least restrictive custody.

Finally, correctional workers are anxious—for various reasons—to improve classification procedures. No single security or custody system is generally accepted, and there is much dissatisfaction and cynicism among correctional staff regarding all classification systems. Staff acceptance of newer objective systems is fairly high once they become familiar with their logic and operations (Gettinger 1982; Holt, Ducat, and Eakles 1982; Austin 1983; National Institute of Corrections 1984). Other reasons for seeking improved systems of classification include the need of top management for better information on which to base short- and long-term planning and pressure from court suits.

C. Current Approaches to Jail and Prison Institutional Classification

The concurrent pressures of court litigation, overcrowding, fiscal problems, and general dissatisfaction with older methods is producing a "new generation" of jail and prison classifications. All aspects of correctional classification have undergone searching scrutiny (Flynn 1982; Austin 1983). There are four components of these newer classifications that are worth describing in some detail. They include variation in the way risk factors are selected, how scores for risk factors are combined, what are some of the advantages of the newer systems, and what are some of the criticisms that have been leveled at them at the applied level.

1. *Selecting Risk Factors.*   A critical first component is the selection of classification variables. Any change in these factors can profoundly change the resulting classification decisions (see Brennan, in this volume). The following current trends are noted regarding the selection of risk factors.

a) Consensus-based Models.   Many prisons and jails lack good longitudinal data on which to base statistical predictions. Thus, in building their classification systems, they rely on professional judgment and consensus. Risk factors in this instance are not chosen for their proven statistical validity and are selected logically without reliance on statistical analysis. Explicitness and face validity are the advantages of this approach. However, while such systems may achieve the goals of standardization and consistency, questions regarding validity remain unanswered.

b) Equity-based Models.   This popular approach restricts classification factors to explicit behavioral and legal variables. Variables are chosen that focus strictly on current and previous criminal behavior and legal variables. Factors that reflect "extraneous" variables (such as social and psychological personality characteristics) are excluded. These systems obviously do not aim to achieve optimal predictive accuracy but rather attempt to maximize consistency and equity. Predictive purposes, in fact, are often discouraged; proponents of these models assert that the science of prediction is insufficiently accurate (Austin 1983). Nonlegal, social, and psychological variables are excluded because there is little consistent research support for their predictive validity (Megargee and Bohn 1979; Clements 1980; Monahan 1981) and on ethical grounds.

c) Predictive Models.   These systems aim to include any and all risk variables thought to predict inmate behaviors such as disciplinary infractions, escape, and suicide. This approach uses a broad mixture of legal, social, and psychological data and past criminal history. The performance of predictive approaches in custody and security classification has been only marginally successful (Chapman and Alexander 1981; Solomon and Baird 1982; Flanagan 1983; Hanson et al. 1983).

d) Psychological Models and Psychometric Tests.   In a few classification systems, well-known psychometric instruments have been adapted for security and custody classification. Megargee and Bohn (1979) offer a typology based on the Minnesota Multiphasic Personality Inventory (MMPI). Carlson (1981) offers a classification system based on psychometric inventory. Eber (1978) has adapted Cattell's personality inventory (Cattell, Eber, and Tatsuoka 1970) and the Clinical Assessment Questionnaire for use in certain custody and security decisions. None of these systems has been widely adopted. The few studies aimed at rigorous evaluation of these psychological approaches have demonstrated inconsistent relations between the psychological factors and inmate disciplinary problems (e.g., Hanson et al. 1983). Correctional staff seem to prefer simpler classification factors based on criminal history or prior institutional adjustment (Levinson 1982).

2. *Combining Risk Factors.* The second critical methodological component is the procedure by which risk factors are combined to make a classification decision. The following are slowly replacing the traditional subjective or clinical approach in jail and prison classification.

a) Linear Additive Point Scales. The scores for each of the selected risk factors are added together. Such additive schemes can be statistically generated using regression and other multivariate methods (Gottfredson and Gottfredson 1980) or simply based on logic or consensus (American Correctional Association 1984). Weighting schemes are often applied for each separate factor to reflect its relative importance. Linear additive models offer only a limited approach to classification (Brennan, in this volume). However, this method is practical, easy to understand, and perhaps the most commonly used form of objective decision making for jail and prison classification.

b) Decision Trees. Decision trees are much less frequently used in jail and prison control classification systems. Decision trees can also be developed statistically or by consensus. Statistical approaches include predictive attribute analysis, the automatic interaction detector, and association analysis (MacNaughton-Smith 1965; Brennan and Huizinga 1975; Gottfredson and Gottfredson 1982; Flanagan 1983). Decision trees have the practical advantages of being intuitive and easy to use. They achieve high interrater reliability in applied work due to their simplicity.

Statistically based decision trees have not received an unequivocal acceptance in the statistical community. They are criticized for the arbitrariness involved in their splitting procedures. However, the same criticism can be leveled at point scales since cutoffs are often arbitrary impositions on continuous distributions. Very few statistical decision trees are in use in practical correctional agencies; one example is the Parole Decision Tree (see Monahan 1981). More logical, or consensus-based, decision tree systems are in use—for example, in the Traverse City Jail and the Florida Department of Corrections.

c) Matrix Classifications. The matrix decision approach involves the cross-classification of two separate point systems (see Baird 1982; Correctional Services Group 1984). Some correctional jurisdictions develop separate scales for security and custody levels and, by cross-classifying these two scales, develop a matrix of cells. This gives a decision rule that integrates both security and custody implications. An advantage is that it incorporates a greater amount of information into one decision system.

d) *Integrating Objective and Subjective Components of Classification.* Wormith and Goldstone (1984) describe two main approaches to integrating clinical and statistical approaches. In the first approach—which is common in jails and prisons—an objective method is applied, followed by a discretionary override. In effect, the objective classification data are used as an input into the subjective decision. In the second approach, the subjective judgment is entered as a variable into a statistical prediction procedure. This represents an extension of the statistical procedure since it inserts a subjective variable into the statistical model. Wormith and Goldstone tested whether such integration could improve on standard objective classification. They concluded that the clinical data did not produce any substantial improvement of prediction in either a multiple regression approach or a unit-weighted point system when cross validation was applied.

e) *Comparing the Decision Methods.* There seems to be no clear advantage between various statistical decision trees or linear additive scales. Arguably, the statistical decision trees have not yet had a chance to prove their superiority because of inadequacies in data and a dearth of comparative studies. Decision tree methods are extremely vulnerable to incorrect data. One incorrect variable can introduce a chain of incorrect decisions. Statistically developed trees, using large data bases, in conjunction with reliable variables, might eventually prove to be a superior predictive classification method.

3. *Advantages of Newer Approaches.* The evidence concerning the impact of objective classification systems comes from a handful of evaluation studies (Austin and Lipsky 1980; Levinson 1982). The following appear to be the main advantages and potential impact of these newer "objective approaches."

a) *Efficiency.* Objective classification models seem, generally, more efficient and less costly to operate. Compared with the traditional model they do not require lengthy diagnostic periods, highly salaried expert staff, or extensive clinical assessments. Using objective systems, appropriately trained line-level staff can administer instruments and reach consistent classification decisions (American Correctional Association 1982).

b) Objectivity and Coherence. The new procedures are more objective and verifiable. Thus they help constrain excessive subjectivity, bias, and prejudice. Although subjectivity still plays a role, that role becomes more explicit and can be made accountable (American Correctional Association 1982).

c) Consistency and Reliability. Most of the newer systems achieve higher consistency within applied institutional settings (Gettinger 1982; Holt, Ducat, and Eakles 1982; Austin 1983; Correctional Services Group 1984).

d) Protection against Litigation. Many of the demands of the courts and legislative and professional bodies are met by these objective methods. This helps allay jail and prison staff anxiety regarding liability and accountability. However, if a facility formally adopts an objective procedure and then fails to apply it properly, they may place themselves in a far more vulnerable position from a legal standpoint.

e) Upgraded Documentation. Appropriate documentation of classification decisions is critically important. The newer objective systems improve documentation and justification by the presence of explicit data collection and decision rules.

f) Ease of Training. The newer methods are rational, understandable, and easily communicated to new personnel. This contrasts with older traditional systems where staff had to work for an extensive period to gain "experienced judgment" (Prottas 1979; Lipsky 1980).

g) Reduction of Classification Errors. Objective systems are not perfect and have not managed to eliminate all classification errors (Flanagan 1983; Hanson et al. 1983). However, the available research suggests that objective systems do better than traditional approaches, particularly in helping to constrain overclassification errors (Flynn 1982; Gettinger 1982; Holt, Ducat, and Eakles 1982).

h) Evaluation and Refinement. The objective approaches can be evaluated, modified, and further developed by successive identification and elimination of weaknesses. This cycle of evaluation and redesign has already been demonstrated in some systems.

i) Cost Control and Fiscal Efficiency. When large numbers of inmates are overclassified, projected needs for new construction will be erroneous and overstated. Austin (1983) indicates that in Nevada a new objective classification system helped identify such projection errors; objective classification indicated a greater need for lower-cost minimum security facilities. At the daily operations level, reducing overclassification helps avoid needless and wasteful provision of expensive high- and medium-security resources.

4. *Criticisms of Newer Approaches.* On the other hand, the newer systems have been criticized on many fronts. My aim here is to examine challenges that are critical at the applied level of institutional control. Methodological problems are examined elsewhere in this volume (Brennan, in this volume).

a) Poor Face Validity. Some objective systems are not easy to understand. They may not fit with intuition and may be inconsistent with staff experience (Gettinger 1982; Holt, Ducat, and Eakles 1982). In some instances, objective systems have been thoroughly undermined by staff resistance and sabotage (Bohnstedt and Geiser 1979).

b) Rigidity, Inflexibility, and Denial of Experience. Jail and prison staff often assert that objective systems leave too little role for professional judgment and discretion. This is sometimes true. Some objective systems completely omit discretion and operate mechanically. Staff feel this rigidity strangles flexibility and denies their professionalism. A common solution for these problems is the use of a staff "override procedure" with appropriate constraints (American Correctional Association 1984).

c) Oversimplification and Reductionism. Objective systems are always limited to a handful of major variables and may not include all relevant variables. Objective classifications can (and often do) oversimplify, by truncating individuality through omission of unique case information. Such exclusion poses ethical problems and may also violate court requirements to include "all relevant" variables. The traditional clinical approach is said to handle uniqueness well, on the assumption that the information handling capacity of a subjective decision maker exceeds that of objective statistical systems. This argument has recently been challenged. Studies of subjective decision making indicate that a common human response to "information overload" is to seize on a few salient variables and dramatically oversimplify (Kahneman and Tversky 1973; Monahan 1981). Thus the information-processing capabilities of objective systems may exceed those of subjective approaches.

d) Probabilistic Classification, Uncertainty, and Error Rates. Subjective approaches often are characterized by an aura of certainty. Objective systems, by contrast, acknowledge uncertainty. They can be evaluated, and are explicitly associated with error rates, probabilities, and degrees of membership. Objective procedures rival or improve on human judgment (Pankhurst 1975; Hand 1981; Monahan 1981), yet they are often challenged on the basis of their "uncertainty" of classification.

e) Staff Rejection of Objective Methods.   Jail and prison staff acceptance of objective methods ranges from high to low. It often is low in the initial stages but improves dramatically with time (Holt, Ducat, and Eakles 1982; Austin 1983). The main staff concerns are loss of autonomy and discretion (Gettinger 1982) and a reluctance to give up subjective intuition regarding inmates (Alexander 1982). The inclusion of an override procedure usually solves these problems.

III. Recent Research Regarding Risk Factors for Security and Custody Classifications

Much recent research has focused on the search for valid risk predictors. However, there is no commonly agreed set of risk factors for custodial and security classifications.

Research regarding classification factors cannot ignore the "differential reaction" hypothesis of Jensen (1977), Poole and Regoli (1980), and others who suggest that "selective enforcement" rather than inmate behavior produces correlations of "risk factors" with custodial problems. The following results, therefore, must be seen as representing an "inmate component" of institutional classification systems.

A. Classification Factors for Custody

Institutional misconduct is assessed in a variety of ways. Some studies have accepted "staff ratings" of troublemakers, while others use various elements of the formal disciplinary record as a criterion of adjustment. Institutions vary in the content, completeness, and accuracy of such records. Most correctional facilities have dozens of bureaucratic rules that, if broken, constitute an infraction. Some are serious. Others are extremely minor. One common approach is to separate "seriousness" from "frequency" of violations and to provide two total scores. However, such totals can be misleading because they lump together quite diverse behaviors. Another method is to form separate general dimensions such as alcohol and drug use, sexual pressuring, and aggression toward other inmates.

The disciplinary record is a critically important document because it governs critical decisions such as assignment to custody levels, housing, and work. The following risk factors correlate with custody adjustment and often enter into custodial classification procedures.

1. *Age.*   Age is a consistent correlate of institutional misconduct.

Younger offenders generally have higher rates of disciplinary infractions than older inmates. Misconduct rates have been found to decline with age and level off after the age of thirty-five (Petersilia and Honig 1980). One study reports that prisoners under twenty-two violate institutional rules at a rate over three times greater than that of inmates over thirty (Flanagan 1979).

2. *Race*.   The relation between race and misconduct is inconsistent and weak with much geographical variation (Petersilia and Honig 1980). Interaction effects complicate the bivariate relation between race and custody problems; being black and having a long sentence may produce high disciplinary problems (Chapman and Alexander 1981). Other work suggests that Hispanic inmates, particularly in California prisons, have a higher likelihood of participating in assaultive incidents than either blacks or whites (Bennett 1972, 1976). Some studies (e.g., Lockwood 1977) suggest that blacks are overrepresented in sexual assaults compared with either whites or Hispanics. However, the main finding here is of weak and inconsistent relationships.

3. *Marital Status*.   Chapman and Alexander (1981) indicate that inmates who have never been married have higher infraction rates than those who are currently married or have been married in the past. However, this may simply be a proxy for age since the younger inmates tend to be unmarried.

4. *Job Stability*.   Job stability is often used as a factor for custodial level classification. Research finds a correlation between steady employment and lower violation scores. For example, Flanagan (1979) indicates that badly behaved inmates were less likely to have been employed during the month prior to arrest.

5. *Drug or Alcohol Use*.   Findings regarding the relation between drug or alcohol use and misconduct are mixed (Chapman and Alexander 1981). Some recent studies using multivariate configural methods indicate that there may be a complex relation between drug and alcohol use and misconduct rates (Flanagan 1983). An interaction between being young and using drugs seems to produce high infraction rates.

6. *Residential Mobility*.   This factor is frequently used in security and custody classifications. The relation between this factor and institutional misconduct is inconsistent or weak (Chapman and Alexander 1981, p. 45).

7. *Criminal History*.   Different elements of criminal history have different correlations with overall disciplinary problems. For example, type of commitment crime and prior incarcerations show inconsistent

results. Some evidence suggests that those who exhibit early juvenile criminality and have high involvement as juveniles with the justice system have higher misconduct scores (Chapman and Alexander 1981). Petersilia (1982) has indicated that habitual criminals do not pose higher custodial risks.

8. *Past Violent Offenses.* This factor is included in most jail and prison custodial considerations. However, validation studies show this risk factor to have inconsistent or weak correlations with institutional behavior. Flanagan (1983) reports that homicide offenders have significantly fewer infractions during the first year of confinement than other inmates. To complicate matters, Chapman and Alexander (1981, p. 84) found that inmates convicted of violent personal crimes other than homicide have higher misconduct rates. These inconsistencies in global correlations between past violence and misconduct indicate the critical importance of unraveling the various types of past violence (spouse killers, serial killers, repeated robbery, etc.) and examining the particular correlations for each separate form of past violence against misconduct rates.

9. *Prior Incarcerations.* The research to date does not suggest any strong link between prior incarcerations and misconduct.

10. *Sentence Length and Time Served.* Chapman and Alexander (1981, p. 85) report that an inverted U-shaped pattern of misbehavior is found—rates are highest during the middle stages of a prison sentence but then sharply decline with the approach of parole board appearances or release dates. However, it seems likely that length of sentence may interact with other variables (e.g., type of offense, age, race, and so on) to influence institutional behavior. Thus simple global correlations may not offer the most appropriate approach to examining the importance of length of sentence.

11. *Psychological Assessments.* Correlations between institutional misconduct and personality dimensions have yielded mixed results (Flanagan 1983). While some studies have failed to find any discriminating power using the MMPI scales in regard to disciplinary problems, others report significant differences. Megargee and Bohn (1979) report that, when their MMPI typology was correlated against institutional adjustments, the various personality types differed significantly in number of days spent in segregation and in rate of violent infractions. Edinger (1979) reports similar findings in aggressive behavior and disciplinary misbehaviors across the MMPI types. However, other studies (e.g., Jaman 1972; Myers and Levy 1978; Hanson et al.

1983) are unable to replicate Megargee's findings. Such inconsistency suggests a relatively moderate or weak connection between personality variables and disciplinary problems.

B. Classification Factors for Security

Security classification shifts the focus from institutional risk to public risk and street behavior. Classification factors are keyed to criteria that involve escape, dangerous recidivism, and habitual criminality. Security classifications emphasize legal variables, history of criminality, seriousness of current offense, and past escape attempts. The following factors have emerged as useful for the prediction of dangerous recidivism and hence for jail and prison security classification. Most are already used as the foundation of newer objective jail and prison security classification systems.

1. *Prior Criminal Behavior.*   Gottlieb (1985) reports that an overwhelming majority (92 percent) of criminal justice practitioners agree that prior criminal history is a key factor in predicting future crime. Most security classification systems already include prior criminal history (Levinson 1980; Holt, Ducat, and Eakles 1982). An important research finding is that the likelihood of recidivism rises with each prior criminal offense. The use of criminal history alone achieves reasonable validity in predicting new offenses (Farrington 1979; Cohen 1983).

There is no consensus on the selection and weighting of specific elements of the criminal record for security considerations. Elements that might be used include the length and seriousness of prior convictions, the frequency of rearrests, the commission of a crime while on bail, and various aspects of the juvenile record. The current charge is regarded by practitioners as an important indicator of future dangerousness and is widely used in security considerations, but there is no consensus on what types or elements of the current charge should be considered (Gottlieb 1985). The various elements are not consistently used across diverse jail and prison systems.

2. *Age.*   Age is included in some well-known security classification systems, such as the National Institute of Corrections model. Research has demonstrated some validity for this practice since the most serious public risks are presented by younger offenders (Monahan 1981, p. 5). Juvenile criminal history provides various predictive indicators of continued habitual offender behavior, including age of first contact with the police, one or more convictions before the age of sixteen, and incarceration at a state juvenile facility. However, due to the difficulty

of gaining access to reliable juvenile reports, these indicators are generally omitted from security classification systems.

3. *Race.* This is generally excluded from security classifications on both ethical and legal grounds. However, it is impossible to eliminate race from informal classification, and many formal objective systems include various "proxies" or correlates of race.

4. *Socioeconomic Status and Unemployment.* Social factors are often used in the new security classifications (National Institute of Corrections 1982). There is also some predictive validity in this practice (Monahan 1981). Similarly, the Rand studies of habitual criminals found that a good predictor of habitual criminal status was whether the offender had been unemployed more than 50 percent of the time during the preceding two years (Petersilia, Greenwood, and Lavin 1977). Although many well-known systems have adopted such social factors, many political, legal, and ethical concerns complicate their use (Monahan 1981).

5. *Drug and Alcohol Use.* The presence of substance abuse problems is frequently used in jail and prison security classifications. This practice is also supported by research that indicates that substance abuse is an important correlate of serious recidivism (Monahan 1981). Furthermore, the joint use of both alcohol and drugs seems to escalate crime rates. Monahan (1981) reports that offenders using both alcohol and drugs commit more than twice the number of crimes against persons than offenders who avoid both of these drugs.

6. *Other Classification Factors.* Numerous other factors have entered the recidivism prediction literature, including residential mobility, marital status, and IQ scores. The above five factors, however, appear to be emerging as the most powerful correlates of serious crimes (Monahan 1981, p. 8). Psychiatric diagnosis and psychological test assessment have not had much success in predicting serious recidivism behavior.

IV. The Diversity of Jail and Prison
Institutional Classifications

The few available surveys (Bohnstedt and Geiser 1979) suggest considerable diversity in classification approaches. The criminal justice system consists of numerous independent and largely autonomous correctional facilities that have developed procedures and definitions in their own ways, addressing their own problems, and employing their own language. There are no standardized definitions of basic data or of custodial and security classes (American Correctional Association 1982).

A. Reasons for Diversity

Jail and prison staff often exhibit a strong desire for autonomy and often prefer to develop their own procedures. If they adopt an existing method, they will customize it to their own particular institution and purposes (Bohnstedt and Geiser 1979; National Institute of Corrections 1985).

As noted earlier, classifications can be geared to different policy priorities. There is no consensus on which particular policies should be optimized. The prioritization of different policies will produce differing approaches to classification (Solomon and Baird 1982). Local community values provide a strong diversifying influence. Corrections administrators are often elected and are sensitive to the politics and needs of local communities.

Jails and prisons vary considerably in architecture, size, funding levels, treatment and program resources, organizational structure, and management style. Such variation can profoundly influence the type of classification system (Glaser 1982).

The local nature of the inmate population is also an important influence and may depend in part on the particular community in which a jail or prison is located. If the facility is part of a larger system, the population mix will depend on the system's referral procedures and policies.

Successful implementation of new classification systems must take account of these above factors as well as local staff values, preferences, and training (Fowler and Rans 1982; Soloman and Baird 1982). Since no particular method is regarded as a "standard," staff seldom adopt any particular approach uncritically (Bohnstedt and Geiser 1979; American Correctional Association 1984). Top administrative officers often impose their own framework of values, methods, risk factors, and decision procedures in designing a classification system. Thus the challenges and constraints confronting classification systems vary. A tentative conclusion is that no single classification solution can be optimal nationally across all jails and prisons.

B. Differences between Jail and Prison Classification

Classification systems in jails are more primitive than in prisons (Gettinger 1982). Most offenders who eventually reside in prisons spend a brief initial time in a jail, while many minor offenders never go to prison. Thus while offender classification is more developed for prisons, the inmate population in jails may be more heterogeneous than those in prison.

The average length of stay in jails is usually much shorter than in prison. Jails do not have the luxury of a thirty- to sixty-day diagnostic period in which intensive testing and clinical assessment can take place. Thus decision criteria and risk factors in jails are simpler and more limited than in prisons. The immediate need for a safe and orderly environment places tremendous pressure on the initial classification procedure in jails.

Classification systems are less elaborate in jails since many lack the resources to conduct extensive medical, psychological, social history, and criminal inventories. Many jails also have severe constraints on the complexity of their classifications due to their limitations of architecture and size (e.g., many jails have fewer than fifty beds). Such limitations, however, do not mitigate the need to separate dangerous from nondangerous offenders. In fact, careful classification may be even more critical in facilites that have inadequate or limited space resources. Many jails restrict their classification to simple demographic and legal separations (e.g., men from women, adults from juveniles, sentenced from unsentenced). Many jails have no formal classification procedures and operate according to staff subjective judgment, or on a "space available" basis (inmates are housed wherever there is an empty bunk). There is, however, a widespread trend among jails to adopt objective classification systems.

C. Brief Reviews of Selected Prison Classification Systems

In this section a number of actual prison systems are briefly reviewed. Comments are added where evaluation or validity studies are available.

1. *Federal Bureau of Prisons Classification System.*   This classification model is objective and uses standardized classification instruments. It has been adopted by a number of states. This system is based on a number of simple principles, including the use of standardized and objective instruments, classification at the least restrictive custody, preference for more recent rather than distant past predictors, use of past behavior to predict future behaviors of the same sort, the separation of security and custody dimensions, and the retention of staff judgment via an override procedure. Reviews of this system are available in Levinson and Williams (1979), Levinson (1982), and Austin (1983).

The risk factors for security classification are limited to type of detainer, severity of current offense, expected length of incarceration, type of prior commitment, history of escapes or attempts, and history of violence. Social and prior institutional behavior factors are omitted. The new inmate is classified into six security levels corresponding to six types of institutions. The Federal Bureau of Prisons (BOP) system designates these six levels using the following criteria: perimeter barriers, towers (length of time staffed), external patrol (presence and constancy), detection devices, type of cells (single or multiple cells; dormitories), and level of staffing. The presence of these explicit distinctions allows for systematic matching with inmates' security needs (Levinson and Gerard 1986).

Four levels of custody supervision are designated within each institution. They are the same for all forty-seven BOP institutions; however, no institution has all four levels. The levels are (1) *Community*—These inmates are given the least secure housing. They can work outside the facility. There is minimum supervision, and the inmate is eligible for community programs or activities and may travel without an escort. (2) *Out*—These prisoners are eligible for outside work but require a specified level of staff supervision. On trips into the community they will be escorted and restraints may be used at the discretion of the accompanying officer. (3) *In*—These inmates cannot work or participate in programs outside the perimeter of the facility. Inside the facility they receive "normal" supervision and have access to all programs and services. At least two officers are required on outside escort and they may use leg chains or handcuffs. (4) *Maximum*—These inmates are viewed as assaultive, predacious, riotous, or high escape risks. Their movement may be restricted within the institution. On trips outside the facility at least two officers are required and restraints will be used. Such trips require the warden's permission.

The risk-assessment component of this system uses a weighted additive point scale. Weights are assigned to each risk factor and cutoff points for security and custody recommendations are imposed. The initial development of this procedure was based on professional consensus rather than statistical analysis; subsequent revisions were based on past experience with the approach. Overrides based on professional judgment are generally constrained to certain predictable issues and must be documented.

The initial security classification establishes custody and a schedule of reclassification reviews. At a scheduled review, a unit team assesses the inmate's progress and behavior using explicit guidelines covering seven reclassification variables: percentage of time served, drug and alcohol involvement, mental/psychological stability, most serious disciplinary reports, frequency of disciplinary reports, responsibility shown by the inmate, and family/community ties. A point system is again used to assess whether the prisoner's current custody level should decrease, remain the same, or increase. Custody level changes (up or down) may trigger moves to higher or lower security institutions.

In evaluating this system, Levinson (1982) assessed its impact on six classification goals. (1) Are inmates appropriately confined in the less secure facilities? (2) Has the new classification brought the total prison system into a better balance? (3) Is there a decrease in the number of transfers? (4) Has the new system reduced the number of inmates requesting protective custody? (5) Has it eliminated or reduced "preferential transfers" between institutions? (6) Is better use being made of available resources?

Levinson found that a larger proportion of inmates can be placed into less secure facilities. This agrees with Austin (1983) who found that this BOP procedure classified only 2.1 percent of inmates into the top two security levels (levels five and six) with a concurrent shift of many inmates into minimum security levels (56.2 percent). Levinson reports no significant increase in either escape or assault rates over a six-month period following the adoption of the new system, despite the greater number of prisoners shifted into low-security facilities. The system-wide racial balance was perceived as "better" by the more even distribution of white and black inmates across the various facilities. Transfers progressively decreased over the months following implementation. Finally, the new system profoundly influenced construction plans since classification data indicated a need for more minimum- rather than more maximum-security cells.

Kane and Saylor (1983), in a related study of the BOP procedure, examined the relative statistical importance of each classification factor in governing security designations and in predicting inmate behavior. They constructed two separate criterion variables: management problems (disciplinary transfers, violent incidents, overall misconduct, and escapes) and severity of conduct. Their results indicate that the total security score as well as the various component factors were predictive of both management problems and severity of misconduct. However, the specific items in the security scale were not of equal predictive power. Management problems were best predicted by prior commitments and a history of violence. Escape was best predicted by current offense and escape history. Severity of misconduct was best predicted by seriousness of current offense, escape history, and violence history.

Austin (1983) compared the BOP model with a traditional subjective prison classification and with the systems in use in California and the National Institute of Corrections model (these are both discussed below). Using the same sample of 1,206 prisoners, he found that the three objective systems classified highly similar proportions of inmates into maximum, close, medium, and minimum levels. In each instance, only a small proportion of the inmates were classified at maximum levels (2.1, 3.5, and 8.2 percent, respectively) while over 50 percent were classified into minimum security. This again demonstrates the massive shift downward into minimum security levels. Austin examined the relevance of each risk factor in reaching the overall security classification by regressing them against the overall security classification level. The BOP model was dominated by current offense, which accounted for 66 percent of the total variation in security classification level, while the other risk factors were of relatively less significance.

2. *Illinois Adult Classification System.* This system also uses standardized instruments and a point system (Adams and Henning 1982; Correctional Services Group 1985). It classifies inmates in terms of stability and dangerousness. Stability refers to behavioral adjustment; dangerousness refers to violence and aggression. Each dimension has its own point system. Three levels of stability are differentiated using the following factors: time until release, current age, age at first arrest, number of prior convictions, past institutional performance, and past performance under supervision. Dangerousness is indicated by level of violence in current offense, past dangerousness, and violence in past institutional records. Again, inmates are differentiated into three levels. The stability dimension governs the level of supervision, and the dangerousness dimension determines the level of security constraint. On both dimensions the risk factors are differentially weighted according to relative importance.

These two dimensions are combined to form a "decision matrix" giving nine potential groups of inmates. Overrides are allowed, although they are governed by specific standards. The reported override rate is 14.7 percent, the majority (9 percent) being moved into higher security levels.

This system has been under development since 1980 and seems to have achieved acceptance by both inmates and staff (Adams and Henning 1982). As with most other objective systems, it appears to have redistributed many inmates into lower security levels.

3. *The National Institute of Corrections Model.* This influential model has been adopted or investigated by many states (e.g., Vermont, Ken-

tucky, Virginia, and New Jersey; see Gettinger 1982; National Institute of Corrections 1982; Austin 1983). The approach is objective and uses standardized scoring. It is largely behavior based, emphasizing the concept of equity (Austin 1983). The system relies on a few explicitly defined legal and behavioral variables. However, it deviates somewhat from a strict equity model by including a few social factors. An attempt was made to select only those risk factors demonstrated by prior research to predict escape and adjustment problems. Thus it goes beyond a consensus-based model by incorporating research findings.

The National Institute of Corrections model meets many requirements of a complete management approach. It includes custody and security issues, needs assessment, program monitoring and assessment, reclassification, and a management information system within its scope. The model distinguishes between street behavior and institutional behavior particularly in the reclassification process, where institutional behaviors and disciplinary infractions assume a larger importance. The model emphasizes least restrictive custody. Prediction is downplayed, particularly in the reclassification phase, which emphasizes the inmate's behavioral adjustment to the institution.

The risk factors in the National Institute of Corrections model include seriousness of current offense, detainers and warrants, prior escapes, prior felony convictions, prior assaultive offenses, prior negative institutional behavior, and social factors (including age, education, employment, and alcohol and drug abuse). It excludes length of sentence.

Length of sentence is a controversial omission and is included in most consensus models. However, research shows no clear relationship between length of sentence and escape attempts. In fact, some findings suggest that inmates with longer sentences have lower infraction rates (Chapman and Alexander 1981). The use of detainers to disallow low custody placement is strictly limited to serious and recent detainers. The National Institute of Corrections system also omits minor institutional infractions that do not involve escape or violence.

Decision rules involve a combination of decision trees and point scores. Initially a point score separates out those inmates who fall into the maximum-security category. Additional risk factors are then used to differentiate the remaining inmates into medium- and minimum-security categories. These additional variables include alcohol or drug abuse, outstanding detainers, prior felony convictions, and stability factors (age, presence of high school diploma, and employment or school prior to arrest).

This model also uses a point system in its reclassification component, but it is based on different factors. Prior history factors are given lesser importance; stability factors and alcohol and drug history are omitted; and institutional behavior, disciplinary reports and their severity are more heavily weighted. The needs assessment instrument focuses on health, intellectual ability, behavioral and emotional problems, alcohol abuse, drug abuse, educational status, and vocational status.

Like other objective systems, this model reassigns a high proportion of inmates to lower security levels. Austin (1983) demonstrated that it classifies about 8 percent of offenders into maximum security levels, 35.3 percent into medium, and 56.6 percent into minimum levels and is comparable to both the California and BOP models. It is reported that some states have made the system more conservative by increasing weights or raising the cutoffs for various security levels (Correctional Services Group 1985).

Austin's (1983) regression analysis suggests that only three factors statistically dominate the overall security decision, that is, seriousness of current offense, prior assaultive offenses, and prior felony convictions. Furthermore, seriousness of current offense has by far the largest weight. This analysis suggests that most of the risk factors used are largely irrelevant to the classification decision and that the model could be reduced to a two-factor system incorporating only seriousness of current offense and seriousness of prior criminal history.

4. *The California Prison Classification System.* The California system (Holt, Ducat, and Eakles 1982) is also objective and uses standardized procedures. The choice of risk factors seems to have been largely consensus based, although many have been shown by research to be related to inmate adjustment. This system includes institutional behavior and social factors and is thus broader than a strict equity-based system. A relatively unusual feature is the use of positive institutional behavior in the point system. This reflects a correctional philosophy of allowing inmates to change their security level through good behavior (see Clements 1981). The risk factors are length of sentence, detainers and warrants, prior escapes, prior juvenile incarceration, prior adult incarceration, positive and negative institutional behavior, and social factors (age, education, employment, marital status, and military record). The current offense is assessed strictly by length of sentence. Since length of sentence and severity are essentially redundant, the inclusion of both (as in the BOP model) overweights this dimension of prior behavior. The California system collapses security and custody into a single di-

mension. Reclassification, however, introduces a greater emphasis on institutional behavior, thus strengthening the custody orientation. At reclassification, points are computed for favorable and unfavorable institutional behavior since the last review and are then added or subtracted from the initial score.

Austin (1983) demonstrated that this system classifies about 53 percent of inmates into the minimum-security status, while only 3.5 percent would be classified into its maximum (level 4). These percentages are comparable with those found with use of the BOP and NIC models. Austin also examined the relative importance of the various risk factors in reaching the overall classification decision. His regression analysis revealed that length of sentence dominates the decision. The remaining risk factors had virtually no impact (although for that small percentage who are assigned to maximum security, prior violence or prior involvement in prison escapes or attempts plays a major role).

Because use of this system showed that many inmates were overclassified (Gettinger 1982), there was a substantial transfer of prisoners between the various California institutions. Movement occurred in both directions, but primarily downward. This also profoundly changed plans for new construction in the California system (Gettinger 1982; Holt, Ducat, and Eakles 1982).

The concentration of troublesome inmates in a few institutions has apparently not caused a discipline crisis. One report shows a generally positive impact on disciplinary rates throughout the system, with tensions subsiding and a reduction of "locked down" days (Correctional Services Group 1985). Racial imbalance among the various institutions has been reduced, suggesting that California's approach is more racially evenhanded than the old system (Holt, Ducat, and Eakles 1982, quoted by Gettinger 1982, p. 37).

5. *Correctional Services Group—Prison Classification System.* The Correctional Services Group (1984) system has been implemented in a number of states. It appears to be a consensus-based system; little information is available regarding its validity. The principle of least restrictive custody is emphasized. It separates security and custody dimensions. Following admission, the new inmate is assessed on eight separate factors or needs: medical needs, mental health needs, security/public risk score, custody/institutional risk, educational needs, vocational needs, work skills, and, finally, proximity to release/family ties. Eight codes provide a comprehensive profile of inmate problems. Treatment plans are designed around this profile of needs. An override procedure can be exercised, with written documentation.

The scoring procedure is based on a five-point rating for all eight dimensions. Specific definitions for each score level are developed consensually, by local corrections staff specialists and Correctional Services Group staff. Thus these definitions may change as the system is adapted to local facilities. The local staff responsible for a particular factor are involved in establishing the definitions for that factor. For example, medical personnel might be involved in preparing medical factor definitional levels.

The Correctional Services Group approach attempts to rate facility resources on the same factors used to evaluate inmates. This organizes and highlights facility resources according to the presence or absence of programming and other resources required to meet inmates' supervision and program requirements.

A useful account of the implementation of this system in Missouri in 1983 is available (National Institute of Corrections 1985). Missouri officials indicate that escape percentages have decreased along with grievances by both staff and inmates. This new approach improves understanding of an inmate's assets and liabilities at reception and provides clearer guidelines for the transfer of inmates once they have entered the system. However, the system requires validation; only a limited amount of statistical evaluative research has been conducted.

D. Brief Reviews of Selected Jail Systems

There has been even less published evaluation research on jail classification systems. One major survey of jail classification by Bohnstedt and Geiser (1979) found that most jails conducted classification in a traditional informal style. Most did not have explicit decision rules; risk factor data were often collected in an unstructured way. More recently, however, many jails have moved toward quantified objective systems using point scales and standardized instruments.

1. *Oxford County Jail.* This jail uses a point system for a combined security and custody classification (National Institute of Corrections 1983). The scale separates inmates into three security levels. Risk factors include severity of crime, prior criminal record, pending court actions, escape risk, medical and drug dependency problems, and a set of stability factors (stable address, stable living arrangements, family ties, educational level, and employment history). The information is verified by phone calls and review of official records. This system has a second phase of classification (within ten days of admission) in which a classification committee may reassign the offender to a more appropriate security level and rehabilitation program.

2. *Bureau of Prisons System for Jail Detainees.* The Bureau of Prisons formed a task force to design a classification system for federal detainees housed in its metropolitan correctional centers and in its jails. As in most jails, detainees are held for just a few days. Thus intensive long-term assessments are impractical and are often not needed. The first aim is to predict if a detainee will stay longer than seven days—this prediction is based on the bond level and the seriousness of current offense. Those inmates having low bail and a minor charge are immediately oriented to release procedures. Those who fall into the "greater than seven day" category are moved to a second, more comprehensive stage of risk assessment.

Risk assessment at this second stage is based on a point scale that includes substance abuse, employment and education in the last two years, anticipated detainers, age at first commitment, history of violence, and history of escape. This security-oriented scale places inmates into three levels (light, average, and heavy). Overrides are allowed but a written rationale must be given and the unit manager's signature is required. Initial classification occurs after fourteen days. The formal instrument uses a point system based on bail amount, severity of charge, number of disciplinary reports, severity of disciplinary reports, current programs (education, job, or industry assignment), false data on the screening form, and level of adjustment during stay (good, average, and poor). Again, light, average, and heavy levels of security are distinguished. This system also recognizes various administrative factors that may warrant an override (suicide risk, mental health problems, communicable diseases, and so forth).

Detainees are reclassified on the forty-fifth day after initial classification. Additional reviews are held every forty-five days until the offender leaves the facility. The reclassification form is identical to the initial classification form and thus includes initial charges and bail amount as well as points for discipline and adjustment while in the facility. An evaluation of this system is being conducted by the BOP research section.

3. *Boulder County Jail Classification.* This classification system is included since it illustrates the hazards of omitting explicit and standardized rating criteria and of omitting a clearly specified decision rule. The system was based on the idea of encouraging good behavior through rewards (Austin and Lipsky 1980). Good behavior was to be rewarded by progressive movement across classification levels from maximum to minimum, to work release. All inmates are initially assigned to the

maximum level and are expected to move progressively through the levels. Criminal history and other criminality variables are eliminated from this classification and replaced by staff observations of inmate behavior (conformity, responsibility, and so forth). Staff are trained to understand the behavioral criteria. However, no formal checklist was developed for these behavioral measures. The omission is critical (Austin and Lipsky 1980) because it leaves this system open to all the failings of traditional clinical assessment (Monahan 1981). Thus this system does not qualify as a fully objective system. It seems to leave a large window of opportunity for impressionistic ratings.

A second problem is that the decision process is not conducted according to formal decision rules such as point scales or decision trees. Rather, personnel who work with the inmates reach decisions on a consensus basis. All staff who work with detainees enter notes and information into a "passbook" regarding the individual's behavior. Each shift routinely examine this passbook and are presumed to be informed regarding the behavior of all inmates.

Reclassification is critical in such a progression system. Downward movement in custodial restrictions can be requested informally by either inmate or line staff. Upward reclassification would stem from behavioral or discipline problems and involve an appeals process and a formal disciplinary hearing. However, Austin and Lipsky (1980) conclude that the progressive movement idea has not worked and is essentially a "charade." They discovered that most inmates had no, or only one, move during their total stay in jail. They also note that the length of stay in this institution is generally too short to produce significant change in behavior and imply that the system appears to have degenerated into a purely subjective approach.

4. *Grand Traverse County Jail System.* This recent classification approach, initiated in late 1984, illustrates the use of a decision tree format for primary security classification in a group of five northern Michigan jails.

The main goal is to determine initial security assignment, housing, and programs or treatment eligibility. This system also assesses special needs during the booking phase (medical, psychological, suicide risk, etc.). The decision tree focuses on security since it is based largely on prior criminality and legal variables. Reclassification occurs later, using a scheme for measuring inmate behavior.

There is some similarity between this decision tree classification system and the well-known Michigan Parole Prediction System (Monahan

1981). The development of the tree was based on consensus and professional judgment in selecting risk factors and division rules for the tree. An override procedure termed a "special conditions option" is allowed for in the primary tree. In small jail systems many inmates are repeat offenders and are well-known to jail staff; thus an override is especially important in small jail settings.

An evaluation is under way to investigate the consistency of decisions under the system, its effectiveness at predicting infractions and behavior, and its fiscal implications. Preliminary results suggest that a high level of consistency is being achieved. An unexpected finding is that use of a standardized classification and "language" to describe inmates has improved the coordination and consistency of transfers between the jails. A further impact, as might be expected, is that a smaller proportion of inmates are being classified into maximum security levels.

V. Sources of Failure in Jail and Prison Classification

Institutional classification is often not used carefully or systematically, either in research or in practice (Clements 1981). The current failures stem from such sources as management and administrative failures, line-level difficulties, and methodological or conceptual problems. A brief examination of problems that undermine jail and prison classification levels follows. Additional reviews are provided in Prottas (1979), Lipsky (1980), American Correctional Association (1982), and Brennan (1984).

Inadequate implementation is a recurrent management failure (Fowler and Rans 1982). Top management may fail to provide the required resources of money, staff, space, training, and political support. Fowler and Rans (1982) note that many top administrators "talk" objective classification but have little commitment or confidence in it. This tendency is bolstered by resistance toward change and ambivalence from those who are comfortable with traditional approaches.

A. Failure to Use Classification

Sometimes classification systems are designed and implemented but then ignored. Data are left in a disaggregated form; and few planning, management, or even line decisions are based on the classification process. Consequently, most decisions remain based on subjective and "space available" approaches. Evaluation, monitoring, quality control, and supervision are all essentially ignored (see Fowler and Rans 1982;

Solomon and Baird 1982), and the formal "objective" classification system remains disconnected from any meaningful institutional policies. Sources of such weak commitment are multiple: there may be no confidence in the new objective systems, a preference for subjective judgment, or fear of encountering resistance from important colleagues.

A variant of this problem occurs when administrators establish classification procedures primarily for legal and political reasons. Their fundamental goal is to avoid litigation and minimize accountability. This produces a "going by the book" approach. The true purposes of classification are often forgotten. This mentality may produce a systematic misuse of the classification process (see Lipsky 1980). For example, this "safety-first" philosophy fosters systematic overclassification.

B. Failure to Understand the Roles and Purposes of Classification

Too often administrative staff do not fully appreciate the complexities and multiple goals of correctional classification (Fowler and Rans 1982). They may see classification as a topic mainly for research or clinical staff. Thus classification remains underused for management purposes and is poorly integrated into the general operations of the facility.

At the line level, failure to understand classification can produce a routinized, overly rigid approach or, at the other extreme, highly subjective approaches (Prottas 1979; Lipsky 1980).

C. Failure to Cope with External Political Pressures

Classification in jails and prisons often becomes the focus of strong political and community pressures. If top management fail to resist these extreme positions, their capitulation may result in overly restrictive or overly lenient practices. Administrators must find a workable balance between extreme positions.

D. Failure to Provide Guiding Initiatives and Clear Policy

Fowler and Rans (1982) argue that the design and maintenance of classification systems require clear management directives regarding aims, policies, procedures, and orientation. The absence of these, along with inadequate training, weak supervision, and low accountability between the line and management staff, will inexorably undermine classification in most jails and prisons. Failure to supervise, or to evaluate the performance of line staff, or to provide clear policies and procedures allows the "informal" policies and subjective procedures of line staff to become dominant "de facto" policy in many institutions (Lipsky 1980).

E. Inadequate Data

Correctional data bases frequently are replete with inadequate and incomplete records (Austin and Lipsky (1980, p. 83), particularly pertaining to criminal history. The collection, verification, storage, and retrieval procedures in jails and prisons are often inadequate to meet requirements for accurate classification.

A major cause of missing data is the inadequate flow of information from other agencies into jails and prisons. Various criminal justice agencies collect separate, independent information and store it in their own data bases. Poor coordination produces redundancies, errors, and very inefficient and costly data collection. Interagency cooperation is often deficient. Adams and Henning (1982) indicate that in certain jurisdictions legislation had to be instituted to facilitate and improve the information flow between agencies.

Austin (1983) has pinpointed the problems that missing data pose for objective methods. Under traditional approaches, where data were seldom used, and inmates were systematically overclassified into higher security, the problem of missing data was tolerable. However, with objective methods the absence of accurate criminal history information can produce erroneous assignments. A further problem is that incomplete records fuel the tendency to use subjective discretion and impressionistic assessments based on "demeanour and attitudes" (Austin and Lipsky 1980, p. 83).

F. Ambiguity of Classification Factors

Many jails' and prisons' classification approaches use ambiguous written definitions of risk factors (Austin and Lipsky 1980). Alexander (1982) points out that line staff often must "guess" at the scores and ratings when confronted with vague definitions. This produces inconsistent interpretations, unreliable data collection, and wide variation and inconsistency in decisions.

G. Inadequate Verification

The major sources of data used in jails and prisons are computerized criminal histories, information from the courts, law enforcement arrest reports, offender self-reports at entry, and inmate behaviors while in-carcerated. Each offers the possibility of unreliability and error. Verification procedures are often time-consuming, cumbersome, and avoided by line staff. Many supervisors do not implement rigorous verification standards, and their decisions are thus vulnerable to errors.

H. Low Predictive Validity

Recent research (Austin 1983; Monahan 1981; Chapman and Alexander 1981) indicates that many risk factors that were believed to predict jail and prison adjustment have no clear relation to custodial problems. The use of irrelevant variables blurs distinctions and creates "noisy" decisions characterized by high numbers of errors (Brennan, in this volume). This problem cannot be laid at the door of correctional practitioners; it is more obviously a concern for the research community.

I. Inappropriate Kinds of Classification Systems

Many failures in past classification practice in jails and prisons were due to the adoption of inadequate or inappropriate forms of classification (Fowler and Rans 1982; Solomon and Baird 1982). In many cases abstract theoretical classification systems were borrowed from the academic arena. They were often based on theoretical or abstract terms that were difficult to use or understand and proved awkward for staff training and general implementation. Such systems were quite inadequate at the operational level. A fundamental problem negatively affecting such "transfer" was that the academic research classification systems were theoretical and explanatory in their intent, and they were never designed to meet the specific custody and security needs of a correctional facility.

As can be seen from the preceding discussion, there are many factors that influence whether an institutional classification system succeeds. Sources of failure are numerous but can be avoided if classification systems are carefully conceived and implemented. Conclusions are discussed in the final section below.

VI. Summary and Conclusions

Until relatively recently, objective security and custody classification methods, which met even minimally adequate standards of validity and reliability, were simply unavailable (see Brennan, in this volume). Thus jail and prison staff were forced back upon their own experience and subjective judgments. Recent improvements in objective systems may change this situation (see American Correctional Association 1982), although some evaluations (Austin 1983) suggest that enthusiasm for the current crop of new methods may be somewhat premature. However, simply moving toward an objective approach carries many advantages and creates the possibility of continual cycles of evaluation, modification, and improvement.

In addition to the likely benefits of careful evaluation, there are a few basic pathways toward improving the scientific quality and practical usefulness of correctional classifications. These include clarification of purposes and goals of classification, improved methods (i.e., improvements in data and in statistical decision procedures), and improvements in the management and training of classification personnel.

There is a need for clarification and separation of the diverse and conflicting purposes of correctional classification. If need be, different kinds of classifications should be constructed to optimize each different policy or correctional decision. An attempt is offered early in this essay to clarify these various goals of classification. Yet the issue is complex and much confusion seems to exist between predictive, treatment, explanatory, and descriptive forms of classification in this field. These different purposes require different methods for their construction, usually require different data, and are usually evaluated using different criteria. The naive use, for example, of a predictive classification for treatment purposes will not usually achieve the desired results.

A further complicating factor is the diversity of correctional philosophies among correctional personnel and between different facilities. Such a diversity—ranging from extremely restrictive to liberal—will produce a variety of classifications straddling the same liberal/restrictive continuum. A differential tolerance of the ratio of false negative to false positive errors will characterize these positions. No common consensus appears to exist. Thus different facilities endorse and develop classification procedures ranging all across this continuum. Some of these will probably violate the principle of least restrictive custody. However, an exact definition of "excessive restrictiveness" seems destined to be governed by political and value considerations. Yet the costs of excessive restrictiveness include bloated inmate populations, crowded facilities, and huge fiscal outlays. These costs eventually force some curtailment of the apparently systemic tendency toward overly restrictive classification. The fundamental issue seems to be that of reaching a balanced policy of classification that seeks to minimize both false negative and false positive errors.

Turning to methods, the path of improvement involves the apparently more tractable tasks of improving our data and discovering improved statistical decision rules. The widespread adoption of standardized reporting, numerical scoring, and computer storage seems likely to steadily upgrade the quality of objective data. This, in turn, should allow more rigorous evaluation of the predictive validity of the risk factors used in classification. Thus the quality of data—assessed as a function of reliability, completeness, accessibility, and predictive validity—may steadily be improved.

The statistical decision rules used in classification are also likely to improve in the next few years. This assertion is based on the fact that in a majority of institutions the formal decision rules currently used are the most primitive (i.e., subjective judgment or consensus-based linear point systems). The shift from the consensus-based point scale to a statistically developed approach should produce improved classification. Furthermore, much academic research in classification is aimed at improving our statistical methods for objective classification. Many new techniques are becoming available (see Gottfredson, in this volume), and some show promise of producing improved classifications.

A further source of improvement may be gained by a strategic moving away from the current practice of "broad range" security and custody classifications. An alternative strategy is to make more use of the variety of "special offense" classifications that are emerging in the literature. For example, there have been many advances in both predictive and explanatory classifications for particular offenses, for example, drunk drivers, homicides, vandals, runaway youth, and so on (Brennan, in this volume). The current practice of using a single security or custody classification to cover an extremely broad range of offenders under one classificatory scheme has certain weaknesses. It is well established that the broader the range of a classification, the less well it can predict or explain a particular event. Special purpose classifications focus on specific problems and generally reach higher validity for the specific behavior they deal with. Thus, as these various special offense classifications are developed, improved, and validated, they may be quickly incorporated into correctional practice for their improved explanatory and treatment implications and also for their enhanced predictive power for the particular types of offenders that fall within their range. This strategy, when used selectively and appropriately, might produce fairly dramatic improvements in both predictive decision making and the development of intervention stategies based on a more detailed delineation and explanation of the dynamics of particular offenses. Obviously, such special offense typologies contain information that is far more clearly focused on the particular behavior under consideration.

A final set of problems, which is underlined by the large number of lawsuits involving inmate classification, is that of personnel training and the management of classification in correctional facilities. There are numerous examples of attacks on the expertise, training, and credentials of line staff and related criticisms of the inability of administrative staff to properly manage, evaluate, and supervise the line officers. It is also clear that much offender classification—particularly in jails—is conducted by relatively inexperienced line officers. To compound these problems there is, as yet, no commonly agreed standard body of knowledge for a classification curriculum and no clear conclusion regarding the certifiable skills of people who are hired as classification officers. These problems are acute for both the line-level skills of classification officers and the skills involved in managing a classification unit, monitoring staff performance, and using classification as a management tool. For example, what criteria of accountability should a manager use to monitor the rate of false positives? Fortunately, valiant efforts are being made by various professional and national groups (American Correctional Association, National Institute of Corrections, and others) to develop such training guidelines. These represent some profound challenges, yet represent certain well-delineated pathways to improvements in the scientific quality and practical usefulness of offender classification.

REFERENCES

Adams, L., and J. Henning. 1982. "Illinois' Adult Classification System Design." In *Classification as a Management Tool: Theories and Models for Decision Makers*, edited by L. Fowler. College Park, Md.: American Correctional Association.

Alexander, J. 1982. "Security Classification in New York State." In *Classification as a Management Tool: Theories and Models for Decision Makers*, edited by L. Fowler. College Park, Md.: American Correctional Association.

American Correctional Association. 1982. *Classification as a Management Tool: Theories and Models for Decision Makers*, edited by L. Fowler. College Park, Md.: American Correctional Association.

————. 1984. "Female Classification, an Examination of the Issues." Unpublished report under grant from the National Institute of Corrections. College Park, Md.: American Correctional Association.

Austin, J. 1983. "Assessing the New Generation of Prison Classification Models." *Crime and Delinquency* 29:561–76.

Austin, J., and P. Lipsky. 1980. "Multi-jail Classification Study." Final report to the National Institute of Corrections, Washington, D.C.

Baird, S. C. 1982. "Probation and Parole Classification: The Wisconsin Model." In *Classification as a Management Tool: Theories and Models for Decision Makers*, edited by L. Fowler. College Park, Md.: American Correctional Association.

Bennett, L. A. 1972. "Classification Requirements in the Process of Social Change." Paper presented at National Institute of Law Enforcement and Criminal Justice Seminar, Washington, D.C.

————. 1976. "The Study of Violence in California Prisons: A Review with Policy Implications." In *Prison Violence*, edited by A. K. Cohen, G. F. Cole, and R. G. Bailey. Lexington, Mass.: Heath.

Bohnstedt, M., and S. Geiser. 1979. "Classification Instruments for Criminal Justice Decisions." Washington, D.C.: National Institute of Corrections.

Bottoms, A. E. 1973. "Methodological Aspects of Classification in Criminology." In *Collected Studies in Criminological Research: Methodological Aspects of Classification in Criminology*, vol. 10. Strasbourg: Council of Europe.

Brennan, T. 1984. *Offender Classification and Its Relationship to Jail Overcrowding*. Boulder, Colo.: National Institute of Corrections Information Center.

————. In this volume. "Classification: An Overview of Selected Methodological Issues."

Brennan, T., and D. Huizinga. 1975. *Theory Validation and Aggregate National Data*. Final report to Office of Youth Development, vol. 12. Boulder, Colo.: Behavioral Research Institute.

Carlson, K. A. 1981. "A Modern Personality Test for Offenders." *Criminal Justice and Behavior* 8:185–200.

Cattell, R. B., H. W. Eber, and M. M. Tatsuoka. 1970. *Handbook for the Sixteen Personality Factor Questionnaire (16 P. F.)*. Champaign, Ill.: Institute for Personality and Ability Testing.

Chapman, W., and J. Alexander. 1981. "Adustment to Prison: A Review of Inmate Characteristics Associated with Misconduct, Victimization, and Self-Injury in Confinement." Working Paper no. 10. Albany: State of New York, Department of Correctional Services.

Clements, C. B. 1980. "Offender Classification: Problems and Prospects for Correctional Management." *Prison Law Monitor* 2:237–42.

————. 1981. "The Future of Offender Classification: Some Cautions and Prospects." *Criminal Justice and Behavior* 8:15–38.

Cohen, J. 1983. "Incapacitation as a Strategy for Crime Control: Possibilities and Pitfalls." In *Crime and Justice: An Annual Review of Research*, vol. 5, edited by M. Tonry and N. Morris. Chicago: University of Chicago Press.

Correctional Services Group. 1984. *Use of Objective Classification Systems in Correctional System Master Planning*. Boulder, Colo.: National Institute of Corrections Information Center.

————. 1985. *Overview of Objective Prisoner Classification*. Boulder, Colo.: National Institute of Corrections Information Center.

Eber, H. 1978. "Case Management Policy and Procedures Manual." Colorado Springs: Colorado Department of Corrections.

Edinger, J. 1979. "Cross Validation of the Megargee MMPI Typology for Prisoners." *Journal of Consulting and Clinical Psychology* 47:234–42.

Farrington, D. P. 1979. "Longitudinal Research on Crime and Delinquency." In *Crime and Justice: An Annual Review of Research*, vol. 1, edited by N. Morris and M. Tonry. Chicago: University of Chicago Press.

Flanagan, T. J. 1979. "Long-Term Prisoners: A Study of the Characteristics, Institutional Experience and Perspectives of Long-Term Inmates in State Correctional Facilities." Ph.D. dissertation, State University of New York at Albany, Department of Criminal Justice.

————. 1983. "Correlates of Institutional Misconduct among State Prisoners—a Research Note." *Criminology* 21:29–39.

Flynn, E. E. 1982. "Classification Systems—Community and Institutional." In *Holistic Approaches to Offender Rehabilitation*, edited by L. J. Hippchen. Springfield, Ill.: Thomas.

Fowler, L., and L. Rans. 1982. "Classification Design Implementation: Technologies and Values." In *Classification as a Management Tool: Theories and Models for Decision Makers*, edited by L. Fowler. College Park, Md.: American Correctional Association.

Gettinger, S. 1982. "Objective Classification: Catalyst for Change." *Corrections Magazine* 8:24–37.

Glaser, D. 1974. The Classification of Offenses and Offenders." In *Handbook of Criminology*, edited by D. Glaser. Chicago: Rand McNally.

————. 1982. "Social Science Perspectives on Classification Decisions." In *Classification as a Management Tool: Theories and Models for Decision Makers*, edited by L. Fowler. College Park, Md.: American Correctional Association.

Gottfredson, S. In this volume. "Prediction: An Overview of Selected Methodological Issues."

Gottfredson, S., and D. Gottfredson. 1980. "Screening for Risk: A Comparison of Methods." *Criminal Justice and Behavior* 7:315–30.

————. 1982. "Risk Assessment: An Evaluation of Statistical Classification Methods." In *Classification as a Management Tool: Theories and Models for Decision Makers*, edited by L. Fowler. College Park, Md.: American Correctional Association.

Gottlieb, B. 1985. "Public Danger as a Factor in Pretrial Release: The Dynamics of State Law Development." Washington, D.C.: U.S. Department of Justice, National Institute of Justice.

Hand, D. J. 1981. *Discrimination and Classification*. New York: Wiley.

Hanson, R., C. S. Moss, R. E. Hasford, and M. E. Johnson. 1983. "Predicting Inmate Penitentiary Adjustment: An Assessment of Four Classificatory Methods." *Criminal Justice and Behavior* 10:293–309.

Hobbs, N. 1975. *Issues in the Classification of Children*. Vol. 1. San Francisco: Jossey-Bass.

Holt, N., G. Ducat, and G. Eakles. 1982. "California's New Inmate Classification System." In *Classification as a Management Tool: Theories and Models for Decision Makers,* edited by L. Fowler. College Park, Md.: American Correctional Association.

Jaman, D. 1972. "Behavior During the First Year in Prison: Report III, Background Characteristics as Predictors of Behavior and Misbehavior." Sacramento: California Department of Corrections, Research Division.

Jensen, G. 1977. "Age and Rule-Breaking in Prison: A Test of Sociocultural Interpretations." *Criminology* 14:555–56.

Kahneman, D., and A. Tversky. 1973. "On the Psychology of Prediction." *Psychological Review* 80:237–51.

Kane, T., and W. Saylor. 1983. "Security Designation: A Validation Study." Report for Federal Prison Executive Staff Meeting, Federal Bureau of Prisons Office of Research, Washington, D.C., July 1982.

Levinson, R. B. 1980. "Security Designation System—Preliminary Results." *Federal Probation* 44:26–30.

———. 1982. "The Federal Prison System's Security Designation/Custody Classification Approach." In *Classification as a Management Tool: Theories and Models for Decision Makers,* edited by L. Fowler. College Park, Md.: American Correctional Association.

Levinson, R. B., and R. Gerard. 1986. "Classifying Institutions." *Crime and Delinquency* (in press).

Levinson, R. B., and J. D. Williams. 1979. "Inmate Classification: Security/Custody Considerations." *Federal Probation* 43:37-43.

Lipsky, M. 1980. *Street-Level Bureaucracy.* New York: Russell Sage.

Lockwood, D. 1977. "Sexual Aggression among Prison Inmates." Ph.D. dissertation, State University of New York at Albany, Department of Criminal Justice.

MacNaughton-Smith, P. 1965. *Some Statistical and Other Numerical Techniques for Classifying Individuals.* London: H.M. Stationery Office.

Megargee, E., and M. Bohn, Jr. 1979. *Classifying Criminal Offenders: A New System Based on the MMPI.* Beverly Hills, Calif.: Sage.

Monahan, J. 1981. *Predicting Violent Behavior: An Assessment of Clinical Techniques.* Beverly Hills, Calif.: Sage.

Myers, L., and G. Levy. 1978. "Description and Prediction of the Intractable Inmate." *Journal of Research in Crime and Delinquency* 15:214–28.

National Institute of Corrections. 1981. *Prison Classification: A Model Systems Approach.* Washington, D.C.: National Institute of Corrections.

———. 1982. *Classification—an Overview.* Washington, D.C.: National Institute of Corrections.

———. 1983. *Jail Classification.* Washington, D.C.: National Institute of Corrections.

———. 1984. *Jail Classification.* Washington, D.C.: National Institute of Corrections.

———. 1985. *Prison Classification.* Washington, D.C.: National Institute of Corrections.

Pankhurst, R. 1975. *Biological Identification with Computers.* London: Academic.

Petersilia, J. 1982. "The Career Criminal Concept: Its Applicability to Prison Management." In *Classification as a Management Tool: Theories and Models for Decision Makers*, edited by L. Fowler. College Park, Md.: American Correctional Association.

Petersilia, J., P. W. Greenwood, and M. Lavin. 1977. *Criminal Careers and Habitual Felons*. Report no. R-2144-DOJ. Santa Monica, Calif.: Rand.

Petersilia, J., and P. Honig. 1980. *The Prison Experience of Career Criminals*. Santa Monica, Calif.: Rand.

Poole, E., and R. Regoli. 1980. "Race, Institutional Rule Breaking, and Disciplinary Response: A Study of Discretionary Decision Making in Prison." *Law and Society Review* 14:931–46.

Prottas, J. 1979. *People-Processing*. Lexington, Mass.: Lexington.

Solomon, L. 1980. "Developing an Empirically Based Model for Classification Decision-Making." *Prison Law Monitor* 217:234–37.

Solomon, L., and C. Baird. 1982. "Classification: Past Failures and Future Potential." In *Classification as a Management Tool: Theories and Models for Decision Makers*, edited by L. Fowler. College Park, Md.: American Correctional Association.

Wormith, J. S., and C. S. Goldstone. 1984. "The Clinical and Statistical Prediction of Recidivism." *Criminal Justice and Behavior* 11:3–33.

Michael Tonry

Prediction and Classification: Legal and Ethical Issues

ABSTRACT

Recent moves toward increased use of preventive detention, selective incapacitation, and predictions of dangerousness have paralleled vigorous debates concerning the legal and ethical implications of those developments. People's views about these matters are often firmly held and not easily changed by empirical evidence or logical argument. In general, those who believe in limited state power and attach high importance to civil liberties tend to oppose these trends; those who believe in extensive state powers and attach high importance to public safety favor them. The major controversies concern the appropriateness of increased punishment or state intrusion into the lives of those predicted to be dangerous, the disparities in outcome that result from use of predictions, the low levels of accuracy of such predictions, and their disparately harsh impact on minorities and the poor. Recent convergence of views among writers supports a system in which the scope for increased punishment or intrusion because of predictions is modest, reliance on information related to social status is forbidden, and primary reliance is placed on prediction variables related to the current offense and prior convictions. Replacement of existing criminal codes based on the *Model Penal Code* with new codes that define offenses in much greater detail and allow shorter maximum sentences would address many of the problems that underlie criticisms of use of predictions in sentencing.

Advances in research methods, newly feasible mathematical and statistical manipulations, and intellectual and ideological developments have

Michael Tonry is managing editor of *Crime and Justice*. Numerous friends, including Albert Alschuler, Marc Miller, John Monahan, Mark H. Moore, Norval Morris, Lloyd Ohlin, Stephen J. Schulhofer, Andrew von Hirsch, and Franklin E. Zimring, offered advice and criticism concerning successive drafts of this essay.

focused attention on use of prediction and classification in the criminal justice system. Research on criminal careers, career criminals, and the prediction of dangerousness has coincided with calls for preventive detention, repeat offender programs, and selective incapacitation. Some prediction and classification uses have been criticized on ethical, legal, or constitutional grounds. Much of the criticism is aimed at preventive detention and selective incapacitation and generally then at problems associated with efforts to predict dangerousness or to identify high-rate offenders. The issues raised are, however, more general and relate to the philosophy of punishment.

People have been arguing about the justifications for punishment and for the criminal law for thousands of years. Modern arguments about the use of predictions are a part of those larger arguments and, like them, are not likely to be resolved. People have deeply bedded beliefs about punishment, and they tend to be the kind of beliefs that are seldom changed by argument or by the marshaling of evidence. The "ethics of prediction" is not unlike the death penalty, the exclusionary rule, or abortion in that regard. Although some people may, for example, be agnostics concerning capital punishment, there are probably many more who will remain fixed in their views whatever the findings of empirical research concerning deterrent effects or the logic of opponents' arguments.

Harvard philosopher Robert Nozick has observed that professional philosophers are in this respect like the rest of us:

> When a philosopher sees that premisses he accepts logically imply a conclusion he has rejected until now, he faces a choice: he may accept this conclusion or reject one of the previously accepted premisses. . . . His choice will depend upon which is greater, the degree of his commitment to the various premisses or the degree of his commitment to denying the conclusion. It is implausible that these are independent of how strongly he wants certain things to be true. The various means of control over conclusions explain why so few philosophers publish ones that (continue to) upset them. [Nozick 1981, pp. 2–3]

If philosophers are little susceptible to persuasion about deeply bedded normative beliefs, it is not surprising that philosophical and ethical arguments often have little persuasive impact on the beliefs of others.

One of the characters in Canadian novelist Robertson Davies's *Fifth Business* notes of philosophers addressing a fundamental question that they "answered it in ways highly satisfactory to themselves; but I never knew a philosopher's answer to make much difference to anyone not in the trade" (Davies 1983, p. 204).

In this essay I attempt to identify contentious issues and to summarize the primary arguments that have been made. In this, as in so many other areas of normative controversy, where one comes out depends on where one begins, and the embarkation points vary greatly. Some start from premises of limited state powers and the primacy of individual autonomy. Others start from utilitarian premises of the primacy of the larger public interest and the need to subordinate individual interests to the collective good. The proportions of the public and of intellectuals subscribing to any particular position vary with place and time, and these differences are unlikely to disappear.

Before turning to the arguments, a few words about uses of predictions and classifications may be in order. The criminal justice system inevitably classifies people. There is nothing special about this. Any social institution that processes large numbers of human beings must sort them into categories or classes, and there is a great deal of constitutional law on this subject.

Most criminal justice predictions generate classifications, but not all classifications derive from predictions. Most recent controversy concerns prediction-based classifications.

Parole guideline systems offer one well-known example of prediction-based classification; prisoners are divided into classes defined by base expectancy rates of recidivism. A base expectancy rate is a statistic, based on past experience, that indicates what proportion of a group will experience some event. For example, a base expectancy recidivism rate of 30 percent means that, in the past, 30 percent of people in a group sharing specified characteristics were recidivists within some follow-up period. Under most parole guidelines, the higher the base expectancy rate of the class into which the offender falls, the longer he is likely to remain in prison.

Base expectancy tables on parole failure have been available since the 1920s and have been used intermittently since that time (see Glaser, in this volume). All targeted "career" or "dangerous" or "high-rate" offender programs divide the universe of offenders into two classes—those who satisfy program criteria and those who do not; fundamental to the classification is the prediction that the targeted offenders will, if not incapacitated, continue to commit serious crimes at unacceptable rates in the future (see Farrington, in this volume).

Other prediction-based classification systems are widely used, and not all concern dangerousness. Bail criteria, for example, traditionally classify defendants in terms of their likelihood of appearing for trial. Some bail systems also now incorporate predictions of reoffending while awaiting trial. Bail guidelines make this prediction-based classification system more evident than ever before (see Goldkamp, in this volume).

Correctional classification systems attempt to allocate prison space and specify appropriate security and custody levels on the basis of predictions about offenders' future behavior. Correctional classifications and the resulting differential treatments are based on predictions of dangerousness to others, on predictions of victimization in prison, and on predictions of escape proneness, suicide proneness, or unlikelihood of institutional adjustment (see Brennan, in this volume, chap. 10; Sechrest, in this volume).

Not all prediction-based classifications are as overt as in the federal parole guidelines or Philadelphia's bail guidelines. Many are nonquantitative. Some are entirely ad hoc and intuitive. Some are based on verbal formulae. Under section 5 of the *Model Sentencing Act* of the National Council on Crime and Delinquency (1963), for example, "the court may sentence a defendant . . . to a term of thirty years, or to a lesser term, if it finds that, because of the dangerousness of the defendant, such period of confined correctional treatment or custody is required for the protection of the public . . . and . . . the court finds that he is suffering from a severe personality disorder indicating a propensity toward criminal activity." This provision has numerous undefined key words and phrases—"dangerousness," confinement "required for the protection of the public," "severe," "personality disorder," and "propensity toward criminal activity." Each individual judge must give them meaning.

Subjective prediction-based classification systems have been vigorously criticized. Most scholars of prediction have concluded that subjective predictions are less reliable than are statistical predictions (see, e.g., Meehl 1954; Monahan 1981; Morris and Miller 1985). The absence of established objective criteria for decision making necessarily results in the application of different criteria, differently weighted by different decision makers, and is susceptible to Justice Marshall's obser-

vation concerning predictions of dangerousness in *Schall v. Martin*, 104
S.Ct. 2403, 2432 (1984):

> excessive discretion fosters inequality in the distribution of
> entitlements and harms, inequality which is especially troublesome
> when these benefits and burdens are great; and discretions can
> mask the use by officials of illegitimate criteria in allocating
> important goods and rights.

Here is how this essay is organized. Section I surveys legal and
constitutional issues related to criminal justice system use of predictions and classifications. The law and the Constitution impose few
constraints. Most of the debate therefore centers not on what is legally
required or forbidden but on what as a policy matter is right or wrong.
Section II canvasses debates concerning the use of prediction-based
classifications in the criminal justice system and attempts to locate some
of these in larger analytical contexts. Section III, the conclusion, proposes some features of an approach to prediction-based classification
generally, and its use in sentencing standards particularly, that may
achieve some of the objectives of such classification systems while
avoiding or, in any case, partially addressing many of the criticisms
that have been made of their use.

I. Legal and Constitutional Issues

This is probably not the place, nor the likely readership of a *Crime and
Justice* volume the audience, for a detailed analysis of legal and constitutional issues germane to prediction and classification problems. Dozens
of articles on these subjects have been published in the law reviews and
in the major treatises on constitutional law and criminal procedure (see,
e.g., Saltzburg 1985), although most analyses do not expressly relate to
the subject of this essay.

Some readers, and probably all lawyer-readers, may wish to skip
Section I altogether and go directly to Section II. As will be seen,
statutes and constitutional doctrines impose few constraints on criminal
justice prediction and classification. I decided that this essay would try
to set out the legal and constitutional frameworks that relate to prediction and classification issues because I have read half a dozen analyses of
"legal and ethical issues in prediction" over the years and invariably
found that legal issues were discussed little or not at all.

Legislatures possess constitutional authority to enact laws that limit use of prediction and classification but seldom elect to do so.[1] When legislatures enact laws governing the purposes of sentencing, for example, they tend either to establish multiple purposes (e.g., as in the *Model Penal Code* [American Law Institute 1962], retribution, incapacitation, deterrence, prevention, and rehabilitation, among others) or, occasionally, to forbid resort to certain factors as bases for classifications (e.g., as under the Minnesota sentencing guidelines, race, sex, education, employment, living arrangements, and marital status [Minnesota Sentencing Guidelines Commission 1980, pp. 37–38]).

State supreme courts possess authority to constrain criminal justice decision making but seldom exercise it; the Minnesota Supreme Court is an exception and has developed an extensive case law on sentencing (Knapp 1985). That court, for example, has held that predictions of dangerousness are not an appropriate justification for imposing a lengthier prison sentence on an offender than Minnesota's sentencing guidelines would otherwise prescribe (e.g., *State v. Magnan*, 328 N.W.2d 147 [Minn. 1983]; *Jackson v. State*, 329 N.W.2d 66 [Minn. 1983]).

Because the statute books are generally silent about limits on uses of predictions, such constraints as exist must be found in the U.S. or state constitutions. According to the U.S. Supreme Court, the U.S. Constitution has relatively little to say on these subjects.[2] Only a handful of generalizations applicable to criminal justice predictions and classifications can be derived from the Supreme Court's interpretations of the U.S. Constitution.

1. Classifications based directly on race, ethnicity, political beliefs, or religion are generally prohibited; reliance on one of these factors must usually be shown to be justified by a "compelling state interest"— a probative standard that is difficult to meet.

2. Classifications based on sex are often prohibited, and attempts to justify such classifications must be substantially persuasive.

3. Classifications based directly on other factors are nearly always

---

[1] When such laws are enacted, they tend to establish or forbid classifications based on fundamental categories such as nationality, race, or sex. Some jurisdictions limit certain benefits to citizens. Civil rights laws forbid use of race, sex, and other factors in classifications. Some jurisdictions forbid use of sex in actuarial classifications used in establishing insurance premiums. Few such laws address criminal justice decision making.

[2] Some of these issues are likely soon to be addressed, however, when the court attempts to resolve conflicts between federal courts of appeals in interpreting the preventive detention provisions of the Bail Reform Act of 1984 (e.g., compare U.S. v. Salerno, 794 F.2d 64 [2d Cir. 1986], with U.S. v. Zannino, 798 F.2d 544 [1st Cir. 1986]).

permitted because all that must be shown is that there is a "rational basis" for the classification; the courts defer to legislative and executive classifications, and it is accordingly very difficult to show that a classification lacks a rational basis.

4. Classifications that result in differential impacts on racial or ethnic groups, but indirectly and without the intention to achieve that result, are nearly always permitted (unless a statutory scheme—e.g., an equal employment opportunity law—is deemed to forbid both intended and unintended differential impacts).

5. Official actions taken before trial involving jail conditions, on the basis of predictions, will generally be sustained even if they infringe on liberty unless they can be shown to be "intended to be punitive."[3]

6. Official actions taken after conviction on the basis of predictions of dangerousness will generally be sustained so long as the sanctions or conditions imposed are within the range authorized by law.

7. Judges (at least; probably all criminal justice system officials) may rely on predictions in making decisions irrespective of the scientific integrity or credibility of the predictive evidence adduced unless they expressly declare that they are relying on evidence that is patently frivolous.

Because statutes have little to say about criminal justice use of predictions and classifications, it is to the Constitution that one must look for guidance. In general, what is not forbidden is permitted, and, as will be seen, in this realm little is forbidden. Most constitutional objections to criminal justice prediction and classification are couched in terms of the Equal Protection and Due Process Clauses of the Fourteenth Amendment to the Constitution, which provides in its first section that

> No State shall . . . deprive any person of life, liberty, or property, without due process of law; nor deny to any person within its jurisdiction the equal protection of the laws.

A similarly worded due process clause applicable to the federal government is set out in the Fifth Amendment. Arguments can also be couched in terms of the Eighth Amendment's prohibition of "cruel and unusual punishment."

---

[3] This statement purposely sidesteps preventive detention; the law and constitutional analysis are in turmoil on this subject as the federal courts sort out issues and cases arising under the federal Bail Reform Act of 1984 (see n. 4 below).

A. *Equal Protection*

The focus of the equal protection arguments is that the basis of a classification offends the Equal Protection Clause. A classification scheme that directed that blacks receive one treatment, whites another, Hispanics a third, and Asians a fourth would give rise to patent equal protection objections. Two broad categories of equal protection objections are made. The first opposes the explicit use of race or other controverted characteristics. The second opposes classifications that, in operation, systematically treat members of different races or groups differently.

1. *The Explicit Basis for the Classification.* The Supreme Court has developed a three-tiered approach for assessing governmental classifications of individuals (actually some constitutional lawyers would assert that more than three tiers exist; for purposes of this essay, the arguably oversimplified three tiers should suffice).

a) Strict Scrutiny and Race. First are a set of highly suspect bases for classifications such as race, ethnicity, political beliefs, and religious affiliation. These are constitutionally regarded as "suspect classes," and a classification based on them will be sustained only if the state can demonstrate that a "compelling state interest" is served by that classification system. The courts subject such classifications to "strict scrutiny." As a practical matter, this probably prohibits the explicit use of these factors in a classification system. If, for a somewhat implausible example, a parole board decided that race (or ethnicity, etc.) was a good proxy for criminal history, employment, and education and for simplicity's sake decided to base release decisions on the offenders' race (zero points for being black, one point for being white), the courts would almost undoubtedly strike down the classification system.

b) Intermediate Scrutiny and Gender. Second are bases for classification, of which gender is the paradigm case, that are subjected to "intermediate scrutiny." This has also been called "minimal scrutiny with bite." The verbal formulae used by the Supreme Court vary with the context, but, in lay terms, if strict scrutiny requires the presence of a "compelling" state interest, intermediate scrutiny requires a substantial state interest. As a practical matter, this probably prohibits the use of gender as the basis for many criminal justice classifications although clearly not all. For example, establishment of single-sex prisons can probably be justified in terms of administrative advantage and avoidance of intersexual victimization and tensions. Whether explicit use of gender to increase or decrease the severity of sanctions in a guidelines system would be permitted is anyone's guess, but to date every major guidelines system has established unisex sentencing standards.

c) Minimal Scrutiny and Most Variables. The courts accord substantial deference to legislative or executive classifications that do not trigger strict or intermediate scrutiny. Such classifications receive "minimal scrutiny," and the state need only demonstrate a "rational" basis for them. Courts do not insist that *the* reason for the classification be rational, merely that *a* reason be rational. Sometimes the courts will search for a hypothetical justification for a disputed classification that, had it been relied on by the classifiers, would have been rational. Most criminal history, offense circumstances, or personal biographical variables that might be used in a classification system do not give rise to substantial equal protection objections.

2. *Facially Neutral but Racially Skewed Bases for Classifications.* A different form of equal protection analysis looks not to the intent or to the explicit basis of the classification but to its effects (see, e.g., Coffee 1975). This analysis derives from equal employment opportunity cases arising under federal statutes that fix on the "differential impact" of disputed employment practices.

Differential impact analysis, were it applicable, would be highly relevant to criminal justice system classifications; many of the variables commonly used in prediction and classification systems adversely and systematically affect minorities (see, e.g., Petersilia and Turner, in this volume; Goldkamp, in this volume, Sec. IV). Many of the standard empirically derived predictors of criminality are correlated with race. Many social status variables, including education, employment, living arrangements, and the like, vary with race; blacks, on average, have less education, fewer marketable skills, and less stable employment and residential records than do whites, on average. Even criminal history information, like age at first arrest and prior arrests and convictions, is correlated with race. However, because differential impact analysis arises under federal statutes, not the Constitution, it can apply only where statutes so specify; no such statutes govern criminal justice decision making. Thus, as a legal or constitutional matter, differential impact analysis is unlikely to limit use of most variables customarily included in prediction or classification formulae. As a policy matter, however, policymakers in a number of jurisdictions have chosen to forbid use in decision making of some social variables relating to education and employment because of their presumed disparate impact on minorities (see, e.g., Minnesota Sentencing Guidelines Commission 1980).

There is some irony in the contrast between this constitutional obliviousness to the equal protection effects of prediction and classification decisions and the criminal law's approach to determination of guilt and innocence. Substantive criminal law doctrine often treats purposive and knowing actions as comparable. The mental states recognized by *mens rea* doctrines as elements of criminal offenses are purpose (intention), knowledge, recklessness, and negligence (this ignores strict liability offenses). Generally, as a precondition to conviction, the presence of a particular mental state must be shown.

Offenders who act with intention or knowledge of a proscribed harm are usually treated as equally culpable and can be convicted of the same offense and receive the same sentence. To intend to kill or to act with knowledge that death will result are analytically different mental states, but morally and legally they are generally treated as equivalents. To burn a house down with the intention to kill a person sleeping inside is legally equivalent to burning a house down with the intention to collect the insurance but with the knowledge that the person sleeping inside will be killed.

Once, however, the context shifts from what must be shown to convict a person accused of crime to what standards govern criminal justice system decisions, the equivalence of purpose and knowledge disappears. A classification whose purpose is to achieve racially disparate impacts, if provable, is unconstitutional; a classification that is adopted with some legitimate purpose in mind but with knowledge of its racially disparate impact is not unconstitutional.

B. Due Process Analysis

"Due process" is the second broad constitutional theory for challenging classifications and predictions. Due process analysis is conventionally divided into "procedural due process" and "substantive due process." As the terms suggest, procedural due process concerns the rules, mechanisms, and procedures by which disputes are resolved or claims are settled, and substantive due process deals with the merits of disputed laws.[4]

---

[4] Substantive due process arguments figure prominently in the most active constitutional litigation concerning prediction in the criminal justice system. The federal Bail Reform Act of 1984 created an overt system of preventive detention in the federal courts.

Two kinds of procedural due process arguments are introduced here. First, some systems for making discretionary decisions have been declared unconstitutional under due process analysis because they were "fixed and mechanical." For example, some federal district court judges during the Vietman War era routinely imposed the maximum authorized five-year sentence on persons convicted of Selective Service offenses. The appellate courts held that such a sentencing policy violated due process because the judge had failed to carry out his responsibility to exercise sound discretion on the basis of the circumstances of individual cases coming before him. Second, some due process analyses challenge decisions as "arbitrary and capricious" because government officials are accorded too great a discretion, unbounded and unguided by governing criteria.

1. *Fixed and Mechanical.*   In circumstances in which legislation confers discretion on decision makers, courts have held that due process requires that discretion be exercised. As the Selective Service cases demonstrate, when decision makers announce that they will not exercise discretion but will act only in a single specified way, due process has been denied.

The "fixed and mechanical" argument has been raised unsuccessfully against the use of parole guidelines. Prisoners have asserted that the effect of the U.S. Parole Commission's guidelines has been to replace the exercise of parole release discretion with a fixed and mechanical system of decision making governed by the guidelines. These assertions, though occasionally successful in lower courts, were rejected by the Supreme Court in *United States v. Geraghty*, 445 U.S. 388 (1980). The Supreme Court held that the federal enabling legislation that authorized establishment of parole guidelines clearly contemplated the creation of a system of structured discretion under guidelines and that decision making under such a system does not deny due process.

2. *Arbitrary and Capricious.*   The converse claim is that due process

The statute's constitutionality has been challenged many times, with different results. The statute's constitutionality has been upheld in the First, Third, Seventh, Ninth, and Eleventh Circuits (U.S. v. Zannino, 798 F.2d 544 [1st Cir. 1986]; U.S. v. Perry, 788 F.2d 100 [3d Cir. 1986]; U.S. v. Portes, 786 F.2d 758 [7th Cir. 1986]; U.S. v. Walker, 40 CrL 2389 [9th Cir. 1987]; U.S. v. Rodriguez, 803 F.2d 1102 [11th Cir. 1986]). The Second Circuit Court of Appeals has declared the statute unconstitutional (U.S. v. Salerno, 794 F.2d 64 [2d Cir. 1986]). The Supreme Court accepted an appeal from *Salerno* and heard arguments in January 1987 (40 CrL 4157); a decision should be announced by June 1987. All of these cases involve close analysis of specific statutory language and are not further discussed here. Interested readers should consult the extensive commentary that will no doubt soon appear in the law reviews.

is denied when too great discretion is vested in decision makers. The paradigm case arises in death penalty litigation. The Supreme Court held in *Furman v. Georgia*, 408 U.S. 238 (1972), that a state cannot, without guiding standards or criteria, constitutionally delegate to a jury or a judge discretion to determine whether capital punishment should be imposed in an individual case. As a consequence, many death penalty statutes now set out specific aggravating and, sometimes, mitigating criteria to be considered by judge or jury in determining whether to impose capital punishment.

In radically different contexts, the Supreme Court has held that conferring too great discretion is unconstitutional. Vagrancy ordinances, for example, are sometimes struck down on vagueness grounds because their generality "permits and encourages an arbitrary and discriminatory enforcement of the law" (*Papachristou* v. *City of Jacksonville*, 405 U.S. 156, 168 [1972]). More saliently to criminal justice problems, the question has been raised in a number of contexts whether the modest reliability of clinical or statistical predictions of dangerousness is sufficiently great to justify official judgments affecting liberty.

The U.S. Supreme Court has several times rejected due process attacks on unreliable systems of prediction of dangerousness. The most far-reaching approval of the use of predictions of dangerousness came in *Barefoot v. Estelle*, 103 S.Ct. 3383 (1983), in which the court upheld the constitutionality of a Texas death penalty statute that allowed a finding of future dangerousness, based on psychiatric testimony, to justify a death sentence. The Texas system was upheld notwithstanding the American Psychiatric Association's express disapproval of psychiatric testimony forecasting future violent conduct in individual cases and the Supreme Court's observation in *Barefoot* that "the single 'best' clinical research currently in existence indicates that psychiatrists and psychologists are accurate in no more than one out of three predictions of violent behavior over a several year period among institutionalized populations that had both committed violence in the past . . . and who are diagnosed as mentally ill." In *Barefoot*, one psychiatrist testified that the defendant "most certainly would" commit future acts of criminal violence and claimed that the degree of probability of criminal acts constituting a continuing threat to society was "100% to absolute." A second psychiatrist, who had neither interviewed nor clinically examined the defendant, testified "within reasonable psychiatric certainty" that there was a "probability that Thomas A. Barefoot . . . will commit criminal acts of violence in the future that would constitute a continuing threat to society."

The Supreme Court also approved of reliance on dangerousness predictions in *Schall v. Martin*, 104 S.Ct. 2403 (1984), in which the Court upheld the constitutionality of New York's juvenile preventive detention statute. The statute permits prehearing detention, without the holding of a probable cause hearing, of any juvenile so long as "there is a serious risk that he may before the return date commit an act which if committed by an adult would constitute a crime." The act provides no criteria to govern the judge's decision that a juvenile presents such a "serious risk." Lawyers, for a variety of reasons, can argue that the decision in *Schall v. Martin* is not applicable to decision making in other settings. The case dealt with juveniles committed for short periods, and the decision was premised in part on the need to "protect the child"; moreover, because "juveniles, unlike adults, are always in some form of custody," the Court's opinion noted that detention would constitute a less substantial intrusion on liberty than would be suffered by an adult. Nonetheless, *Schall v. Martin* expressly addressed the due process arguments that would arise in other contexts when the limited reliability of predictions of dangerousness is alleged. The district court, after reviewing the scientific literature, had observed that "no diagnostic tools have as yet been devised which enable even the most highly trained criminologist to predict reliably which juveniles will engage in violent crime" and, as a consequence, had concluded that the absence of such guidance made decisions under the New York Preventive Detention statute "arbitrary and capricious." Although the Supreme Court discussed many legal issues in deciding *Schall v. Martin*, it concluded, citing *Jurek v. Texas*, 428 U.S. 262 (1976), that

> our cases indicate, however, that from a legal point of view there is nothing unattainable about a prediction of future criminal conduct . . . and we have specifically rejected the contention, based on the same sort of sociological data relied upon by appellees and the district court, "that it is impossible to predict future behavior and that the question is so vague as to be meaningless." [P. 274]

The court asserted that judicial predictions of future criminal conduct constitute "an experienced prediction based on a host of variable factors," listed a wide variety of considerations that a trial judge might take into account, and found no constitutional objection to the absence of specific statutory criteria to guide the family court judges in reaching their decisions.

Factual circumstances in *Schall* make it an especially powerful endorsement of reliance on prediction. First, in contrast to adults held under preventive detention statutes, there had been no determinations that probable cause existed to conclude that the juveniles had committed the crimes with which they were charged. Second, the hearings at which detention was ordered were informed by very limited information and often lasted only a few minutes. Third, two-thirds of the cases in issue in *Schall v. Martin* resulted in the detained juveniles being released before or immediately after trials, suggesting that public safety did not require that they be detained before trial. All of these circumstances, however, serve only to underscore that, in pursuit of the "legitimate and compelling state interest in protecting the community from crime" (104 S.Ct. 243, 2410), the Supreme Court is unlikely to take seriously due process attacks on prediction and classification devices premised on either their low levels of validity or the presence or absence of specific criteria to govern decision making.

Even were the Supreme Court to limit the reach of *Schall*'s "predictions of dangerousness" discussion to juvenile matters, it is unlikely that due process attacks on predictions in other contexts would succeed. Supreme Court decisions have announced, for various stated reasons, that the Court will allow great latitude to the discretionary decisions of judges, prosecutors, correctional administrators, and parole authorities.

A series of modern cases (e.g., *Bordenkircher v. Hayes*, 434 U.S. 357 [1978]) indicates that the courts should defer to the prosecutor's discretion in charging, bargaining, and dismissing charges. This deference is explained partly in separation-of-powers terms and partly in practical terms. The deference surely extends to prosecutorial decisions to allocate resources to concentrate on "dangerous" offenders.

The trial judge's broad discretion is justified negatively and positively. The "negative" justification, discussed in the next section, is that the Eighth Amendment "disproportionality" doctrine prohibits only aberrantly severe sentences; anything not warranting those modifiers is constitutionally acceptable. The "positive" justification is generally identified with *Williams v. New York*, 337 U.S. 241, 247 (1949), in which the Court observed that sentences should be based "on the fullest information possible concerning the defendant's life and circumstances." In a whole series of cases (*Jurek v. Texas*, 428 U.S. 262 [1976]; *Jones v. United States*, 103 S.Ct. 3043 [1983]; *Barefoot v. Estelle*, 103 S.Ct. 3383 [1983]; *Schall v. Martin*, 104 S.Ct. 2403 [1984]), the Court has explicitly included dangerousness predictions of disputed reliability within the permitted "fullest information possible."

The courts have consistently for forty years followed a policy of deference to the expertise and statutory mandates of parole boards and have generally refused to consider the substantive merits of parole release decisions (e.g., *Greenholt v. Inmates of the Nebraska Penal and Correctional Complex*, 442 U.S. 1 [1979]). The deference is premised partly on separation-of-powers concerns and partly on the rationales of individualized sentencing that appear in *Williams v. New York*.

Prison and jail administrators, also, receive extreme deference under modern doctrine. The Supreme Court has recently tried to reduce judicial involvement in prison matters and has announced in a number of leading cases (most notably, *Bell v. Wolfish*, 441 U.S. 520 [1979]) that courts should, wherever possible, defer to the competence and special expertise of correctional administrators.

Thus, like the equal protection arguments, due process arguments are unlikely significantly to constrain the use of prediction and classification devices in the criminal justice system.

C. Cruel and Unusual Punishment

The third basic constitutional argument that might arise concerning prediction and classification is that especially severe actions or sanctions resulting from classification as a high-rate or dangerous offender violate the constitutional injunction against "cruel and unusual punishment."[5] There are "before-trial" and "after-trial" versions of this argument.

The before-trial argument, which would apply to pretrial release and preventive detention, is that special treatment of those predicted to be dangerous violates the Fifth and Fourteenth Amendment Due Process Clauses' prohibition of cruel and unusual punishment. A defendant who is jailed because he is "dangerous" can argue that he is being "punished" because of the prediction. Although the Supreme Court has held, in *Bell v. Wolfish*, 441 U.S. 520, 535 (1979), that "it is axiomatic that '[d]ue process requires that a pretrial detainee not be punished,'"

---

[5] This argument has been raised, generally unsuccessfully, in attacks on the preventive detention provisions of the federal Bail Reform Act of 1984.

it has also held (p. 538) that "a court must decide whether the disability is imposed *for the purpose of punishment* or whether it is but an incident of some other legitimate governmental purpose" (emphasis added). Unless an express intention to punish can be shown (which is highly unlikely in most cases), the state need only show that some legitimate purpose will be served by the special treatment. By this standard, few confined pretrial detainees are likely to win a "cruel and unusual punishment" claim.

The after-trial argument is based on the Eighth Amendment's prohibition of "cruel and unusual punishment." Since *Weems v. United States*, 217 U.S. 349 (1910), the Supreme Court has held that the Eighth Amendment forbids punishments that are disproportionate to the crime for which they are imposed. In *Weems*, a sentence of fifteen years at hard labor in chains for "falsifying a public document" was held unconstitutionally disproportionate. Since 1910, the disproportionality doctrine has waxed and waned.

We are now in a waning era. In *Rummel v. Estelle*, 445 U.S. 263 (1980), involving imposition of a life sentence under a habitual offender statute, after a third nonviolent felony conviction, the court held that for felonies "the length of the sentence actually imposed is purely a matter of legislative prerogative" (p. 274). In other words, the Court held that the disproportionality doctrine did not apply to prison sentences if they were lawful in that they were authorized by statute (other cases have held that this distinction does not apply to some death sentences). More recently, in *Solem v. Helm*, 463 U.S. 277 (1983), another case involving a life sentence imposed on a nonviolent offender under a habitual offender statute, the Court, by a 5–4 vote, revived disproportionality analysis without overruling *Rummel* on the basis of a distinction that only a lawyer could love (in *Estelle v. Rummel* the defendant's life sentence allowed for possible parole release; the *Solem v. Helm* defendant's life sentence allowed only for commutation).

Notwithstanding the fine lines by which disproportionality analysis is now applied, it clearly applies only to aberrant cases, such as life sentences for nonviolent social nuisances. It is most unlikely that the courts will strike down as unconstitutionally disproportionate sentences that result from a prediction that an offender is a repetitive violent offender.

D. Summary of Constitutional Issues

There are virtually no constitutional impediments to the use of prediction and classification devices in the criminal justice system. Although a few bases for classifying offenders, such as race, ethnicity, religion, possibly sex, and maybe one or two others, would likely not be permitted, the use of other variables whose application would have disparate impacts apparently presents no serious problem. Similarly, except in very special contexts, like the death penalty, the presence or absence of criteria to guide discretionary decisions is unlikely to raise constitutional issues, and reliance on predictions of dangerousness, whatever their scientific validity, is permitted.

A critic of an earlier draft of this essay noted that "the whole constitutional analysis exudes disapproval of the current state of the law without explaining the reason for this disapproval." My principal aim is not to register disapproval but to observe that the U.S. Constitution, as currently interpreted, has little to say about prediction and classification. From some civil liberties perspectives, this can only be seen as unfortunate. To a person who believes that individual liberty is the paramount value protected by our constitutional system, the burden of demonstrating the need to intrude on liberty (or further intrude, as by delaying a release decision for predictive reasons) should generally rest on the state. Under the current constitutional case law, the probative burden on the state concerning predictions is slight and the permitted intrusions on liberty are great. Earlier I noted that there exist widely divergent normative views on the justifications for punishment and criminal law powers, some premised primarily on concern for individual liberty and others premised primarily on concern for public protection and the larger public good. The disapproval noted by my first-draft critic derives from my belief that the cases one-sidedly adopt the "public safety" perspective over the "individual liberty" perspective even though in the larger society and in the Supreme Court, as evidenced by Justice Marshall's dissent in *Schall v. Martin* that was quoted above, there is disagreement about the choice between these goals.

The absence of controlling statutes and constitutional doctrines means that analyses of the appropriateness of use of predictions and classifications must be phrased in ethical and policy terms. These arguments are the subject of the next section.

II. Ethical and Policy Issues

Most of the debate over the use of prediction-based classifications has focused on predictions of dangerousness, particularly concerning preventive detention, sentencing, and parole; I maintain that focus here. Comparable police and prosecutorial programs of targeting resources on high-rate offenders provoke less controversy, perhaps because these are law enforcement agencies, which must allocate scarce resources, and because their decisions are in theory subject to later review by impartial judges. In any case, police and prosecutors can take action against an individual only when there is probable cause to believe a crime has been committed and subject to obtaining judicial approval. A targeted special offender program signifies that no favors or leniency will be granted, but, since the prosecution is in respect of an alleged crime, a known repeat offender is not well placed to argue that he should not be prosecuted with vigor.

Judges, however, make bail and sentencing decisions, and those decisions differ crucially from police and prosecutorial decisions in two important respects. First, judges are supposed to be impartial decision makers, and, except concerning procedural issues, in most jurisdictions their decisions are not subject to further review (except where appellate sentence review has taken root); judicial mistakes can have long-term, often irreversible, consequences. Second, judges deciding about preventive detention or incapacitative sentencing make decisions not only about alleged or proved offenses but also about possible future offenses. Some would argue that an offender who commits an offense can be said to make himself vulnerable to full and vigorous prosecution for that offense and that a comparable assumption-of-risk analysis justifies decisions to impose or extend incarceration because of predicted future offenses. Because selective incapacitation and preventive detention have been the subjects of most of the controversy over uses of prediction, the following discussion addresses the ethical and policy issues in those contexts.

A. A Framework for Philosophies of Punishment

Much of the debate over predictions of dangerousness in sentencing turns on the debaters' differing views of the importance of equality and proportionality in the distribution of punishment. These different views, in turn, derive from different theories of the justification and properties of criminal punishment.

More than twenty-five years ago, H. L. A. Hart (1968) proposed a taxonomy of punishment philosophies. Writing at a time when rehabilitative rationales for punishment were widely accepted but were beginning to come under attack, he tried to show that thinking and arguing about punishment were often muddled by statements that took the form of "the purpose of punishment is. . . ." Statements in that form were inadequate, Hart urged, because there are several different aspects of punishment that require justification, and one might coherently offer different justifications for different aspects.

These are the separate questions.

1. What is the general justifying aim of criminal punishment?
2. Whom should the state punish?
3. How much punishment should be imposed?

These are referred to, respectively, as questions of "general justifying aim," "liability," and "amount." The importance any writer attributes to pursuit of equality and proportionality in punishment may be implied or determined by how he justifies the amount of punishment. For example, whether comparably situated offenders convicted of the same offense receive the same sentence will be of high importance to a retributivist who believes that an offender's degree of culpability should determine his punishment. To punish equally culpable, like-situated offenders differently would be objectionable as would it be to punish in the same way and amount offenders of differing culpability: punishing like offenders in unlike ways is as objectionable as is punishing unlike offenders in like ways. By contrast, to a utilitarian who justifies punishment in terms of the general public good, equal treatment of like-situated and comparably culpable offenders may not seem an especially important objective. Hart himself "allows some place, though a subordinate one, to ideas of equality and proportion in the gradation of the severity of punishment" (1968, p. 233).

H. L. A. Hart's analytical framework is now part of the jurisprudential landscape.

For some writers, the answers to Hart's three questions must be consistent. For a "thoroughgoing retributivist," for example, the justifying aim is the moral requirement that suffering be imposed on wrongdoers; only those who are conscious wrongdoers should be liable to punishment, and the amount of punishment should be "as much as is deserved." For most writers, however, the three questions may coherently be given different answers. Thus Hart himself, who trod a "middle way," urged general prevention of crime as the justifying aim, limited punishment to conscious wrongdoers (a retributivist position), and would permit utilitarian goals of incapacitation, deterrence, and rehabilitation substantially to influence the amount of punishment imposed on any individual.

No single punishment philosophy predominates in the United States among politicians, professionals, academics, or writers on punishment.

Lack of concurrence does not mean that everyone must be agnostic and accept all positions as being of equal merit or justness. Nor does it mean that legislatures or criminal justice institutions should refuse to adopt overriding purposes or premises. It does mean, however, that debates over punishment issues tend to be resolved by compromises and seldom by unqualified acceptance of any single set of views.

B. Retributive and Utilitarian Theories

In the interest of efficiency, the issues commonly raised concerning prediction are considered here primarily from two polar hypothetical positions—that of the ultimate utilitarian (UU) and that of the thoroughgoing retributivist (TR), which are stereotyped exemplars of two kinds of philosophical views called, respectively, teleological (or "consequentialist") theories and deontological theories. In general, teleological theories are concerned with justification for actions as means to ends, deontological theories with justification of actions in themselves. For the purposes of this essay, those terms are not important. I mention them only to make clear that utilitarianism and retributivism, while examples of teleological and deontological theories, respectively, are not the only punishment theories that might be devised or elaborated.

1. *Utilitarian Theories.*   Utilitarianism is the best-known teleological theory and is concerned ultimately with maximizing social utility and the aggregate public good. In the arcane reaches of utilitarianism, there is considerable debate about how one could best measure social utility, but for the purposes of this essay "the greatest good for the greatest number" should suffice. Applied to crime, UU would support the crime control strategy that costs least in economic and social terms when one takes fully into account the cost of crime and fear of crime; the cost of law enforcement and sanctioning; the cost to offenders, their families, and associates, and the state of the offender's being punished.

Utilitarians believe in incentives and rationality and therefore see the punishment of offenders as a device for reducing the incidence and cost of crime through deterrence, incapacitation, and rehabilitation. To UU, then, what is important in punishing individual offenders is not anything about them but rather the likely crime-preventive effects of their punishment. Strictly speaking, if no crime prevention effects would be realized from punishing an individual, no punishment would be justified. Jeremy Bentham, the archetypal utilitarian, subscribed to a principle of "parsimony," under which punishment imposed beyond that necessary for prevention is immoral; anyone's suffering is undesirable, and to impose suffering gratuitously, to no utilitarian end, is immoral. Conversely, if punishment of an individual will on balance increase social utility, then that punishment should be imposed even if, for example, a severe punishment is needed for a petty offense. Thus, for UU, equality and proportionality are relatively unimportant properties or objectives of punishment.

2. *Retributivist Theories.* The thoroughgoing retributivist, TR, finds UU's views shocking and believes that people must be viewed as ends, not means. Punishments must be deserved; the relevant moral calculus concerns the offender and his culpability and not the consequences of his punishment. People deserve punishment because they knowingly and wrongly inflict injury to the person or interests of others. Exactly why this is so varies for different theorists, just as the methods for measuring social utility vary among utilitarian theorists.

For some retributivists, the knowing infliction of a wrong upsets the equilibrium of society, and the punishment of the wrongdoer is needed to restore that equilibrium. For others, respect for individual autonomy means that individuals are treated as persons capable of making moral choices; failure to punish those who knowingly commit wrongs implies that they are not responsible adults capable of making moral choices and therefore denies their autonomy as individuals. For still others, punishment connotes censure, and persons who commit offenses deserve to be censured. Finally, for some, punishment is simply a consequence of taking individuals seriously and asking, Were I the one being punished, on what basis would I accept it as just that I be punished? From an offender's perspective, acceptance of one's suffering may be eased by the knowledge that one is being treated exactly as any other like-situated wrongdoer would be. It may seem more persuasive morally that one is punished "the deserved amount," which is the same amount suffered by others who committed the same offense rather than "the amount needed to deter others (or rehabilitate or incapacitate, etc.)," which may be substantially different from amounts suffered by others who committed the same offense.

Of course, TR and UU are stereotypes. In terms of Hart's framework, UU would offer social utility as the justifying aim of punishment, and liability and amount would be assessed in terms of what is needed to maximize social utility; TR would say that retribution is the justifying aim of punishment, liability must be premised on conscious wrongdoing, and the amount of punishment in any case is "precisely as much as is deserved."

A number of criticisms of prediction-based classifications have been offered. These are summarized in the following pages with, where appropriate, the different views of UU and TR set out alongside those of major contemporary writers.

C. Problems with Predictions

The mainstream case made for use of predictions of dangerousness goes something like this. Judges, parole boards, and correctional administrators have *always* taken an offender's apparent dangerousness into account in making critical decisions, although, of necessity, they have done so in an intuitionist way with wide divergence in the decisions reached; it is far better explicitly to rely on general predictive rules that are based on the best available evidence and that are systematically applied than to go on as before; so long as the resulting penalties do not exceed what the offender deserved, he has no ground for complaint, and the rest of us will be better off because crime will be incrementally reduced by virtue of the incapacitation of offenders predicted to be dangerous. If the accuracy of predictions can be significantly improved, we may be able to target resources on dangerous offenders, to extend greater leniency to nondangerous offenders, to reduce prison populations, and thereby to achieve greater crime control at less financial cost. Thus the public's interests in crime control and economy will be served, sentencing (or bail release or parole release) disparities will be diminished, and offenders will suffer punishments that are not undeserved. It is not the best of all possible worlds, but it is better than what now exists.

Arguments for marginal improvements in justice and efficiency are hard to resist because we know that more ambitious efforts tend to fail. Nonetheless, powerful arguments have been offered against reliance on predictions.

1. *Simple Injustice.* Some simply reject prediction's incapacitative premise. If, like TR, one believes that the offender's blameworthiness or culpability determines how much punishment he should suffer, an increase of that punishment for incapacitative reasons is, by definition, unjust. The promised decrease of punishment for the nondangerous is not necessarily a good thing; the resulting differences between punishments of dangerous and nondangerous offenders who have committed the same offense exacerbate existing inequalities in punishment.

A standard rejoinder is that, for obvious metaphysical reasons, it is impossible to say precisely what punishment is deserved for any particular offense and, consequently (barring aberrantly severe punishments), it is difficult ever to say that a punishment is undeserved. Norval Morris, for example, has argued that one can meaningfully speak of punishments as being "undeservedly lenient" or "undeservedly severe" but can say of punishments within the range thereby defined only that they are "not undeserved": "Hence, a deserved punishment must mean a not undeserved punishment which bears a proportional relationship in the hierarchy of punishments to the harm for which the criminal has been convicted" (1982, p. 150).

John Monahan has extended this argument by noting that, because neither moral theory nor empirical research on public attitudes and opinions can precisely determine crime seriousness, "it is affirmatively preferable [to consider crime control in making punishment decisions], in that, justice to the offender being equal (within our large measurement error), a scheme which promotes justice to potential victims is superior to one that does not" (Monahan 1982, p. 104; see also Bedau 1977, p. 65).

Andrew von Hirsch has offered a surrejoinder to arguments like those of Morris and Monahan. He concedes that no available moral calculus will allow one to identify the single punishment appropriate in any individual case. However, he argues that moral principles can give much more guidance than does Morris's "not-undeserved" punishment. Von Hirsch distinguishes between "cardinal" and "ordinal" desert (1985, pp. 39, 43–46). With Morris he agrees that cardinal desert—that is, some absolute metaphysically appropriate punishment—is beyond the knowledge of mortal mind. Ordinal desert, however, deals with relations between punishments, and regarding this man's moral principles can offer guidance. Robbery, most people agree, is more serious than is petit larceny and should be more severely punished, and similar comparative statements can be made about most offenses. If one concedes that, other things equal, more serious offenses should precipitate more severe sanctions, then the logic of a comprehensive listing of offenses scaled to reflect notions of their comparative seriousness carries with it an ordinal ranking of deserved punishments.

Norval Morris responds to this by observing that the "ranges" for deserved punishments for particular offenses must be quite broad and overlap substantially because the least severe version of higher-rated offenses may be less deserving of punishment than the most severe version of lower-rated offenses: "some rapes are less serious than some aggravated batteries that are not rapes" (Morris 1982, p. 151).

The force of Morris's response to some extent depends on the kind of criminal law sentencing system one has in mind. In systems in which criminal offenses are defined broadly and in which judicial sentencing discretion is not structured by guidelines or a meaningful determinate sentencing law, surely Morris is correct. Some batteries are more serious than some rapes, and a generalization that all rapes must be sentenced more severely than any battery would be morally unconvincing and unduly rigid.

Many states have adopted criminal codes based on the *Model Penal Code* (American Law Institute 1962). The definitions in the *Model Penal Code* were purposely broad and generic and were premised on the existence of individualized indeterminate sentencing in which the judge could, in setting sentences, take into account morally significant factors that distinguished offenses from one another. *Model Penal Code* offense definitions, however, are not inevitable, and jurisdictions that wished to do so could establish much more detailed offense definitions that would distinguish among rapes or robberies of differing gravity. The sentencing commissions that have promulgated guidelines to date have invariably found offense definitions too general to be useful in a determinate sentencing system and have crafted and differently ranked relevant subcategories.

In a jurisdiction with tightly specified offense definitions, Morris's argument loses much of its force: various grades of rape could be distinguished, as could various grades of battery, and it would not be surprising if some battery subtypes were regarded as more serious than some rape subtypes. Even then, exceptional cases can be imagined in which offenses of a less serious type (e.g., vindictive destruction of property known to have enormous sentimental value to the owner) seem worse than offenses of a more serious type (e.g., mercy killing of an aged spouse who has clearly and repeatedly asked to be relieved of intense incessant pain and who will in any event soon die), but these will be exceptional cases, and any sensitive ethical or legal system must allow for the existence of difficult special cases.

Thus Morris's rebuttal can be avoided mechanically, if imperfectly. Inevitably, there must be marginal cases and gray areas, but in the main it should be possible to establish an offense ranking of sufficient detail to permit a coherent system of "ordinal" desert.[6]

---

[6] There is another complication here. Even if offense categories are precisely delineated, variations in offender characteristics may for some decision makers result in very different sentences. This problem is actually a conflict over premises. For those who

If one sees desert or retribution as defining principles governing the amount of punishment, as von Hirsch largely does,[7] then achievement of equality and proportionality in punishment are paramount goals. Predictive sentencing conflicts with achievement of equality and proportionality in outcomes and violates the limits set by concern for ordinal desert.

However, von Hirsch in my view wins the skirmish but loses the conflict unless he can persuade Morris or others to adopt his premise that desert *should* be both a justifying aim of punishment and the primary defining principle in determining amounts of punishment. Almost by definition, proponents of predictive sentencing subscribe to a significant degree to utilitarian premises of punishment and so, rejecting von Hirsch's premises, can reject his critique of predictive sentencing.

2. *Past and Future Crimes.*   A second, more general, criticism of predictive sentencing is that it punishes people for crimes they have not yet committed and might not commit if released (von Hirsch 1985, pp. 2, 167–69). This criticism is related to, but different from, the argument that predictions of dangerousness are unacceptably unreliable: this latter claim is the empirical basis for the assertion that some of those "incapacitated" would not reoffend, but the "false positive" argument is a different argument.

On this point, TR and UU simply differ in principle. To TR, deserved punishment for the current crime can be calibrated reasonably precisely; extension of punishment beyond that amount is not deserved in respect of the current offense and can be seen as an additional increment of punishment for a crime not committed. Von Hirsch (1981) argues that some increase in punishment is permitted in respect of prior offenses (actually, that offenders should be given the benefit of the doubt and given more lenient sentences than they deserve for the first, or first few, offenses); to the extent that accumulated prior convictions predict future offending, some incapacitative effect will be coincident with increased penalties for successive convictions and is to that extent not objectionable. For von Hirsch, the values of equality and propor-

---

believe that punishment should be based solely, or primarily, on the offender's culpability and the harm that resulted, offender characteristics by definition should play only a small role. For those who believe that culpability and harm are but some of the factors that should shape punishment decisions, then, by definition, a tight offense-based punishment scheme will be too confining.

[7] "Largely" because von Hirsch would permit prior criminal history to play a modest role in setting appropriate punishments. See von Hirsch (1981, 1985).

tionality are not seriously undermined since all offenders convicted of the same offense and with the same criminal history will receive the same sentence.

Norval Morris and Marc Miller would go further because their position of "limiting retributivism" does not require equality of suffering. It seems to them entirely proper "within the range of not unjust punishments, to take account of different levels of dangerousness of those to be punished; but the concept of the deserved, or rather the not undeserved, punishment properly limits the range within which utilitarian values may operate" (Morris and Miller 1985, p. 37). The imprecision of "the range of not undeserved punishments" makes it difficult to say precisely where the Morris-Miller view would limit the scope of predictive sentencing; however, if for a hypothetical offender any prison sentence from within the range of two to five years would be not undeserved, an incapacitative sentence not to exceed five years would be acceptable. There the line would be drawn, however, and an incapacitative sentence of ten years would be unjust, even if it would optimize the incapacitative effects of punishment.

The Morris-Miller view can be tested by trying to apply it in a determinate sentencing jurisdiction that has narrow ranges of approved sentences for individual cases. If, as a matter of authoritative policy-making, the applicable range has been set at thirty-two to thirty-six months, can predictive considerations be looked to only within that narrow range? If so, much of their disagreement with TR and von Hirsch disappears. The underlying issue is whether "not-undeserved punishment" is a normative and cultural question or whether it is a policy-making question. If it is the former, the thirty-two- to thirty-six-month boundaries are not confining if cultural norms would regard a sixty-month sentence for the offense (to which the thirty-two- to thirty-six-month range applies) as "not undeserved." If this is the argument, it is hard to see how it can be incorporated into legal rules because it is difficult to see what source of credible authoritative declarations of moral and cultural views of not-undeserved punishment there can be other than legally constituted policymakers.[8] If authorized policymakers are the determiners of "not-undeserved" punishment, there may be little practical difference among TR, von Hirsch, and Morris-Miller, at least in determinate sentencing jurisdictions.

---

[8] At the reductionist extreme, the answer is that each decision maker must decide which punishment is "not undeserved" in each case, but this answer effectively rejects the value of general rules and culpability-influenced punishment.

Finally, UU, who cares nought for equality and proportionality, would opt for a ten-year sentence if that would most enhance social utility even if two to five years is the agreed range of not-undeserved punishment in an individual case. Richard Posner, for example, has argued that the utilitarian principle of parsimony may require stark inequality (Posner 1977, pp. 163–73). He argues that, if crime prevention goals required imposition of ten years of punishment, it would be preferable to sentence one person to a ten-year term than to sentence ten people to one-year terms. This is because subjective suffering would diminish as the years passed, and, consequently, the ten, each suffering an especially grievous first year's loss of freedom, would suffer more in the aggregate than would the one over time. To impose the greater aggregate subjective suffering on the ten is unnecessary and therefore unjust. (The converse argument from retributive premises has been made by John C. Coffee, Jr. [1978], and Richard Singer [1979] that if crime prevention could be maximized by sentencing two of ten like-situated offenders to two-year sentences, although desert would require only a one-year sentence, there are only two morally justifiable solutions: forgo prevention by sentencing all ten to one-year terms or sentence all ten to two-year terms even though the effect is to *increase* the overall amount of penal suffering; this is because retributive concern for equality in penal suffering for like-situated offenders requires that all be treated alike.)

Thus, like the previous criticism that predictive sentencing is prima facie unjust, the argument against sentencing in respect of future crimes turns out to be another disagreement over the premises of punishment. Only for UU is there no problem—UU, however, is a mythological beast, and few people subscribe to this polar view. For "limiting retributivists" like Norval Morris, predictive sentencing is unjust only when the resulting aggregate sentence is "undeserved." Von Hirsch allows much less scope for predictive considerations than does Morris's range of "not undeserved punishments."[9] Finally, to TR, predictive sentencing is prima facie objectionable because it treats individuals as means to crime control ends.

3. *False Positives and the "Conviction-of-Innocents" Analogy.* By this

---

[9] But it is not clear whether this is true. If, as is discussed in the text, Morris would defer to policymakers, such as a sentencing commission, to specify what is "not undeserved," there is little difference in their views, and the seemingly large difference is an artifact of their assumptions about the kind of sentencing system in which each addresses his arguments.

point in the argument, TR has rejected predictive sentencing. To Andrew von Hirsch, predictive sentencing is acceptable only insofar as it can be achieved in ways that are consonant with the limited scope that he would permit for increased sentence on account of prior convictions. For those who remain unconvinced or skeptical, another major problem remains—predictions of violence are not very accurate. The conventional wisdom for some years has been that for every three persons predicted to commit serious violent offenses, only one will do so, and the other two will be "false positives" (see, e.g., Morris and Miller 1985 [citing Monahan 1981]; Floud and Young 1981). Perhaps this 33 percent accuracy rate has improved, but even at 50 percent accuracy, an argument can be made that this is too inaccurate to serve as the basis for denying liberty.[10]

To some extent, people's views of this criticism are subsumed within their views on "punishment for future crimes" but not completely. For Norval Morris and Marc Miller, even within the range of not-undeserved punishments, predictive sentencing is appropriate only if:

> the base expectancy rate of violence for the criminal predicted as dangerous must be shown by reliable evidence to be *substantially higher* than the base expectancy rate of another criminal *with a closely similar criminal record* and *convicted of a closely similar crime* but not predicted as unusually dangerous. [Morris and Miller 1985, p. 37; emphasis added]

This is a very demanding test that few proposals for predictive sentencing could satisfy. Information concerning past criminality has repeatedly been shown to be the best predictor of future criminality (see S. Gottfredson, in this volume; Petersilia and Turner, in this volume). If, as the Morris-Miller formula prescribes, one controls for criminal history and the nature of the current crime, the offender's remaining characteristics are seldom likely to lead to predicted base expectancy rates "substantially higher" than those for other individuals with comparable criminal histories convicted of comparable crimes. Thus the

---

[10] It is true that predictions of participation in *any crime* can be made at much higher rates of accuracy (see Farrington 1979; Blumstein, Farrington, and Moitra 1985). Most discussions of dangerousness prediction focus on violent crime. This seems reasonable to me. Liberty—even that of property offenders—seems to me a sufficiently important value that one should rely on deterrence as a crime prevention strategy for property crimes and not extend offenders' incarceration because of property crimes they might later commit.

Morris-Miller view concedes that the false-positive problem is a serious problem and sidesteps it by setting a test for predictive sentencing that few, if any, systems could meet.

A number of arguments are commonly made about the false-positive problem. The first, the "conviction-of-innocents" analogy, is to analogize *extension* of incarceration to conviction by contrasting the standards of proof that apply at a criminal trial and the levels of predictive accuracy that now characterize violence predictions. Proof beyond a reasonable doubt is seldom quantified, but surely it is equivalent at least to a 90 percent probability. Thus, one can argue, the requisite *90 percent probability* of commission of a *past crime* that must be proven before a person can be convicted and deprived of liberty should be contrasted with the best case *33 percent probability* of commission of a *future crime* that can be used to extend incarceration. If liberty is an important value, the argument goes, we should not extend deprivations of liberty on so much lower a probative standard than justifies its deprivation in the first place.

The standard response to this, as given by Floud and Young (1981) and Morris and Miller (1985), is that the analogy is misconceived. Per Floud and Young, "The question is not 'How many innocent persons are to sacrifice their liberty for the extra protection that special sentences for dangerous offenders will provide?' but 'What is the moral choice between the alternative risks: the risk of harm to potential victims or the risk of unnecessarily detaining offenders judged to be dangerous' " (1981, p. 49). This argument, again, is an argument about premises. To TR or Andrew von Hirsch, the deserved punishment imposed for the current offense is relatively specific, and conviction of the offense is an essential condition precedent; Floud and Young's balancing of harms is simply inappropriate. A significant increment added to the deserved punishment for those predicted to commit future crimes is imposition of an additional term of incarceration, and, so seen, a 33 percent probability standard of proof is shockingly low. Floud and Young, by contrast, simply assume that a limited utilitarian calculus is appropriate.

To limiting retributivists, the increment of punishment added for predictive reasons may be acceptable so long as the total punishment is "not undeserved" (though recall that the Morris-Miller test is so stringent that it could seldom be met). Whatever the level of predictive accuracy, an aggregate sentence exceeding the upper limit of not-undeserved punishment would be unjust. For UU, Floud and Young are absolutely correct, and the trade-off between offenders' liberty and crimes prevented is simply another appropriate utilitarian calculus.

A second response to the conviction-of-innocents analogy that is sometimes offered by proponents of predictive sentencing is that the false-positive problem is itself misconceived. This argument has two components. The first component is that "statistical predictions are made for groups and not for individuals" (Farrington and Tarling 1983, p. 20). The false positives, say Floud and Young (1981, p. 26), "are statistical errors and it is fallacious to think of them as misjudged individuals." All members of the group predicted to be violent (assuming reliable information) were correctly identified as having the characteristics that, in general, are possessed by those predicted to commit future violence. One could say that there was 100 percent correct identification of members of a group that has a 33 percent violence probability.

The second component of this argument is that "a statistical prediction of dangerousness, based on membership in a group for which a consistent and tested pattern of conduct has been shown, is the statement of a *condition* [membership in the group] and not the prediction of a result [future violence]" (Morris and Miller 1985, p. 18).

Clearly, neither component of this second argument would convince TR or Andrew von Hirsch. I doubt that they would convince an agnostic or a skeptic either for the distinctions offered beg the critical question. That this argument does not resolve the false-positive problem can be shown by imagining that a criminal code expressly authorized an incremental prison term for dangerous offenders to be served after the "deserved" sentence imposed for the current offense (as English habitual offender laws once did; see Morris 1951). The question to be decided would be "is there an X percent [possibly 33 percent, possibly 50 percent] probability that this individual will commit future acts of serious violence?" That the defendant had the attributes of membership in a group with a 33 percent base rate would be admissible in evidence to show what is equivalent to membership—that the probability of that individual committing serious violence is 33 percent. The legislative draftsmen in their wisdom could specify 33 percent or 50 percent or 90 percent as the required probability, but the policy question concerning the punishment of individuals must surely be focused on the individual's probability of future violence, and that question is the same whether one considers group or individual probabilities (see also Monahan and Wexler 1978).

A third response to the conviction-of-innocents analogy put by proponents of predictive sentencing is that the seemingly low "false-positive" rates are misleading. Some seeming false positives may be true positives who were overlooked either because their violent acts did not come to the attention of the authorities or researchers or because, for some reason, police, prosecutor, judge, or jury elected to overlook violent acts. Other false positives may in fact have committed no violent acts, not from innocence but from the lack of appropriate opportunities or circumstances.

Here too I think the proponents of prediction offer a weak case. The effective argument is that the false-positive problem is less serious than it appears to be because the predictions are more accurate than they appear to be. Given the attention that violence predictions have received, it seems reasonable to place on prediction's proponents the burden of proving predictive accuracy higher than the state-of-the-art appears to allow. If substantially more accurate predictions can be made, that could significantly alter the debates over predictive sentencing, and it seems only fair that the higher accuracy levels be demonstrated empirically rather than be surmised.

4. *Inappropriate Predictors.*   One major criticism of predictive sentencing (or paroling or bailing) is that many factors correlated with future violence are controversial. Although the Constitution apparently precludes use only of race, religion, ethnicity, political affiliation, and possibly sex as sentencing factors, many people object to other factors on policy grounds.

a) Factors beyond the Offender's Control.   Many people believe it unjust to base punishment decisions on factors over which the offender has no control. For example, sex is seen by many to be an inappropriate factor, even though it is highly predictive of violence, because it has no moral relevance to punishment. Similarly, race, age, ethnicity, intelligence, and national origin are factors beyond the offender's control and are therefore not logically related to culpability. Some people would also place drug or alcohol addiction (as contrasted with nonaddicted use) in the same category.

b) Status Variables.   A considerable number of social and economic status variables are correlated with recidivism and violence probabilities but are nonetheless widely regarded as inappropriate factors for consideration in punishment decisions. These include various measures of educational attainment, vocational skills and experience, residential stability, and income. Incorporation of such variables in decision-making criteria systematically adversely affects people of lower income and social status. On policy grounds, the sentencing commission in Minnesota expressly prohibited reliance on such factors in sentencing precisely because of their socially skewed impact. The U.S. Parole Commission has responded to such concerns by eliminating social variables from the "Salient Factor Score," by which recidivism risks are determined. The Harvard Dangerousness Project report (Moore et al. 1984) reached the same policy conclusion.

Patently, retributivists in principle oppose consideration of such factors, and utilitarians in principle should not object, though in practice many do. Many people object to consideration of such factors, and, to the extent that they are purged from prediction formulae, their accuracy will be by that much reduced (and the false-positive problem thereby exacerbated).

c) Nonconviction Criminal History. Past involvement in crime is the best single predictor of future involvement in crime (see, e.g., Blumstein et al. 1986). Numerous research findings confirm this conclusion. Generally, however, researchers' analyses incorporate self-reports or information on arrests that did not result in convictions.

Arrests and alleged criminality not resulting in an arrest present one kind of problem. Researchers generally justify use of arrests in their analyses in three ways. First, arrests are much closer in time than are convictions to the commission of crimes, and in the aggregate they offer a fuller picture of crime. For analyses of aggregate data, the fullest picture of crime involvement is best, and it is not important to know which of those arrests proved unfounded. No harm will come to any individual because of research use of arrests (or self-reports) as indicators of crime. Second, relatively few arrests result in convictions, and reliance solely on convictions as crime indicators would impoverish the analyses. Third, there is no reason to doubt that most people who are arrested for crimes committed those crimes.

The problem results from the interaction of several of the preceding propositions. From a predictive perspective, the more indicators there are of past criminality, the more likely that a prediction of continued involvement in crime will be accurate. From the defendant's perspective, and from a civil liberties perspective, that is beside the point. If past crimes are to influence current sentencing, then they should be considered only when they have been admitted or proved beyond reasonable doubt (see, e.g., Monahan 1982). Reliance on arrests creates an unacceptable risk that the defendant will be additionally punished now for offenses he did not commit (or that could not have been proven to have committed) then.

From an incapacitative perspective, reliance solely on past convictions defeats the system. Many much-arrested individuals have been seldom convicted and, without arrest information, will escape the incapacitative net.

The split resembles that on many prediction issues. While UU would have little doubt about the appropriateness of use of arrests in making predictive judgments (though were he a proceduralist, he would want to establish procedures for assessing defendants' claims that their apparent arrest records were incorrect), TR would probably say that the benefit of the doubt should operate for the individual and against the state and, therefore, that taking liberty seriously requires that punishment be imposed or extended in respect only of criminal behavior admitted or proved beyond a reasonable doubt.

d) Juvenile Court Records. The issue here is straightforward. Some believe that, compared with the adult criminal court, the juvenile court has different, primarily rehabilitative, purposes and that adults should be able to leave the record of their juvenile misconduct behind them. Many states' laws make juvenile court records confidential. Other commentators argue that juvenile crime is highly predictive of adult crime and that lack of access to juvenile court records unacceptably weakens predictions (for a summary of these arguments, see Greenwood [1986]).

5. *Disparate Racial Impacts.* For both constitutional and policy reasons, no one has proposed that race be used as a factor in setting sentences or implementing incapacitation programs, even though race is significantly correlated with recorded criminality. Indirectly, however, race effects may occur in prediction systems if those systems incorporate variables that are correlated with race. Insofar as class is associated with race, many of the status variables described in the preceding subsection will, if used in sentencing as prediction factors, systematically adversely affect blacks. Many criminal history factors are also correlated with race (Petersilia and Turner, in this volume).

Although in this context there are apparently no constitutional problems in adopting policies known (but not intended) to affect minorities systematically and adversely, there may be powerful policy grounds for wanting to purge criminal justice decision making of practices that operate to the systematic detriment of minorities. This is one reason why the Minnesota Sentencing Guidelines Commission elected to prohibit reliance on status variables in sentencing.

There would be some loss in predictive accuracy if all status variables were purged from prediction systems and substantial loss if racially skewed criminal history variables were also purged. (Goldkamp [in this volume] and Petersilia and Turner [in this volume] attempt to demonstrate how much predictive accuracy is lost when race and race-correlated variables are omitted from predictive formulae.)

This particular problem is not much of a problem for TR or Andrew von Hirsch because a retributive sentencing system can comfortably rely on the conviction offense alone or in conjunction with criminal history information. For utilitarians, this is a dilemma, for the elimination or diminution of systematic racially disparate impacts can be bought only at the cost of sacrifices in predictive accuracy.

To conclude this section where it began, whether the ethical and policy criticisms of predictive sentencing summarized here are regarded as devastating depends largely on the premises that shape one's views of punishment. Retributivists tend strongly to disapprove of predictive sentencing; utilitarians tend to accept it. However, almost every analyst of predictive sentencing is uncomfortable with some of its features. Section III offers some tentative proposals for rethinking incapacitative policies that may avoid some of their defects and achieve some of their aims.

III. Something Old, Something New

This section proposes measures for addressing some of the major criticisms that have been made of reliance in decision making on prediction-based classifications. The discussion focuses primarily on sentencing and parole release because these are the most visible such decisions and the ones for which systems of structured decision making have most commonly been developed.

Almost everyone who writes about predictive sentencing seems uncomfortable with it. This would be expected of its critics, of course, but even its adherents would impose conditions that show their unease. The Harvard Dangerous Offenders Project (Moore et al. 1984, p. 184), for example, would allow "only information about prior criminal conduct [to be] used in discriminating among offenders, because no other variables provide a just basis for punishment." Monahan (1982) takes a similar position. Both the Harvard Project and Floud and Young (1981), authors of the report of the British Howard League for Penal Reform Working Party on Dangerous Offenders, would limit vulnerability to predictive sentencing to a small percentage of offenders who meet stringent screening tests (for Moore and colleagues, two violent crime convictions and either two property crime convictions or two additional violent crime arrests within three years of "street time"; for Floud and Young, two offenses of "grave harm" [p. 155]).

This section offers a series of proposals for reconciling the views of modern mainstream punishment philosophies. The proposals address many of the objections levied against predictive sentencing and would limit what its critics see as its worst excesses. The first two proposals are premised on the view that many problems with modern American sentencing (and proposals for predictive sentencing) occur because of criminal codes that were designed to facilitate indeterminate sentencing. Proposals 1 and 2 call for recodification of the criminal law and reduction of the maximum lengths of authorized sentences. Proposal 3 calls for replacement of predictive sentencing with a system of graded increments of punishment for successive offenses. Proposal 4 would prohibit use in predictions of any but criminal history variables, thereby avoiding direct class biases and some indirect race biases. Proposal 5 would prohibit use in predictions of criminal history variables that are not the result of convictions; specifically, arrests and indictments would not be allowed.

A. *Replace Indeterminate-sentencing Criminal Codes*

The gap between retributivist and utilitarian punishment theory may be greater in America than elsewhere. No other Western European or North American country adopted indeterminate sentencing with American enthusiasm or scope. The institutionalization of discretionary individualized sentencing had a number of unfortunate consequences. First, because both judges and parole boards were given authority to individualize sentences, prison sentences announced by judges were often nominal or symbolic. If the judge's decision about sentence length often had little practical effect, there was no reason for judges to give it the careful consideration that is given decisions that do have practical consequences—ad hoc intuitive decision making was acceptable. Second, partly because judges were supposed to impose sentences uniquely suited to the facts of individual cases, and partly because the parole board made the crucial time-to-be-served decisions anyway, there was no need to develop standards for sentencing (judges did, however, have sole legal responsibility for deciding who went to prison). This meant that, third, there were no available standards by which appellate courts could have reviewed the appropriateness of sentences in individual cases, even had the appellate courts been inclined to do so. In any event, fourth, the appellate courts had a ready excuse for their not attempting to regulate sentencing and to reduce disparities: the parole boards had authority to fix release dates and could even out sentencing disparities and, often, vitiate the effects of aberrant sentences. Finally, fifth and sixth, the legislatures established extremely long maximum sentences and, beginning with the example of the *Model Penal Code* in the 1950s, enacted criminal codes that contained broadly defined, generic definitions of offenses: both of these statutory features were designed to permit judges and parole boards to make individualized decisions. If the statutory definition of robbery encompassed acts as different as professional armed robbery and forcible schoolyard appropriation of a basketball, and authorized punishment from probation to twenty years in prison, that was all right because the judge, in sentencing, would treat those different robberies differently and appropriately. If the judge imposed a prison sentence, the parole board would take a second look.

These features of American indeterminate sentencing exaggerate the differential ramifications of various punishment philosophies. In European countries, where prison sentences exceeding one year are uncommon and those exceeding five years rare, the different consequences of retributive and utilitarian approaches must generally be measured in months or a few years at most. In the United States, however, where announced sentences of five, ten, or twenty years are not uncommon, the difference between a retributive and a utilitarian sentence can routinely be measured in years and sometimes in decades.

The criminal codes designed for indeterminate sentencing are a major impediment to sentencing reform efforts generally and to efforts to bring principle to sentencing whether those principles be retributive or utilitarian. That this is so can be seen in the experience of the Minnesota Sentencing Guidelines Commission, which, first, felt obliged to subdivide generic criminal code offense definitions into more discrete and meaningful categories and, second, though it adopted "modified just deserts" as the rationale of its prison guidelines and repudiated the use of predictions as the rationale for its policies, adopted a guideline matrix that seems only slightly compatible with retributive notions.

Table 1, a reproduction of the Minnesota grid, demonstrates its less-than-perfect retributiveness in two important respects. Retributive punishment philosophies attach substantial value to treating likes alike—to achievement of equality in punishment. Some retributivists would base punishment solely on the current offense, arguing that prior punishments have wiped the slate clean of prior offenses; to increase punishment for the current offense because the offender was previously convicted is, in effect, double counting and violative of double-jeopardy notions. Others would allow some increase of punishment in respect of prior convictions but only some. Yet, and notwithstanding the narrowness of the Minnesota guideline ranges, individuals convicted of the same offense may be imprisoned for terms that vary by as much as a factor of five. For example, persons convicted of a "Level VII offense" can, depending on their criminal history, receive guideline prison sentences ranging from twenty-three to 104 months. This scale of difference for persons convicted of identical offenses seems hard to reconcile with retribution or "modified just deserts."

As with many of these issues, whether one cares about these comparisons depends on one's punishment premises. Utilitarians who are prepared to weigh criminal history information heavily may not care about a factor-of-five difference in prison sentences for persons convicted of the same offense, but those who want criminal history weighed lightly, or not at all, will disapprove.

The Minnesota matrix seems also incompatible with the retributive value of proportionality, the complement of equality. If likes should be treated alike, then unlikes should be treated differently. Yet, if one looks diagonally across table 1 from lower left to upper right, it will be seen that people convicted of offenses of widely various wickedness can receive the same sentence. For example, persons convicted of offenses ranging from Level IV to Level VIII can receive a guideline sentence of forty-five months as a consequence of their criminal history scores.

This illustration is given not in criticism of the Minnesota guidelines, for their inconsistency with equality and proportionality was probably unavoidable. Public and official sentiment for increased punishments for repeat offenders would be substantial anywhere in America and politically dangerous to deny. More important, because of the extremely long sentences authorized in Minnesota's criminal code, a powerful logic calls for radically increased sentences for repeat offenders in order to "fill in" or "use up" the lawful range of authorized sentences. In brief, the limited consistency of Minnesota's guidelines with a retributive punishment scheme occurs in part because of the nonfit between a determinate sentencing system and a criminal code crafted for use in an indeterminate sentencing system.

Thus two first steps toward achieving more principled sentencing (whether retributive or utilitarian) aim to reduce the dissonance between determinate sentencing institutions and indeterminate statutory frameworks.

PROPOSAL 1.   **Replace generic offense definitions with much more detailed and less inclusive definitions that substantially reflect the different moral gravities of the criminal behaviors they describe.**

Alan Dershowitz's commentary to *Fair and Certain Punishment*

TABLE 1

Minnesota Sentencing Guidelines Grid (Presumptive Sentence Length in Months)

Security Levels: Conviction Offenses	Criminal History Score						
	0	1	2	3	4	5	6 or More
I: Unauthorized use of motor vehicle; possession of marijuana	12*†	12*†	12*†	13†	15†	17†	19 (18–20)
II: Theft-related crimes ($250–$2,500); aggravated forgery ($250–$2,500)	12*†	12*†	13†	15†	17†	19†	21 (20–22)
III: Theft crimes ($250–$2,500)	12*†	13†	15†	17†	19 (18–20)	22 (21–23)	25 (24–26)
IV: Nonresidential burglary; theft crimes (over $2,500)	12*†	15†	18†	21†	25 (24–26)	32 (30–34)	41 (37–45)
V: Residential burglary; simple robbery	18†	23†	27†	30 (29–31)	38 (36–40)	46 (43–49)	54 (50–58)
VI: Criminal sexual conduct, second degree	21†	26†	30†	34 (33–35)	44 (42–46)	54 (50–58)	65 (60–70)
VII: Aggravated robbery	24 (23–25)	32 (30–34)	41 (38–44)	49 (45–53)	65 (60–70)	81 (75–87)	97 (90–104)

VIII: Criminal sexual conduct, first degree; assault, first degree	43 (41–45)	54 (50–58)	65 (60–70)	76 (71–81)	95 (89–101)	113 (106–120)	132 (124–140)
IX: Murder, third degree; murder, second degree (felony murder)	105 (102–108)	119 (116–122)	127 (124–130)	149 (143–155)	176 (168–184)	205 (195–215)	230 (218–242)
X: Murder, second degree (with intent)	120 (116–124)	140 (133–147)	162 (153–171)	203 (192–214)	243 (231–255)	284 (270–298)	324 (309–339)

SOURCE.—Knapp (1985, p. 107).

NOTE.—Numbers in parentheses denote the range within which a judge may sentence without the sentence being deemed a departure. Offenders with nonimprisonment felony sentences are subject to jail time according to law. First-degree murder is excluded from the guidelines by law and continues to have a mandatory life sentence.

* One year and one day.

† At the discretion of the judge, up to a year in jail and/or other nonjail sanctions can be imposed as conditions of probation. Data not followed by a † denote presumptive commitment to state imprisonment.

(Twentieth Century Fund Task Force on Criminal Sentencing 1976) made a start at this; his proposals for statutory determinate sentencing based on a fine grading of offense seriousness were probably too rigid, but his effort illustrates the possibility of the creation of a statutory substantive criminal law designed to be compatible with a determinate sentencing system.

PROPOSAL 2.   **Revise criminal code sections that establish extremely long felony sentence maximums (typically, six years, twelve years, twenty-four years, and life) to permit much shorter maximums.**

This could be done in any of several ways. First, it could be done openly. Three felony classes (six-, twelve-, and twenty-four-year maximums) in an indeterminate criminal code might be replaced with five felony classes with maximums of, say, two years, three years, five years, seven years, and ten years.[11] If that is politically impracticable, the same result could be achieved in other ways. The [British] Advisory Committee on the Penal System (1978), for example, proposed establishment of short maximums for most cases but, when specified special findings are made, would allow longer sentences (subject to the defendant's right of appellate sentence review). The National Commission on Reform of Federal Criminal Laws (1970), through the combination of a mandatory period of parole supervision that is included within the maximum sentence and a special findings requirement, reduced an apparent fifteen-year maximum sentence for Class B offenses (which would have included most serious crimes) to a maximum four years (unless the special findings were made).

Adoption of proposals 1 and 2 would make choices between predictive and nonpredictive sentencing more intelligible and their ramifications less dramatically different. For example, if "robbery not involving use of firearms or infliction of bodily injury" were a "Class M offense" subject to a three-year maximum sentence, a retributive scheme might insist that all like-situated offenders receive eighteen-month sentences; a predictive scheme might allow sentences up to the maximum of thirty-six months. This scale of difference, eighteen to thirty-six months, might make predictive sentencing much more palatable to its critics than in a system in which the predicted "nondanger-

---

[11] Several readers pointed out that ten years is too short a maximum for a Richard Speck or a Charles Manson. These cases could be dealt with by means of consecutive sentencing for multiple charges or perhaps under a special "depraved conduct" offense bearing an extraordinarily long maximum.

ous" offenders received eighteen months anɑ the predicted "dangerous" offenders ten years.

B. A Predictive/Retributive Synthesis

A synthesis between the policy preference of supporters of predictive and retributive sentences might be possible, especially if maximum lawful sentences were greatly reduced. Many supporters of both retributive and predictive sentencing would permit some increase in sentences for persons with prior convictions. The rationales vary: for Andrew von Hirsch, first and second offenders are given the benefit of the doubt and receive discounts from the deserved punishment; for Mark Moore (1985), repetitive offending shows bad character; for Norval Morris (1982, p. 185), prior convictions demonstrate wickedness, contempt of law, or the failure of past leniency.

Empirical research shows that criminal history is the best predictor of future crime. Thus a system of established increments of punishment in respect of successive offenses would be compatible with many retributivists' beliefs and would also serve incapacitative ends. Yet, when coupled with reduced sentence maximums, enormous differences, like Minnesota's factor of five, would be prevented.

PROPOSAL 3.   **The severity of sanctions imposed on offenders should be increased incrementally with each successive offense, but never result in the imposition of a sentence more than double what would be imposed were the conviction for a first offense.**

For example, policymakers might establish first-offense sanctions for all offenses and then provide for scheduled increases for subsequent offenses.

If X is the sentence for a first conviction of a subcategory of robbery, the sentences for second, third, or fourth convictions of that offense might be $1.2X$, $1.4X$, and $1.6X$.

This proposal is presented in simple bare-bones terms. It could be made more complex; the weight by which the base sentence is multiplied could vary with the number, nature, and patterns of prior convictions. For example, multipliers might rise much more rapidly for violent than for property offense convictions. Or the multiplier for a current violent offense might vary depending on the number of prior convictions and whether some or all were also for violent offenses. For purposes of this essay, the simplest illustration should suffice.

Such a system established under the constraint of reduced sentence maximums might be widely acceptable. Because all persons convicted of the same offense and having the same prior record of convictions would receive the same sentence, the retributive goal of equality would be realized. Because the "multipliers" would always apply to the base sentence and might (hypothetically) never be allowed to exceed 2.0, proportionality far superior to existing practice would be achieved. Because, at least to a point, each successive conviction would raise the multipliers and thereby increase the sentence, some incapacitative effects would be achieved. It might be possible to calculate the weights on the basis of incapacitative effects. Prior offenses whose commission is especially highly correlated with future crime might receive higher weights. (Retributivists and utilitarians might disagree vigorously here unless the high correlation offenses were relatively wicked offenses.) Although retributivists who believe that prior record should play no role in punishment would disapprove of this system—as would utilitarians who believe that the offense of conviction should not limit predictive restraint—most other punishment theorists should be able to live with it.[12]

C. Social Variables

All variables directly related to class or income should be forbidden. Although, in principle, utilitarians should want to use any information that has predictive value, the social status variables are readily abandoned by legislators and policymakers.[13] Notable examples include the U.S. Parole Commission and the sentencing commission in Minnesota. As noted earlier, this position was also taken by the Harvard Dangerous Offenders Project. Jacqueline Cohen (1983) has proposed a system of "categorical incapacitation," in which predictive sentencing would be based only on the current conviction and the offender's criminal history.

PROPOSAL 4.   Sentencing criteria, including those relating to pre-

---

[12] One law enforcement strategy that would be handicapped under this set of proposals is the "Al Capone Strategy" of convicting villains of trifling offenses and imposing long prison sentences. Zealous prosecutors may want to be able to increase Al Capone's sentence for tax evasion ten times over the norm. These proposals would frustrate that. That strategy can be justified only in terms of expediency, and reasonable people differ as to whether it is in principle justifiable.

[13] The U.S. Congress, for example, in enacting the Sentencing Reform Act of 1984, expressed a strong preference for nonuse of such variables: "The Commission shall assure that the guidelines and policy statements, in recommending a term of imprisonment or length of a term of imprisonment, reflect the general inappropriateness of considering the education, vocational skills, employment record, family ties and responsibilities, and community ties of the defendant."

diction of violence and incapacitative crime control strategies, should not include social status variables but instead should be limited to criminal history items.

D. Criminal History Variables

There is disagreement among scholars over which criminal history items are appropriate for use in sentencing. Mark Moore and his colleagues (1984, p. 183) would, in some circumstances, take arrests and indictments into account, primarily because both the duration and the intensity of offending are related to prediction, and considering indictments would "increase both the accuracy and the practical value of the tests" (p. 74).

Others disagree, arguing that only convictions should be taken into account. This is a natural subject for retributive/utilitarian disagreement. Only a conviction evidences an authoritative announcement of guilt, a declaration of blameworthiness. Although the Supreme Court has held that the "presumption of innocence" is merely an evidentiary rule (*Bell v. Wolfish*, 441 U.S. 520 [1979]) and has no substantive implications for the treatment of persons accused but not convicted of crime, many people disagree and argue that punitive state action based on arrests or indictments is simply unacceptable.

PROPOSAL 5.   **Sentencing criteria should not include any criminal history variables that do not consist of, or depend on, a conviction.**

There is inexorably a trade-off between achievement of retributive and utilitarian goals of punishment. Better predictions are likely if arrests or indictments may be relied on in fixing punishments. Yet, patently, convictions are more reliable indicators of past criminality than are arrests and indictments. After all, there must be reasons why arrests and indictments do not result in convictions; sometimes these reasons have nothing to do with the defendant's innocence, but sometimes they do. "Litigation" of the reasons why past arrests or indictments yielded no convictions is seldom likely to be feasible or wise; however, reliance on past nonconvictions without full investigation of the circumstances could result in an increase of the sentence for a current offense because of a prior arrest that was not pursued because the police knew they arrested the wrong person.

Critics of predictive sentencing have argued that it is anomalous to increase sentences on the basis of a 33 percent probability of future violence when greater than 90 percent predictability (proof beyond a reasonable doubt) is required for conviction. This anomaly is exacerbated if the increased sentence for a 33 percent probability of violence is based on a past crime that may not have occurred. The standard response is to observe, as Mark Moore does (1985, p. 49), that "the wider scope given to the use of prediction in sentencing also has a great deal to do with the fact that the liberty interests of an offender are taken less seriously once he has been convicted of a criminal offense." An extension of that analysis would urge that by committing the offense of current conviction the offender assumed the risk of increased punishment based on inaccurate information.

My view is that, if the increment of punishment for predictive reasons is predicted on evidence of prior criminality, then that prior criminality should be convincingly established. However, proposal 5 is not entirely incompatible with predictive sentencing. Besides prior convictions, which could be differentially weighted depending on their nature and frequency, such information as "custody status" (whether on parole, probation, and possibly bail at the time of the current offense) could be considered.

E. Coda

Seemingly intractable differences about punishment are amenable to resolution, for despite the differences between the views of writers as different as Andrew von Hirsch, Norval Morris, John Monahan, Mark Moore, and Floud and Young, they share much in common.

With differences in emphasis, all these writers could probably agree on the appropriateness of a punishment system that based sentences primarily on the current conviction offense, that eschewed reliance on ascribed traits or social status indicators, and that increased punishments on account of reliable indicators of past criminality. Such a system would be retributively defensible yet would serve incapacitative ends.

To be sure, all the writers cited would give different justifications for their support of the main elements of such a scheme. Andrew von Hirsch, arguing from a "just deserts" perspective, would explain increased punishment for successive offenses as the gradual elimination of a benefit of the doubt extended to criminal amateurs. The penalty for a first offense can be less than is deserved because the offender's behavior may have "been out of character." "That's not like me," he might say. That confession in avoidance would be less credible after a second or third offense and at some point would lose all credibility and result in imposition of the full deserved punishment.

From Norval Morris's "limiting retributivist" perspective, an increase in penalties for predictive purposes is acceptable so long as punishment is not increased beyond that which would be justified as a deserved punishment independently of that prediction. This means that the resulting aggregate punishment would be "not undeserved." Part of the explanation for this is that the past offenses are evidence of wickedness, defiance, or more.

Mark Moore's argument is substantially different from those of the others for he urges that most people's intuitions, and analysis of the criminal law, concur that widely shared perceptions of the bad characters of repeat offenders are what justifies increased punishment: "a series of offenses reveals an offender as clearly more willing to commit crimes than others, and therefore more deserving of punishment" (Moore 1985, pp. 77–78). Moore sees this shared perception as the explanation for the willingness of most retributivists and all utilitarians to accept as legitimate a sentencing system that increases punishments on account of prior crimes.

Moore's conclusion that perceptions of offenders' bad characters explain most people's willingness to take past crimes into account, with which I agree, is based on an argument about the substantive criminal law with which I disagree. His argument, in brief summary, is that a theory of crime and character is immanent in the criminal law's *mens rea* doctrines, particularly the general requirement that an unlawful intention be established, the treatment of uncompleted attempts as crimes, and the excusing and justifying defenses. Where Moore sees preoccupation with character, I see a criminal law struggling to make manifest individualist contractarian notions of individual moral responsibility and autonomy, including the notion that men are entitled to retain their liberty unless it is convincingly shown that they are morally responsible for committing acts whose commission justifies a deprivation of liberty. The focus on intentionality is a way to assure that wrongful acts do reflect a moral lapse and not merely accident or negligence.

The five "proposals" set out above may or may not be practical. The first two, concerning recodification of the criminal law and reduction of statutory sentence maximums, are probably the least realistic and the most important. The apparent lack of principle in criminal justice decision making, especially sentencing, is not merely apparent, but real, and structurally determined. If the structural setting of sentencing could be improved, the prospects for more principled and more effective sentencing would be greatly enhanced, for the differences between proponents of various punishment philosophies are more apparent than real.

REFERENCES

Advisory Committee on the Penal System. 1978. *Sentences of Imprisonment—a Review of Maximum Penalties.* London: H.M. Stationery Office.

American Law Institute. 1962. *Model Penal Code.* Proposed official draft. Philadelphia: American Law Institute.

Bedau, Hugo. 1977. "Concessions to Retribution in Punishment." In *Justice and Punishment,* edited by J. B. Cedarblom and William Blizek. Cambridge, Mass.: Ballinger.

Blumstein, Alfred, Jacqueline Cohen, Jeffrey Roth, and Christy Visher, eds. 1986. *Criminal Careers and "Career Criminals."* Washington, D.C.: National Academy Press.

Blumstein, Alfred, David P. Farrington, and Soumyo Moitra. 1985. "Delinquency Careers: Innocents, Desisters, and Persisters." In *Crime and Justice: An Annual Review of Research,* vol. 6, edited by Michael Tonry and Norval Morris. Chicago: University of Chicago Press.

Brennan, Tim. In this volume. "Classification for Control in Jails and Prisons."

Coffee, John C., Jr. 1975. "The Future of Sentencing Reform: Emerging Legal Issues in the Individualization of Justice." *Michigan Law Review* 73:1361–1462.

———. 1978. "The Repressed Issues of Sentencing, Accountability, Predictability, and Equity." *Georgetown Law Journal* 66:975–1107.

Cohen, Jacqueline. 1983. "Incapacitation as a Strategy for Crime Control: Possibilities and Pitfalls." In *Crime and Justice: An Annual Review of Research,* vol. 5, edited by Michael Tonry and Norval Morris. Chicago: University of Chicago Press.

Davies, Robertson. 1983. *Fifth Business: The Deptford Trilogy.* Harmondsworth, England: Penguin.

Farrington, David P. 1979. "Longitudinal Research on Crime and Delinquency." In *Crime and Justice: An Annual Review of Research,* vol. 1, edited by Norval Morris and Michael Tonry. Chicago: University of Chicago Press.

———. In this volume. "Predicting Individual Crime Rates."

Farrington, David, and Roger Tarling. 1983. *Criminal Prediction.* Albany: State University of New York Press.

Floud, Jean, and Warren Young. 1981. *Dangerousness and Criminal Justice.* London: Heinemann.

Glaser, Daniel. In this volume. "Classification for Risk."

Goldkamp, John S. In this volume. "Prediction in Criminal Justice Policy Development."

Gottfredson, Stephen D. In this volume. "Prediction: An Overview of Selected Methodological Issues."

Greenwood, Peter W. 1986. "Differences in Criminal Behavior and Court Responses among Juvenile and Young Adult Defendants." In *Crime and Justice: An Annual Review of Research,* vol. 7, edited by Michael Tonry and Norval Morris. Chicago: University of Chicago Press.

Hart, H. L. A. 1968. *Punishment and Responsibility.* New York: Oxford University Press.

Knapp, Kay. 1985. *Minnesota Sentencing Guidelines and Commentary Annotated.* St. Paul: Minnesota CLE Press.

Meehl, Paul E. 1954. *Clinical vs. Statistical Prediction: A Theoretical Analysis and a Review of the Evidence.* Minneapolis: University of Minnesota Press.

Minnesota Sentencing Guidelines Commission. 1980. *Report to the Legislature.* St. Paul: Minnesota Sentencing Guidelines Commission.

Monahan, John. 1981. *Predicting Violent Behavior: An Assessment of Clinical Techniques.* Beverly Hills, Calif.: Sage.

———. 1982. "The Case for Prediction in the Modified Desert Model for Criminal Sentencing." *International Journal for Law and Psychology* 5:103–13.

Monahan, John, and David B. Wexler. 1978. "A Definite Maybe: Proof and Probability in Civil Commitment." *Law and Human Behavior* 2:37–42.

Moore, Mark. 1985. "Purblind Justice: Normative Issues in the Use of Predictive or Discriminating Tests in the Criminal Justice System." Paper prepared for the National Academy of Sciences Panel on Criminal Careers and "Career Criminals." Cambridge, Mass.: Harvard University, John F. Kennedy School of Government.

Moore, Mark H., Susan Estrich, and Daniel McGillis, with William Spelman. 1984. *Dangerous Offenders: The Elusive Target of Justice.* Cambridge, Mass.: Harvard University Press.

Morris, Norval. 1951. *The Habitual Criminal.* London: London School of Economics.

———. 1982. *Madness and the Criminal Law.* Chicago: University of Chicago Press.

Morris, Norval, and Marc Miller. 1985. "Predictions of Dangerousness." In *Crime and Justice: An Annual Review of Research,* vol. 6, edited by Michael Tonry and Norval Morris. Chicago: University of Chicago Press.

National Commission on Reform of Federal Criminal Laws. 1970. *Study Draft of a New Federal Criminal Code.* Washington, D.C.: U.S. Government Printing Office.

National Council on Crime and Delinquency. Advisory Council of Judges. 1963. "Model Sentencing Act." *Crime and Delinquency* 9:337–69.

Nozick, Robert. 1981. *Philosophical Explanations.* Cambridge, Mass.: Harvard University Press.

Petersilia, Joan, and Susan Turner. In this volume. "Guideline-based Justice: Prediction and Racial Minorities."

Posner, Richard A. 1977. *Economic Analysis of Law.* 2d ed. Boston: Little, Brown.

Saltzburg, Stephen. 1985. *American Criminal Procedure.* 2d ed. St. Paul, Minn.: West.

Sechrest, Lee. In this volume. "Classification for Treatment."

Singer, Richard. 1979. *Just Deserts: Sentencing Based on Equality and Desert.* Cambridge, Mass.: Ballinger.

Twentieth Century Fund Task Force on Criminal Sentencing. 1976. *Fair and Certain Punishment.* New York: McGraw-Hill.

von Hirsch, Andrew. 1981. "Desert and Previous Convictions in Sentencing." *Minnesota Law Review* 65:591–634.

———. 1985. *Past or Future Crimes: Deservedness and Dangerousness in the Sentencing of Criminals.* New Brunswick, N.J.: Rutgers University Press.

Author Index

Subject Index